"*Paul and the Good Life* is a highly creative and perceptive study of Paul in his own cultural context and in ours. Julien Smith reveals how Paul sees Jesus as the suffering savior-king, launching a 'new regime' that provides an alternative social imaginary and an alternative *polis* for human flourishing. The good life means cruciform allegiance to Christ, transformed character, liturgical community, and care for both humans and all creation as integral aspects of salvation and mission—both then and now. A critical book for both the academy and the church."

—**Michael J. Gorman**, *Raymond E. Brown Professor of Biblical Studies and Theology, St. Mary's Seminary & University*

"Headwaters are elusive. So, essential streams are navigated separately: the gospel, spiritual practices, politics, church life, philosophy. But in this exciting and important study, Julien Smith goes farther back and deeper in. He shows that the gospel invites us not merely to trust a savior, but to give allegiance to the *ideal king* for the sake of human flourishing. The separate streams are joined to the headwaters and mapped afresh."

—**Matthew W. Bates**, *author of* Gospel Allegiance *and Associate Professor of Theology, Quincy University*

"Julien Smith makes a compelling case that Paul's gospel centers upon Christ's kingship and its implications for human flourishing. We need more books like this one—books which combine the best of biblical exegesis and ancient historical context in order to marshal contemporary visions of what it means for us as humans to live 'the good life.'"

—**Joshua Jipp**, *Associate Professor of New Testament, Trinity Evangelical Divinity School*

Paul and the Good Life

Transformation and Citizenship in the Commonwealth of God

Julien C. H. Smith

BAYLOR UNIVERSITY PRESS

Unless otherwise stated, Scripture quotations are from the New Revised Standard Version Bible, copyright 1989, Division of Christian Education of the National Council of the Churches of Christ in the United States of America. Used by permission. All rights reserved.

Cover and book design by Kasey McBeath
Cover image: Portrait of Saul of Tarsus known as Saint Paul the Apostle (Tarsus, 5/10-Rome, 64/67), painting by Giuseppe Franchi (1565–1628), oil on canvas, 66×51 cm. (Inv. 1519), © Veneranda Biblioteca Ambrosiana/ Mondadori Portfolio / Bridgeman Images

Paperback ISBN: 978-1-4813-1310-0
Library of Congress Control Number: 2020024591

NATIONAL
ENDOWMENT
FOR THE
HUMANITIES

Paul and the Good Life has been made possible in part by a major grant from the National Endowment for the Humanities: NEH CARES. Any views, findings, conclusions, or recommendations expressed in this book do not necessarily represent those of the National Endowment for the Humanities.

Printed in the United States of America on acid-free paper with a minimum of thirty percent recycled content.

To the students, faculty, and staff who make Christ College a house of learning and friendship.

CONTENTS

ACKNOWLEDGMENTS

Beginning in graduate school, I developed the habit of reading the acknowledgements of just about any book I picked up. Soon it became a compulsion. At first, I suppose, it was just idle curiosity, a kind of gossipy desire to learn whom the author knew. But then it turned into a genuine interest in *how* the author came to know what she knew. What was the path of discovery like? What pitfalls did she manage to avoid? What dark nights of the soul did she endure? Often, I learned, the path of discovery involved a measure of felicity. While searching for something, the author stumbled across something else. While wrestling with one problem, the solution to another gently came to mind. An offhand remark from a colleague helped to crystallize her thinking. Amidst the hard and often lonely labor of working with words, such gifts from above—happy accidents I now think of them—are to be received with gratitude and wonder. This book came about by many such happy accidents, two of which deserve mention.

The first occurred when I was at the very early stage of writing. I had gone out to California to visit some old and dear friends from college and found myself one evening talking about the book project with Susi, who was at the time working on a science fiction novel. I was just about to deliver the well-prepared pitch when Abby, Susi's daughter and a college student, asked, "Why are you writing a book about Paul?" I froze. Had she asked what the book was *about*, I might well have gone on at some length. But *why* write a book about Paul? The question had never entered my mind. Several silly answers started to creep from my brain towards my mouth: Why *not*? . . . Because that's what folks with Ph.D.'s in my field *do* . . . Because there aren't *enough* books about Paul already . . .

Before I blurted out any of these asinine responses, Susi—perhaps mistaking my long silence as an index of the complexity of my forthcoming response—intervened: "Just explain it like you would to a college student." From that point on, a different book from the one I had been thinking of began to emerge, a book that might help explain the Apostle Paul to a college student. While I hope that other sorts of readers will find this book helpful and interesting—scholars, seminarians, churchgoers, and the intellectually curious—I have come to envision them as "reading over the shoulder" of college students.

The second happy accident was joining the faculty of Christ College, the interdisciplinary undergraduate honors college of Valparaiso University. This decision has proven "happy" in the fullest sense of the word. It was an "accident" only in the narrow sense that I had neither foreseen teaching and writing in such a place, nor could I have predicted the ways this place has shaped me as a teacher and a scholar. These two accidents are integrally related: the one helped me discover my audience; the other, what I might have to say. This is not the place to give an account of this formative journey. Here I merely acknowledge my debt of gratitude to my students, too numerous to mention, and to my co-laborers in the task of teaching, without whom this *particular* book would never have been written: Gretchen Buggeln, Marcia Bunge, Samuel Graber, Agnes Howard, Tal Howard, Slavica Jakelić, Mel Piehl, Jennifer Prough, Matthew Puffer, Mark Schwehn, Edward Upton, and David Western.

Within the first month of joining the faculty, my dean Mel Piehl sat me down and gave me a charge at once liberating and terrifying. He encouraged me to allow the interdisciplinary nature of my teaching in the college to influence the direction of my scholarship. This book represents my earnest effort to take that encouragement to heart. The two deans who succeeded Mel, Peter Kanelos and Susan Van Zanten, have created a nurturing place for the faculty in the college to think and write. I am grateful as well to the other administrators and staff at the college for the good work they do each day of the week to make Christ College an extraordinary place to teach and learn: Sharon Dybel, Margaret Franson, Linda Schmidt, Anna Stewart, and Patrice Weil.

I am grateful to Valparaiso University for the combination of a sabbatical and the awarding of a University Research Professorship, which together afforded me an entire academic year to begin research and writing. A number of scholarly societies gave me the opportunity to present my work in progress and offered valuable criticism: the Society of Biblical Literature; the Scripture and Hermeneutics Seminar; the Forum on Missional Hermeneutics; the Baylor Symposium on Faith and Culture; and the Chicago Society of Biblical Research.

Several individuals and groups deserve special thanks for reading and commenting upon portions of the book: my students in the Paul seminar in spring 2019, the anonymous readers from Baylor University Press, Ellen F. Davis, Andrew Byers, Stephen Barton, and Michael Rhodes. Mel Piehl generously read every word of this book—and much else that I have written over the past decade—and his thoughtful comments have taught me much about good writing. I have received guidance and encouragement from a number of people at Baylor University Press, whose passion and expertise in bringing books to life is evident: David Aycock, Maddee Barbier, Bethany Dickerson, Jenny Hunt, Cade Jarrell, and Carey Newman.

Many friends and family members have provided me with an invaluable service, perhaps even without their knowing. Across cafe tables, in quiet corners at parties, on long road trips, these patient and attentive listeners provided me the space to work out my argument on my feet. Their raised eyebrows often indicated precisely where my thinking was unclear. Among this crowd, several merit honorable mention: Doug Hahn, Jim Mitchell, Claire Smith, Jason Varsoke, and Rich Wachsmann. My wife Hope, and two sons, Eben and Ian, have made life sweet during the writing of this book in ways that surpass telling.

The community of believers who gather each week to worship at St. Andrew's Episcopal Church have been a constant source of encouragement and inspiration, not just in the writing of this book, but in living life in faithful allegiance to Jesus. Father Roger Bower, the rector of St. Andrew's, has graciously invited me to share in the preaching ministry of the church, and these opportunities to proclaim the gospel over the years have profoundly influenced the arc of this book. Nearly every Sunday morning for the past two years, David Jones has looked me in the eye, shaken my hand and said, "You will finish it."

Valparaiso
Epiphany 2020

IN THE IMAGE OF PAUL

The Journey So Far

I confess that I was uninterested in the Apostle Paul right up through my early thirties. In my youth I suppose I was just ignorant. On a multiple-choice test, I would probably have guessed that Paul was one of Jesus' twelve disciples. (I eventually learned that he wasn't.) By the time I was in college, I had learned who Paul was, but didn't care too much for him. Being a Christian was (and still is) all about following Jesus, in my view. Paul seemed a lightning rod for controversy, primarily of interest to the sort of people who liked arguing about doctrine, which I didn't. For my money, the best book in the New Testament was the Gospel according to Mark, because it offered a direct, vivid picture of Jesus, and so could serve as the paradigm for discipleship. I wouldn't have wanted to strike Paul's letters from the canon exactly, but I wasn't much interested in reading them.

Eventually I wound up going to seminary, where I was obliged to read and study Paul's letters. By that point I didn't mind; the Apostle had by then become something of an intellectual curiosity and challenge to me. In the course of my studies, I became aware of a rather significant chronological fact: the earliest extant Christian writings are Paul's letters to the fledgling churches he planted.[1] Interesting, you might say, but not exactly life changing.

But when you set Paul's letters next to Mark's Gospel (or any of the four canonical Gospels), a far more important observation comes into focus. Paul was grappling with the significance of Jesus a good twenty years before the first Gospel was written (Mark, ca. 70 CE). To read Mark and then pick up, say, Galatians, is like stepping into a time machine. Reading the Gospels, we discover a rich, multi-layered portrait of Jesus' life. Reading Paul's letters, we encounter the earliest written effort to work out the theological *significance* of Jesus' life, an achievement that doubtless influenced later writers who saw fit to preserve that portrait for posterity.[2] My seminary epiphany, if you like, was the realization that my paradigm of discipleship had not simply emerged from the pages of the Gospels. Rather, I had been reading the Gospels—albeit without fully realizing I was doing so—through the lens of Paul's theology. The Gospels had beckoned me to come follow Jesus; Paul's letters gave me the resources for the challenging work of figuring out how this might be done in my daily life.

After seminary and subsequent doctoral studies came another epiphany of sorts. Having spent six grueling years learning as much as I could about the New Testament, I joined the faculty of an interdisciplinary undergraduate honors college within a Midwestern church-related university. In addition to courses on theology and biblical studies, each semester I began to teach an introductory seminar on the humanities to first-year students. To my chagrin, I quickly discovered that my doctoral studies had prepared me to teach only a fraction of the texts on the reading list—Genesis, Mark, John, Augustine. Others I had a passing familiarity with—Plato, Aristotle, Sophocles, Aeschylus. But with respect to quite a number of texts, I was a rank neophyte—Confucius, Mencius, Xunzi, Zhuangzi, Machiavelli, and Shakespeare. And that was just the first semester.[3]

My saving graces that first semester, and every semester since, have been twofold. First, my gracious colleagues and students taught me that a good teacher can also be a learner. Second, the overarching question of the seminar—What is the good life?—helped me find the common threads between these vastly different textual tapestries. Over time, this question began to animate my reading of biblical texts, as I began to ponder the church father Tertullian's age-old question, "What indeed has Athens to do with Jerusalem?"[4] Thus I stumbled upon my second epiphany, namely that the philosophical pursuit of the life of human flourishing and the life of Christian discipleship have much in common.

This, then, is a book about the Apostle Paul, but at its heart it is also a book about Jesus. To be more precise, and slightly technical, this is a book about Paul's *Christology,* how the Apostle made sense of Jesus the Christ. For this reason, the book is not concerned with Paul's life and ministry *per se.* Nor will it offer a systematic interpretation of Paul's letters or derive from them an overview of his theology.[5] Rather, this book strives to better understand the significance Paul attributes to the death, resurrection, and ascension of Jesus, and to grasp why this constitutes for Paul good news to be proclaimed to all creation. Importantly, this book makes the case that Paul's good news concerning Jesus the Messiah is integrally connected to the pursuit of the good life, the life of *eudaimonia*, or human flourishing.[6] To do so, Paul must be coaxed into conversation with Aristotle and the wider Greco-Roman philosophical tradition of virtue ethics.[7] Such a conversation reveals significant areas of overlap, but also the ways in which Paul offers a christological redefinition of the aim, or *telos*, of the good life for human beings, what the good life actually *aims for*.

Even though the very *telos* of the good life would thus have been contested by Paul's contemporaries, I contend that there was an accepted framework within which this goal was understood to be pursued. There are four elements to this framework. First, the good life is a communal, social, even *political* project rather than merely an individual one.[8] For Aristotle, the good life must be pursued within the city-state, or *polis*, and for Paul, this social context is the heavenly commonwealth, or *politeuma*, as he writes to the church in Philippi (Phil 3:20). For both Aristotle and Paul, the life of human flourishing thus implies membership, or *citizenship*, within a commonwealth directed towards this end.

Second, citizenship within this commonwealth requires moral transformation, the acquisition of a *character* that reliably leads one to discern and choose the good for oneself and the *polis*. Aristotle contends that one acquires this sort of character by pursuing *aretē*, a term we normally translate as "virtue" but which refers to a type of excellence suited to a given task.[9] Although Paul uses the term *aretē* only once (Phil 4:8), he likewise understood that citizenship in the heavenly *politeuma* both required and resulted in a transformation of character.

Third, as anyone who has lived with at least one other individual for any length of time knows, shared life leads typically, if not inevitably, to conflict. Thus the political pursuit of the good life requires political unity, or—to preserve alliteration—the preservation of *community*. The concern for unity amidst diversity within the *polis* is a constant refrain amongst political philosophers in Mediterranean antiquity and also a recurring motif of Paul's letters.

Fourth and finally, although the pursuit of the good life is anthropocentric, it is not *anthropomonistic*; that is, it does not conceive of humans as "unique and uniquely solitary, cut off from the community of creation."[10] Humans are "implaced" creatures, existing only within a larger framework of physical and biological processes, and thus the life of human flourishing must attend to ecology, the interconnected web of relationships comprising all of life.[11] Within the Greco-Roman philosophical tradition, the environment within which humans live was understood as *nature*. Paul, informed and shaped by Israel's Scriptures, understood this rather as *creation*.[12]

Thus the thematic foci of this book—*citizenship, character, community, and creation*—constitute what I consider to be a shared framework within which Paul and his contemporaries saw themselves to be pursuing the good life. Admittedly, this is an artificial framework constructed for heuristic purposes. Certain elements, moreover, would not have been universally shared. The notion, for example, that human beings exist within the community of God's creation and are responsible to God for the care of creation is probably only intelligible within the context of Israel's, and Paul's, Scriptures—what Christians commonly call the Old Testament. In other words, this framework does not fall from heaven; I shall have to argue for it by showing how central it all is to Paul's interpretation of Jesus and what it means to follow him.

Whether or not this framework finally has any utility—the proof of the pudding, so to speak—depends upon whether the following can be demonstrated. The framework must resonate with the wider discourse in Mediterranean antiquity regarding the good life, and it must make intelligible within this wider discourse Paul's christological vision of the good life. Specifically with respect to the latter goal, the argument intends to show that Paul understands Jesus as a type of ancient ideal king, a figure who both saves and rules—two functions that were often considered integrally connected with the pursuit of the good life in antiquity. These twin functions of Jesus—saving and ruling—suggest that Paul's soteriology might provide an illuminating entrée into his Christology. Starting here illustrates one of the ways in which Paul's legacy is both vitally important and, as I will show, worryingly confusing.

CHAPTER 1

SALVATION AND THE GOOD LIFE

Ancient Conversations

1. Salvation: Eternal Life and/or the Good Life?

What must I do to inherit eternal life? What must I do to obtain the good life? The first question is posed by a young man to Jesus in Mark's Gospel (Mark 10:17). The second is the implicit question animating Aristotle's *Nicomachean Ethics* and much of the Greco-Roman philosophical tradition of what is commonly called "virtue ethics."[1] On the face of it, these two questions are not remarkably different. Both inquire into the means by which a desirable or richly full life may be acquired. And yet, within the Christian tradition, these two questions have frequently been understood to be asking vastly different things. The first question has often been understood to concern salvation, conceived of as an existence that begins after death. One is saved, or granted entrance into this postmortem existence, by the atoning death of Jesus, believed by faith, received by grace.[2] The second question has often been understood by many believers, and others, to pertain to the quality of life prior to death. In response to this question, Aristotle and others insisted that one strive to obtain and exemplify the moral virtues, or excellences of character.[3] On this account, eternal life and the good life are reckoned to be two different sorts of life, acquired in two radically different ways.

Nevertheless, rather confusingly, the first question has sometimes been answered in a way that depends upon the second question. That is, some within the Christian tradition have claimed that one is saved by some combination of grace and moral effort. On this account, eternal life depends in some measure upon the pursuit of the good life. The evident tension between these two understandings of salvation has given birth to great confusion, not to mention wrenching conflict, throughout the history of the church.[4] And this confusion can be at least partially attributed to Paul himself. To the church in Ephesus he writes, "For by grace you have been saved by faith, and this is not your own doing; it is the gift of God" (Eph 2:8).[5] But he exhorts the Philippian believers to "Work out your own salvation with fear and trembling" (Phil 2:12). Which is it—salvation by grace, moral effort, or some combination of the two? The roots of the confusion, however, go deeper than Paul's own apparent vacillations. It is not simply a question of whether or not salvation requires moral effort in addition to divine grace and what the relationship between grace and moral effort might be. It is rather a question of whether or not eternal life and the good life are in any way comparable concepts. The following analogy may help clarify the issue.

Consider the question, "If one wants go to Disney World for vacation, is it better to travel by car or by boat?" This question aims to find out which mode of transportation enables one to reach the destination in the most efficient manner. One could debate the merits of travel by car or boat, taking into consideration the starting point of the voyage, season of the year, weather, price of gasoline, and so forth. This question of the best means to reach a given, desired destination is analogous to the way the church has typically understood the relationship between eternal life and the good life. The analogy works this way: Disney World is the destination (eternal life), and the car (pursuing the good life through moral effort aimed at the acquisition of virtue) and the boat (grace) are two modes of reaching the same destination.

Now consider the question, "Which would be a better vacation—a road trip or cruise?" This question is not interested in the efficiency of transportation (no destination is predetermined or even mentioned), but rather the choice hinges only on the quality of the experience of traveling. The debate here would consider which mode of travel conforms best to the traveler's idea of a vacation. In the first question, the car and the boat only relate to the destination insofar as they allow a traveler to reach it. The destination and the mode of travel are not comparable. In the second question, the car and the boat offer comparable experiences—each is being considered as a type of vacation. The second question offers an analogy for understanding the relationship between eternal life and the good life as comparable terms or experiences of life. The analogy works this way: a road trip (the good life) and a cruise (eternal life) each represent a type of experience in and of themselves, similar in that both are types of vacation, but different in the quality of vacation (or life) that they represent.

Back to Paul. This tension between grace and moral effort in Paul's soteriology stems, at least in part, from the assumption that eternal life and the good life are incomparable concepts for Paul. The latter relates to the former, if at all, merely instrumentally. In other words, many modern Christians approach Paul's letters as though he is answering the question "What must I do to be saved?", which they interpret to mean "How can I get to heaven when I die?"[6]

My argument in this book suggests that this assumption ought to be reconsidered. For Paul, eternal life and the good life are inextricably bound together in his concept of salvation. The good life is not a means to another, different destination, but a part of the process.

What, then, is the nature of salvation? That depends upon whether one is being saved *from* something or *to* something. We can think of salvation as "rescue *from* life-threatening peril"—for example, saving a drowning person. But we can also think of salvation as "restoring *to* wholeness"— for example, saving someone from addiction to drugs. These concepts of salvation are obviously related, and one could indeed argue that the first concept (rescue) is already contained within the second (restoration). To restore a person to wholeness who is addicted to drugs already implies some kind of a rescue from the daily activity of drug use and its attendant problems.[7] But the reverse is not necessarily true. There might well be nothing "un-whole" about the drowning person that would require restoration. Paul, I believe, has *both* these concepts in mind when he writes about salvation through the death of Jesus.

But in many Christian circles, the former—rescue from imminent peril—is emphasized to the neglect of the latter—a process of restoring wholeness amidst damage. Many Christians rightly believe that Jesus died to save one from sin, but are puzzled by whether and how this death also restores one's humanity to a better and richer condition. Holding together these two aspects of salvation is difficult for non-Christians as well, but for the opposite reason. Many outside the church, for example, would acknowledge that human beings often need to be restored to wholeness. Even as I write, our nation is suffering an epidemic of opioid addiction from which many thousands need both rescuing and restoring. Yet those outside the church would likely be puzzled by the suggestion that the demonstrable problem of opioid addiction might have anything to do with the hypothetical problem of sin—a deeper deficiency underlying particular ailments. From the Pauline perspective from which I am arguing, confusion regarding the nature of salvation thus pervades our thinking not only within the church but also outside it.[8]

In fact, confusion outside the church may stem from confusion within it. Consider this thought experiment. Imagine asking a non-Christian, "What do Christians, in your view, believe about the following concepts: guilt, sin, God, Jesus, heaven, and hell?" You might well receive an answer that runs something like this: "The Christian God is a distant celestial record-keeper who is endlessly offended by human moral failure, or sin, and scrupulously demands that all offenses must be punished. Since you are guilty of sin, you will be punished in hell when you die. If you believe in Jesus, however, you will be saved and go to heaven."

Now imagine asking your interlocutor whether she finds this account of salvation persuasive, or even plausible. I expect the answer would be, "Not so much."

A dramatic literary tale may illustrate the pervasiveness of this kind of thinking about salvation. I recently watched a television adaptation of a short story by the late American science-fiction writer, Philip K. Dick. The episode, entitled "Real Life" and based upon Dick's story "Exhibit Piece," explores the mysterious correspondence between the lives of two characters who interact with one another by means of virtual reality. One is a female cop from the future, the other a male virtual-reality designer living in the present. In fact, over the course of the story we discover that the two characters are one and the same person. Only one, however, is a real person; the other exists only in the realm of the real person's subconscious. The viewer soon realizes the central question of the story: Which person is real?

The female cop from the future lives a "perfect" life, yet she is haunted by vague feelings of guilt, which in the end prove to be illusory. She has not, in fact, done anything to deserve these feelings of guilt. By contrast, the present-day male tech mogul lives a miserable life, wracked with actual guilt—a keen awareness of his own sin.[9] When the future cop descends from her perfect world into the virtual world of the guilt-wracked tech mogul, it seems as though she is paying for the "heavenly" life she does not deserve by experiencing the "hellish" misery of another. If *this* character is the real one, then she ought to "wake up" to the reality that her feelings of guilt and unworthiness are merely an illusion.

When the present-day tech mogul escapes into the virtual world of the future cop, this perfect life affords him a brief respite from the miserable consequences of his moral failing and the guilt that plagues him as a result. If *this* character is the real person, then the story would suggest that guilt is the appropriate consequence to sin. For this character, to "wake up" and live in the real world would be to deal with the real consequences of sin.

Both characters in this short story are seeking a salvation of sorts by means of virtual reality; they each hope to escape—to be rescued from—their feelings of guilt. But which of these characters is real? Put differently, which of these stories seems most plausible within the modern Western world we inhabit? Do we live in the world of the cop from the future, in which sin and guilt are really just figments of our imagination, a hangover from the days of bad religion? Or do we live in the world of the present-day tech mogul, in which sin and guilt are realities we must face, and perhaps even pay for?[10]

The episode's dramatic conclusion answers this question (spoiler alert).[11] The tech mogul (whose guilt for sin is real) turns out to be a figment of the imagination of the cop from the future (whose guilt is merely illusory). Thus the story implies that sin and guilt are not realities that must be addressed but merely false projections of our subconscious that can be safely ignored. If sin is not real, what need is there to be rescued from its consequences? Insofar as this story captures something of the contemporary *Zeitgeist* ("spirit of the age"), it suggests that the modern Western world finds the Christian notion of salvation—such as it understands it—thoroughly implausible.[12]

The world did not get this picture of salvation from nowhere. It got it from the church, and the church got it from Paul. This picture, I hasten to add, is not incorrect so much as incomplete. Paul himself says, "For the wages of sin is death, but the free gift of God is eternal life in Christ Jesus our Lord" (Rom 6:23). The first part of this sentence clearly indicates that sin is a life-threatening peril from which one must be rescued. No argument there.

The problem lies in how the church has often understood the second part of that sentence. Some Christians over the centuries have tended to assume that eternal life refers exclusively to life after death. If one is saved by Jesus' death, then when one dies, one receives not the just penalty for sin, eternal damnation, but rather the free gift, eternal life. On this under-standing, eternal life is largely if not entirely divorced from the good life, the day-to-day life we now live in the present. Paul, however, sees eternal life rather as a christologically redefined version of the good life, a type of life that one enters in the present and which continues eternally.[13]

To be saved, then, is not merely to be rescued from the penalty of sin so that we go to heaven rather than hell when we die. To be saved, in Paul's words, is to be "rescued . . . *from* the power of darkness and transferred . . . *into* the kingdom of his beloved Son" (Col 1:13). To be saved clearly im-plies a divine rescue operation, but it equally involves being made whole as one lives under the reign, and in the power, of Jesus the king.

2. Jesus: The King Who Liberates and Transforms

This book is about what it *meant* for Paul to view Jesus as the Messiah of the God of Israel, as God's anointed king over his people Israel, and ultimately over all creation. It is also about what that fact might *mean* for contemporary readers of Paul in the present. In the ancient Mediterra-nean world, kings were routinely thought of as saviors (Greek: *sōtēr*). But an ancient Mediterranean auditor would not have understood that term to mean "one who saves others from the consequences of sin so that they can go to heaven when they die." Rather, the term *sōtēr* evoked a victorious king who had defeated a tyrant in battle and liberated those held in thrall by the tyrant.[14] The orator and popular philosopher Dio Chrysostom (ca. 40–120 CE) describes the good king as "the savior (*sōtēr*) and protector of men everywhere" (*Or.* 3.6)[15] In this vein, Dio claims that Heracles deserves the epithet *sōtēr* for having delivered the entire world from tyranny:

> This . . . was what made him Deliverer (*sōtēr*) of the earth and of the human race, . . . the fact that he chastised savage and wicked men, and crushed and destroyed the power of overweening tyrants. And even to this day Heracles continues this work and you have in him a helper and protector of your government as long as it is vouchsafed you to reign. (*Or.* 1.84)

Naturally, when Paul refers to Jesus as *sōtēr* (e.g., Phil 3:20), he would ex-pect his audience to hear in that term its wider cultural resonance. To gain an understanding of that perspective widely shared by Paul's first-century hearers and readers, I shall present throughout this book a good

deal of literary material illustrating how people in Mediterranean antiquity thought about the ideal king, that is, the king or emperor as he was *supposed* to be, not necessarily as actual rulers were. It should not be inferred
thereby that either Paul himself or his audience had read these texts; rather, they help us assemble what we might think of as an ancient auditor's
cultural repertoire concerning the reign of the ideal king. In so doing our
goal is to attain a level of cultural competence necessary to become the
"authorial audience" of Paul's letters and so gain a better understanding of
what he was conveying at the time he wrote.[16]

Does Paul really think of Jesus as a king? On the surface, the evidence
in his letters might seem rather thin. Paul never, in fact, uses the common
Greek word for king, *basileus*, to refer to Jesus.[17] Furthermore, in comparison with the canonical Gospels, Paul rarely speaks of the *basilea tou
theou*, the kingdom of God.[18] Rather, Paul frequently refers to Jesus with
the term *christos*, a Greek verbal adjective literally meaning "greasy." The
descriptor does not evoke Jesus' complexion, but rather his status as one
who has been anointed, or rubbed with oil. In ancient Israelite religion,
the ritual of anointing was used to consecrate an individual to a particular
office, such as priest, prophet, or king. English translations of the Bible
routinely transliterate this term into what is often seen as a part of Jesus' name: Christ. Occasionally, translations will opt for a transliteration
of the equivalent Hebrew term for "anointed," *mashiach*: Messiah. Thus
Paul's "christ language" must be understood first of all as an example of
ancient Jewish "messiah language."[19] Such language often, if not always,
carried royal connotations because the Messiah, in Jewish tradition, was
frequently envisioned as a royal figure, and inheritor or restorer of Israel's
royal house of King David.[20] In order to grasp the significance of Paul's
designation of Jesus as *christos*, then, one must read his letters against the
backdrop of Greco-Roman and Jewish political discourse.

As an example of this, let us briefly consider this notion of a savior as
a victorious general and apply it to the passage quoted above, Col 1:13.
Imagine for a moment what transpires after the triumphant general, understood as a "good king," liberates the oppressed subjects of a foreign
tyrant. Would a truly good general or king then turn around and ride back
to his own country, wishing those poor souls the best of luck in finding a
new king who is better than the last one? Certainly not. He becomes their
king and works to bring them a new order of justice and peace. The original act of salvation—liberation from a hostile and wicked tyrant—always

implies the transference of those subjects of the former tyrant into the kingdom of the saving king.

This is precisely what Paul declares to be the case in the salvation won through Jesus' death. Humanity has been liberated from the oppressive and deforming tyranny of sin and has been brought under the transforming reign of Jesus, who has not only overthrown the evil power but instituted an entirely new regime. Reflect for a moment upon the nature of the savior-king's rule, and how it must prove different from the rule of the tyrant, if this liberation is going to be counted as salvation in any real sense. Clearly, the kingdom of the savior-king must be superior—by whatever metrics one chooses—to that of the tyrant. To see Jesus as a savior in this sense is to see eternal life not only as the defeat of evil but also as the sort of life one experiences under the reign of Jesus, the new and ideal king.

With this in mind, let me return now to the puzzle with which we began: Does Paul think we are saved by grace or moral effort? To claim that both are true, as Paul apparently does (Eph 2:8; Phil 2:12), appears to be a plain contradiction. Yet, as I shall argue, a view of salvation that holds together grace and moral effort does not constitute a contradiction, but rather a paradox.[21] Paul understands the death of Jesus as necessarily signaling the divine act of God that both rescues us from the dominion of sin *and* simultaneously transfers us into the utterly new kingdom of his victorious Son. We (the once powerless and oppressed subjects) contribute nothing to the liberation but must be involved in the new king's reign with every fiber of our intelligence and moral effort.

These two elements of salvation, integrally related yet often separated in the church and in different theologies, are brought into balance and focus when we see Jesus—as Paul's audience would have—as a savior-king who has both defeated an enemy and launched a new regime. But then why is it relevant to modern readers of Paul whether or not he conceived of Jesus as a king? Monarchy is, after all, largely a defunct form of human governance in our time. (A few kings and queens still exist, but they are, for the most part, powerless figureheads.) Even if it was natural for Paul to conceive of Jesus' function in such terms culturally relevant for his audience, does it make any sense for us to do so, given the *ir*relevance of monarchy in the twenty-first century?

This question is more complex than it might seem, since it relates not just to the secular institution of monarchy, but also to the divine kingship of God, upon which, in the ancient understanding, the human institution rested.[22] But this particular question—the relevance of Paul's royal messianic conception of Jesus—leads us to a broader question. Why is Paul relevant at all to an understanding of any "good life" that modern people, technologically and media-savvy, would want to lead?

3. What Does the Good Life Look Like for Us?
A Discussion "In Conversation" with Paul

Over the past several years of teaching seminars on the Apostle Paul to undergraduates, I have experienced the following scenario a number of times. Students will come to my office to discuss potential paper topics, usually of considerable interest to them. What would Paul say about stem cell research? Gene-editing therapies? Social media? Frequently I find myself needing to explain to students that these highly urgent questions that burden them would likely never have occurred to Paul and might well have been incomprehensible to him. Might they instead wish to pursue a research topic more germane to the sort of research strategies their professor knows something about? What about Paul's relationship to Judaism? Did Paul write Ephesians? How many trips to Jerusalem did Paul make? How reliable is the narrative of the Book of Acts? Quickly, the students' eyes glaze over as their hunch is confirmed: Paul is irrelevant to me and likely to any bright young person today.[23] The suspicion of Paul's irrelevance emerges not simply from the fact that a great historical and cultural chasm separates him from us—a chasm, I must admit, which I have not always helped my students to bridge—but also from the assumption that Paul would not be interested in the questions of human flourishing.[24] The following story may shed some light on the roots of this suspicion.

In the introductory seminar in the humanities that I regularly teach, the faculty routinely observe the following phenomenon as we transition from the Greek unit (Plato, Aristotle, and Sophocles or Aeschylus) to the biblical unit (Genesis, Mark, sometimes John or Galatians). Up to this point in the semester, the dynamic of the seminar has typically been lively, cordial, respectful, and engaged. Students and faculty have felt a growing partnership in teaching and learning with one another about a serious concern we all share: How can we live a "good," rich, full life? We are glad for the privilege of reading such important, culture-shaping texts that address this subject with a new group of fast-forming friends.

But as we open the pages of Genesis or other biblical texts, something odd happens. (It *doesn't* always happen in quite this way or to this extent, but I'll give you the extreme scenario to make the point.) All of a sudden, the tight-knit group of young scholars fractures, splitting into two, and sometimes three, groups. One group starts to feel distrustful of both the professor and fellow students, fearing that the sacred text of the Bible will now be read in a way that undermines its spiritual authority. Another group is incredulous that a blatantly religious text has somehow snuck in alongside the great texts of the Western and East Asian philosophical tradition. Before long, these two groups come to class with knives sharpened, ready for a fight. Sometimes a third group, rightly feeling that such acrimonious discourse doesn't belong in the classroom (and perhaps not anywhere), checks out entirely or pronounces "a plague on both your houses"—though they may also blame the faculty for introducing the plainly controversial religious ideas into a previously friendly conversation.

The first two groups, and often the third, despite their obviously different assessment of the Bible, typically hold at least one important conviction in common. Each feels that the Bible (and perhaps also religion in general) has no place in a curriculum of liberal arts studies. My colleagues and I respond to this unwelcome dynamic—more often than not successfully—by urging our students to approach the Bible as another voice in a long *conversation* about the nature of human flourishing—the "good life"—and how best to pursue it. That is, we invite them to see the Bible as taking up the same task—albeit with different understandings about who we are as humans and the world we live in, and the problems we all face—as all the other texts on the syllabus.

I share this perpetually repeated story to make two points. The first is because it captures both my goal in writing this book and the method behind my argument. My hope is not so much to explain definitively what Paul meant as it is to place Paul in conversation with a number of other voices, both ancient and contemporary, who will help us better understand how Paul might have been heard in his own context, and how we (especially but not exclusively the Christian church) might hear Paul today in our own context.[25] The ancient voices consist primarily of those interested in what life might look like under the reign of the good king—in this case the good king Jesus. I have presented these voices at some length in an earlier monograph, and draw upon that research throughout the present book.[26] The contemporary voices, as represented by the almost universally shared assumptions and perspectives of bright young people, although typically absent from the discussions of Paul by professional biblical scholars, have been profoundly helpful to me in hearing the voices of Paul and Jesus afresh in my own context.[27] More to the point, such voices have helped me place Paul in conversation with the sorts of difficult, urgent modern ethical and social questions my students have posed to me when they come to my office.

The second point, which also speaks to the reader of this book who wonders whether Paul is at all relevant, has to do with what I suspect is the underlying reason my students object to reading the Bible in a liberal arts curriculum. We live, as I mentioned earlier, in a secular age in which both religious and non-religious ways of life are considered equally valid (see note 10 above). One of the defining characteristics of this postmodern, Western world is the dichotomy between the public and private spheres. Public life is the realm of objective facts; private life is the realm of subjective values. Science belongs to the domain of public truth, religion to the domain of private values. So, the claim concerning the equal validity of both religious and non-religious ways of life is actually merely describing the private sphere. My students feel uneasy about discussing the Bible in a liberal arts curriculum because, I suspect, it intuitively seems that we are transgressing the border between public and private. Our social location, within a liberal arts classroom at a university—a public, intellectual setting—dictates that we should be assessing the public truth claims of the texts that we interrogate. And yet the society that legitimizes this educational activity generally deems the Bible, as a religious writing, to be the sort of text whose insights are properly limited to the realm of private values—"personal" or at most "churchly."[28]

This issue of the relevance of the Bible, and by extension a book about Paul, within the public sphere, brings me to the first of the contemporary interlocutors I now bring into conversation with Paul, the late British missiologist Lesslie Newbigin (1909–1998). After spending some twenty-five years as a missionary in India, Newbigin returned home in 1974 to a Britain vastly more secularized than the one he left in 1936. The church that had sent him to India regarded its mission to be the proclamation of the gospel to foreign peoples among whom there was not yet an established church. The church to which he returned needed to take up once again (or perhaps for the first time) the task of missional engagement with the gospel towards its *own* culture.[29]

The returned Newbigin quickly perceived that the church in the Western world had largely become content to retreat into the realm of private values, offering to its members the hope of a blessed life after death, a hope that did not intrude into the realm of public truth as it once had. The church had conceded to the "modern" ground rules of what Newbigin calls "agnostic pluralism," which is "the kind of pluralism in which truth is regarded as unknowable, in which there are no criteria for judging different kinds of belief and behavior."[30]

And yet, Newbigin insists, the gospel cannot be reduced to a private value, but rather demands to be proclaimed as public truth. He firmly acknowledges, however, that this demand does not and cannot imply a return to the theocracy of medieval Christendom—as many think it must. Rather, Newbigin contends that the church should embrace what he calls "confident pluralism," a "vision of knowledge as neither purely objective nor purely subjective but as that which is available to the person who is personally and responsibly committed to seeking the truth and publicly stating his findings."[31] How might the church take up this task? By becoming, in Newbigin's memorable phrase, the "hermeneutic of the gospel."[32] Local congregations, by living out in public their allegiance to a new king, can provide the world with an interpretive key that unlocks the gospel proclamation of Jesus' reign.[33]

An atrophied vision of salvation—"going to Heaven when you die"—is of concern not just for the church but for the world. When the church thus reduces the content of the gospel to an individualistic and otherworldly transaction, and then reduces the scope of its proclamation to the sphere of private values, the world comes to see the gospel as implausible. This was the point behind the earlier discussion of the short story by Philip K. Dick. Reading Paul in conversation with Newbigin opens the possibility of recovering a full-orbed vision of salvation in which eternal life and the good life on this earth, once cleaved asunder, are brought back together. The task before the church, as it lives out this vision, is to make plausible the gospel by its embodied allegiance—*pistis*, often translated as "faith"—to Jesus as king.[34] The task of "missional hermeneutics," as this burgeoning interdisciplinary sub-field has come to be known, concerns not merely the reading of the Bible, but also the way the church lives out its reading of the Bible.[35] Accomplishing this task requires that the church, corporately and individually, be transformed into the image of Christ, as Paul writes to the church in Corinth: "And all of us, with unveiled faces, seeing the glory of the Lord as though reflected in a mirror, are being transformed into the same image from one degree of glory to another; for this comes from the Lord, the Spirit" (2 Cor 3:3).

The well-known words of Jesus at the conclusion of Matthew's Gospel summon the church to the world- and person-transforming vocation of making disciples:

> "All authority in heaven and on earth has been given to me. Go there-
> fore and make disciples of all nations, baptizing them in the name of
> the Father and of the Son and of the Holy Spirit, and teaching them
> to obey everything that I have commanded you. And remember, I
> am with you always, to the end of the age." (Matt 28:18–20)

Sadly, one would be justified in pointing out that there are few churches that intend to teach their members to obey all of Jesus' commandments, and fewer still that could articulate a practical plan for doing so. Such is the lament of the late Dallas Willard (1935–2013), philosopher and leader in the field of spiritual formation.[36] This neglect arises partly as a consequence of the atrophied vision of salvation ubiquitous in the church, as discussed above. If salvation is reduced to the promise of a blessed postmortem existence received on the basis of believing in the atoning death of Jesus, then learning to live the life that Jesus lived—a christocentric version of the good life, if you will—seems quite beside the point.[37] In fact, the moral effort required to live such a life might even be regarded as antithetical to salvation by grace alone.

There is, moreover, another problem behind the church's characteristic failure to produce disciples transformed into the image of Jesus: the lack—or rather, the loss—of a realistic plan. For centuries, Willard argues, the church understood that the practice of spiritual disciplines was the means by which Christians were transformed through the power of the Holy Spirit. This practical tradition, reflected throughout both the OT and NT, is not uniquely Christian or Jewish, but also has roots in the spiritual exercises common to Greco-Roman philosophical schools, and to some other philosophical and religious traditions as well.[38] Since the Reformation, the progressive abandonment of such practices has resulted in widespread bewilderment within the church regarding the means by which one can reliably put on the character of Christ.[39] If the church is to function effectively as the "hermeneutic of the gospel," it must recover the means by which such character transformation happens.[40] To this end, Willard illumines what he calls Paul's "psychology of redemption," a psychologically realistic process by which God's transformative power is actualized in human persons.[41]

If Dallas Willard insists that we are transformed through spiritual disciplines that are generally (although not exclusively) individualistic, philosopher James K. A. Smith contends that we are also shaped communally through liturgy.[42] Humans are more than "thinking things" shaped by rational thought; we are *homo adorans*, shaped by the things we love. One of the key insights of Smith's work on "cultural liturgies" is that this shaping of our selves happens liturgically, through both sacred and secular rituals. Football games and shopping malls form people no less than religious ceremonies such as the Eucharist.

Because secular liturgies have such great potential for forming—and deforming—us without engaging our rational thought processes, Smith argues, the church should give careful thought to the formative potential of its liturgy. Above all, the liturgy of Christian worship "stories" us, enfolding us in the story of God's creation and redemption of the world through Christ.[43] In so doing, worship aims to give us "sanctified perception," the ability to reimagine ourselves in the world as God perceives it, rather than in a world as defined by advertisers seeking to form us as more efficient consumers.[44] This liturgical formation is missional: worship sends us into the world to participate in God's restoring (and "re-story-ing") of creation.[45] To this end, liturgical and missional formation must result in a church that is politically engaged, that is, deeply and prayerfully concerned with the flourishing of the *polis*. This engagement takes the form of *paideia*, or education.[46] Smith's examination of "cultural liturgies" thus commends a reading of Paul that is attentive to the formative and missional function of the Apostle's ubiquitous exhortations to worship.[47]

Newbigin insists that the church, by its embodied allegiance to Jesus as king, interprets the gospel for society. Willard and Smith further insist that the church must be transformed, individually and communally, for this missional task. The poet, writer, and social critic Wendell Berry, the fourth and final conversation partner I am introducing for Paul, suggests that such a task entails making whole, or mending, that which has been torn apart. In a recent documentary about his life and work, Berry says to filmmaker Laura Dunn:

> This is an age of divorce. Things that belong together have been taken apart. And you can't put it *all* back together again. What you do is the only thing that you *can* do: you take two things that ought to be together and you put them back together. *Two* things, not *all* things![48]

Berry is no doubt echoing Jesus' well-known words regarding the union of a man and a woman in marriage: "Therefore what God has joined together, let no one separate" (Mark 10:9). Yet Berry's remarks reflect a concern for a broader, more pervasive problem in Western society, the sundering of all manner of relationships, but especially the relationship between human communities and the land that sustains our very lives. Although all human societies share some measure of responsibility for the destruction of creation, Berry believes that the church is particularly culpable because, in the light of its inherited biblical traditions, it *ought* to have known better.[49] And yet:

> Despite its protests to the contrary, modern Christianity has become willy-nilly the religion of the state and the economic status quo. Because it has been so exclusively dedicated to incanting anemic souls into Heaven, it has been made the tool of much earthly villainy. It has, for the most part, stood silently by while a predatory economy has ravaged the world, destroyed its natural beauty and health, divided and plundered its human communities and households.[50]

In repentant response for its willful neglect, Berry proclaims, the church must turn afresh to the biblical tradition, which, properly understood, can instruct and inspire us to our divinely bestowed vocation, the care of creation. It is worth noting that Berry is not inclined to turn to the Apostle Paul as a spokesperson for that tradition; indeed, for Berry, Paul represents the worst of the Christian tradition—exclusivity, chauvinism, and slavish obedience to the state.[51] While Berry might therefore resist engaging in deep conversation with Paul, I am convinced that they would in fact have a great deal to say to one another.

What convictions might Berry and Paul hold in common? They would both agree that "incanting anemic souls to Heaven" is not the proper business of the church, and would therefore equally lament the destruction that this atrophied vision of salvation has wrought. They would also affirm the essential goodness of creation. While they both, in different ways, express hope that God is at work to restore the goodness of creation, they part ways in their understanding of how this task will be accomplished. Paul expresses the hope thus:

> For the creation waits with eager longing for the revealing of the children of God; for the creation was subjected to futility, not of its own will but by the will of the one who subjected it, in hope that the creation itself will be set free from its bondage to decay and will obtain the freedom of the glory of the children of God. (Rom 8:19–21)

Berry is not as sanguine as Paul regarding the outcome of this hope, and less explicitly "religious" in his mode of expression.[52] Yet he too pins his hope for the survival of creation upon the survival and renewal of Christianity. He expresses hope that Christianity

> should survive and renew itself so that it may become as largely and truly instructive as we need it to be. On such a survival and renewal of the Christian religion may depend the survival of the Creation that is its subject.[53]

Berry and Paul would agree that, although the achievement of this hope is not finally dependent upon us, it nevertheless requires our intention and effort.[54] Although not as explicitly interested as Newbigin, Willard, and Smith in the role of the church in moral formation, Berry is keenly interested in how we are formed as human beings. Across the corpus of his poetry, essays, and fiction, Berry argues that the basic human vocation is to care properly for creation, and that our individual and communal lives are alternately formed or deformed as we attend to, or ignore, that task.[55] Inviting Berry into the conversation with Paul helps us to see that the heavenly commonwealth in which we are citizens, and in which we are formed individually and communally, is a teleologically shaped community. And the *telos* towards which we yearn is the restoration of creation.

What might a conversation look like between the Apostle Paul, Lesslie Newbigin, Dallas Willard, James K. A. Smith, and Wendell Berry? Obviously, these four figures (and we could add many more who think and write along with them or in their wake) are asking questions and addressing particular modern problems that, to varying degrees, likely never occurred to Paul. By bringing them into conversation with Paul, I certainly do not mean to imply that their questions are also Paul's. Rather, their questions can function as a kind of leaven throughout my own argument, allowing insights to rise from Paul's letters that do address the world we live in—though those letters were written in a very different historical time.

Yet Paul, as I will endeavor to show, would have shared much in common with the convictions of these later thinkers. With Newbigin, Paul viewed the church as a missional outpost bearing witness to the wider world of the good news that Jesus is king. With Willard and Smith, Paul believed that the church is made fit for its witness only as it is transformed individually and communally into the image of Christ. And like Berry, Paul understood the human vocation as the "exercise of skillful mastery" over creation as God's image-bearers.[56] Although this vocation has been marred by sin, Paul insists (although perhaps not Berry) that through the reign of Christ, God is now at work in restoring us to this vocation.[57] That is, I shall endeavor to show that these four emphases (missional engagement, individual and communal moral transformation, and the care of creation) find a genuine home in Paul's thought world, in particular the way that Paul imagined life under the reign of King Jesus.[58]

4. How Can We Picture the Good Life? Recalibrating Our Imagination

The ultimate aim of this book is to help us imagine the world differently. Often we think of our imagination as a creative, liberating, even fantastical power. Our imagination gives birth to clever inventions and novel solutions to vexing problems. Captivating stories and entire worlds—Narnia, Wakanda, Middle Earth—spring forth from the human imagination. So do our spectacular technological inventions. Yet our imagination is also a formidable restricting power. Our imagination often closes off to us possibilities that appear to us impractical or implausible. Indeed, it can paradoxically keep us from even thinking about such possibilities. All of us imagine the world to be a certain way, and the way we do so will make certain choices appear attractive, necessary, or even inevitable, while others will seem ludicrous, repugnant, implausible, or even impossible.[59] These "social imaginaries" exist often just below the surface of our consciousness and are widely (although not necessarily universally) shared within cultures.[60] We can see the evidence of these social imaginaries by paying close attention to the way advertisements subtly seek to make products appeal to potential consumers without ever needing to clearly state the logic of the appeal. Consider the pervasive cultural appeal of fast food: the very notion that food served quickly is a good only makes sense if we assume that, as a culture, we imagine ourselves to be busy and short of time.[61]

The ways in which we imagine our world can have calamitous consequences. I first sat down to write this chapter a week after another mass shooting in which seventeen high school students were murdered. These unspeakable tragedies have become so commonplace that many of us cannot imagine a world in which such things don't continue to happen with numbing regularity. The following headline from the satirical website *The Onion* captures the sense of hopelessness bred by the way we imagine the world actually is: "'No Way to Prevent This,' Says Only Nation Where This Regularly Happens."[62] Although the reasons behind mass shootings and potential solutions to preventing them are both complex, one thing is clear: as a nation, we have shown ourselves incapable of imagining a world where such things no longer happen. At present there is a group of high school students, survivors of this most recent attack, who appear determined to imagine the world differently. I pray desperately that they succeed.

As our nation's grim history of mass shootings show, we often imagine ourselves to inhabit a world in which certain things are simply inevitable. At present, cars are largely driven by human beings, but at some point in the near future, we are assured, cars will drive themselves. Some welcome this technological advancement while others are inclined to regard it with skepticism, a nostalgic sense of loss, or fear. Yet nearly all of us, I would wager, look upon the advent of self-driving cars as, sooner or later, inevitable. Along with the conviction that our destiny is set, we are inclined to believe that we cannot turn back. In many respects this is doubtless true, especially with respect to the material world. Strip mining, for example, has inflicted irreparable damage on mountains and their surrounding ecosystems. Finite resources such as oil or coal, once consumed, cannot be renewed. With respect to the social world, it is probably also impossible to return to the way things were prior to the industrial revolution, or at least impossibly difficult to imagine such changes occurring.

Paul's letters challenge the assumption that our common future must follow a path that is inevitable. They do so by offering a vision of creation restored under the leadership of Jesus, and inviting us to recalibrate our imagination according to that vision. Paul provides us with a new social imaginary in which we are citizens of a heavenly commonwealth, in which we are being transformed individually and communally into the image of the king Jesus, and in which we eagerly await the restoration of creation through the consummation of Jesus' reign. But in so doing, Paul is not suggesting that we—as individuals, communities, institutions—have the power to change our future by ourselves. The future, as the diverse voices from Scripture tell us in unison, is in God's hands. This of course in no way suggests that we must therefore idly wait for God to act. Rather, this vision of the future has implications for how we live in the present. We are to eagerly await, to anticipate, to live into the new creation—God's Kingdom on earth—that God is assuredly bringing to fruition. The Gospels tell us that Jesus came announcing that the Kingdom of God has come near (Mark 1:15). Revelation offers us a vivid, if cryptic, description of this Kingdom consummated (Rev 11:15; 12:10). What does it look like to live in this already-but-not-yet Kingdom? How shall we imagine it? To answer such questions this book enlists the aid of the Apostle Paul in the disciplined task of recalibrating our imagination.

5. Heavenly Living on Earth: Citizenship, Character, Community, and Creation

What is the central bind that this book intends to address? Recall the image of salvation I described earlier, of the king as *sōtēr* who both liberates the *polis* and transforms the citizenry to a new pattern of living under his reign (page 10). If Paul, as I argue, regards Jesus as such a liberating and transformative king, he also regards Jesus' reign as inaugurated but not yet consummated. This results in a practical problem: how do we live under the transformative power of Jesus' reign while the tyrant—the oppressive and deforming reign of sin from which we have been liberated—continues to wield power and influence?

The problem of being ruled by a tyrant is not simply the tyrant's active oppression but also the fact that his oppressed subjects have actually been formed (or deformed) into the image of the tyrant. The fundamental bind the book aims to resolve is how to live in this in-between time, how to be reformed through allegiance (*pistis*) to Christ rather than through allegiance to the tyrannical power of sin. As Paul explains to the church in Philippi, the Messiah's people now belong to an alternative political community, a heavenly *politeuma*, or commonwealth (Phil 3:20). This book therefore explores Paul's transformative vision of membership within this community, and examines how to live in the tension between the old regime and the new emerging one.

Chapter 2 argues that citizens within this commonwealth must conform their pattern of living to that of Jesus, who renounced status and embraced suffering. Citizenship in this heavenly commonwealth is the necessary political and social corollary of the gospel, the glad tidings of Jesus' reign. Chapter 3 addresses the vital question, What enables citizens of this commonwealth to flourish within it? How are God's people made fit for heavenly life? The answer Paul presents in 2 Corinthians is that the church is transformed into the image of Jesus the king. This also means that the church is transformed into the image of God, which is another way of saying that we are restored to our authentic humanity (cf. Gen 1:26–28).

Chapter 4 looks at the social and political consequences of this transformation from the perspective of the closely related letters Ephesians and Colossians. There one sees that unity within the diverse community of the church is dependent upon clothing oneself with the character of Jesus the king. The unity within the church, understood as an alternative *polis*, is further intended as a witness to the wider *polis* of the reconciliation achieved through the Messiah Jesus. Chapter 5 addresses the relationship between this heavenly commonwealth, a social structure comprised of human beings, and the non-human creation with which we share our home. Paul's letter to the church in Rome presents a vision of salvation in which the human family is restored to its divinely bestowed vocation as stewards of God's creation.

In sum, the consequences of Jesus' reign, in parallel to the fourfold framework of the good life discussed briefly in the introduction, are the following: (1) citizenship within Jesus' heavenly commonwealth (the good life as a political project); (2) transformation into the image of Jesus that is thereby enabled and required (the good life as the acquisition of moral virtue); (3) unity amidst diversity that thereby results (the good life as requiring political unity); and (4) the *telos* of this community, the restoration of humanity to its God-given vocation (the good life as the flourishing of humans in harmony with the non-human creation).

Throughout these four chapters, the questions and insights of the four modern conversation partners I have invited in—Newbigin, Willard, Smith, and Berry—act as leaven, allowing important implications of Paul's own letters to rise to our attention. Chapter 6 places these four interlocutors—and the contemporary concerns they represent—into a more explicit conversation with Paul.[63]

How am I using Paul's letters as a window into this thinking? After all, Paul's letters cannot be read as a unified theological treatise; rather, each one addresses a contingent circumstance. Nevertheless, I understand the contingency of his letters to be grounded in the coherence of his gospel.[64] I have chosen to focus upon passages from Philippians, 2 Corinthians, Ephesians, Colossians, and Romans because they illuminate some vital aspect of the ancient Mediterranean concept of the good king that assists us in understanding Paul's picture of Jesus. Moreover, there is a gradual movement in the course of this book from Paul's world to ours. The next four chapters focus heavily on Paul's world and the argument he makes in his letters, all the while making suggestive nods towards our own context. Chapter 6 endeavors to help the reader bridge the gap between Paul's context and our own. But the goal of this book is not simply to help modern readers, Christian or not, understand Paul. Ultimately, my goal is to help the church think alongside Paul about God's mission for the church in our contemporary context.

6. Why Does the Church Need Paul (and Not Just Jesus)?

As I mentioned above, in my early adult life I thought that as a Christian it was vitally important to focus on Jesus, while at the same time perfectly permissible to quietly ignore Paul. If being a Christian is about following Jesus, and if the Gospels give us four rich portraits of Jesus, why do we need the additional layer of Paul's theologizing? The answer, as N. T. Wright has suggested, has to do with the difference between their respective *contexts and tasks*.[65] The relationship between Jesus and Paul can be compared to that between composer and performer, or architect and builder. Jesus and Paul, each within their context, labored at tasks that were distinct but complementary. Jesus, within a Jewish context, announced and inaugurated the kingdom of God. Paul, largely but not exclusively within a Gentile context, worked out the implications of living under the reign of God's resurrected Messiah Jesus. Jesus is king; Paul is his royal emissary. Jesus is the *sōtēr* who liberates us from the oppressive and deforming tyranny of sin and makes us citizens of his heavenly commonwealth. Paul is his ambassador sent to assist us in working out the implications of this salvation for our daily lives.

A vast cultural and chronological chasm separates the world of Jesus and Paul from our own world. There is, however, one crucial sense in which our world is similar to Paul's—both we and Paul inhabit the same chapter in the narrative of God's story of redemption. Jesus has inaugurated God's kingdom on earth, and both we and Paul must figure out how to live in it. In this respect, Paul's letters may prove more helpful to us in following Jesus than the Gospel narratives.[66] Thus Paul's questions are often, in principle, our own. What are the qualities of citizenship within the commonwealth of the Messiah's rule? How is one made fit to be a citizen within this commonwealth? How can citizens within this commonwealth forge a common life amidst diversity? And how, as citizens of this commonwealth, do we eagerly anticipate the restoration of the created world in which we live? These questions—citizenship, moral transformation, unity amidst diversity, care of creation—were as relevant to Paul as they are to us.

CHAPTER 2

CITIZENSHIP

Allegiance to the Suffering King in Philippi

Where do I belong? To what, or whom, do I give my ultimate allegiance? These are the two questions that animate this chapter. A third question relates these two questions to the larger questions of this book. What do belonging and allegiance have to do with salvation and the life of human flourishing?

In Paul's world, these questions were bound up with the central ideas of *polis* and *pistis*. The term *polis* originally referred to the city-state of classical Greece. In Greek philosophical discourse, the *polis* played an instrumental role in the pursuit of the good life. By Paul's day, the political institution of the *polis* as it was known in classical Greece had long since ceased to exist, and the term was instead used to refer to an urban habitation, something like a large town or city. In my usage of the term, I intend to invoke the older idea of the community, broader than one's extended family, within which one's identity and values are formed.

The term *pistis* appears throughout the letters of Paul (and the NT) and is frequently translated "faith" or "belief." Yet the semantic domain of this Greek noun is considerably broader, encompassing the overlapping concepts of trust, loyalty, and allegiance. Matthew Bates has recently argued that, in many instances throughout the NT, the term *pistis* denotes *embodied allegiance*, a concept comprised of three dimensions: "*mental affirmation* that the gospel is true, *professed fealty* to Jesus alone as the cosmic Lord, and *enacted loyalty* through obedience to Jesus as the king."[1] Understood in this sense, *pistis* does not mean something less than or other than faith or belief, but rather something more—the embodied loyalty to Jesus that is founded upon faith and belief. In turn, *polis* and *pistis*—belonging and allegiance—were wrapped up in the larger concept of *citizenship*.

As an entrée into Paul's world, permit me to share a little about my own. I am a dual citizen. Born in England to English parents, I emigrated to the United States (at my parents' behest) when I was two years old. I did not become naturalized—an odd expression, when one thinks about it—until my early thirties, however. Why the long wait? As a child, I inherited my parents' love of their native land and culture and felt myself to be more English than American. (When we moved from New Hampshire to California—I was nine at the time—my new classmates briefly mocked me for my strange accent.) As a teenager and young adult, I continued to cherish this ever-waning "exotic" cultural identity. (My university considered me an international student!) In my early thirties, I realized that I was American in every respect but my passport. It was high time to take on responsibilities of citizenship such as voting and jury duty. Also, following 9/11, I became increasingly worried about the status of non-citizens in this country. So I filled out the application, paid the fee, took the test and passed.

About six months later I found myself, one brilliantly sunny spring morning, sitting in the packed auditorium of a federal government building in San Francisco, waiting to take the oath of citizenship. That morning, I discovered that citizenship means different things to different people.

With time to kill before the ceremony began, I struck up a conversation with the man sitting next to me. His story could not have been more different than mine. In broken English, he told me that he had trained to become a doctor in his native Somalia but had left the country due to mounting violence and waning economic opportunities. Despite his education, he had thus far only managed to find employment as a parking garage attendant. The journey to reach this ceremony had been long, arduous, and costly. His United States citizenship had come at a high price, and yet he was brimming with gratitude to finally become a member of what he clearly regarded as a great country. By contrast, my journey had been swift, effortless, and inexpensive.

The marked difference in our paths to citizenship can be attributed, no doubt, to the fact that I had by then been living in the United States for over three decades. But if we compare this man to my father, some interesting contrasts emerge. Like this man, my father had trained to be a doctor. Unlike this man, however, my father was welcomed with open arms. The small town in New Hampshire where we settled had bent over backwards to expedite his medical license (and even his driver's license). My father entered the professional career for which he had trained with remarkable ease, while this Somali man struggled to find a job for which even a high school drop-out would have been qualified.

How to explain this? In part, the world had changed vastly in thirty years, and the United States had become more restrictive in its immigration policies, especially after 9/11. But it is also important to note that my father's medical degree came from a highly esteemed London medical school, which opened many doors for him. I am no expert on the matter, but I suspect that a medical degree from a Somali university does not have quite that effect. In brief, it was easy for me to become a citizen (as it would have been for my father had he so desired) because I was already a citizen of a comparably wealthy and highly esteemed nation. Coming from such a privileged background, the path to citizenship was effortless because we were regarded as potential assets. Absent this pedigree of privilege, one is apt to be regarded as a potential liability. Hence, I think, the arduous path to citizenship for the Somali man I met that day.

Two points from this story help us understand the Apostle Paul's social context. The first is: privilege begets privilege. As the old adage goes, it is easier to get a job if you already have one. The second is: citizenship in the United States, and in other prosperous, economically developed countries, is a privilege. Paul's argument in Philippians challenges the normative status of both of these common clichés. How does the privilege-begetting privilege of citizenship help us understand Paul's context? Luke, the author of Acts, informs us upon three occasions that Paul is a citizen of Rome (Acts 16:37–38; 22:25–29; 23:27).[2] Moreover, he holds dual citizenship, being a native, as Acts tells us, of "Tarsus in Cilicia, a citizen of an important city" (21:39). Paul relates to his status as a dual citizen in a way that I identify with. In fact, my conversation with the Somali man bears a faint resemblance to the conversation Paul has with a Roman tribune towards the end of Acts.[3]

Paul has arrived in Jerusalem for the feast of Pentecost, and his presence in the Temple courts has elicited a riot. The Roman tribune has taken him into protective custody and ordered that he be flogged. Paul then asks the centurion on duty whether it is legal to flog an uncondemned Roman citizen. Alarmed, the centurion summons the tribune. Apprised of the situation, the tribune and Paul share words: "The tribune came and asked Paul, 'Tell me, are you a Roman citizen?' And he said, 'Yes.' The tribune answered, 'It cost me a large sum of money to get my citizenship.' Paul said, 'But I was born a citizen'" (Acts 22:27–28). Two men who have experienced strikingly different paths to citizenship—the tribune paid dearly for the privilege, but Paul was born into it.[4] What I find most significant about Paul's Roman citizenship is not that he was born into the privilege, but how he uses it. In this instance, playing the citizenship card saves Paul from a flogging.

Earlier in the narrative, imprisoned in Philippi with Silas, Paul had informed his captors of his Roman citizenship, demanding of them a public apology for the severe (and illegal) flogging he had received (Acts 16:35–40).[5] In both episodes, Luke reports that the authorities were afraid when they learned that they had mistreated a Roman citizen. Clearly the status of Roman citizenship afforded Paul some measure of greater protection under the law, and Paul used this privilege to his advantage. But Acts also suggests that Paul was ambivalent about this privilege insofar as the reciprocal responsibilities of citizenship were concerned.

This extended discussion of citizenship and the privileges it confers may seem to have taken us miles away from the issues brought up in the introduction of this book—Paul's vision of the good life and its relationship to salvation. In fact, however, this circuitous journey has brought us to a vantage point from which we will be able to see the fraught relationship between Paul's privileged Roman citizenship and the way of salvation he proclaims. This tension emerges during Paul's visit to Philippi and subsequent visit to Thessalonica.

In Philippi, Paul and Silas are followed for several days by a slave-girl who possesses a spirit of divination, a gift which earns her owners a great deal of money. She loudly proclaims, "'These men are slaves of the Most High God, who proclaim to you a way of salvation'" (Acts 16:17). In irritation, Paul commands the spirit to leave the girl. Deprived of their ability to profit from the girl, her owners respond in anger by dragging Paul and Silas before the magistrates. Their accusation is surprising: "'These men are disturbing our city; they are Jews and are advocating customs that are not lawful for us as Romans to adopt or observe'" (Acts 16:20–21). What customs are they talking about? Luke does not tell us, but one wonders whether the accusation—assuming it was not merely trumped up—has something to do with the "way of salvation" they had been proclaiming.

The likelihood of this possibility depends upon what we understand Luke to mean by "salvation." Recall this distinction from the introduction: salvation *from* life-threatening peril, or salvation *to* a life of flourishing? Or both? The question of salvation emerges on the lips of the Philippian jailer, following an earthquake that—he erroneously presumes—has allowed all the prisoners to escape. Believing he has failed in his duty, he prepares to take his own life. When Paul informs the jailer that all the prisoners are still there, the relieved jailer inquires, "Sirs, what must I do to be saved?" Paul and Silas respond, "Believe on the Lord Jesus, and you will be saved, you and your household" (Acts 16:30–31). The jailer is most assuredly not asking how he might go to heaven when he dies, but rather how, having narrowly avoided a certain death sentence, he can be rescued from further trouble. The response to his question, to "believe (*pisteuson*) on the Lord Jesus" is not a command merely to give intellectual assent to a proposition (Jesus' atoning death), but rather to give an entirely new allegiance to Jesus as king.[6] This is not the sort of message a loyal citizen of Rome goes about saying.

This politically charged reading of Paul's message of salvation receives further support from what comes next in the narrative of Acts. After the magistrates politely but firmly ask them to leave, Paul and Silas head to Thessalonica. Over the course of three weeks, Paul proclaims that Jesus is the Messiah, a message eliciting both positive and negative responses. Eventually a mob forms and brings Paul's host Jason before the magistrates with this accusation: "'These people who have been turning the world upside down have come here also. . . . They are all acting contrary to the decrees of the emperor, saying that there is *another king* named Jesus'" (Acts 17:6–7; emphasis added). Another king? Assuming once again that the charge is not entirely specious, what does it imply about Paul's gospel proclamation that Jesus is Messiah? According to Luke, the "way of salvation" entailed *pistis* (faith, belief, allegiance) in Jesus, a king to whom allegiance constituted a political threat against Rome.[7]

Reading this portion of the narrative, I detect tension between Paul's proclamation of the gospel—the "way of salvation"—and his attitude towards his Roman citizenship. Notice, first of all, the parallelism between the accusations lodged against Paul in both Philippi and Thessalonica. "Customs that are not lawful for us as Romans" is echoed by "acting contrary to the decrees of the emperor" (Acts 16:21; 17:7). Paul's message of *pistis* in Jesus is seen as incommensurate with the commitments of Roman citizenship. And yet, sandwiched in between these two accusations, we find Paul in prison, parlaying the privilege of his Roman citizenship to his advantage, as he demands a public apology from the magistrates for his mistreatment.

What might account for this ambivalence in Paul's understanding of citizenship? And what might Paul's view of citizenship have to do with his gospel proclamation of the "way of salvation"? These questions require us to reflect further on the interrelationship between *polis*, *pistis*, and the good life. The concept of citizenship denotes membership within a *polis* as well as *pistis* (understood as allegiance) to laws and customs characteristic of the *polis*. Within certain streams of Greco-Roman political thought, the king was conceived as the living embodiment of good laws, a living, ensouled, or animate law (*nomos empsuchos*).[8] Allegiance to the laws of a *polis* could therefore be focused on the person of the king. Citizenship—the interrelationship of *polis* and *pistis*—was integrally connected to the pursuit of the good life, which was understood to be a *political* project, that is, taking place within the social context of the *polis*.

So, to the extent that salvation is bound up in the question of the good life for Paul, it should come as no surprise that salvation is also bound up in the question of citizenship. And what better place to explore the tension between citizenship and salvation than in Paul's letter to the church in Philippi, where Paul's imprisonment had led him to reflect upon the competing claims of *polis* and *pistis*.

1. Location, Location, Location: *Polis* and the Good Life

The Apostle Paul lived in a world in which philosophy, virtue, and citizenship were integrally connected. Even though Paul would not have seen himself as belonging to, or attempting to establish, a philosophical school, one may observe parallels between Paul's purposes and those of philosophy in antiquity.[9] Unlike the modern academic discipline of philosophy, in the ancient world philosophy was regarded as a way of life, an art of living aimed at a "profound transformation of the individual's mode of seeing and being."[10] Moreover, philosophy was a communitarian undertaking, by which philosophers (usually living and teaching together) sought to have "an effect on their cities, transforming society, and serving their citizens."[11] In brief, philosophy concerned itself with both the individual and corporate transformation of human life. This goal well describes "Paul's all-encompassing vision of what human society could be when structured around men and women walking in the fullness of Christ," a vision which "solved the problems human government always fails to solve."[12] Thus both Paul and ancient philosophers were animated by two questions: How can human character be formed? And what sort of human society both fosters, and results from, such formation?

The integral relationship between these questions is aptly illustrated by the interplay between two of Aristotle's seminal works, *Nicomachean Ethics* and *Politics*.[13] Writing in the fourth century BCE, Aristotle sets forth in the *Ethics* his understanding of *eudaimonia*—human flourishing—and how it may be achieved. To live the good life, he contends, one must be able to act reliably in accord with reason.[14] Such right moral action requires above all the possession of virtue (*aretē*).[15] Aristotle understands virtue to be a particular excellence of character (*ēthos*), acquired through habituation (*ethos*).[16] Generosity, for example, is the excellence in character pertaining to the disposition of material goods. In order to acquire a generous character, one must habitually practice generosity, imitating the practices of those who have already acquired this excellent state.[17]

Habituation through imitation naturally requires virtuous friends, a subject to which Aristotle devotes great attention in books 8–9 (*Nic. Eth.* 1155a–72a). The need for friends notwithstanding, a modern reader may be excused for thinking that Aristotle's project in the *Ethics* is highly individualistic. Although there are hints to the contrary throughout, he largely seems concerned with producing individuals possessing all the requisite virtues for human flourishing. Moreover, he does not think many will succeed in this endeavor. Yet towards the end of the *Ethics*, Aristotle tips his hand to his larger, more communal end, the establishment of the good *polis*.[18] In the *Politics*, Aristotle undertakes a rigorous, empirical inquiry into the best form of governance, yet the success of this endeavor depends upon the ability of the *polis* to reliably produce citizens worthy of itself.[19] Thus the end of the *Ethics*—the production of flourishing persons—serves the end of the *Politics*—the governance of a flourishing *polis*.[20]

But this is not just a one-way street, in which the virtuous citizen contributes to the good of the city. As Aristotle intimates towards the end of the *Ethics* and develops more fully in the *Politics*, the inculcation of virtue and the governance of the *polis* mutually reinforce each other (*Nic. Eth.* 1179b–1181b; *Pol.* 1252a–1253a). Indeed, it is impossible to actualize one's full potential outside of the *polis*, because, in Aristotle's memorable words, "man is by nature a political animal" (*Pol.* 1253a2).[21] One's sense of virtue depends greatly upon the *polis* one is formed in.[22] Although habituation is the primary mechanism by which the virtues are acquired, the larger concept of what constitutes moral excellence is fostered by the *polis*.[23] If one has been formed in a *polis* characterized by a deformed sense of the good, one's earnest pursuit of virtue ineluctably leads rather to vice.[24]

So, while the good *polis* requires morally virtuous citizens to function properly, such persons can only be reliably found within a *polis* that fosters the inculcation of moral virtues.[25] *Polis* and virtue are inextricably linked. Indeed, in the fifth through fourth centuries BCE, the concept of virtue itself takes on a political nuance: "It was seen primarily as the ability to rule other men, to desire what was *kalon* [fine] and *agathon* [good] and the power to obtain it."[26] If the good life, the pursuit of moral virtue, requires the order of the *polis*, how is this political order best achieved? That is, who should govern the virtuous *polis*? And what sort of relationship ought to exist between those who govern, and those governed? This brings us to the question of *pistis* and its importance for human flourishing.

2. I Pledge Allegiance: *Pistis* and the Good Life

If the function of the *polis* is to inculcate virtue within the citizenry, then those preeminent in virtue ought to govern. Considered alternately an elitist or merely a realist, Aristotle was under no illusion that the pursuit of virtue would be easy. Consequently, those possessing the virtues required to rule—the aristocracy—would be few. In fact, both Aristotle and Plato before him allowed for the theoretical possibility that one person supreme in virtue (should that person be found to exist) might rule alone: the philosopher-king.[27] The theoretical possibility of monarchical rule in classical Greece became a political fact after the conquest of Alexander the Great. In his wake, Hellenistic political philosophers (principally the Neopythagoreans) adapted the classical tradition to this new political reality, formulating an ideology of ideal kingship that was later appropriated within the Roman principate, or empire.[28]

Central to this ideology was the conviction that the good king, or emperor, the one preeminent in virtue, was essential to the inculcation of virtue within the citizenry. Such a person ruled as the vicegerent—one appointed to rule—of the god(s), receiving divine virtue as a gift that he transmitted as a benefit to his people.[29] The transformative effect of association with the good king followed from the "general Mediterranean belief that one's being in the presence of a deity causes transformation of the self."[30] This belief was also applied to the relationships between disciples in a philosophical school and their master, and helps us understand why political philosophers repeatedly insisted that kings must be philosophers.[31] As one who transmitted the divine benefit of virtue to the citizenry, the good king functioned as a benefactor.[32]

The fitting response to such benefaction was allegiance. The ancient Mediterranean phenomenon of benefaction, or euergetism (from *euergetēs*, the Greek term for benefactor) is rooted in the notion of magnificence (*megaloprepeia*), the virtue concerning the disposition of great wealth.[33] A person of surpassing excellence is not only magnificent, but must also cultivate magnanimity (*megalopsuchia*), the virtue concerned with the appropriate estimation of honor to oneself.[34] An important question emerges at this point: Given that virtuous friendships are instrumental to pursuing the good life, can the typical person ever truly become friends with a benefactor, an individual of such towering magnificence and magnanimity? I often contextualize this question for my students in this way: What manner of friendship can a freshman have with the president of our university?

Aristotle believed that, although an individual of modest virtue and means could and should endeavor to cultivate friendship with a truly magnificent and magnanimous person, such a relationship would always be asymmetrical. Benefactor and beneficiary were obligated to one another in a reciprocal, although unequal, relationship. In exchange for the benefactor's gift, the beneficiary was obliged to return gratitude, and above all, honor (*Nic. Eth.* 1163b15).[35] A similar dynamic existed between a king—the figure of surpassing virtue—and his subjects: "Both sides were keeping records, so to speak, on giving and receiving."[36] A king's benefactions engendered the loyalty of his subjects, as the Athenian orator Isocrates (436–338 BCE) somewhat cynically observes: "His friends he made subject to himself by his benefactions, the rest by his magnanimity he enslaved" (*Evag.* 45).[37] By metaphorically attributing to magnanimity an enslaving power, Isocrates highlights the vastly asymmetrical relationship engendered by royal benefaction. Rome's emperors adopted the Hellenistic ideology of kingship, offering divinely bestowed benefits to their subjects in exchange for their allegiance.[38]

Clarifying the principal thread of the argument thus far may be helpful before proceeding. The role of the king within the virtue-forming community of the *polis* is to confer upon the citizenry the divinely bestowed benefit of virtue. The citizens respond appropriately by giving allegiance to their benefactor the king. What, then, does this reciprocal relationship between benefaction and allegiance have to do with *pistis*, a word often translated as "faith" in Paul's letters?

The concept of allegiance owed to a king was often expressed in Mediterranean antiquity through the word *pistis* and its cognates.[39] As noted earlier, this term is frequently rendered as "faith" or "belief" when it appears in the New Testament; yet, as the following examples from Maccabean literature attest, *pistis* also appropriately expresses political loyalty.[40] First Maccabees is a history of the Hasmonean dynasty, from its origins in the revolt of Judas Maccabeus ("the hammer") in 167 BCE to the accession of John Hyrcanus in 134 BCE. The dramatic action arises from the Jewish effort to remain faithful to their ancestral religion in the face of the Hellenizing pressure of Greek kings. In 152 BCE, two rival claimants to the Seleucid throne, Alexander Epiphanes (also called Balas) and Demetrius I court the alliance of Jonathan, the brother of Judas (now dead). King Demetrius writes Jonathan the following:

> Since you have kept your agreement with us and have continued your friendship with us, and have not sided with our enemies, we have heard of it and rejoiced. Now continue still to keep faith (*pistin*) with us, and we will repay you with good for what you do for us. We will grant you many immunities and give you gifts. (1 Macc 10:27–28)

Note the reciprocal exchange here: Jonathan pledges *pistis* and in return the king offers to repay this expression of political loyalty with immunities and gifts, a lengthy list of which follows (vv. 29–45).[41] Included in this list is the offer for Jews to "be put in positions of trust (*pistin*) in the kingdom" (v. 37). Again, the term is used to convey political loyalty.[42]

Fourth Maccabees is set during the time of the Maccabean revolt and offers an extended philosophical reflection upon the martyrdom of a Jewish mother and her seven sons. These faithful Jews refuse to capitulate to the demands of King Antiochus IV Epiphanes that they abandon their religious practices.[43] The king entreats their obedience with the promise of reward:

> I also exhort you to yield to me and enjoy my friendship (*philias*). Just as I am able to punish those who disobey my orders, so I can be a

benefactor (*euergetein*) to those who obey me. Trust me (*pisteusate*), then, and you will have positions of authority in my government if you will renounce the ancestral tradition of your national life. (8:5–7)

Note again the reciprocal nature of the transaction being described. The king describes himself as a benefactor, one who is in a position to give gifts. In this instance, the king is offering political favor, *philia*, a technical term in Hellenistic political discourse to denote the status of advisors to a king.[44] But even if the seven sons pay nothing, the gift is by no means free. It is given in exchange for political loyalty, *pistis*.[45] Indeed, the whole rationale behind Antiochus Epiphanes' program of enforced Hellenization was likely to foster a deeper sense of cultural unity among a mixed population with the ultimate goal of making his subjects more loyal to himself.[46]

Further examples from the Maccabean literature could be added to this brief survey.[47] Nevertheless, it should be clear that *pistis*, normally rendered "faith" or "belief" in English translations of the Bible, is also used to denote political loyalty more broadly within Hellenistic literature that is roughly contemporaneous with Paul's letters.[48] It does not thereby follow that *pistis* should be translated "allegiance" or "loyalty" whenever we encounter it in Paul's writing. Rather, my hope is that by putting Paul into conversation with this political discourse—and the broader discourse concerning human flourishing with which it is related—we might hear afresh the political overtones of Paul's argument in Philippians. Consider these three instances of *pistis*, all in close proximity, in the opening chapter of that letter:

> I know that I will remain and continue with all of you for your progress and joy in faith (*pisteōs*). . . . Only, live your life (*politeuesthe*) in a manner worthy of the gospel of Christ, so that, whether I come and see you or am absent and hear about you, I will know that you are standing firm in one spirit, striving side by side with one mind for the faith (*pistei*) of the gospel. . . . For he has graciously granted you the privilege not only of believing (*pisteuein*) in Christ, but of suffering for him as well. (Phil 1:25, 27, 29)

It certainly makes good sense to think that Paul wants the audience to live their lives in a way that reflects faith or belief in Christ. But the task of "living one's life" is for Paul also a matter of "conducting oneself as a citizen," the normal meaning of the verb *politeuesthe*. In what kind of *polis* does Paul imagine his audience to be living as citizens? Does such citizenship require faith in Christ? Loyalty to Christ? Or both?

The argument so far can be summed up in the following points. The project of human flourishing in Mediterranean antiquity was a communal endeavor, involving membership in the *polis*. The function of the *polis* was to make virtuous people, a process that entailed habituation, imitation, and the collaboration of virtuous friends. Fully flourishing people in turn contributed to the flourishing of the *polis*. The leadership of the *polis* was entrusted to those preeminent in virtue; initially in theory, and later in fact, this ideal person was conceived of as a king. As a benefactor, the good king inculcated divinely bestowed virtue upon his subjects, and in return his beneficiaries owed him *pistis*, or allegiance.

Paul, I believe, would have accepted the conventional wisdom reflected in these commonly (if not universally) held assumptions. This is not to imply that Paul would have agreed with Aristotle's account of the virtues, or even his more basic claim that the human *telos* or function is *eudaimonia*.[49] Rather, as I shall argue, Paul would have seen this wisdom dramatically reconfigured through his *pistis* (faith? allegiance?) in Jesus the Messiah. Before exploring the way Paul does so, we must take account of the changes in the way virtue, *polis*, *pistis*, and above all, citizenship, were thought about in Paul's day as a result of an ascendant global superpower, Rome.

3. Citizenship in the Roman *Colonia* of Philippi: A Theology of Victory

The political landscape in the Mediterranean basin changed dramatically in the four centuries between Aristotle and Paul. By the middle of the fourth century BCE, the world of the historic Greek *polis* was in decline. In the wake of the military successes of Philip II of Macedon and his son Alexander, monarchical government spread throughout much of the Hellenized world. Rome, originally founded as a monarchy and reconstituted as a republic, eventually suffered a bitter civil war, the aftermath of which saw the establishment of a constitutional monarchy.[50] Individual *poleis* continued to exist, but with a much reduced degree of political autonomy under the rule of the new *cosmopolis*, or world city, Rome.

As a republic, Rome had begun the practice of extending the rights and responsibilities of Roman citizenship to cities in Italy, and increasingly during the principate, in the Hellenized provinces of the east.[51] The privilege of Roman citizenship, granted at times to individuals, at times to entire cities, involved the observance of Roman civil law and provided protection from magisterial *imperium*.[52] Citizens in the provinces were sometimes granted the right to vote should they ever reside in Rome. Often citizens enjoyed a relatively favorable tax status. Over the course of the first two centuries of the principate, as citizenship was offered more liberally, the practical advantages of Roman citizenship declined.[53]

Increasingly during this period, citizenship was sought not for its political significance but rather for the honor it conveyed. Citizenship was a mark of loyalty to Rome and was a component of the larger phenomenon of Romanization.[54] Thus, for example, a *municipium* might be rewarded for its loyalty and be granted the higher civic status of a *colonia*. Of particular relevance to the developing argument of this chapter, "in the hellenized East loyalty takes a less material form, its conspicuous characteristic or badge being devotion to the emperors."[55] Just as, in the Hellenistic era, the good king as benefactor was owed *pistis*, so now the honor of Roman citizenship implied allegiance to the emperor.

What was the significance of this changed political arrangement for the whole project of human flourishing? Remember that the Greek pursuit of the good life was undertaken in a *polis*, with the assistance of virtuous friends, under the leadership of those preeminent in virtue. How was this project conceived by citizens of the *cosmopolis* of Rome? The Hellenistic ideal of the king who inculcated virtue among the citizenry was adapted by Roman philosophers and poets and applied to the emperor. Rome's first emperor Augustus was routinely praised—indeed, he praised himself!—not merely for possessing the virtues requisite for a ruler, but for his ability to transmit these divinely bestowed virtues to the Roman people.[56] This phenomenon must be understood within the context of what the classical historian J. Rufus Fears has described as the Roman "Cult of Virtues."[57]

Grasping this aspect of Roman religious and political culture requires a somewhat technical discussion of the concept of virtue and, in Roman thought, its connection to the divine. The Apostle Paul lived in a world charged with divinity; how, then, did Greeks and Romans think about the concept of divinity? Fears offers the following definition:

> Within the framework of Greco-Roman paganism, a divinity may be defined as a supernatural power which is capable of rendering

benefits to the community of worshipers and which manifests its divinity by specific actions producing a characteristic result. For Symmachus, *utilitas*—benefits conferred—provided the clearest proof of the existence of gods.[58]

Romans would therefore establish cults to embody the proper relations between the people and the various gods, thereby ensuring the ongoing favor of the gods and the continued provision of the needed benefits. This practice was known generally as *theologia civilis*.[59] While all gods were believed to confer benefits, certain gods were known solely by the specific, concrete benefits they provided for humankind: *Concordia, Pax, Victoria*, and the like.[60] The specific practice of venerating such gods is referred to as the Cult of Virtues.[61]

This particular use of the word "virtue" requires further explanation. The Latin term *virtus*, derived from *vir* (man), originally described the sense of "manliness." The term was also used, however, to translate the Greek *aretē*, which comprised the broader conception of human excellence.[62] Thus the Latin term came to describe a composite sense of moral virtues such as *prudentia* (prudence), *iustitia* (justice), *fortitudo* (courage), and *temperantia* (temperance). Within the Hellenistic world, the good king was a model for subjects, and by his virtues, the commonwealth was preserved. Indeed, the king's character was defined by virtues he possessed, and he was thought to be able to bring these conditions into being; for this he was honored, sometimes in ways approaching divine honors, sometimes explicitly so. It must be remembered, however, that such honors functioned as a kind of idealized statement about what the king *should* be like rather than an accurate depiction of what he actually was.[63]

Both Greeks and Romans divinized rulers for possessing virtues; additionally, Romans divinized the virtues themselves, viewing them as divine benefits that the emperor, in his role as benefactor, would confer upon his people. During the first three centuries of the principate, the Virtues became shorthand for denoting "the universal beneficence of the *princeps* and the specific blessing bestowed upon the human race through the imperial saviour."[64] The following examples, related to the virtues of Concordia and Pax, illustrate the way in which the Roman Cult of Virtues served to legitimate imperial rule.

In 45 BCE, the Roman Senate decreed that a temple devoted to Concordia was to be established in Rome in honor of the civil concord brought about by Julius Caesar. The peace which arose out of Caesar's victory was also personified, and Pax appears for the first time on Roman coinage during this period. Caesar was also known for the virtue of Clementia, due to the mercy he showed to enemies; this virtue was recognized by the Senate a year later by the establishment of a temple devoted to Clementia Caesaris.

Augustus, Caesar's adopted son, inherited and formalized Caesar's virtues. He furthermore received great honor for his military victories as well as for restoring the *res publica* after a period of bitter civil war. In honor of this achievement, in 10 CE Augustus' adopted son Tiberius rededicated the temple to Concordia—it was known thereafter as the temple of Concordia Augusta. By restoring peace among the Roman people, Augustus was celebrated as having restored the *pax deorum*, the peace understood to exist between the gods and humanity. Thus, the *Pax Augusta* did not merely refer to the peace that Augustus had achieved, but the "divine power which produced *pax*: the godhead Pax performed her function within the sphere of Augustus' activity."[65] The Roman Cult of Virtues had the effect of making the emperor indispensable in the eyes of the public for bringing about the concrete conditions needed for prosperity and human flourishing. In effect, "the Augustan Virtues bespoke clearly the establishment of monarchy at Rome. . . . creating a mythology of imperial power capable of supporting the framework of oecumenical monarchy."[66]

While the emperor was widely celebrated for possessing an entire panoply of virtues, one reigned supreme: the virtue of Victory (*Victoria*).[67] So important were the emperor's divinely enabled military victory and the tangible benefits they realized for the Roman citizenry that they gave rise to an aspect of *theologia civilis* appropriately termed the Roman "theology of victory." This expression denotes a complex set of themes creating a political myth that legitimized imperial rule. There was not a dichotomy in the ancient world between the religious and the political; religion provided a sociological function—establishing the basis for social order—as well as a spiritual one.[68] This "theology of victory" both legitimated the emperor's rule and persuaded the populace that it was sharing in the fruits of a restored "golden age" of peace and prosperity.[69] This official propaganda, disseminated widely through the imperial cult, coinage, and monumental architecture, vouchsafed for citizens throughout the empire the stability and harmony of both the cosmic and social order.[70] The importance of this religious and political phenomenon cannot be overstated. Fears concludes: "Victoria came to be the center of a rich and complex political mythology, the most critical element in an ideology to support the immense and *fragile* fabric of the empire."[71] Not without good reason does Fears regard the enormous edifice of the Roman empire as fragile, requiring a well-crafted and continuously maintained apparatus for its legitimation.[72]

To see evidence of this fragility we need look no further than Philippi, where evidence of Rome's "theology of victory" would have been keenly felt, if perhaps not always believed. Founded as a Roman colony after the Battle of Philippi in 42 BCE and re-named *Colonia Iulia Augusta Philippensis* after the Battle of Actium in 31 BCE, Philippi preserved its Roman ethos well into the first century and beyond. Veterans from both of these battles had been rewarded through imperial land grants and settled in Philippi.[73] Although the proportion of veterans relative to the overall population of the city was likely not as large as has frequently been asserted, their presence nevertheless was significant.[74] Veterans belonged to the class of *honestiores*, those regarded as possessing honor (*dignitas*) within Roman society, a status that afforded them privileged standing within the legal system.[75] Veterans had contributed to the emperor's victory and were tangibly enjoying its benefits. Their presence in Philippi would have served as a potent symbol of the reigning political ideology.

It is not likely, however, that many veterans, or other elites, comprised the membership of the Philippian church that received Paul's letter. That congregation no doubt reflected the larger socioeconomic make-up of the town, which consisted of something like 97 percent commuting peasants, service groups, the poor, and slaves, with only about 3 percent affluent elites.[76] The letter itself gives evidence that the church was suffering, likely as a result of proclaiming the gospel to family, friends, and associates.[77] Put differently, their special suffering was the direct result of proclaiming the advent of a worldwide kingdom whose king was *not* Caesar. Given the economic vulnerability of the congregation, there is good reason to believe that this suffering was economic in nature.[78] Thus Paul's letter would have been heard by those for whom the ubiquitous symbols underlining the Roman theology of victory rang false.

The point of the preceding discussion has been to situate Paul's letter to the church in Philippi within overlapping discourses concerning the life of human flourishing and the nature of citizenship in the Greco-Roman world. To help sum up, let us imagine how someone who actually lived in this world might have answered the following questions. How would you describe the good life? *Living in a community of individuals who together seek the excellences of character—moral virtues—that contribute to individual and communal flourishing.* How should such a community be governed? *Those preeminent in virtue ought to govern, thereby inculcating virtue within the citizenry.* How does such a leader inculcate virtue? *The gods bestow virtue upon the king, and as benefactor, the king bestows the benefit of virtue on the people.* How does one relate to the good king? *By giving to him one's embodied allegiance.* Where can such a king be found? *The true king, the vicegerent of the gods, the benefactor of humankind, the guarantor of victory, is of course none other than Rome's glorious emperor.* The pursuit of the good life in Paul's day thus entailed citizenship in the *cosmopolis* of Rome as well as allegiance to Rome's emperor. To help us think about the importance of such allegiance in Paul's day, consider what allegiance means today.

4. Citizenship in the Heavenly Commonwealth: A Theology of Suffering

"I pledge allegiance to the flag of the United States of America." Can you remember where and when you first learned to recite that pledge? I can: Ms. Chick's kindergarten classroom at Marston Elementary School in Berlin, New Hampshire. Every morning, we faced the front of the classroom where the flag was hung. A bank of windows to my left flooded the classroom with light. Since I had not yet reliably learned left from right, I had to look to the windows to get my bearings before placing my right hand over my heart as we began every school day with this solemn oath.[79] I was four years old when I started to learn the Pledge of Allegiance. To the best of my memory, I could not as of yet tie my shoes, read, add or subtract, or recite my home address or telephone number. I am certain that I did not comprehend the words "pledge" and "allegiance" or what I was committing to by joining these words together in a sentence. I was unable to grasp the symbolic significance of a flag and had not the faintest idea of what a republic was, and how the one might stand for the other. And yet my teachers and parents, no less than the more distant bureaucrats and politicians responsible for the larger system of education, all saw fit to begin making a good citizen out of me at this tender age. At the heart of this practical and symbolic education lay the Pledge of Allegiance.

Why do we regard allegiance to be of such paramount importance for citizenship?[80] Many helpful answers could be given to this question, no doubt, but I propose the following one, not only because I think it has good explanatory value, but also because it helps us understand the way Paul might have negotiated the demands and privileges of citizenship in his own world.

Allegiance is a necessary condition for the shaping of a virtuous character. The concept of allegiance presupposes a relationship of some kind, either to an individual, a group of people, or an entity larger and more complex, yet still composed of people. One cannot meaningfully pledge allegiance to an inanimate object such as a car, or to an abstract concept such as freedom. The flag is only worthy of allegiance insofar as it is a symbol of "the republic for which it stands," as the Pledge of Allegiance itself says.[81]

This relational dimension of allegiance is important, because relationships shape us in myriad ways, for good or ill. It thus follows that to pledge one's allegiance to a person or community is to open oneself to being shaped through relationship with such people. Recall Aristotle's insight that the flourishing *polis* and the flourishing person are mutually reinforcing goals. You cannot pursue one without the other. To become a virtuous participant in a virtuous society is a deeply relational project, one that shapes character through relationships between people whose lives are wedded to a common project in a shared place. Allegiance is obviously a practical necessity for the success of such a project: the difficult path of pursuing the good life requires profound commitment to the good of others, the settled conviction that one's destiny is inextricably bound up with the destiny of one's neighbors and one's neighborhood. But allegiance is also necessary because relational commitment is a powerful vehicle (although certainly not the only one) for the transformation of character.

To illustrate this point, consider how allegiance to Christ plays a role in forming the Philippians' understanding of generosity. Philippians may best be read as a letter of thanks.[82] Paul is writing from prison, probably in Ephesus, although a later imprisonment in Rome is also possible. The Philippian believers have undertaken to support Paul's physical needs by sending a member of their congregation, Epaphroditus, to him with a gift. The gift likely consisted of money with which to buy food as well as the services of Epaphroditus. Given that prisoners were responsible for their own food while in prison, it is no exaggeration to say that Paul owes his life to the Philippians' sacrificial generosity.

It is important to underscore that this gift probably came at great cost to people whom, as noted, were likely close to the margins of existence themselves.[83] One of the principal aims of the letter, then, is to express Paul's profound gratitude. Given this goal, it is strange that Paul does not even explicitly mention the Philippians' gift until the very end of the letter (4:10–20). And when he does finally thank them for their gift, his tone seems reserved, even off-handed. He rejoices that they have "at last" revived their concern for him, suggesting perhaps that they had earlier promised a gift and had failed to deliver (4:10). Paul is furthermore quick to add that he is not actually concerned about his own needs, having learned the secret of contentment with both little and plenty (4:11–12). "In any case," he adds coolly, "it was kind of you to share in my distress" (4:14). To paraphrase: "Thanks for your gift, which was late, and which I didn't need—but a kind gesture nonetheless." Saying thank you can often be awkward, but Paul seems to be having a terrible time of it!

There are, of course, rhetorical conventions in antiquity that would have made Paul's words sound less strained than they do to modern ears. But the explanation goes deeper than style and has to do with what motivates Paul to say thank you to the Philippians in the first place.[84] He is not driven merely by a sense of propriety, or even a deeper sense of personal gratitude. He is most keen to interpret for them the christological significance of their gift: "Not that I seek the gift," he explains, "but I seek the profit that accumulates to your account" (4:17).

Speaking of "profit" in the same breath as giving thanks for a gift may strike us as particularly gauche, but the turn of phrase picks up on one of the important themes of the letter. Right from the opening lines, Paul sets out to redefine how the Philippians are to think of profit and loss, victory and defeat. Although in prison on a serious charge—seemingly a defeat—Paul rejoices because the gospel is being proclaimed—a surprising victory (1:12–18). Although formerly confident of his status within God's covenant people Israel, he now regards these putative gains as loss (3:4–7).

It is not the case that Paul is merely a sunny optimist by nature. Rather, Paul has come to experience the world differently as a result of coming to "know Christ and the power of his resurrection" (3:10). The pretext of giving thanks (not that I doubt his heartfelt sincerity) gives Paul the opportunity to interpret for the Philippians why their sacrificial giving—doubtless a loss in strict economic terms—constitutes a profit within the political economy of Christ's reign. To phrase this goal in terms of the discourse discussed earlier, Paul aims to redefine the good life of human flourishing in a way that implicitly critiques the Roman imperial "theology of victory."

The nature of this christologically redefined good life can be discerned by attending to three closely related claims that Paul makes in the course of the letter. First, Paul exhorts the Philippians to conduct themselves worthily as citizens. Initially, however, it is not clear *where* their citizenship is held. Worthy conduct is not defined with respect to a *polis* (for example, Rome, or Philippi) but rather with respect to *pistis*. The evidence of their proper conduct as citizens is that Paul will know that they are "standing firm in one spirit, striving side by side with one mind for the faith (*pistei*) of the gospel" (1:27).

Second, Paul gives shape to this *pistis* by calling the Philippians to be of the same mind as Christ Jesus. Worthy conduct by citizens is characterized by conformity to the pattern of Christ's life: refusing to exploit status, he emptied himself to the point of death and was ultimately exalted by God (2:5–11).

Third, this conduct—cruciform living in the pattern of a crucified king—makes sense only because the Philippians are actually citizens of a different *polis*, a heavenly *politeuma*, or commonwealth (3:20). Paul indeed wants to thank them for their sacrificial gift, but even more he wants to interpret for them that such cruciform generosity is actually paradigmatic of the good life, a life characterized by allegiance to a crucified king who reigns over a heavenly commonwealth.

4.1. Conduct Worthy of Citizenship (Phil 1:27)

Earlier in this chapter, I suggested that, according to the narrative of Acts, Paul had conducted himself in a way unbecoming of a Roman citizen during his first visit to Macedonia. In Philippi, Paul had cast out a spirit of divination from a slave-girl who had been loudly announcing that Paul and his associates were proclaiming "a way of salvation (*sōtērias*)." Deprived of their source of revenue, the girl's owners brought Paul before the magistrates, accusing him of "advocating customs that are not lawful for . . . Romans to adopt or observe." These charges were subsequently echoed in Thessalonica, where Paul's hosts were accused by an angry mob of "acting contrary to the decrees of the emperor, saying that there is another king named Jesus" (Acts 16:18, 21; 17:7). While the charges were prejudicial, there was more than a grain of truth to them. Paul's new way of *sōtēria* entailed allegiance to another *sōtēr*. Loyalty to Jesus challenged the loyalty due to Rome's emperor. The charges against Paul in Philippi had resulted in a severe beating and imprisonment. Now, as Paul writes this letter of thanks to his friends and supporters in Philippi, he finds himself once again in prison.

Paul does not need to inform the Philippians of this fact; after all, they had already sent Epaphroditus to him with the gift. He does, however, need to help them think through the implications of his current circumstances. Paul's chains are not, as perhaps the Philippians might fear, evidence of Paul's recidivist behavior—he is not in prison once again simply because he loves to make trouble. Nor is Paul's imprisonment evidence that the gospel proclamation has somehow failed. Rather, Paul's plight has actually served to spread the gospel, and this is cause for rejoicing rather than lament (1:12, 18).

This perspective is crucially important for the Philippians to grasp because they are, as Paul reminds them, partners, or sharers, in God's grace (1:7). The term Paul uses to describe their relationship—*sugkoinōnos* —bespeaks a business partnership.[85] Although the Philippians have indeed invested their limited financial resources to care for Paul in prison, the aim of their partnership is not, however, any financial profit. The "business" venture in which they are partners is nothing less than "the defense and confirmation of the gospel" (1:7), an enterprise in which they have invested their very selves.[86]

The Philippians, in other words, have a vested interest in understanding the reasons for Paul's imprisonment. It is not simply that they care for his well-being; rather, they are his *partners* in the gospel and are therefore entitled to an accounting. How can the gospel message be succeeding when its proponent languishes in prison? Of what value is a "way of salvation" that leads one to the very real possibility of violent death?[87] How should such failure be interpreted in a world awash in the "theology of victory"? And what might Paul's conduct and its consequences imply for the Philippians' own destiny?

Paul well understands that he must interpret his imprisonment in order to address such questions. This is why he prays for the Philippians' discernment, in order that their "love may overflow more and more with knowledge and full insight" (1:9). Such wisdom will enable them not only to understand the implications of Paul's imprisonment with respect to their shared gospel mission, but also to reflect upon their own conduct as citizens.

Having explained that his imprisonment has actually served to spread the gospel and does not therefore indicate the failure of their partnership (1:12–26), Paul makes the following request:

> Only, live your life (*politeuesthe*) in a manner worthy of the gospel of Christ, so that, whether I come and see you or am absent and hear about you, I will know that you are standing firm in one spirit, striving side by side with one mind for the faith (*pistei*) of the gospel, and are in no way intimidated by your opponents. For them this is evidence of their destruction, but of your salvation (*sōtērias*). And this is God's doing. For he has graciously granted you the privilege not only of believing (*pisteuein*) in Christ, but of suffering for him as well—since you are having the same struggle that you saw I had and now hear that I still have. (1:27–30)

It might seem that Paul is moving on to a new subject—having addressed the problem of his imprisonment, he now pivots to the subject of ethics. This is not the case, however: it merely seems so because many English translations render the verb *politeuein* as though it simply connoted proper moral conduct.[88] Yet in virtually every other instance in extant Greek literature, the verb means something like "to live as a citizen."[89] Paul, moreover, is aware of verbs that straightforwardly and simply describe proper moral behavior, and uses such verbs often.[90] It therefore seems reasonable to believe that Paul is aware of the political nuance of the verb *politeuein* and selects it for this very reason.[91]

Why might he do so? On one level, Paul may well understand the question of moral conduct to be simply a matter of politics, in the sense that the flourishing of individuals and the *polis* are inextricably intertwined. I suspect, however, that Paul's purpose goes deeper than a mere nod to this piece of conventional wisdom. Paul may be drawn to the verb *politeuein* precisely at this point in his argument because he wishes to underline the political significance of the gospel. While Paul uses the term "gospel" in a variety of ways, the basic meaning of the term denotes a "glad proclamation" (*eu-angelion*). The word was used frequently in this sense to announce or celebrate the reign of a new emperor. So, for Paul, the "gospel of Christ" constitutes a political announcement, the glad tidings of the present-and-coming reign of Christ.[92] Paul's intent in using the verb *politeuein* may well be to urge the Philippian church to a particular sort of *political* conduct in light of this new *political* announcement.

What might such conduct entail? And in what sense would it count as *political*? The immediate context reveals several dimensions of this conduct worthy of citizens of the new kingdom. First, it requires unity of purpose, expressed in "striving side by side (*sunathlountes*) . . . for the faith (*pistei*) of the gospel" (1:27). Does it make sense here to interpret *pistis* as *embodied allegiance*? Such a translation would seem to yield a very odd sentence indeed: "striving for the allegiance of the gospel." The oddness, however, may be more perceived than actual. Most English translations take the relationship between the verb "striving side by side" and the noun "faith" to be one of advantage: striving together *for* the faith. One could just as well understand the relationship between the verb (*sunathlountes*) and the noun (*pistei*) in a causal sense: striving side by side *because* of allegiance to the gospel.[93] Allegiance, in this sense, is what motivates the striving. Considering that the gospel is the glad announcement of Jesus' reign, one is justified in thinking that Paul expects his audience to express their embodied allegiance to Jesus as king.

Second, directly following from the first, the Philippians are to stand firm together against their opponents. Unity in the face of opposition constitutes, surprisingly, the evidence of their salvation and their opponents' destruction. Such evidence is by no means *self*-evident. Paul writes from the experience of standing firm himself against those who oppose him by proclaiming Christ "out of selfish ambition," attempting to increase his suffering while he is in prison (1:17).[94] Third and finally, conduct worthy of citizens entails suffering, which Paul shockingly claims to be a privilege graciously granted by God (1:29)! Suffering, moreover, is related to *pistis*, which is reflected in the parallel syntax of Paul's sentence. To translate it woodenly:

> To you it has been graciously granted, on behalf of Christ,
> not only unto him to give *pistis* (*to eis auton pisteuein*)
> but also for him to suffer (*to huper autou paschein*). (1:29)

The precise nature of this relationship is not exactly clear. Reflecting on Paul's own circumstances, however, one might think of suffering as the expected consequence of embodied allegiance to Jesus. Indeed, Paul encourages the Philippians to see their own struggles as analogous to his own (1:30). Living as a citizen of this new kingdom would thus seem to imply at the very least a posture of unity, giving allegiance to Jesus, and suffering for him.

In what sense does Paul view such conduct as political? At this point in the letter, the answer is not yet clear, although we can discern hints that point in the direction of his developing argument. Already the Philippians have been called to strive side by side towards a common goal. Throughout the letter, Paul will reiterate the importance of their unity (2:1–4; 3:15; 4:2–3). This emphasis can be understood within the wider philosophical and political discourse that regarded the flourishing of the individual and of the *polis* to be inseparable. By calling his audience to conduct themselves worthily as citizens, then, Paul is intimating that their conduct has a larger *telos*, the well-being of the *polis*.

Their conduct can also be understood as political in the sense that it derives from their allegiance to Jesus as king. In a truly puzzling move, however, Paul correlates this allegiance with suffering. Not only that, but he characterizes suffering for Christ as a divinely granted privilege. The strategy is puzzling not simply because suffering would seem to be, at least conventionally, at odds with divine privilege. Paul, remember, is endeavoring to explain to the Philippians why their partnership in the gospel has not been in vain. A strategy more likely to persuade would have been to downplay his sufferings, to acknowledge them but regard them with equanimity.[95] Instead he rejoices in them (1:18; 2:17).

This attitude to suffering would surely have seemed absurd in the context of Rome's theology of victory. Rome's emperor was regarded as blessed with *felicitas*, the combination of happiness and divine good fortune. Consequently, "such a blessed mortal becomes a saviour to his nation, and the manifest possession of such *felicitas* is sufficient reason to entrust him with unprecedented authority."[96] By contrast, Paul's suffering would appear to be unquestionable evidence of divine *dis*favor. Paul, however, plainly argues otherwise, and his argument rests on his portrayal of Jesus as a suffering king.

4.2. Imagining Downward Mobility (Phil 2:5–11)

Intuitively, suffering seems antithetical to the good life. Recall the conversation I had with the Somali man prior to my naturalization ceremony. It was his suffering—both physical danger and economic privation—that had led him to seek citizenship in the United States. The privilege of citizenship in a prosperous *polis* is, according to all ordinary wisdom, a sensible strategy for *avoiding* suffering. What, then, can Paul mean by claiming that suffering for Christ is, in itself, a *privilege*? Such a notion is so vastly out of step with the prevailing assumption of his age—that citizenship confers the rich benefit of sharing in the emperor's *Victoria*—that it demands an explanation.

Yet explanation or rationale is not exactly what Paul gives. Rather, he undertakes the task of disciplined *imagination*. By this I do not imply that Paul engages in a flight of fantasy. Far from it. Paul aims to recalibrate the imagination of the Philippian believers, showing them that what they previously imagined to be absurd is not only possible but actual: suffering is the way of Jesus the king.

Having exhorted the Philippian believers to unity in suffering (2:1-4), Paul makes clear what resources he expects will fund this unity. Believers are to have "the same mind . . . that was in Christ Jesus" (2:5-11):

> [A] who, though he was in the form of God, did not regard equality with God as something to be exploited,
>> [B] but emptied himself, taking the form of a slave, being born in human likeness.
>>> [C] And being found in human form, he humbled himself and became obedient to the point of death—
>>>> [D] even death on a cross.
>>> [C'] Therefore God also highly exalted him and gave him the name that is above every name,
>> [B'] so that at the name of Jesus every knee should bend, in heaven and on earth and under the earth,
> [A'] and every tongue should confess that Jesus Christ is Lord, to the glory of God the Father.

I have chosen to lay out this portion of the letter in a way that underlines its poetic qualities (as some modern Bible versions also do). Paul is probably quoting a hymn here, likely one that the Philippian believers were familiar with, possibly one they had learned from Paul.[97] The hymn tells the story of Christ's descent to the point of death on a cross, and his subsequent ascent, or exaltation. The parallelism between Christ's descent and ascent provides the basic structure of the hymn.[98] In the first unit, Christ is declared to be in the form of God [A]. This is paralleled in the final unit by the universal recognition that Jesus Christ is Lord [A']. The interior units describe Christ's stepwise descent, first taking on human form [B], and then humbling himself to the point of death [C]. This is mirrored by a stepwise ascent: God exalts Christ [C'], such that every knee bows before him [B']. The parallel structure, sometimes described as *chiastic*, after the shape of the Greek letter *chi* (X), draws the eye to the central element, which is without parallel: "even death on a cross" [D]. The poetic structure and language of the hymn, underlining Christ's shameful death, well serves Paul's rhetorical purpose at this point in his argument.

Indeed, it would not be an exaggeration to claim that this hymn's imaginative appeal constitutes the center of gravity for the entire letter.[99] The story of Christ's descent and ascent in the hymn is paradigmatic for Paul; it is his "master story."[100] The paradigm consists of two narrative movements: humiliation and exaltation. Christ's humiliation consists of the following components: possessing status ("in the form of God"); renouncing status ("did not regard equality . . . exploited"); and self-abasement ("emptied himself . . . obedient to the point of death"). Exaltation consists of two components: divine vindication ("God . . . exalted him"); and universal acknowledgement ("every tongue should confess").[101]

This voluntary renunciation of status, embrace of suffering, and trust in God's vindication constitute for Paul not just the story of Christ but also the paradigm for discipleship. Paul believes that his suffering in prison conforms to this pattern (1:12–26), as do the examples of Timothy and Epaphroditus raised later in the letter (2:19–30). The "enemies of the cross" whom he opposes are such precisely because they reject this pattern of suffering (3:18–19).[102] Euodia and Syntyche, two members of the Philippian congregation, are exhorted to display the same cruciform love as Christ demonstrates in the hymn (4:2–3).[103]

Given the centrality of the hymn to the letter, how does it relate to Paul's earlier claim regarding citizenship? Two answers can be given. First, and most obviously, the story of Christ's voluntary renunciation of status helps Paul to explain his own suffering and imprisonment, and in so doing also addresses the implicit question about Paul's own conduct vis-à-vis his Roman citizenship. Having learned of Paul's second imprisonment, the Philippians would have had reason to worry about the viability of their gospel partnership: can one trust the announcement that Jesus is king when his apostle languishes in a Roman prison?

Second, they would also have had reason to question whether allegiance to this king would ineluctably lead to the same fate as Paul. This concern is especially acute since Paul unabashedly holds himself up as an example to be followed: "Brothers and sisters," he writes, "join in imitating me, and observe those who live according to the example you have in us" (3:17).[104]

The Christ-hymn addresses both of these concerns. Paul's imprisonment does not cast a shadow over the plausibility of the gospel, because Christ himself embraced the sort of shameful suffering Paul is now experiencing. And allegiance to Jesus will likely—if not necessarily—lead the Philippians to share in Paul's suffering. Indeed, to some extent they are already doing so (1:30). Having recalled for them the story of Jesus the suffering king, Paul in effect implies that living life as citizens entails suffering because it is the path of allegiance to Jesus.

But how is allegiance to Jesus implied in the Christ-hymn? After all, *pistis* is never mentioned, nor is there any explicit command to imitate Jesus' suffering. The Philippians are, however, enjoined to "let the same mind be (*phroneite*) in you that was in Christ Jesus" (2:5). This short sentence has actually presented quite a difficulty for translators.[105] Yet however the verse is translated, the meaning of the imperative (*phroneite*, "think") is clear. Paul is calling them to cultivate the virtue of *phronēsis*—practical wisdom, prudence, or "moral insight"—after the pattern of Jesus' own *phronēsis*.[106]

The virtue of *phronēsis* enables one to deliberate well between multiple seemingly good choices to arrive at a course of action leading to a good end.[107] Acquiring the virtue of *phronēsis* requires (as do all the moral virtues) both habituation and the examples of virtuous friends to follow. The ideal king was thought to be preeminent in virtue, and as such the benefactor of humankind. Friendship with such an individual, however, was invariably asymmetrical. To one's benefactor the appropriate response was allegiance. Earlier I had suggested that allegiance was important to the entire project of human flourishing because the relational aspect of allegiance was critical to the task of character formation. Learning the *phronēsis* of Jesus is an excellent example of the way allegiance and character formation work together.

Acquiring the virtue of Jesus' practical wisdom points to the second way in which the Christ-hymn relates to Paul's earlier exhortation to live as citizens of the new regime. The pursuit of the good life in Greco-Roman society, based upon the acquisition of virtue, was in many respects an "agonistic," or competitive, pursuit.[108] And as is frequently the case in competition, this pursuit was a zero-sum game. The limited quantity was not the virtue itself, but rather the honor that accrued to those who possessed virtue. In fact, Aristotle regarded the ability to properly esteem the honor due oneself to be a virtue in itself: magnanimity (*megalopsuchia*).

Because honor was, and indeed was understood to be, a very limited good, the elites within Greco-Roman society competed fiercely for it. Benefaction was one of the many activities by which one could accrue honor for oneself. Distributing massive amounts of wealth to the *polis* was also intrinsically a virtue: magnificence (*megaloprepeia*). Such virtues we might term "ruling" virtues, in the sense that they were associated with the ruling elite. These "ruling" virtues could be—and often were—manipulated for political ends, as evidenced by the emperor Augustus' boasting of his benefactions to the Roman people (*Res gest.* 15–24).[109]

Aristotle also argued that one must possess—or endeavor to possess—*all* the virtues in order to truly flourish. Justice (*dikaiosunē*), while constituting a critical virtue in its own right, was also the state in which all the virtues worked together in harmony. So for Aristotle, at least, "ruling" virtues could have their appropriate place only when harmonized with all the others. Yet one can easily imagine the natural human tendency to recognize the sort of virtues that accrue honor—magnanimity and magnificence—more than the other virtues.[110] Isocrates, writing in the fourth century BCE, remarked that many—falsely in his view—regarded kings to be the equal of the gods because of their great wealth, honor, and power (*Ad Nicoclem* 5).

How does Paul's Christ-hymn address these popular conceptions of the "ruling" virtues? In brief, Paul rejects them. The requisite virtues for the good king are not the powerful ruling virtues of magnificence and magnanimity. The way to acquire great honor is not to pursue it head on, but rather to renounce status and embrace suffering. Although by the end of the hymn, Christ is exalted by God and is universally honored, the focal point of the hymn is not Christ's honor but rather his shame. The hymn's chiastic arrangement focalizes not merely Christ's death, but his *shameful* death on a Roman cross.

For the Philippians reading, singing, or listening to this hymn, giving *pistis* to Jesus will thus require a radical recalibration of their imagination. Even as their thinking changes, so must their actions. Allegiance to Jesus as king, as I argue above, consists in acquiring the virtue of Jesus' *phronē-sis*. This virtue enables one to deliberate wisely among possible courses of action, selecting the one that will most reliably lead to the desired outcome. With respect to the exercise of rule, a Christ-formed *phronēsis* will lead one not to exploit status for greater honor, power, and wealth. Rather, the "ruling" virtue espoused by Jesus the king and those loyal to his reign is suffering.

To speak of suffering as a virtue immediately raises a number of questions, not least of which is whether the category of "virtue" is ever even appropriate to the experience of suffering. Such questions will be addressed below. For the present, I merely wish to emphasize how *strange* it is to characterize suffering in this way. For Paul to present Jesus as a king who voluntarily renounced status and chose suffering would have been entirely antithetical to the entire theology of victory regnant throughout the Roman empire. Enabling his audience to imagine a world in which such a claim is plausible leads Paul to recall for them the striking poetry of this familiar hymn. And yet imagining a suffering king is only half the battle. The Philippians must also imagine the commonwealth over which Christ reigns.

4.3. A Commonwealth in the Heavens (Phil 3:20): What and Where?

At the beginning of the *Politics*, Aristotle makes the argument that the *polis* is logically antecedent to other forms of human community—family, village—and even to the individual. The whole, he reasons, is prior to the part. "The complete community," he insists, "is the *polis*. It reaches a level of full self-sufficiency, so to speak; and while coming into being for the sake of living, it exists for the sake of *living well*" (*Pol.* 1.2.8 [1252b; emphasis added]).[111] The *polis* exists "by nature," by which Aristotle means that the *polis* is that community in which humankind's natural function may be realized. Therefore it follows "that man is by nature a political animal (*politikon zōon*). He who is without a *polis* through nature rather than chance is either a mean sort or superior to man" (*Pol.* 1.2.9 [1253a]). To be a political animal without a *polis* is like being a fish out of water; it is to be fundamentally incomplete:

> For if the individual when separated from it is not self-sufficient, he will be in a condition similar to that of the other parts in relation to the whole. One who is incapable of sharing (*koinōnēn*) or who is in need of nothing through being self-sufficient is no part of a city, and so is either a beast or a god. (1.2.14 [1253a])

For a human to live well requires community (*koinōnia*), a sharing of common purpose. Without this, one is hardly more than a beast.

I bring us back to Aristotle's thoughts on the *polis* in order to highlight a deficiency up to this point in Paul's argument. He has exhorted the Philippians to conduct worthy of citizens (1:27). He has made clear to them the countercultural nature of their king's suffering reign (2:6–11). But where is the *polis*? If Christ is a king, over what does he rule? As noted, the good king in Mediterranean antiquity was portrayed as a savior (*sōtēr*), which envisioned both his liberation of the *polis* and subsequent rule over it. Without a *polis* to rule, the reign of Jesus would seem to be incomplete or even nonsensical, and the Philippians would seem to fall short of living well. With such questions in mind, Paul explains:

> But our citizenship (*politeuma*) is in heaven, and it is from there that we are expecting a Savior (*sōtēr*), the Lord Jesus Christ. He will transform the body of our humiliation that it may be conformed to the body of his glory, by the power that also enables him to make all things subject to himself. (3:20–21)

The Greek word rendered "citizenship" by the NRSV and many other translations is not *politeia*, as one might expect. Rather, Paul speaks of a *politeuma*, a word that connotes a wider sphere of meaning than our English word "citizenship." What does he mean by it?

The word *politeuma* was used in a variety of distinct yet related ways during the Classical, Hellenistic, and Roman periods.[112] Basic to all of the derived meanings is the concept of political activity or action. While the term could indeed denote the concept of citizenship, this meaning is not well attested in the first century CE and it is therefore not likely that Paul used it in this way.[113] In Paul's day the term *politeuma* frequently denoted the *polis* itself, understood as the state or commonwealth.[114] Behind this meaning stands the concept of the *politeuma* as the government, or the ruling administrative organization of the *polis*.[115] It is not difficult to imagine that Paul intends his audience to see themselves as members of some sort of heavenly *polis*. Yet can we imagine that Paul also is encouraging the Philippian church to envision themselves as somehow involved in the *government* of this commonwealth?

It is simply laughable, on the face of it, to imagine that Paul expects members of a fringe religious group of low socioeconomic status to see themselves as having a vital role in the administration of any *polis*, whether heavenly or terrestrial. The notion is thoroughly implausible, but perhaps no more so than the exhortation to participate joyfully in the suffering of the Messiah Jesus. In what world would either of these claims make sense? Certainly not in the world of Roman imperial propaganda, in which the emperor's victory has brought power and prosperity, at least to the elites within the empire. But Paul insists that Christ-followers do not live in that world. The *politeuma* to which they belong exists "in the heavens."

There are two important dimensions to this expression which will help us understand what sort of *politeuma* Paul is talking about. When Paul locates this *politeuma* "in the heavens" (*en ouranois*) he is speaking both temporally and spatially, even though these elements exist in tension with each other. Heaven is the realm in which God reigns, the domain of God's effective authority. In temporal terms, God's reign *on earth* lies in the future; it will not come into being in fullness until the *eschaton*, or end time. Paul believes, however, that this future consummation has been brought forward into the present through the death and resurrection of God's Messiah Jesus.

Thus, incipiently, the transcendent realm of God's authority now exists spatially on earth through the reign of the Messiah.[116] By claiming to belong to a *politeuma* existing within the transcendent realm of God's authority, inaugurated yet waiting its future consummation, Paul implies that two assumptions behind Roman eschatology are false. Rome's eschatological vision was decidedly presentist: the emperor's virtue had *already* established the *pax deorum* and there was therefore no need to await a future consummation.[117] Furthermore, the very existence of this blessed state of affairs entailed allegiance to Rome's emperor as the savior (*sōtēr*) who had achieved it. Paul's confident expectation of a coming savior from the heavens undermines both of these Roman assumptions.

It must furthermore be stressed that Paul is by no means simply expressing the hope to "go to heaven when he dies." Paul's vision of salvation is not "incanting anemic souls to heaven."[118] He is indeed facing the imminent possibility of death and expresses confidence that death would usher him into the presence of Jesus (1:20–24). At this point in the argument, however, he is not preparing his audience for death, but rather giving instructions for living. He exhorts them: "Join in imitating me, and observe those who *live* according to the example you have in us" (3:17; emphasis added). In so doing, he says, they will avoid the error of those who live as "enemies of the cross of Christ," refusing to conform to the cruciform pattern of Christ's reign (3:18).[119] Paul is not encouraging the Philippians with the hope that they will be evacuated from earth to meet their *sōtēr* in some distant celestial realm. He rather confidently expects the *sōtēr* to come *from* heaven to effect transformation in their communal life on earth (3:20–21).[120]

Citizenship in the heavenly commonwealth is therefore *christomorphic*: the goal is for the citizens to become conformed to the likeness of their king. This is both a present and future reality.[121] Heavenly citizenship moreover concerns *mundane*—in the sense of "pertaining to earth"—activity.[122] Paul, in other words, has in mind the same sort of thing he emphasized when he earlier exhorted them to conform their *phronēsis* to that of Christ.

Locating the *politeuma* within the transcendent realm of God's authority and reign opens up the possibility that Paul may indeed be encouraging his audience to see themselves as having a vital role in the governance of the *polis* where they live—both the *cosmopolis* of Rome and its *colonia* Philippi. Clearly, such a suggestion would sound like nonsense within the plausibility structure of the Roman empire. But as Newbigin insists, the gospel intends not to justify itself within the bounds of whatever a particular culture deems plausible, but rather announces a new reality in light of which the reigning plausibility structure must itself be reconsidered.[123]

I am not suggesting that Paul intends his audience to launch a political movement by which people of low socioeconomic status like the believers in Philippi take hold of the levers of local government or mount an insurrection against Rome. Of course, Paul *does* expect that as a consequence of the gospel announcement of "another king named Jesus," the church will indeed turn "the world upside down," but not through a political revolution as such movements have been regularly conceived and enacted in human history.[124] Rather, I am arguing that Paul wants the church in Philippi to see itself as a political entity—a collective body, that is, concerned with the flourishing of the *polis*—and to arrange its common life accordingly.

To reiterate, Paul writes to the church in Philippi to both thank them for their partnership in the gospel and to interpret their shared suffering, not as evidence of the failure of their partnership, but rather as paradigmatic of allegiance to Jesus as king. By thus recalibrating their imagination, he intends them to see themselves *politically*, that is, invested in and participating in the life of the wider *polis* (understood both as the *colonia* of Philippi and the *cosmopolis* of Rome). The new reality of the Messiah's death, resurrection, and reign has effected a new commonwealth, and the Philippian church must endeavor to live worthily as citizens therein. In contrast to magnificence, magnanimity, and above all, victory, the "ruling" virtues of the Roman *polis*, the distinguishing virtue of the heavenly *politeuma* of the Christian community is suffering. This virtue is exemplified in the cruciform pattern of the Messiah's life, which Paul and his associates follow, and which the Philippians must imitate.

Several important questions remain: Why is the virtue of suffering important? How is this virtue inculcated? And in what sense can a heavenly *politeuma* marked by this virtue be considered missional?

4.4. Suffering: The Countercultural Virtue of the Heavenly Commonwealth

Before addressing either of these questions, however, we must first ask whether suffering can even be considered a virtue. Certainly Aristotle and the wider Greco-Roman philosophical tradition would not have thought so.[125] Indeed, the idea that one should follow the Messiah's pattern in renouncing status (Phil 2:6–7) would appear to be merely a deficiency in the crowning virtue of magnanimity, a defect Aristotle referred to as pusillanimity (*Nic. Eth.* 1123b10). Suffering, moreover, is not something that one can cultivate through habituation; it merely happens to one.

But if we speak of an *attitude* towards the possibility of suffering and a *character* that is able to undergo suffering in a particular manner, then it might be possible to understand these qualities as a type of excellence *(aretē)* that can be formed within a person.[126] Why would this countercultural virtue be desirable within the heavenly *politeuma*?

Briefly, we can formulate two interrelated reasons. First: the virtue of suffering would be based upon truth, not propaganda. Paul lived in a world awash with propaganda advertising the golden age won through the *Victoria* of Rome's emperors, themselves noisily touted as exemplars of virtue. While Rome, like any empire, could point to tangible benefits of its rule (absence of military conflict, roads, grain subsidies, and the like), the propaganda was, in a larger sense, manifestly false. The vast majority of the population lived near the subsistence level, slavery was ubiquitous, and pacification of Rome's enemies was achieved at the point of the spear. The agonistic pursuit of status and its attendant wealth and power had long been considered to varying degrees essential to the pursuit of *eudaimonia*, but were beyond reach of all but the few. For those who heard Paul's letter, a life of suffering cohered with reality far more than the chimera of Rome's theology of victory. Yet Paul was not merely interested in validating the daily suffering experienced by so many over against the propaganda of prosperity; he was urging the church to suffer "for Christ" (Phil 1:29).

This brings us to the second reason: the new regime would be based on love, not coercion. The *pax Romana* had been plainly achieved at the point of the spear. Its vaunted administration of justice notwithstanding, Rome's primary power over its enemies (without and within the empire) was coercive in nature. Indeed, throughout human history, this is largely the way of empires and nations. But Paul was announcing an empire and an emperor of a different kind, one whose sovereign power was exercised not through coercion but through love. Such love correlates not with victory achieved by violence, but rather with suffering. Thus in urging the church to suffer *for Christ*, Paul intends for it to symbolize and embody the world-changing power of God's love, demonstrated through the cruciform pattern of the Messiah's suffering.

How, then, is the church to be shaped into the likeness of God's suffering Messiah Jesus? Such transformation is the task of Jesus himself, who, Paul writes, "will transform the body of our humiliation that it may be conformed to the body of his glory, by the power that also enables him to make all things subject to himself" (Phil 3:20–21). Yet the formation of moral character is also, as Aristotle and the wider classical tradition remind us, the task of the *polis*. Thus we can conceive of the heavenly *politeuma* as a sort of "*polis* within a *polis*" whose citizens are being transformed into the image of their king, Jesus. This "transformation by vision," as will be seen, focuses on Paul's astonishing claim to the Corinthian church: "And all of us, with unveiled faces, seeing the glory of the Lord as though reflected in a mirror, are being transformed into the same image from one degree of glory to another; for this comes from the Lord, the Spirit" (2 Cor 3:18). Here, it suffices to say that this process resembles the way in which apprentices in the ancient philosophical schools sought, through both association with their teacher and disciplined and thoughtful undertaking of spiritual exercises, to conform their lives to the ideal.[127]

If indeed this heavenly *politeuma* can reliably form its citizens into the image of its suffering Messiah Jesus, how would the very existence of such a community contribute to the furthering of the *missio Dei*? Consider first what the divine mission is: the restoration of the human family to its pristine vocation to wisely govern God's good creation (cf. Gen 1:26–28) under the leadership of God's Messiah Jesus.[128] Such a task requires the destruction of personal and cosmic evil. Yet God has chosen to accomplish this task not through coercive power, but rather through the self-giving, sacrificial love of the Messiah and through the people who are transformed into his image.

This account of God's mission in the world challenges the way in which most human societies normally "do business," namely by means of coercive power.[129] To frame this in the context of the dominant first-century Roman propaganda, it was simply absurd to claim that a crucified Jewish peasant (who looked nothing like Rome's awe-inspiring emperor) had, through his suffering and death (not through the emperor's victory) inaugurated God's kingdom on earth, which would be fully realized at the *eschaton* (not the present golden age).

Precisely because of this perceived implausibility, it was vitally important that the church see itself as the community within which this vision was being practically lived out. In other words, if the heavenly *politeuma* could reliably produce a people who have been formed in such a way as to make them fit for the wise governance of the *polis*, then this fact would corroborate the plausibility of the larger narrative of this community. The formation of public virtue makes believable the church's claim of public truth.[130]

This chapter has sought both to explain and promote Paul's claim that the church must see itself as a heavenly *politeuma* whose citizens are marked by *pistis*—embodied allegiance—to Jesus as king. Citizenship within this commonwealth calls for the imagination of a new reality or plausibility structure, as well as commitment to a countercultural set of virtues, epitomized by suffering over against victory.

From this, several powerful claims follow. First, citizens of this commonwealth must be transformed into the image of its king, realized by the practice of spiritual exercises or disciplines. Second, this transformation at the level of the individual enables unity amidst diversity at the level of the entire community. Third, citizens of this new regime should be formed into a commonwealth that has as its *telos* the stewardship of God's creation. These claims form the basis of the subsequent chapters.

CHAPTER 3

CHARACTER

In the Presence of the Transformative King in Corinth

What is the first thing you do in the morning when you wake up? If you reach bleary-eyed for your phone, you are in good company. Nearly half of all Americans report checking their smartphone before getting out of bed. For millennials, the number is higher: 66 percent of those between the ages of 18–24 perform this daily ritual while still under the covers. Overall, 74 percent of respondents in a recent survey indicated that they have gazed upon that glittering screen by the end of breakfast.[1] Such observations might prompt us to wonder: how is our relationship to our phones, tablets, computers, televisions—the variety of screens that surround us daily—shaping us as persons? While a complete response to this question is complex and deserving of greater attention than can be given here, recent research does suggest an answer that is far from encouraging. Frequent use of social media, it seems plain, has been correlated with a range of unhealthy symptoms including anxiety, depression, poor self-esteem, and body dissatisfaction.[2]

There is something both old and new about the pernicious effects of the attention we lavish upon our phones. Tim Wu's riveting book, *The Attention Merchants: The Epic Scramble To Get Inside Our Heads*, traces the story back to Benjamin Day's publication of the *New York Sun* in 1833, the first daily newspaper to advance a new business model: "reselling the attention of his audience, or advertising."[3] In other words, instead of that original penny newspaper itself being the product sold to readers, the readers *themselves* became in effect the product sold to advertisers—the real source of the publication's profits. Since then, advertisers have found ever-more ingenious and intrusive ways to harvest our attention for commercial gain, turning us into products to be sold to ever-more-clever marketers. So in one sense, waking up to your phone is merely the extrapolation of the intrusion of the television, unprecedented at the time, into the sanctum of the family living room.[4] Yet as advertisers creep closer and closer towards ever more private sanctums, offering us ever more enticing visions of happiness in exchange for our rapt attention, we open ourselves up to their person-shaping powers in unprecedented ways, not just in degree but in kind.

Consider the example of Instagram. Founded in March 2010 by Kevin Systrom and Mike Krieger, Instagram's genius was rooted in simplicity, a platform to share photos and, optionally, messages on mobile devices, creating an image-centric social network. When it was purchased by Facebook for $1 billion in April 2012, Instagram had 30 million monthly users. Today it boasts 1 billion users and 500 million daily stories.[5] Users of this smartphone app can also become "followers" of other users, and with the click of a heart-shaped icon, one can "like" a posted photo, giving instant feedback to the user who posted it. Such a platform has obvious utility for celebrities already well-versed in capturing attention and intent on marketing themselves. Although the vast majority of Instagram users are obviously not the famous or even the "microfamous," the app encourages and rewards the efforts of ordinary people to aspire towards the trappings of celebrity.[6]

In a society saturated with social media, gaining attention becomes not a means to an end but rather the end in itself. Tim Wu explains:

> For most, the effort is an end in itself, and the ultimate audience is the very subject of the camera's interest. Understood this way, Instagram is the crowning achievement of that decades-long development that we have called the "celebrification" of everyday life and ordinary people, a strategy developed by attention merchants for the sake of creating cheap content.[7]

Wu suggests that Instagram perhaps represents the "logical endpoint" of "a century of the ascendant self": "the self as its own object of worship."[8] Even if the average person's use of Instagram and other social media platforms might not rise to the level of self-worship, we nevertheless ought to be concerned about the fact, in the words of philosopher James K. A.

Smith, that "the competitive world of self-display and self-consciousness is always with us. . . . We are no longer seen doing something; we're doing something to be seen."[9] Our intimate relationship with such technology is surely shaping us in ways we may not even fully appreciate, not just as individuals, but as a society. We are in danger of becoming "a chaotic mutual admiration society . . . without real precedent in human history."[10]

What do smartphones and social media have to do with the Apostle Paul, you may be wondering? The key link between the first-century Apostle and our twenty-first-century obsessions lies in the shared centrality of *images*. My intent here is not to launch a jeremiad against technology. I myself own a smartphone and my friends who work in the high-tech field are quick to remind me of the many ways in which human existence has benefited by the wise application of technology. I simply wish to make the point that we are formed by the objects of our attention. Think of all the times in the past week in which you found yourself with a few minutes—or even seconds—in which your attention was not actively engaged—in a doctor's office, waiting for class to start, in a subway car, eating a meal by yourself (or with someone else!), walking somewhere. Chances are high that you, and a good number of those around you, were gazing upon a small screen in your hand.

Although Paul would have been mystified by this particular cultural phenomenon, he was well aware of the power of images to transform us. In Greco-Roman antiquity, beholding the statue of a god, for example, was thought to bring one into the transformative presence of that divine being represented by the statue.[11] Paul, writing to the church in Corinth, seems to have such a notion in mind as he describes the process of being formed into the likeness of Jesus:

> And all of us, with unveiled faces, seeing the glory of the Lord as though reflected in a mirror, are being transformed into the same image from one degree of glory to another; for this comes from the Lord, the Spirit. (2 Cor 3:18)

One may object that "seeing the glory of the Lord as though reflected in a mirror" is a far cry from staring at a smartphone—these would seem to be completely incomparable activities. In reality, however, the two activities—staring at an image—are similar, as is the necessarily attendant process of formation; yet the *nature* of the images is so divergent that the resulting image-formed character is also radically different. Beholding the glory of the Lord and beholding the glory of a smartphone are likely to form us in strikingly divergent ways! In order to understand, and possibly to experience, the sort of formation that Paul describes, we must carefully consider the sorts of things upon which we habitually fix our gaze, asking how the objects of our attention shape us.

Paul's concern for the transformation of the Corinthians' character is the beating heart of his "second" letter to them, animating its argument.[12] When he writes to the church in Corinth, he is seeking to repair a relationship that, tempestuous from the beginning, has now turned sour. Although Paul introduced them to Jesus and nurtured their infant faith for a year and a half, the Corinthian believers have now come to doubt his apostolic credentials. "Doubt" is the polite way to put it; in fact, they have told him not to come back unless he can provide for them a letter of recommendation that backs up his claim to be an ambassador of Jesus the king. Paul's response is to turn their request right back in their faces:

> Surely we do not need, as some do, letters of recommendation to you or from you, do we? You yourselves are our letter, written on our hearts, to be known and read by all; and you show that you are a letter of Christ, prepared by us, written not with ink but with the Spirit of the living God, not on tablets of stone but on tablets of human hearts. (2 Cor 3:2–3)

What Paul means by a "letter written on the heart," as will be explained in greater detail below, is that their hearts have been transformed by Jesus the Christ. Beholding the glory of the Lord, Paul continues, they have become transformed into the same image (2 Cor 3:18). What more evidence do they need that Paul is Jesus' royal ambassador?

But what precisely does he mean? He cannot mean that either he or his audience have actually physically beheld Jesus with their own eyes. He must be speaking of vision metaphorically. And while his use of metaphor indicates that he has reached the limits of literal meaning, it is not the case that he has abandoned the meaning of words altogether. He is no doubt trying to explain a process whose working is beyond the grasp of his understanding, but it does not therefore follow that he understands *nothing* about it. When Paul speaks here of "seeing the glory of the Lord as though reflected in a mirror," he means something more than the ability to take in the reality of the world through one's eyes, something greater even than the faculty of attention that allows one to focus upon and interpret visual sense data. Paul, as I shall argue, asserts the transformative capacity of *association with Jesus*. Throughout this chapter, I will refer to this process of character formation as "transformation by vision"—specifically, the vision of a particular "image" of Christ.[13]

To begin to grasp this concept of transformation through association, suppose that you intend to acquire the virtue of bravery, one of the cardinal virtues that Aristotle considers essential to a fully flourishing human.[14] You might well set yourself the task of doing something brave each day, gradually habituating yourself to brave action until it became, as it were, second nature. Alternately, you might decide to associate with a brave individual, trusting that as you immerse yourself in that person's world, doing the sort of brave things she habitually does, you yourself would begin to acquire the character of bravery.[15] Then again, you might decide to enlist in the army and sign up for the infantry, confident that association with other soldiers—undergoing training, the strict regimen of martial discipline, combat experience—is precisely the sort of activity that inculcates bravery. Each of these three scenarios share the following three components: *envisioning* a particular outcome, *deciding* to pursue it, and *employing* a strategy calculated to achieve it.[16]

In the first scenario, all three steps are dependent upon you; in the latter two, the implementation of the strategy depends upon association with others. In these scenarios, you are deciding to fix your attention upon those whom you perceive already to possess the virtue you seek. In Aristotle's words, you are seeking the company of virtuous friends (*Nic. Eth.* 9–10). The author of Proverbs puts it this way: "Iron sharpens iron, and one person sharpens the wits of another" (Prov 27:17).[17] When Paul speaks of being transformed into the image of Jesus by beholding "the glory of the Lord as reflected in a mirror," then, he has in mind this transformative capacity of association with Jesus.

What does being transformed into the image of Jesus have to do with living the good life? Recall, from the introduction, the fourfold framework I proposed for conceiving of the good life in holistic terms. Such a project: (1) is rooted in a shared political, or communal, life; (2) envisions the transformation of character, such that individuals can fruitfully participate in this community; (3) requires the preservation of unity within the community; and (4) exists in harmony within the larger community of creation. This schema corresponds closely with the consequences of Jesus' reign as king.

As argued in the previous chapter, Paul portrays the church as a heavenly commonwealth characterized by allegiance (*pistis*) to its suffering king Jesus. Allegiance, the asymmetrical relationship of loyalty between king and subject, is crucially important to the pursuit of the good life because the inculcation of virtue is a fundamentally relational project.

The present chapter explores how such allegiance to Jesus transforms the character of his "citizens," those who have in effect sworn allegiance to him. This argument also carries forward the missional thread of the previous chapter, in which I claimed that the church functions as the "hermeneutic of the gospel," the means by which the gospel challenges the plausibility structure of postmodern society by creating an alternative social imaginary. Transformation into the character of Jesus is the means by which the church is equipped for this task.[18]

The argument in this chapter unfolds in three steps. The first step prepares the ground by establishing the historical context in which Paul wrote and in which his contemporary readers all lived. Paul's portrayal of Jesus as king would have resonated with widely held notions in the first-century Roman Empire concerning the function of the "ideal king." Second, with this context in view, I investigate Paul's defense of his apostleship to the Corinthian church (2 Cor 2:14–4:6) to better understand his portrayal of Jesus as the king who transforms his subjects into his own image. Finally, I explore the bodily practices by which "citizens" of the new regime become disposed to the transformative presence of Jesus the king.

1. Philosopher-kings and Moral Transformation

Our initial perception that Paul, apparently, seldom evokes the overt language of "kingship" is largely due to our own tone deafness: we do not share the cultural repertoire of Paul's authorial audience and so have difficulty hearing the proper cultural cues. Understanding Paul's defense of his apostleship to the church in Corinth requires us to learn those cues. Indeed, the rhetoric of his argument here depends upon his assumed conceptual background of the "ideal king." This is because the heart of his argument involves a *synkrisis*—an evaluative comparison—between Jesus and Moses, who are presented as ideal kings (2 Cor 3:7–18).[19] To grasp the significance of this comparison for the larger question of moral transformation, we must understand several salient characteristics of the ideal king in Greco-Roman antiquity. First, such a king was broadly conceived not simply as a political ruler but also as a philosopher. Second, the king was regarded as the living, animate, or ensouled law—that is, some-one who "embodied" in his very person the best possible rules of justice and harmony for society. And finally, the king effected a transformation among his subjects through their vision of him—by seeing and imitating him they also took on his ideal qualities and rich life. Each of these aspects requires further explanation and discussion.

1.1. Why Kings Should Study Philosophy

Plato famously asserts in the *Republic* that the good *polis*—the *kallipolis*—will never be realized without the good ruler. Such a person must be both a king and a philosopher:

> Unless . . . either philosophers become kings in our states or those whom we now call our kings and rulers take to the pursuit of phi-losophy seriously and adequately, and there is a conjunction of these two things, political power and philosophic intelligence . . . there can be no cessation of troubles . . . Nor, until this happens, will this constitution which we have been expounding in theory ever be put into practice within the limits of possibility and see the light of the sun. (*Rep.* 473D; cf. 499B; 519D; 540D [Shorey, LCL])

Philosophy in antiquity, we must remember, denoted not merely the intel-lectual pursuit of wisdom and knowledge. Rather, philosophy was under-stood to be a way of life that embodied wisdom and virtue. The wedding of "political power and philosophic intelligence" thus envisions a ruler who is committed to the project of *eudaimonia*, human flourishing. If we imag-ine this philosopher-king spending all his days in the library with his nose buried in a book, we will have entirely the wrong image in mind. Plato's picture here is of a statesman devoted to a political end conceived of in philosophical terms, the flourishing of the virtuous *polis*.[20]

Plato makes this clear by comparing the rule of the tyrant with that of the philosopher-king. With respect to "virtue (*aretē*) and happiness (*eu-daimonia*) . . . there is no city more wretched than that in which a tyrant rules, and none more happy (*eudaimonestera*) than that governed by a true king" (*Rep.* 576C, E). Indeed, the character of the *polis* reflects the character of its ruler:

> The best (*ariston*) man and the most righteous [is] the happiest, and . . . he is the one who is the most kingly and a *king over himself*;

... the most evil and most unjust is the most unhappy, who again is the man who, having the most of the tyrannical temper in himself, [is] most of a *tyrant over himself* and over the state. (*Rep.* 580B–C; emphasis added)

In order to make the *polis* virtuous, then, the king must first inculcate virtue within himself.[21] The making of virtuous people—king and subjects together—can thus be understood as the quintessential royal art, or *technē*.[22]

In the *Statesman* [*Politicus*], Plato uses the more earthy image of a shepherd to describe this essential function of the king: the "single art called both kingly and statesmanlike" is that of "herding human beings" (*Pol.* 267C).[23] But the "herding" of a good shepherd involves much more than simply driving the sheep and teaching them to obey. The true shepherd's art bespeaks a way of caring for his flock that is both holistic and intimate:

The herdsman himself tends the herd, he is their physician, he is their matchmaker, and he alone knows the midwife's science of aiding at the birth of their offspring. Moreover, so far as the nature of the creatures allows them to enjoy sport or music, no one can enliven or soothe them better than he. (*Pol.* 268A–B)

Like the god Cronus, the divine shepherd, the king cares "for the whole human community" (*Pol.* 276B). Yet humans, as Plato well knows, are not merely grazing animals but rather complex beings whose flourishing requires not simply feeding but care (*Pol.* 276D). Therefore, unlike the tyrant, who rules through compulsion, the good king exercises "voluntary care of voluntary bipeds" (*Pol.* 276E). The role of the philosopher-king is to enable his subjects *voluntarily* to pursue the good life.

Later in the *Statesman*, Plato differentiates the kingly art from its chief rivals and imitators, the arts of the rhetorician, judge, and general. These particular arts, or skills of leadership, Plato argues, are subservient to the statesman's art, "the art that is truly kingly" (*Pol.* 305C):

But the art which holds sway over them all and watches over the laws and all things in the state, weaving them all most perfectly together, we may, I think, by giving to its function a designation which indicates its power over the community, with full propriety call 'statecraft.' (*Pol.* 305E)

Plato further develops the image of weaving introduced in this passage, likening the kingly art to that of the weaver. The "whole business of the kingly weaving" is to produce a harmonious *polis* that can be compared to a "well-woven fabric" (*Pol.* 310E):

> This, then, is the end, let us declare, of the web of the statesman's activity, the direct interweaving of the characters of restrained and courageous men, when the kingly science has drawn them together by friendship and community of sentiment into a common life, and having perfected the most glorious and the best of all textures, clothes with it all the inhabitants of the state, both slaves and freemen, holds them together by this fabric and omitting nothing which ought to belong to a happy state, rules and watches over them. (*Pol.* 311B–C)

These passages from Plato's dialogues, which were widely known in the ancient Mediterranean world, thus proclaim an ideal of kingship that can be summarized briefly as follows. The good king must be a philosopher in the sense that he inculcates virtue within himself and leads his subjects into the good life that he himself pursues. The kingly art thus aims to produce a harmonious, flourishing *polis* of virtuous persons.

The practices of philosophic schools in antiquity shed some light on the means by which a king's art might be accomplished. In the first century CE, the practice of philosophy was characterized by four different approaches, or schools, which had formed around the teaching and way of life of their founders. The school of Plato was known as the Academy; that of Aristotle, the Lyceum; that of Epicurus, the Garden; and that of Zeno, the Stoa. To these four can be added the more complex philosophical movements of the Skeptics and the Cynics, which did not form schools, but articulated a way of life that was regarded as a mode of "doing philosophy"—even though they represented in some ways an anti-philosophy.[24]

Amidst the wide variety of doctrines espoused by these diverse schools and movements, two elements were shared universally by all who undertook the philosopher's way of life. The first is that, although philosophy was marked by discourse aimed at the acquisition of wisdom and knowledge, this intellectual pursuit actually served a greater goal, *the inculcation of a way of life*. Plato observes, for example, that the philosopher Pythagoras (mid-sixth c. BCE) transmitted to posterity a way of life recognized widely in Plato's time as distinctively "Pythagorean" (*Rep.* 600B). Teachers and students within Plato's own school understood the *telos*, or goal, of philosophy to be the good life. This is confirmed at the conclusion of the *Republic*, wherein the importance of choosing such a life is represented mythically in the story of Er. Socrates recounts to Glaucon the story of a young soldier, Er, who dies and comes back to life, reporting all that he witnessed in the underworld. In the afterlife, the dead must wisely choose another life, a task for which the only adequate preparation is having already gained wisdom through the pursuit of philosophy. Socrates explains:

> And this is the chief reason why it should be our main concern that each of us, neglecting all other studies, should seek after and study this thing—if in any way he may be able to learn of and discover the man who will give him the ability and the knowledge to distinguish the life that is good from that which is bad . . . so that with consideration of all these things he will be able to make a reasoned choice between the better and the worse life. (*Rep.* 618C–D)

The intrinsic reward of philosophy, Plato implies, is the wisdom it inculcates, which enables one to both perceive and choose the good life.

Although the activity most often associated with Plato's school is the Socratic dialogue, "the object of discussion and its doctrinal content are of secondary importance. What counts is the *practice* of dialogue, and the transformation it brings."[25] In other words, while Plato's dialogues always involved Socrates' questioning and discussion with others about some subject, their real purpose was to model the kind *life* that Socrates exemplified and enacted.

To speak of practices is to anticipate the second feature shared by philosophical schools in antiquity. From one common perspective, the practice of theoretical philosophical discourse can be considered an intellectual exercise aimed at determining truth, or acquiring knowledge.[26] While the goal of discourse often appears to be the articulation of some idea or dogma, sometimes its end was not so much intellectual as spiritual.[27] Discourse can thus be seen as a type of exercise that "tended to produce an aptitude, or *habitus*, in the interlocutor's soul, and to lead him to a determinate choice of life."[28] Within all the philosophical schools, one finds evidence of what philosopher Pierre Hadot terms *spiritual exercises*, "voluntary, personal practices intended to cause a transformation of the self."[29] These exercises were denoted by the Greek terms *askēsis* and *meletē*.[30]

The brief treatise *On Training* (*Peri Askēseōs*) by the Roman Stoic philosopher Musonius Rufus (ca. 30–101 CE) likens the "practical training (*askēsin*)" of a student of philosophy to the physical exercises of an athlete. For the athlete or similar performer, physical training is obviously needed "because often the virtues make use of this [the body] as a necessary instrument for the affairs of life." The "training which is peculiar to the soul," on the other hand, consists in "learning to recognize the things which are truly good and in becoming accustomed to distinguish them from what are not truly good."[31] Although Musonius' *On Training* is the only extant treatise of its kind, references to such exercises within philosophical schools are plentiful, as the following examples illustrate.

Plato, for example, recommends the exercise of meditation prior to sleep in order not to be disturbed by the "beastly and savage" desires that typically arise during sleep (*Rep.* 571–572). In the *Phaedo*, the "exercise of death" (*meletē thanatou*) enables one to be "of good courage when he is to die" (63E–64A, 80E–81A). Epicurus, in the conclusion of his *Letter to Menoeceus*, urges his reader to meditate day and night upon all his teachings, habituating himself to the thought of death and thereby freeing himself from worry.[32] Philo gives evidence of the Stoic practice of *praemeditatio*, the meditation upon potential future evils one might experience, in order that one might suffer them with equanimity when they inevitably come (*On the Special Laws* 2.46).[33] Examples of such "spiritual exercises" could be multiplied. In short, all the philosophical schools in Greco-Roman antiquity taught a "therapeutic of the passions," a practical method by which desires and fears could be mastered, leading to a "profound transformation of the individual's mode of seeing and being."[34]

Understanding the aims of these widespread, ancient philosophical schools and the means by which they were achieved sheds light on the "ideal king's" role as philosopher in the world that Paul and his readers knew. Such schools, as we have seen, sought to inculcate their students into an entire way of life and taught them spiritual exercises to assist in achieving that end. A king who rules with "philosophic intelligence," it may be inferred, possesses not merely wisdom, but virtue. The king's own excellence in living must furthermore be both *taught* and *caught*. Within the philosophical schools, discourse and dialogue were the primary vehicles by which doctrine was taught. But doctrine always endeavored to explain, justify, and motivate students not only to understand but to pursue a way of life.[35] Spiritual exercises were among the means by which this way of life was inculcated, or caught.[36] The prevalence of such a mode of inner transformation suggests that the philosopher-king's virtuous way of living could similarly be caught by his subjects. In other words, the ideal of the philosopher-king implies both a way of living and the practical means by which that life could be obtained.

If this explains why Plato's statesman must study—or rather *practice*—philosophy, why must the philosopher also be *king*? Here, Plato's student Aristotle sheds some light on the question. In the *Politics*, Aristotle contends that the best-governed *polis* is one in which good laws are promulgated by good men: an aristocracy (*aristokratia*), or rule by the best (*aristos*), or most virtuous (1286a8–1286b8).[37] Such a view reflects the crucial role of law in inculcating virtue in the *polis* (*Nic. Eth.* 5.1129b20–26, 1130b25–27; 10.1180a21–23).[38] Laws, if you will, were one of the practical means by which virtue could be caught, or inculcated.[39]

Yet Aristotle also recognized that even the best of laws are of necessity general in nature. Thus, while one can and must look to good laws in order to flourish, one must more importantly look to virtuous people as exemplars of the virtue the laws seek to inculcate. Aristotle followed his teacher Plato's conviction that "the best thing is not that the laws be in power, but that the man who is wise and of kingly nature be ruler" (Plato, *Pol.* 294A–B [Rackham, LCL]). Such a man, the "best man" in society, would in Aristotle's view "naturally be as a god among men" (*Pol.* 1284a3–11).[40] In brief, the philosopher must be *king* because the prerogative of rule belongs to the most virtuous man, the one who has so patterned himself after the spirit of the law.

1.2. The King as "Living Law"

If good laws make the *polis* virtuous, then those in power must rule in accordance with, or in submission to, the law. Yet the one most capable of rule is not in fact subordinate to an external rule, or law outside of himself, but rather governs himself by means of the law *within* him. This paradoxical relationship to law is perhaps made clearer by the Roman poet Virgil's vision of a return to a golden age, which has come about, he believes, through the virtues of Octavian, who would subsequently become Rome's first emperor, Caesar Augustus.[41] In book 6 of Virgil's *Aeneid*, this age of harmony and bliss is envisioned as a return to the age of the god Saturn (6.791–797). Later, King Evander relates to Aeneas the founding myth of Latium: "First from heavenly Olympus came Saturn . . . He gathered together the unruly race, scattered over mountain heights, and gave them laws" (8.321).

Yet Saturn's *giving* laws to the Latins (the original native people in the vicinity of Rome) seems incongruous with the way in which Latinus had earlier described his own people: "The Latins are Saturn's race, righteous not by bond or laws, but self-controlled of their own free will and by the custom of their ancient god" (7.202–204). On the surface, these two accounts—Saturn giving laws and the people behaving righteously without need of laws—seem in tension with each other. This tension resolves, however, when we realize that there is a *progression* in view between Evander's founding myth and Latinus' description of his people's habitual behavior. Saturn's giving of laws appears to be the necessary first step of moral education. The eventual ability to act morally without the compulsion of laws characterizes a people among whom this moral education has reached its apogee. Thus, as one who lived in harmony with the law because he had internalized it, the ideal king was commonly thought of as the "ensouled," "animate," or "living" law, the *empsuchos nomos* or *empsuchos logos*.[42]

Among Greco-Roman political philosophers, this notion gains currency during the Hellenistic era and remains current through at least the reign of Trajan (98–117 CE).[43] Thus, for example, we see the king portrayed as the animate law from writers as diverse as the Neopythagoreans to the Roman Stoic philosopher Musonius Rufus, the biographer and moralist Plutarch, and the Jewish philosopher Philo.[44] Two dimensions of the king as living law emerge from the evidence. The first is reflected in Plutarch's brief treatise, *To an Uneducated Ruler* (*Moralia* 779D–782F), in which the author addresses the reluctance of rulers to be ruled by reason, fearing that their power will be curtailed and they will thus become "slaves to duty." As it is commonly thought, the supreme advantage of ruling is not to be ruled. Yet if this is the case, Plutarch insists, the following question emerges:

> Who, then, shall rule the ruler? The "Law, the king of all, both mortals and immortals," as Pindar says—not law written outside him in books or on wooden tablets or the like, but reason endowed with

life within him (*empsuchos ōn en autō logos*), always abiding with him and watching over him and never leaving his soul without its leadership. (*Mor.* 780C)[45]

The king is not enslaved to the law, but rather has internalized the morally educative intent of the law. In other words, he has inculcated virtue within himself. He not only knows the good, but desires, wills, and habitually does the good.

The significance of the king as living law can further be explained in terms of two approaches to ethics. A *deontological* approach derives right moral action from duty to an external code. One *knows* the right because it is communicated through authoritative laws or commands. One *does* the right because one is bound by duty to obey such authority. A *virtue ethics* approach, as articulated by Aristotle, contends rather that one knows right moral action by observing the behavior of the fully virtuous individual. One is able reliably both to *know* and to *do* the right by cultivating the virtues exemplified by such a person. Plutarch appears to contrast these approaches: the ideal king rules through "reason endowed with life within him" (virtue ethics), rather than through obedience to the "law written outside him in books or on wooden tablets" (deontological). The idea is not that good laws can simply be flouted by the king—that would merely be tyranny. Rather, the king internalizes the law and it functions to reliably guide his actions.

The second dimension, or rather implication, of the king as living law is also captured in the same treatise by Plutarch. The guidance of ensouled law or reason enables the king to fulfill a crucial prerogative: "the sovereign must first gain command of himself, must regulate his own soul and establish his own character, then *make his subjects fit his pattern*" (*Mor.* 780B; emphasis added). It is not enough for the king himself merely to act virtuously; he must inculcate virtue within his subjects. This aspect of the king as living law can be understood in terms of the role of the philosopher-king, as discussed above. A philosopher endeavors to lead the students in his school into a fully flourishing way of life, and a king has the same duty with respect to his subjects. In terms of the distinction between deontological and virtue ethics, we can say that a king must enable his subjects to act morally not through obedience to an external code but through the guidance of ensouled reason. To speak of the king as a living law is to recognize not only the king's virtue, but his ability to inculcate virtue within his subjects. Yet the practical question remains: How does the king effect this transformation?

1.3. Transformation by Vision

As early as Xenophon (ca 429–357 BCE), we find evidence of the belief that the good leader transforms those in his charge by virtue of his very presence. At the conclusion of *Oeconomicus*, a treatise dealing with the management of the household economy, Xenophon considers what is essential in the ability to command, influence, and transform others. A good commander brings forth effort and sacrifice willingly:

> For example, on a man-of-war . . . some boatswains can say and do the right things to sharpen the men's spirits and make them work with a will, while others are so unintelligent that it takes them more than twice the time to finish the voyage. Here they land bathed in sweat, with mutual congratulations, boatswain and seamen. There they arrive with a dry skin; they hate their master and he hates them. (*Oec.* 21.3)

Here it is the boatswain's intelligence that summons the willing effort of his men. Yet the mark of a good leader is not merely the practical ability to instruct others in order to realize a goal. The "genius, the brave and scientific leader," actually effects the inner moral transformation of those under his charge:

> They are ashamed to do a disgraceful act, think it better to obey, and take a pride in obedience, working cheerfully, every man and all together, when it is necessary to work. . . . he is the strong leader . . . who can make his soldiers feel that they are bound to follow him through fire and in any adventure . . . and truly great is he who can do great deeds by his will rather than his strength. (*Oec.* 21.5–8)

Key to this inner transformation is the very presence of the leader himself. Xenophon concludes this discussion with an example from agriculture:

> If the *appearance* of the master in the field . . . makes no striking impression on the men at work, I for one cannot envy him. But if *at sight of him* they bestir themselves, and a spirit of determination and rivalry and eagerness to excel falls on every workman, then I should

say: this man has a touch of the kingly nature (*ēthous basilikou*) in him. (*Oec.* 21.9–10; emphasis added)

These examples from Xenophon demonstrate that already in Classical Greece, the charismatic presence of the leader was regarded as playing a role in transforming the characters of those he led. This ability, as Xenophon observes, is the quintessence of the kingly nature.

This idea gains currency among the Neopythagorean philosophers, whose writings and influence span the Hellenistic and Roman eras.[46] Diotogenes, for example, claims, "A good king should be able to charm those who behold him, no less than the sound of a flute and harmony attract those that hear them" (4.7.62 [Guthrie]).[47] The same idea finds expression in Plutarch's *Life of Numa*. Plutarch waxes eloquent describing the golden age of peace and harmony under the reign of Rome's legendary king:

> For not only was the Roman people softened and charmed by the righteousness and mildness of their king, but also the cities round about, as if some cooling breeze or salubrious wind were wafted upon them from Rome, began to experience a change of temper, and all of them were filled with longing desire to have good government, to be at peace, to till the earth, to rear their children in quiet, and to worship the gods. . . . honor and justice flowed into all hearts from the wisdom of Numa, as from a fountain, and the calm serenity of his spirit diffused itself abroad. . . . For there is no record either of war, or faction, nor political revolution while Numa was king. (*Numa* 20.3–5)

Plutarch portrays Numa as effecting harmony not coercively but by inculcating virtue within his subjects. It is worth noting the metaphors Plutarch employs to convey this transformation: the wafting of a cooling breeze, the flowing of water from a fountain, the diffusion of a vapor. Virtue seemingly arises naturally, organically, within the hearts of the people under the reign of the good king.

Plutarch further remarks that the transformation effected by Numa's blessed reign confirms the later insight of Plato, "namely that human ills would only then cease and disappear when, by some divine felicity, the power of a king should be united in one person with the insight of a philosopher, thereby establishing virtue in control and mastery over vice"

(*Numa* 20.7). Beholding the king's virtue is of decisive importance in effecting the universal return to virtue among the king's subjects:

> But when they *see with their own eyes* a conspicuous and shining example of virtue in the life of their ruler, they will of their own accord walk in wisdom's ways, and unite with him in conforming themselves to a blameless and blessed life of friendship and mutual concord, attended by righteousness and temperance. Such a life is the noblest end of all government, and he is most a king who can inculcate such a life and such a disposition in his subjects. (*Numa* 20.8)

Although Plutarch's hyperbolic description is part and parcel of the legend surrounding Numa, nevertheless it conveys accurately the *ideal* of the king's role in moral transformation by virtue of his presence.

There is, moreover, a note of realism in this portrayal, which is more easily understood when one remembers the king's intimate connection to the divine in the ancient mindset.[48] This philosophical tradition saw

> the ruler as the embodiment or agent or representative on earth of the Law or Reason or Logos of God. . . . [whose] task was to be in his own life the ensoulment of cosmic order and thereby bring it down to earth, so that the earthly state might mirror the cosmic harmony.[49]

To be in the presence of the king was to be, at least in some sense, in the presence of the divine. The king was often regarded as descended from the gods, and sometimes held to be a god himself.[50]

Indeed, the king's radiant visage and virtuous character were regarded as a reflection of divine glory. In this regard, witness the effusive praise lavished upon the emperor Domitian by his admirer, Statius:

> So eager was I to gaze upon himself, ay himself, calm-visaged and in majesty serene tempering his rays and gently veiling the glory of his state; yet the splendour that he would fain conceal shone in his countenance. . . . nor can I yet find any rival to thy countenance, O Germanicus: such is the monarch of the gods. (*Sylv.* 4.2.40–44, 53–55)[51]

Moreover, the king was widely understood to be the gods' vicegerent—the one divinely appointed to rule in the place of the gods.[52] Thus it was natural to attribute to such a figure the instrumental role of inculcating divine virtue through his very person.

There is, to be sure, an element of mysticism as well as idealization here, an aspect of transformation that eludes the grasp of human comprehension. But it is a mistake to dismiss this way of thinking as merely superstitious. The transformation effected by the presence of the king is not instantaneous, as though by magic.[53] Rather, consistent with Aristotle's understanding of the way character is transformed deliberately and habitually, transformation appears to occur progressively.

The concept of transformation by vision is, despite its mystical garb, a way of talking about the transformative power of association. We can understand this by turning once again to the practices of the philosophical schools of antiquity. These schools offered, first and foremost, a distinctive way of living, articulated in the teachings of the philosopher, and modeled by his life. Disciples within these schools learned how to live not through discourse alone, but equally through friendship with the philosopher and the community gathered around him.

Seneca (d. 65 CE), a Stoic philosopher and adviser to Emperor Nero, offers the following assessment of the transformative power of association within philosophical schools:

> Of course, however, the living voice and the intimacy of a common life will help you more than the written word. You must go to the scene of action, first, because men put more faith in their eyes than in their ears, and second, because the way is long if one follows precepts, but short and helpful, if one follows patterns. Cleanthes could not have been the express image of Zeno, if he had merely heard his lectures; he shared in his life, saw into his hidden purposes, and watched him to see whether he lived according to his own rules. Plato, Aristotle, and the whole throng of sages who were destined to go each his different way, derived more benefit from the character than from the words of Socrates. It was not the class-room of Epicurus, but living together under the same roof, that made great men of Metrodorus, Hermarchus, and Polyaenus. (*Ep.* 6.6)

Doctrines can obviously be taught through books and lectures, but the philosopher's way of life must, above all, be *caught*. This process happens most effectively, Seneca insists, when one is in the living presence of the philosopher and the community of those who have inculcated the philosopher's life. It was, moreover, precisely this process of transformation that the philosophical practice of spiritual exercises sought to facilitate.

Certain spiritual exercises appear calculated to bring a student, after a manner of speaking, into the presence of the philosopher. Before discussing them, it is necessary to distinguish between two related figures: the philosopher and the sage. The former can be used to describe both a teacher within a philosophical school and also a student. The latter, however, refers uniquely to the philosopher *par excellence*: "In each school, the figure of the sage was the transcendent norm which determined the philosopher's way of life."[54] The true sage was a rarity; indeed, among the philosophical schools in antiquity, Socrates appears to have been the only universally recognized sage.[55]

Given the paucity of living sages, schools sought to bring before students the lives of past sages, the emphasis being not on the historical details of the sage's life but on the sage's idealized behavior. The question to consider—to revise a popular contemporary Christian slogan—was: "What Would Socrates Do?" Stoics, for instance, discussed theses related to the paradoxes of the life of a sage:

> These demonstrated not only that the sage is the only being who is infallible, impeccable, impassive, happy, free, handsome, and wealthy, but also that he is the only one who can truly and excellently be a statesman, legislator, general, poet, and king. This means that the sage, by his perfect use of reason, is the only person capable of carrying out all these functions.[56]

Such philosophical discourse appears on the surface to be primarily an intellectual exercise, but it is profoundly also a spiritual one, in that it endeavors to bring before the student the transformative persona of the sage with the intent of inculcating the sage's way of life.[57]

This intent is clearly reflected in the following exercise, recommended by Seneca in one of his letters. The goal is to bring the transformative presence of the sage before one's thoughts:

> Hear and take to heart this useful and wholesome motto: "Cherish some man of high character, and *keep him ever before your eyes*, living *as if he were watching you*, and ordering all your actions *as if he beheld them*." Such, my dear Lucilius, is the counsel of Epicurus; he has quite properly given us a guardian and an attendant. We can get rid of most sins, if we have *a witness* who stands near us when we are likely to go wrong. The soul should have someone whom it can

respect, – one by whose authority it may make even its inner shrine more hallowed. Happy is the man who can make others better, not merely when he is in their company, but even when he is in their thoughts! And happy also is he who can so revere a man as to calm and regulate himself by calling him to mind! One who can so revere another, will soon be himself worthy of reverence. Choose therefore a Cato; or, if Cato seems too severe a model, choose some Laelius, a gentler spirit. Choose a master whose life, conversation, and *soul-expressing face (ipse animum ante se ferens vultus)* have satisfied you; *picture him* always to yourself as your protector or your pattern. For we must indeed have someone according to whom we may regulate our characters; you can never straighten that which is crooked unless you use a ruler. (*Ep.* 11.8–10; emphasis added)

This is clearly on one level an intellectual exercise: Lucilius is instructed to bring the sage into his thoughts in order that the pattern of the sage's life might regulate his own character. But Seneca's exercise is also profoundly affective. The visual imagery, which I have emphasized, is hardly incidental to the success of the exercise. Note especially the focus on the sage's face as the part of his body that reveals his inner character.[58] Significantly, the visual activity is mutual: Lucilius is to behold the sage, and live as though the sage were watching him. This is not mere recollection, but rather an exercise that aims towards association, being in the presence of another. After all, it is only in another's physical presence that mutual beholding can take place.

Similarly, Lucian of Samosata (b. ca 120 CE) advocates the regular practice of bringing to mind the teachings and persona of the philosopher Nigrinus. In his *Wisdom of Nigrinus*, Lucian responds to a friend's puzzled observation that he has returned from a recent visit to Rome "lordly and exalted."[59] Lucian explains the cause of the change: "I have come back to you transformed by the wayside into a happy (*eudaimōn*) and blissful (*makarios*) man" (*Nigr.* 1).[60] Whilst in Rome to obtain treatment for an ocular malady, Lucian had visited the Platonic philosopher Nigrinus, who had spoken to him at length of the freedom that true philosophy brings. As a result, Lucian now experiences an astonishing transformation: he reports having forgotten his eye ailment, "and by degrees grew sharper-sighted in my soul; which, all unawares, I had been carrying about in a purblind condition till then" (*Nigr.* 4). Listening to the philosopher's "ambrosial speech (*logōn ambrosian*)" had been intoxicating, such that Lucian now goes about "enraptured (*entheos*) and drunk with the wine of his discourse (*logōn*)" (*Nigr.* 3, 5).[61]

When the friend inquires whether Lucian can recall in further detail the words of Nigrinus, he responds affirmatively. Lucian's memory is aided by a particular exercise, which he describes fulsomely:

> I take pleasure in calling his words to mind frequently, and have already made it a regular exercise (*meletēn*): even if nobody happens to be at hand, I repeat them to myself two or three times a day just the same. I am in the same case with lovers. In the absence of the objects of their fancy they think over their actions and their words, and by dallying with these beguile their lovesickness into the belief that they have their sweethearts near; in fact, sometimes they even imagine they are chatting with them and are as pleased with what they formerly heard as if it were just being said, and by applying their minds to the memory of the past give themselves no time to be annoyed by the present. So I, too, in the absence of my mistress Philosophy, get no little comfort out of gathering together the words that I then heard and turning them over to myself. In short, *I fix my gaze on that man as if he were a lighthouse* and I were adrift at the sea in the dead of night, *fancying him by me* whenever I do anything and always *hearing him* repeat his former words. Sometimes, especially when I put pressure on my soul, *his face appears to me and the sound of his voice abides in my ears*. (*Nigr.* 6–7; emphasis added)

Lucian's vivid and evocative description of this spiritual exercise beautifully illuminates the concept of transformation by vision and further suggests how it relates to the philosophical way of life. He has experienced a conversion through the philosophical discourse of Nigrinus and now endeavors to bring himself into the presence of the philosopher in order to guide and enable his newly chosen way of life. The success of the exercise depends upon the transformative capacity of association and seeks to recreate the original life-changing encounter with the philosopher. His comparison to a lover bereft of his beloved is particularly revealing, as it suggests that the exercise engages not just the intellectual, but the affective faculty as well. This spiritual exercise aims at the transformation of the whole person.

Before going further, it will be useful to sum up the role of the king in moral transformation and begin thinking about how this cultural milieu is relevant to Paul's argument in Second Corinthians. First, to conceive of the genuine king as a philosopher is to assert that the business of ruling is nothing less than the making of fully flourishing human beings. The ideal king stands in relation to his subjects as the sage to his students. Second, to envision the king as a "living law" is to locate the king within the process of virtue formation. Laws were regarded as having a morally educative intent and effect. However, the effect could best be achieved if the laws themselves were internalized. As the paragon of virtue, the king was guided by the animate law within himself and also capable of inculcating virtue within his people. Finally, to speak of the "transformation by vision" effected by the king is to acknowledge the transformative capacity of association. To be in the presence of the king or the sage—indeed, each of these figures can be understood as fulfilling some of the functions of the other—was a transformative experience, which the spiritual exercises practiced within philosophical schools sought to recreate.

It should be stressed that we have only been discussing aspects of the philosophical *ideal* of the king in Greco-Roman antiquity. The preceding discussion has little bearing on what actual kings—or emperors—in antiquity were like, but rather tells us what they *should* be like. Much of the literature pertaining to kingship in antiquity conforms to the logic of the *Fürstenspiegel* ("mirror for princes"), holding before the ruler the ideal behavior in the hopes that he will be inspired to conform himself to it.[62] I make this point not only in the spirit of historical accuracy, but also because I wish to correct a potential misunderstanding of Paul's theological project, and by extension, my own. I do not make the claim that Paul was an enthusiastic supporter of monarchical government as a specific form of political organization. The previous chapter argued that Paul's portrayal of Jesus as a suffering king stood in sharp contrast to the "theology of victory" that propped up the reign of Rome's emperors. It should be clear that Paul was no great admirer of Caesar.

For my own part, let me be clear that I am not in any way a closet monarchist, nor do I intend, by the preceding discussion, to romanticize the human institution of monarchy. Like Aristotle, I am not sanguine about the prospects of finding a good king among the ranks of humanity; history has offered us far too many tyrants. My project is rather to cast Paul's talk about Jesus against the backdrop of kingship discourse that was prevalent in his world, because in Paul's view, Jesus fulfilled that ideal in a way that no human had or could. To see how Paul does this in his letter to the church in Corinth, we must pay close attention to the way in which Paul compares Jesus to Moses, who was himself regarded as a king *par excellence*. To this figure we now turn.

1.4. Moses the Philosopher-king

The ideal of the philosopher-king was closely correlated with the acquisition of moral virtue in Mediterranean antiquity, as seen above, but why is this fact relevant to Paul's defense of his apostolic credentials (2 Cor 2:14–4:6)? Paul does speak of being transformed into the image of the Lord, but why should this claim be seen against the backdrop of kingship discourse, as I propose? The answer has to do with the *synkrisis* (evaluative comparison) Paul develops between Jesus and Moses (2 Cor 3:7–18). Paul compares these two figures with respect to the way in which each reflects, or transmits, divine glory. Note the contrasting claims Paul makes at the beginning and conclusion of this *synkrisis*:

> Now if the ministry of death, chiseled in letters on stone tablets, came in *glory* so that the people of Israel could not gaze at Moses' face because of the *glory* of his face, a *glory* now set aside, how much more will the ministry of the Spirit come in *glory*? (3:7–8)

> And all of us, with unveiled faces, seeing the *glory* of the Lord as though reflected in a mirror, are being transformed into the same image from one degree of *glory* to another; for this comes from the Lord, the Spirit. (3:18)

Moses, in the eyes of the Jewish philosopher Philo of Alexandria (ca 20 BCE–50 CE), ruled over God's people as the quintessential philosopher-king (*Mos.* 2.2).[63] Although Philo's presentation of Moses as a kind of monarch goes far beyond what can be gleaned from the biblical record, it accords nicely with the conceptualization of the ideal king in Greco-Roman political philosophy. Paul's treatment of the Mosaic covenant in 2 Corinthians 3 also appears to be trading in the common currency of this widespread cultural repertoire. Indeed, his audience's ability to grasp Paul's *synkrisis* of Jesus and Moses as two ideal kings would have been essential to their being persuaded by the larger argument of Paul's apostolic defense.[64]

Written to persuade his audience that Moses conformed to the pattern of the ideal Hellenistic king while yet demonstrating the highest ideals of

Judaism, Philo's *On the Life of Moses* portrays the patriarch as the quint-essential monarch in ways that resonate with the sketch provided above: a philosopher-king whose possession of the animate law enables him to inculcate virtue through vision.[65] Echoing Plato's *Republic*, Philo indicates the way in which Moses was uniquely suited to the royal office :

> For it has been said, not without good reason, that states can only make progress in well-being if either kings are philosophers or philos-ophers are kings. But Moses will be found to have displayed, and more than displayed, combined in his single person, not only these two faculties—the kingly and the philosophical—but also three others, one of which is concerned with law-giving, the second with the high priest's office, and the last with prophecy. (*Mos.* 2.2 [Colson, LCL])[66]

Although the offices of legislator, priest, and prophet could all be under-stood as of fundamental importance to the role of king, in Philo's view it is Moses' royal philosophical *education* (*Mos.* 1.20, 23; cf. 2.212, 215) that enables him to acquire virtue and transmit it. Through such education, he learns to master his passions (*Mos.* 1.25–26, 29), and his feet are set on the path toward virtue, "having a teacher within himself, virtuous reason" (*Mos.* 1.48; cf. 2.66). Despising material wealth, he greatly desires the true wealth of virtue (*Mos.* 1.154).[67] Moses' life thus exhibits "perfect harmo-ny . . . like people who are playing together in tune on a musical instru-ment" (*Mos.* 1.29). As a reward for his virtue and benevolence towards his people, God grants him authority to rule (*Mos.* 1.148, 155).

As the person preeminent in virtue, Moses provides the model of vir-tue to be imitated by his people, who take "a faithful copy of this excel-lence in their own souls" (*Mos.* 1.159). Yet this ability is intrinsically linked to his capacity as legislator, since it is fundamentally the law that enables virtue (cf. *Mos.* 2.36, 43, 189). This innate and extraordinary capacity for virtue enables him to compile, at God's prompting, the sacred books of the law, "likenesses and copies of the patterns enshrined in the soul, which be-came the laws which he revealed and established, displaying in the clearest manner the virtues which I have enumerated and described above" (*Mos.* 2.11; cf. 1.158; 2.45; cf. *Abr.* 275–276).

So Philo appears to suggest that the written law is but a copy of the "living law" residing innately within Moses. It would thus follow that if the purpose of the law is to inculcate virtue, the king who is also a perfect leg-islator is best equipped to carry out this task, because he has internalized the morally educative intent of the law. Philo, in fact, says as much in his concluding comments on the king-lawgiver's ability to provide the perfect example of virtue for the people to imitate: "but, perhaps, since Moses was also destined to be the lawgiver of his nation, he was himself long previously, through the providence of God, a living and reasonable law (*nomos empsuchos te kai logikos*)" (*Mos.* 1.162; cf. *Abr.* 5). Consistent with the broader Hellenistic concept of the ideal king, Philo's Moses enables the people to copy his virtue.

Furthermore, the mode by which God's image is transferred to Moses and ultimately to those who imitate him requires vision. God, who alone is sovereign, nevertheless gives Moses a share in divine governance, evidence of their mutual friendship (*Mos.* 1.155–156). As God's "friend," Moses is uniquely able to behold God's invisible nature, and thereby "established himself as a most beautiful and Godlike work, to be a model for all those who were inclined to imitate him" (*Mos.* 1.158; cf. *Sac.* 9; Exod 7:1).[68]

The role of vision in the imitation of virtue emerges in the following passage, in which Philo remarks that a virtuous man, city, or nation will quickly rise to a position of preeminence, "as the head is to the body occupying the pre-eminence of situation, not more for the sake of glory than for that of advancing the interests of those that see (*tōn horōntōn*). For continual appearances of good models stamp impressions closely resembling themselves on all souls which are not utterly obdurate and intractable" (*Praem.* 114). Philo is here referring to "those who wish to imitate models of excellent and admirable beauty . . . so that they may be able to effect a return to virtue and wisdom" (*Praem.* 115).[69]

Within Philo's portrayal of Moses, we may perceive several salient points of correspondence with the larger Greco-Roman understanding of kingship. Fundamentally, the ideal king is understood to possess the prerogative of making his people virtuous. Moses is ideally and uniquely equipped for this task because he is a philosopher-lawgiver, possesses the ensouled law, and may even be understood to transform his subjects by virtue of his glorious presence. The significance of these functions of Moses as king are vitally important in understanding Paul's *synkrisis* of Jesus and Moses, to which we now turn.

2. Paul, Apostle of the King who Transforms (2 Cor 2:14–4:6)

Although our central task is to understand how this *synkrisis* between Moses and Jesus functions in Paul's defense of his apostleship and what it might imply about the nature of moral formation, we must first grasp why Paul felt the need to defend his apostolic legitimacy in the first place. To do so we must attempt to reconstruct Paul's tempestuous relationship with the church in Corinth. I say "attempt" with good reason, for the task is fraught with difficulties. Our data consists of inferences drawn from the text of Second Corinthians itself and, to a lesser degree, corroborative data from the Acts of the Apostles. But, as noted above (n. 12), the literary integrity of Second Corinthians is in dispute. While any historical reconstruction must therefore remain tentative, the following broad sketch seems relatively clear.[70]

Paul established the church during his first visit to Corinth, ca. 51–52. Some time later, Paul apparently wrote to the church. That initial letter is no longer extant, but Paul refers to it in 1 Corinthians 5:9. In response to reports of problems in the church, Paul then wrote again, the letter known as First Corinthians (which would be "Second Corinthians" if the lost letter had survived), ca. 53. Shortly thereafter, Paul paid a brief and painful visit to the church; he was confronted and grievously offended (about what or by whom we do not know) and left in a hurry, ca. 54. Rather than returning to resolve the issue, Paul wrote a "tearful" third letter, also lost (see 2 Cor 1:15–2:4; 7:8).[71]

In the midst of negotiating this fraught relationship, Paul was imprisoned for some time in Ephesus, ca. 55–56. Upon release from prison, Paul received a report from his collaborator Titus (and possibly others afterwards) indicating an improvement in the Corinthians' attitudes towards him. In response, Paul now writes again, the surviving letter known as Second Corinthians, ca. 56. This letter addresses the question of Paul's apostolic authority (chs. 1–7), provides directions concerning money to be collected for the suffering church in Jerusalem (chs. 8–9), and points to the lingering opposition to Paul himself (chs. 10–13). If the letter's literary integrity is presumed, Paul's apostolic *apologia* would therefore seem to be a necessary first step to addressing the issues of the collection and remaining opposition.[72]

If this explains *why* Paul needs to defend his credentials as a minister of the gospel, how does his argument actually work? In brief, Paul asserts that the Corinthians should accept Paul's apostleship on the basis of the incontrovertible evidence of their own moral transformation. Paul should not need a letter of commendation because, he reminds them, "you yourselves are our letter . . . written not with ink but with the Spirit of the living

God" (3:2–3). In other words, because they have been, and continue to be, transformed into the glorious image of Christ (3:18), they must acknowledge Paul as Christ's apostle.

The preceding portrait of the ideal king with respect to moral formation illuminates our reading of Paul's *apologia* in two ways. First, Paul's implied contrast between a mere commendatory letter and the letter written upon the Corinthians' hearts (3:1–6) is sharpened by the concept of the ideal king as a "living law" who enables the inculcation of virtue. Second, the subsequent *synkrisis* of Christ and Moses as two ideal kings (3:7–18; 4:6) relies upon the notion of the ideal king who transforms his subjects through his presence. The audience's cultural repertoire concerning the transformative role of the ideal king thus both undergirds Paul's argument and sharpens its rhetorical effect.

Yet before Paul can even begin this argument, he must address the bewildering fact of his own suffering, which had also cast doubt upon his apostolic legitimacy (2:14–17). The following provides an interpretive overview of the entire argument that anticipates my further analysis of its constituent parts (2:14–17; 3:1–6; 3:7–18; 4:1–6).

Paul's *apologia* begins with an arresting metaphor: the Apostle likens himself to a captured prisoner being paraded behind a victorious Roman general (2:14–17). Paradoxically, it is through this spectacle that the "aroma" of Christ is made known (2:15–16). Insisting that he speaks sincerely before God, Paul distinguishes himself from those who merely peddle God's word (2:17).[73]

Paul is quick to insist, however, that he is not simply commending himself, as though he needed a letter of introduction (3:1). The Corinthians *themselves* are such a "letter" (3:2). By this he means that their lives provide clear evidence of the transformative work of the spirit of the living God (3:3). By implication, the Corinthians must acknowledge that Paul is a legitimate emissary of the God by whose spirit they have been transformed. Again, Paul hastens to clarify that his worthiness as an apostle does not derive from himself but from God, who has appointed him to administer this new covenant of the spirit (3:5–6). As Paul next launches into a comparison of the old and new covenants, he is clearly thinking of this very contrast drawn by the prophet Jeremiah, in which the new covenant, implanted within Israel's heart, actually *enables* the fidelity to God that the old covenant merely commanded (Jer 31:31–34 [38:31–34 LXX]).[74]

Paul also has in mind the contrast between the two purveyors of these covenants, Moses and Jesus. The glory of the covenant that brings death is eclipsed by the glory of the covenant that brings life (3:7–10). Neither Paul nor Jeremiah imagine that a new covenant *actually* replaces an old one; what is *new* is the enablement of fidelity to the one covenant.[75] Likewise the glory of Moses' radiant face—a mere reflection of God's glory (3:7, 13; cf. Exod 34:29–35)—is outstripped by the glory of the Lord's radiant visage (3:18; 4:6). The former was veiled, both actually and more significantly metaphorically: it was incapable of transmitting God's glory (and fidelity to Torah) to Israel. The latter by contrast is unveiled: Paul and the Corinthians alike directly behold the Lord's radiant image and are transformed into its likeness (3:18).

Therefore, in light of this transforming encounter, Paul renounces all manner of shameful behavior unbefitting a true apostle (4:1–2). Some, he concedes, have been blinded to this enlightenment, the announcement of this glorious transformative encounter with Christ (4:4). But Paul is confident that if the Corinthians will only look within to their own hearts they will find incontrovertible proof of this transformation (4:6). Simply put, Paul's apostolic defense *depends upon* the Corinthians' recognition that they have been unmistakably transformed as a result of their encounter with the spirit through Paul's ministry. As I shall now endeavor to demonstrate, Paul's ability to *persuade* the Corinthians of this fact relies upon the shared cultural repertoire concerning the transformative ability of the ideal king.

2.1. Emissary of a Suffering King (2 Cor 2:14–17)

Paul introduces his argument by obliquely addressing the confounding nature of his own suffering. He well knows that the evident marks of his hard life (see 2 Cor 11:23–29) cast doubt on his apostolic *bona fides*. How, it had apparently been asked, could such a pathetic figure imagine himself to be the ambassador of the glorious king Jesus? How could he be taken seriously when his suffering followed him like the stench of death? Paul insists that olfactory recalibration is required—this odor is rather the fragrance of life. The Apostle begins with a metaphor that is at once surprising and perplexing:

> But thanks be to God, who in Christ always leads us in triumphal procession (*thriambeuonti*), and through us spreads in every place

the fragrance that comes from knowing him. For we are the aroma of Christ to God among those who are being saved and among those who are perishing; to the one a fragrance from death to death, to the other a fragrance from life to life. Who is sufficient for these things? For we are not peddlers of God's word like so many; but in Christ we speak as persons of sincerity, as persons sent from God and standing in his presence.[76] (2:14–17)

At first blush, especially in the NRSV translation here quoted, the image of being led by Christ in triumphal procession strikes one as an image of victory. Paul seemingly evokes the Roman *pompa triumphalis*, or "triumph" as it is commonly referred to, a victory parade led by a conquering Roman general through the streets of the capital Rome, his jubilant soldiers and humiliated captives in tow.[77] Christ would thus appear to be cloaked in Rome's "theology of victory," his followers celebrating and participating in his triumph.[78]

In fact, the older King James Version makes this point with even greater force and clarity: "Now thanks be unto God, which always *causeth* us to triumph in Christ." Here, Christ's followers not only celebrate Christ's victory, but through him are themselves rendered victorious.[79] The problem with the KJV translation is that there is no lexical evidence to support a causative meaning of the Greek verb *thriambeuō*. The verb most commonly referred to the celebration of a victory, such as in the Roman *pompa triumphalis*.[80] But the problem goes even deeper: when used transitively, the verb actually means "to lead about *as a captive* in a triumphal procession."[81] In other words, the object of the verb should not be understood as a celebrating soldier but rather a defeated prisoner of war destined for execution.[82] What could Paul possibly mean by this metaphor?

We can begin to see how the imagery works by remembering the striking and countercultural image of Jesus as a suffering king that Paul provides in Philippians 2:5–8. There, Jesus does not "exploit" his status, but rather "empties" himself of all his status in obedience to God, embracing suffering even to the point of his shameful death by crucifixion. In marked contrast to conventional aristocratic or royal virtues such as magnanimity and magnificence, Christ exemplifies a willingness to suffer. In the face of propaganda extolling the *Victoria* of Rome's emperor, Paul exhorts the citizens of the heavenly commonwealth to conform themselves to the pattern of their suffering king Jesus.

I concluded the previous chapter by raising the question: How might these citizens be *enabled* to follow their king in the way of suffering? Paul, I argue, has this very question in mind when he portrays himself not as an exultant soldier but rather a humiliated captive. He knows that his use of this metaphor will likely confound his readers, but that is precisely his objective. He is following a rhetorical strategy memorably described by the writer Flannery O'Connor:

> When you can assume that your audience holds the same beliefs you do, you can relax a little and use more normal ways of talking to it; when you have to assume that it does not, then you have to make your vision apparent by shock—to the hard of hearing you shout, and for the blind you draw large and startling figures.[83]

The startling image of a captive being led to his execution intends to startle and shock, because Paul cannot assume that his audience understands the true character of his apostleship—indeed, he has good reason to believe that they *misunderstand* what it means to be the emissary of a suffering and crucified Messiah.

A royal emissary should reflect in his own person the dignity of the office that he represents. This was as true in Paul's day as it is in ours: diplomats ought to be well-dressed, well-manicured, well-mannered, and above all, well-spoken. The self-evident need for diplomats to be articulate and persuasive is reflected in the fact that we describe as a "diplomatic solution" one in which a mutually satisfying agreement is reached through the art of dialogue between esteemed emissaries of a sovereign government. The correlation between apostolic legitimacy and rhetorical ability seems to have been regarded as axiomatic within the church in Corinth.

In First Corinthians, Paul had already addressed the sharp divisions that had arisen, at least in part, out of his perceived rhetorical ineptitude in comparison to other apostles such as the eloquent Apollos.[84] In Second Corinthians he must counter the profoundly false notion that suffering is incompatible with apostleship. This can be seen in his brilliantly ironic "boasting" of his suffering and weakness, which he claims actually demonstrates the power of Christ dwelling in him (11:16–12:13). Paul anticipates that later argument here by paradoxically likening himself to a humiliated captive being led to death.[85]

The nature of the paradox is suggested by the imagery of burning incense, which to some might signal the reek of death, and to others the fragrance of life.[86] The pungent aromas of incense, cinnamon, and frankincense accompanied the visual spectacle of the Roman *pompa triumphalis*. These pronounced odors broadcast throughout the city the military victory that was being celebrated along the parade route stretching from the *porta triumphalis* (triumphal gate) to the temple of Jupiter in the heart of Rome.[87] Was this a pleasant smell? That would depend primarily not upon olfactory preference, but rather upon location.

To those celebrating the general's military triumph, these aromas conveyed the sweet smell of victory, or as Paul puts it, "a fragrance from life to life." They both recalled the immediate victory now being celebrated, as well as promised the ongoing victory of Rome's armies. Yet to those bedraggled captives paraded in front of the general's chariot, these odors also recalled their crushing defeat and—to some prisoners at least—ominously portended their imminent execution: "a fragrance from death to death."[88]

Observe how Paul mixes up the metaphor at this point: he is no longer the defeated captive but rather has himself become the pungent aroma broadcasting a highly ambivalent message of life or death. Why does he make this rhetorical move? Perhaps to suggest that his audience's perception of him is characterized by the same confounding ambivalence as the aroma of incense in the *pompa triumphalis*. Now to an observer of this victory parade, it would have been blindingly obvious which participants were heading to death and which to life. The splendid trappings of victory would have stood out in sharp contrast—in most cases—to the shabby rags covering the captives.[89] But making the same sort of judgement with respect to the Apostle's life is not so easy.[90]

Paul well knows that some in the church regard his sufferings, rhetorical shortcomings, and general lack of conventional *bona fides* as raising a huge question mark over his claim to apostolic legitimacy. As the emissary of the true philosopher-king, he is keen to distinguish himself from the mere sophists who peddle (2:17) or adulterate (cf. 4:2) God's word.[91] His concern goes further than this, however. If they reject the ambassador on the grounds that he reeks of death, how much more will they reject the king for the very same reason? Recall how Paul, in his letter to the church in Philippi, must confront those who "live as enemies of the cross of Christ," that is, individuals who oppose discipleship in conformity with the pattern of Christ's own suffering (Phil 3:18; see previous chapter). Likewise, his concern here is that the church properly grasp the image of Jesus, the special kind of king into which they are being transformed.

Paul makes this abundantly clear towards the end of the letter, when he asks his audience whether they comprehend his pastoral intent: "Have you been thinking all along that we have been defending ourselves (*apologoumetha*) before you? We are speaking in Christ before God. Everything we do, beloved, is for the sake of building you up" (2 Cor 12:19).[92] Paul's apostolic *apologia* aims not merely to restore his personal legitimacy, but rather serves the greater goal of restoring the image of Jesus as suffering king. Thus Paul employs the metaphor of the Roman triumph in a manner *deliberately* ambivalent.[93] His intent is to say: "I know that some of you reject me, and by extension the king whom I represent, because you smell upon me the stench of death. But your noses betray you. The aroma of my suffering is actually the sweet-smelling means by which, in every place, Jesus is made known." Paul, in other words, calls for the recalibration of their imagination.[94]

2.2. Written on the Heart: Law and Letter (2 Cor 3:1–6)

Having cast himself, provocatively and ambivalently, as the suffering ambassador of a suffering king, Paul now directly addresses one of the Corinthians' presumed objections, namely that he had not presented to them a letter of recommendation authorizing his ministry among them. This he does by setting up a contrast in 3:1 between two sorts of letters: the standard commendatory letter one might have expected Paul to present to (or request from) the Corinthians, and the figurative letter they themselves represent.[95] Lacking the former, Paul claims the latter is written upon his very heart (3:2), the implicit proof of his apostleship. As the next verse makes clear, Paul could well have claimed that this letter was in fact written upon the hearts of the Corinthians as well.[96]

Here, Paul makes deft use of *antanaklasis* ("bending back"), a rhetorical figure of speech in which a word—in this case, *epistolē* (letter)—is repeated while its meaning subtly shifts.[97] Thus Paul writes:

> Surely we do not need, as some do, *letters* of recommendation (*ē mē chrēzomen hōs tines sustatikōn epistolōn*). . . . You yourselves are our *letter* (*hē epistolē hēmōn humeis este*) . . . you show that you are a *letter* of Christ (*phaneroumenoi hoti epistolē Christou*). (3:1–3)

The commendatory letter is supplanted by the letter the Corinthians themselves represent, which is then further characterized as a letter of Christ. Paul's skillful use of repetition goes beyond mere rhetorical adornment; rather, it signals the inner logic of his argument.

The word *antanaklasis* can mean either "reflection of light" or "bending back," and the latter meaning suggests the way this figure of speech indicates the sort of argument Paul is making. The audience demands evidence of Paul's apostleship in the form of a commendatory letter, and Paul "bends back" upon them their own demand by insisting that they themselves constitute the very evidence they seek.[98] This rhetorical strategy commends itself for two reasons. First, it relieves Paul of the perilous burden of needing to justify himself before a skeptical audience. Second, since the evidence of Paul's apostolic fitness resides within the Corinthians themselves, they would have to deny that they constitute a "letter of Christ" in order to reject Paul's argument.[99] What then, might the phrase "letter of Christ" imply about the audience's self-understanding?

Such a letter written on the Corinthians' heart connotes the enablement of virtuous behavior. This becomes clear through Paul's evocation of the two types of covenants contrasted by the prophet Jeremiah. The first covenant, given at Sinai, had proven powerless to enable fidelity to Israel's God: Israel broke it. The second covenant, Jeremiah insists, the LORD will implant *within* Israel, indeed will write it upon Israel's heart. As a result of this second covenant, Israel will no longer need to be taught of the LORD; rather they shall in fact know the LORD:

> The days are surely coming, says the LORD, when I will make a new
> covenant with the house of Israel and the house of Judah. It will not
> be like the covenant that I made with their ancestors when I took
> them by the hand to bring them out of the land of Egypt—a covenant
> that they broke, though I was their husband, says the LORD. But this
> is the covenant that I will make with the house of Israel after those
> days, says the LORD: I will put my law within them, and I will write it
> on their hearts; and I will be their God, and they shall be my people.
> No longer shall they teach one another, or say to each other, "Know
> the LORD," for they shall all know me, from the least of them to the
> greatest, says the LORD; for I will forgive their iniquity, and remember their sin no more. (Jer 31:31–34 [38:31–34 LXX]).[100]

For Jeremiah, the covenant written upon the heart is a metaphor for the enablement of covenant fidelity: Israel will not only *know* Torah, but will be able to *perform* Torah. This metaphor is employed in similar manner by the prophet Ezekiel.[101] In claiming that the Corinthians are a letter written not on stone tablets but on the tablets of human hearts, then, Paul evocatively makes the same claim. The Corinthians' transformation represents the promise of Jeremiah's prophecy.

Paul's allusion to Jeremiah has, of course, long been recognized. What has gone unnoticed, however, is that a law written upon the heart—the ensouled or animate law—was also a way of talking about the unique function of the ideal king in antiquity. The king both loves and obeys the law because the law resides innately within him.[102] Such a person is therefore uniquely qualified to inculcate virtue among his subjects. Thus Philo regards Moses as the quintessential philosopher-king who is able to provide for Israel a perfect example of virtue to imitate because he himself is "a living and reasonable law (*nomos empsuchos te kai logikos*)" (*Mos.* 1.162).

How is this conceptualization of the ideal king relevant to Paul's developing argument? If Paul contends that the Corinthians themselves are Paul's "letter of recommendation," so to speak, what warrant does he provide for such a bold claim? "Such is the confidence we have *through Christ (dia tou Christou)* towards God," Paul insists (3:4). These words, taken in light of ancient kingship discourse, would seem to indicate that God's anointed king—Jesus, the Christ (the Anointed One)—is the means by which the Corinthians' own transformation is effected. Such a warrant only functions persuasively if one understands the king as a "living law," one who embodies and inculcates the spirit of the written law. Jeremiah's proleptic vision of a law written on Israel's heart has come true among the Corinthians by means of Israel's true king, himself a living, ensouled law.[103]

To the extent that Paul can rely on his audience's cultural literacy with respect to political discourse, the trope of kingship also provides a degree of "informational" or "functional" redundancy to his argument.[104] One might well wonder whether a largely Gentile audience would be able to perceive Paul's allusions to Jeremiah or Ezekiel; their failure to do so would jeopardize the success of Paul's argument. Were they not to perceive the correlation between stone tablets and the inefficacy of the Torah to inculcate virtue, they would not grasp the import of Paul's point, namely that Christ has fulfilled the transformative promise of Torah. In this event, the trope of the ideal king who inculcates virtue by means of the ensouled law would function as another, hence redundant, mode of communication. Thus Paul's argument can hope to succeed among a Gentile audience, despite their possible ignorance of the larger scriptural hermeneutical framework Paul employs.

To view the Messiah, or Christ, as the means by which the Corinthians are transformed also helps to understand Paul's distinction between letter and spirit. While the contrast between letter and spirit allows Paul to distinguish his own ministry from that of Moses,[105] it further provides a vehicle to convey the efficacy of Christ's transformative ability. The old covenant, "of the letter" (*grammatos*), he declares, brings death, while the new covenant, "of the spirit" (*pneumatos*), brings life (3:6; cf. 3:3). One can thus understand the function of the king as effecting the transformation from "letter" (that which the law commands) to "spirit" (enablement to obey the law).

"Letter" and "spirit" here can of course be understood simply as metaphorical ways of describing the difference between command and enablement. Yet "spirit" in this argument also carries considerably heavier theological freight. The Corinthians are, in Paul's rich metaphor, a "letter" written not with ink (*ou melani*) but rather with (or by) the spirit of the living God (*pneumati theou zōntos*) (3:3). Here, "spirit" is not a generic term indicating merely God's enablement but rather a way of denoting God's agency. Again, this would likely have been seen, through the lens of ancient political discourse, as a function of the king, the vicegerent of God (or the gods).[106] The Messiah is the one through whom God acts, resulting ultimately in the transformation of the Corinthians, described by Paul, fittingly, as a "letter of Christ" (*epistolē Christou*) (3:3).

If the "spirit of the living God" in 3:3 is a way of denoting God's agency, and if ancient political discourse would have attributed such agency to the king, God's vicegerent, then we have grounds to believe that Paul is identifying the spirit in this argument with Jesus the Messiah. Such appears to be the case in 3:17, when he plainly asserts that "the Lord is (the) spirit" (*ho de kurios to pneuma estin*). Of course, there are also grounds for taking the referent for *kurios* in 3:16–18 to be God rather than Jesus. The larger context, however, points to the identification of Jesus with the spirit.[107]

2.3. *Synkrisis*: Two Covenants, Two Faces, Two Kings (2 Cor 3:7–18; 4:6)

Realizing that "the spirit of the living God" is to be identified with Jesus is decisively important for grasping Paul's intention in the following *synkrisis* of the administration of two covenants (3:7–18). This is not a needless digression that can be excised without any real damage to the argument.[108] Nor is Paul merely responding to some kind of allegation of the superiority of the Sinaitic covenant (although he may be doing that as well). Rather, this evaluative comparison intends to make clear *how* the Corinthians have been transformed through Jesus the Messiah, God's anointed king.

On the surface, Paul compares the administration of two covenants in 3:7–18—that of the covenant of death, and that of the covenant of the spirit. His *synkrisis* appears to set side by side Moses and Paul, as is evident in 3:7–8. Yet looming behind this comparison is the comparison of two shining faces, one belonging to Moses, the other most definitely *not* belonging to Paul. Given that Paul's apologetic goal in this section is to defend his own apostleship, why does he refrain from attributing glory to himself? The logic of the *synkrisis*, after all, would seem to require it.[109]

The glory of the old covenant resulted in Moses' radiant visage, which is made clear through the subtext of Paul's argument, Exodus 34:29–35:

> Moses came down from Mount Sinai. As he came down from the mountain with the two tablets of the covenant in his hand, Moses did not know that the skin of his face shone because he had been talking with God. When Aaron and all the Israelites saw Moses, the skin of his face was shining, and they were afraid to come near him. But Moses called to them; and Aaron and all the leaders of the congregation returned to him, and Moses spoke with them. Afterward all the Israelites came near, and he gave them in commandment all that the LORD had spoken with him on Mount Sinai. When Moses had finished speaking with them, he put a veil on his face; but whenever Moses went in before the LORD to speak with him, he would take the veil off, until he came out; and when he came out, and told the Israelites what he had been commanded, the Israelites would see the face of Moses, that the skin of his face was shining; and Moses would put the veil on his face again, until he went in to speak with him.

In this passage, Moses' face shines brilliantly after his encounter with God on Mt. Sinai. As a result, he must veil his face when speaking with his fellow Israelites, only removing the veil when he goes before the LORD in the tent of meeting. Should not the glory of the new covenant likewise result in Paul's own greater glory?

There are a good number of reasons Paul is loath to thus characterize himself. It would seem precisely the sort of self-commendation he is self-consciously attempting to avoid (e.g., 3:1). Moreover, Paul regards external weakness rather than strength, or visible glory, to be the marks of the true apostle (2:14). On the other hand, Paul is not unknown to boast when the situation calls for it (10:7–18), and ancients were acquainted with the appropriate ways to engage in inoffensive self-praise.[110]

Beyond the question of whether such self-praise is congruent with Paul's larger argument and ethos, there is another reason for his refusal. Paul does not portray himself as possessing radiant glory because that would be dangerously misleading. This radiant figure is properly identified, as 3:18 makes clear, as the Lord himself.[111] If behind the *synkrisis* of the administrations of two different covenants lies a more fundamental comparison of two different *persons*—Moses and the Lord—what then is the point of this comparison?[112] Why is such an implied comparison essential to Paul's larger apologetic argument?

We find a clue by observing what Moses and the Lord have in common: a radiant visage (3:7, 13; 4:6).[113] This detail is not incidental, but rather absolutely crucial to Paul's presentation. Indeed, the heart of the argument in this section concerns both what these radiant visages share in common and how they are, in the final analysis, fundamentally different. And given the wider discourse related to the ideal king, Paul can confidently assume that his audience would recognize the importance of a radiant visage as it relates to moral transformation.

Although Moses' glorious face results directly from his face-to-face meeting with the LORD on Mt. Sinai, this glory is somehow deficient, and is thus being set aside. That a king should reflect divine glory is common coin in ancient kingship discourse, yet to claim that such glory is in the process of being set aside or abolished (*tēn doxan . . . tēn katargoumenēn*, 3:7; see also 3:11, 13, 14) seems unique to Paul's argument here.[114]

What Paul intends by this claim can be understood by recalling the two covenants contrasted by Jeremiah. The first covenant proved incapable of enabling the obedience it commanded, thus calling forth a new covenant. Therefore, the reason for setting aside the first covenant is, perhaps paradoxically, so that its intent can be fulfilled. Paul makes an analogous argument with rhetorical deftness: just as Moses' face was veiled, he claims, so a veil lies over the reading of the old covenant (3:13–14). So close is the identification between the covenant and Moses in Paul's mind, that one can indeed "read Moses," and when one does so, a veil yet lies over the heart (3:15). The veil over Moses' face prevents the Israelites from beholding the reflection of divine glory that presumably would blind them (3:7, 13).

What, then, is prevented by the veil that lies over the heart? Following the hint provided by Jeremiah, I propose that such a veil indicates that the transformation required by the covenant has somehow been prevented. In other words, the veiled face of Moses and the veiled heart of Israel can both be read as metaphors pointing to the inability of the first covenant to effect the transformation it requires. It is for this reason that Moses' glory and the glory of the first covenant is deficient and must, in a manner of speaking, be set aside.[115] Paul declares that this has been done in, or better through, the Messiah (*mē anakaluptomenon hoti en Christō katargeitai*, 3:14).

The glory of the Messiah's face is incomparably greater than that of Moses' face because it effects that which Moses' glory could not. Paul prepares for this climactic conclusion by continuing the metaphor of the veiled heart: when one turns to the Lord, this veil is lifted (3:16). Paul's meaning is made abundantly clear in the following sentences: when one beholds the Messiah's glorious visage—"as though reflected in a mirror (*katoptrizomenoi*)"—one is transformed into "the same image (*tēn autēn eikona*)" (3:18).[116] Now, at last, the point of the preceding *synkrisis* emerges. The vision of the glorious Messiah effects the change that the glorious Moses could not. The former was veiled, both literally and metaphorically. That is, the divine glory reflected in Moses' face was incapable of effecting transformation.

By contrast, one beholds the Lord's glory with *unveiled* face (*anakekalummenō prosōpō*, 3:18) and is transformed into his image. This image, this "face of Christ" (4:6) is nothing other than the "image of God" (*eikōn tou theou*) (4:4). In claiming that Christ is the "image of God," Paul appears to echo the language of Genesis 1:26, in which God says, "'let us make the human (*anthropon*) according to our image (*kat' eikona hēmeteran*).'"[117] By this echo, Paul recalls his earlier letter to the church in Corinth, in which he had explicitly compared Christ to Adam, the first *anthropos*: "Thus it is written, 'The first man, Adam (*ho prōtos anthropos Adam*), became a living being'; the last Adam became a life-giving spirit" (1 Cor 15:45).[118] As he makes clear in his later letter to the church in Rome, Paul understands Adam to be "a type of the one who was to come," namely Christ (Rom 5:14).[119]

By conceiving of Christ as a "second Adam," Paul makes an important theological claim, that the glorious divine image bestowed upon the first human, although disfigured by sin, will be restored in the resurrection through Christ.[120] In presenting Christ as the image of God, Paul further recalls the royal vocation of the first human created in God's image, namely to "have dominion over the fish of the sea and over the birds of the air and over every living thing that moves upon the earth" (Gen 1:28). To be transformed into the image of Christ is thus to be restored to the human vocation, to become truly human.[121]

Taken in light of ancient kingship discourse, which understood the king to be able to effect moral transformation by virtue of his sheer presence, Paul's conclusion makes the point of the preceding comparison clear. When one compares Moses and Jesus, two "kings" who both reflected in some measure God's glory, one concludes that Jesus is incomparably more glorious because only the vision of King Jesus' glory effects one's own moral transformation.[122]

My argument thus far can be summarized as follows: The Corinthians should recognize Paul as an emissary of Jesus the king because they themselves have been, and continue to be, transformed as a result of Paul's ministry (3:1–6). Indeed, they have been transformed into the glorious image of Christ (3:7–18). Yet two interrelated questions remain.

First, how are we to understand what Paul actually means by this phenomenon of "transformation by vision"? Scholars have remarked that such a concept seems entirely foreign to Paul, with the exception of 2 Corinthians 3:18.[123] If the cultural concept of transformation through the presence of the ideal king is to be of any value in grasping Paul's argument, we must endeavor to understand its practical implications. Second, if Paul had indeed intended to compare two kings, Moses and Jesus, surely he could have done so in a more straightforward manner. Why, if my reading is correct, does he muddy the waters by introducing the comparison between "letter" and "spirit"? Does not the plain reading of the text—a comparison of two administrations, Moses' (of the letter) and Paul's (of the spirit)—undermine my argument? Several observations will help us address these questions.

First, Paul's argument suggests a keen desire to correct a potential misunderstanding with respect to the significance of Moses' glory. Indeed, some have argued that Paul's opponents had promulgated what was in Paul's view a false Christology modeled upon Moses' *physical* glory.[124] We cannot, however, know with certainty the identity of such opponents, nor whether they were the source of such a Christology. Nevertheless, on the basis of Paul's argument itself, some inappropriate attribution of physical glory onto Christ by the Corinthians seems likely. Paul must therefore make a clear distinction between Moses' physical radiance, which does not transform, and Christ's spiritual radiance, which does. This is the intent behind the contrast between "letter" and "spirit." Such a contrast achieves its goal through resonance with the notion of the ideal king as living law, one who is able to inculcate fidelity to the spirit of the written law.

Second, Paul is aided in this task of translating a metaphor by the critique of physical royal splendor already in existence. Plutarch, for example, abhors the manner in which certain kings attempt to display their divine nature through the excessive brilliance of their appearance. True divinity is reflected, he claims, in that which resides internally, the king's virtuous character (*Demetr.* 10.2–3; 30.4–5). This observation may explain, moreover, why Moses' glorious visage is incapable of effecting moral transformation. Human glory imitates the divine after a fashion, but it does so in a way that is fundamentally misleading. A resplendent human figure may at once signal divine favor and inspire imitation. But to the extent that one strives to acquire the same glory for oneself, one pursues transformation inauthentically. The sort of transformation that Paul envisions is intimated by the image of a humiliated king (or other captive) with which his *apologia* begins (2:14). For these reasons, Paul chooses to characterize the Messiah as the sort of king who effects the Corinthians' moral transformation by means of the spirit.

Third, and finally, Paul must account for the obvious fact that the Corinthians have never beheld Christ physically. Thus he must deftly translate the concept of "transformation by vision" into the spiritual realm. Paul's argument envisions a sort of visual piety that depends neither upon the literal beholding of a physical person nor upon a mystical encounter such as might be found within Hellenistic mystery religions.[125] Nevertheless, one must resist the assumption that "seeing" can be reduced to some other non-visual mode of transformation such as simply hearing.[126] Elsewhere, for example, Paul appeals to visual evidence, as in 2 Corinthians 10:7, in which the injunction to "look at what is before your eyes" aims to provide the evidence that the Corinthians belong to Christ.[127]

The way in which transformation results from "beholding" Christ actually depends upon another aspect of the ideal king's character: his role as a philosopher. Earlier it was observed that philosophy in antiquity denoted a way of life devoted to the pursuit of truth and the acquisition of virtue. A philosopher's disciples internalized or "learned" his way of life through a sustained association in which they had ample opportunity to observe him in the world. When the sage was not present, various spiritual exercises practiced within philosophical schools endeavored to bring students into the non-physical "presence" of the sage in order to effect moral transformation. Paul's oddly phrased admonition in Ephesians betrays his awareness of this sort of practice: "That is not the way you learned Christ" (Eph 4:20).[128] The same kind of moral transformation through association with Christ, mediated through the spirit rather than a physical body (2 Cor 3:17), is in view here. That is, the Messiah's spiritual, rather than physical, presence effects true transformation.

2.4. From Unveiled Face to Unveiled Gospel (2 Cor 4:1-6)

Having concluded his comparison of Moses and Jesus as two ideal kings, Paul returns in this final paragraph of his *apologia* to several important themes introduced at the beginning. He brings up the question of his own integrity as a minister of God's word (4:2; cf. 2:17), the improper perception of Paul and his gospel by "those who are perishing" (4:3; cf. 2:15–16), and the spreading of the knowledge of God (4:6; cf. 2:14).[129] Chiefly, Paul brings to the forefront the question of his legitimacy, what *commends* him to the church in Corinth. Once again, Paul turns their question on its head. He does not need, as they had supposed, letters of recommendation (3:1). Rather, he insists:

> We have renounced the shameful things that one hides; we refuse to practice cunning or to falsify God's word (*dolountes ton logon tou theou*); but by the open statement of the truth we commend ourselves to the conscience of everyone *in the sight of God* (*enōpion tou theou*). (4:2; emphasis added)

Paul echoes the earlier contrast he had drawn between himself and his sophistic opponents. Unlike such "peddlers of God's word (*kapēleuontes ton logon tou theou*)," Paul speaks as one "standing in [God's] presence (*katenanti theou*)" (2:17).

The prepositions *katenanti* (2:17) and *enōpion* (4:2) can sometimes simply denote position with respect to some other object: "before," "in front of," or "opposite." In these two instances, however, Paul wishes to convey the idea of being "in the presence of" or perhaps even "in the sight of" God.[130] Rather than the conventional trappings of apostolic authority—commendatory letters, rhetorical sophistication, and the like—association with God marks Paul as an emissary of the king. This is a corollary of his argument that he (and the Corinthians) have been transformed through the presence of Christ. Paul implies that it should be *obvious* to the Corinthians why he is a herald of the king: he stands in the presence of the one who transforms him.[131]

Yet Paul knows very well that his identity as a herald, one who proclaims the gospel, is a confounding puzzle to some. Indeed, it is not just Paul's status, but the very nature of the gospel itself that is in question. There are some in the church who are blind to both:

> And even if our gospel is veiled, it is veiled to those who are perishing (*en tois apollumenois*). In their case the god of this world has blinded the minds (*ta noēmata*) of unbelievers (*tōn apistōn*), to keep them from seeing the light of the gospel of the glory of Christ, who is the image of God (*eikōn tou theou*). (4:3–4; emphasis added)

This veiled quality of the gospel recalls the double meaning of the aroma of incense in the Roman *pompa triumphalis*—to those being saved, it smells of the fragrance of life, but among those perishing (*en tois apollumenois*), it is the stench of death (2:15–16). Things are not what they superficially appear—this has been the subtext of Paul's argument throughout the *apologia*. What then, enables one's faculty of seeing to work properly? The polyvalent metaphor of the veil provides a clue.

Moses veiled his face because the Israelites could not bear to gaze upon the intense radiance of its glory after Moses' encounter with the LORD on Mt. Sinai (3:7, 13; Exod 34:30). Here, the veil functions to occlude divine glory, presumably as a merciful concession to human finitude or weakness. But then Paul subtly shifts the meaning of the word "veil" to denote metaphorically the inability of some to perceive the true intent of the covenant with Israel:

> But their minds (*ta noēmata*) were hardened. Indeed, to this very day, when they hear the reading of the old covenant, that same veil is still there, since only in Christ is it set aside. Indeed, to this very day whenever Moses is read, a veil lies over their *heart* (*tēn kardian*). (3:14–15; emphasis added)[132]

Just as the people of Israel suffered from hardened minds (*ta noēmata*, 3:14), so there are some in Paul's day whose minds have been blinded (*ta noēmata*, 4:4). This failure of vision is not merely cognitive, however, but also volitional, not simply of mind but of heart (3:15).[133] The veil, as I have argued, symbolizes the failure of the covenant with Israel to effect the transformation that it requires. Torah, the covenant's divine instruction intended to lead to flourishing, has not become a "living law" animating Israel's behavior from the inside out.[134] This "veil is removed" when one "turns to the Lord" (3:16); only then, with "unveiled face" is one transformed into the image of Jesus the king (3:18). And yet there are some, Paul acknowledges, for whom this "gospel of the glory of Christ" remains veiled.

Paul describes those whose sight has been occluded with the adjective *apistos* in 4:4. The term denotes one who lacks the quality of *pistis*. As we have seen, *pistis* connotes a range of related concepts: belief, faith, loyalty, allegiance. One who is *apistos* may thus be described as unbelieving, faithless, disloyal, or failing to embody allegiance. The NRSV's translation suggest that Paul has in mind "unbelievers," those completely outside the belief structure of the church. This is indeed Paul's habitual use of the term.[135] While *apistos* primarily *denotes* such people in this instance, I suggest that Paul also *connotes* the wider semantic field of the term. That is, "unbelief" in the gospel is bound up in the failure to properly give allegiance to Jesus the king. As with the failure of Israel, Paul puts his finger on a problem that is both cognitive (unbelief) and volitional (allegiance). In other words, the *apistoi*—those blind to the nature of both the gospel and Paul's apostleship—may exist both outside and inside the church.[136]

On its face, it may seem unlikely that Paul would refer to certain members of the church in Corinth as *apistoi*. But recall the way in which Paul writes to the church in Philippi about those who reject the cruciform pattern of discipleship as "enemies of the cross of Christ" (Phil 3:18). Such individuals—both in Philippi and in Corinth—lack not merely "belief," understood as cognitive assent to a set of propositions, but they also lack embodied loyalty, or allegiance, to Jesus the suffering king. This deficit in *pistis* ultimately results in a failure to perceive that "the glory which is seen, as in a mirror [3:18], in Paul's ministry is the glory which shines through suffering."[137] There are some, Paul suggests, who have not been transformed through association with Christ and therefore neither recognize Christ nor his Apostle.

Now at last one sees the force of the intentionally ambivalent metaphor of the "triumph" with which Paul began his *apologia*. By presenting himself as a captive led to slaughter, the Apostle aims to recalibrate the imagination of those who believe that suffering is the mark of his apostolic illegitimacy. In so doing, his aim is not simply to restore his eroded authority, but even more so to persuade believers in Corinth to see the suffering Christ "with unveiled faces" (3:18), that they may be transformed into his likeness.[138]

3. Beholding the Philosopher-King: Paul's Practices of Transformation

Paul, I have argued, regards Christ as the philosopher-king *par excellence*. Through transformative association with Christ, one is made authentically human as the divine image is restored in those who behold and imitate it. Although Paul's metaphorical description of this process verges on the mystical, the traditions of Greco-Roman philosophical schools suggest that, in fact, concrete practices may have been the vehicle by which such transformation was effected. In order to investigate this possibility, we must first reflect on the nature of the human body (such as Paul understood it) that might undertake such practices.

The body is, in Dallas Willard's memorable phrase, "a storehouse and transmitter of power."[139] Anyone who has witnessed the explosive power of a sprinter—or any elite athlete—knows this to be true at the physical level. Less clear, however, is whether and how the body might function as a repository and agent of *spiritual* power. This idea, Willard insists, is rooted in the biblical accounts of God's creation of the human, a creature who reflects God's image and is animated by God's breath.[140] Unlike other creatures, the human was created for a specific task, to rule over the zoological realm and to "tend" the Garden of Eden in a way that reflects and represents God's rule over all things; this unique human vocation expresses what it means to be created in the *imago Dei*, even if it does not exhaust the meaning of that phrase (Gen 1:26–28; 2:15).[141]

Also unlike other creatures, the human was made a living being through God's own breath, or spirit: "The LORD God formed man from the dust of the ground, and breathed into his nostrils the breath of life; and the man became a living being" (Gen 2:7).[142] One ought not read this text in a way that implies a fundamental dualism between body and soul, or matter and spirit.[143] It rather suggests that humans "have a nature that is suitably adapted to be the vehicle of God's likeness."[144]

Like all living creatures, the human possesses a limited capacity of independent, self-sustaining power, which resides in the body. Such power is essential to the task of governing over creation that has been entrusted to humans. To a certain extent, one can master this power, as Willard explains:

> In us some small part of the potential power in our body stands at the disposal of our conscious thought, intention, and choice. In essence an individual's *character* is nothing but the pattern of habitual ways in which that person comports his or her body—whether conforming to the conscious intentions of the individual or not.[145]

Here Willard is simply reflecting Aristotle's insight, shared broadly within the tradition of virtue ethics, that one is naturally able to shape one's habitual pattern of activity—the exercise of one's independent power—in conformity with one's thoughts and intentions. "Virtue," Aristotle insists, "is also up to us, and so also, in the same way, is vice" (*Nic. Eth.* 1113b7).

Yet the Bible's creation accounts imply that, unlike other creatures, the human possesses the capacity for dependent, *spiritual* power in addition to the independent physical and mental powers residing within the human body. This sort of power can be described as *spiritual* because it derives from the spirit of God that animates a human being. It is dependent in the sense that it depends upon relationship with God, its source, in order to function.[146] Genesis 2 presents a picture of the first humans endeavoring to undertake the task they had been given, in the strength of the dependent spiritual power at their disposal through relationship with God in the garden.[147] Genesis 3 presents the tragic consequences of human disobedience: alienation from God's presence and the resulting severe diminution of their powers. Their unique vocation now becomes vastly more difficult to accomplish (Gen 3:16–19), as Willard explains:

> In Eden, one of those specifically *human* powers was the power to interact, not only with the organic, the other living beings such as the creatures of the air, earth, and water, or even with the inorganic, the nonliving matter, but also with God and *his* powers. But the death that befell Adam and Eve in the moment of their initial sin was also the death of this interactive relationship with God, the loss of this central closeness as a constant factor in their experience (Gen. 3). And with this loss came the loss of the power required to fulfill their role as God's rulers over the earth.[148]

In this post-Edenic state of alienation from God, humans must "carry out his rule by meshing the relatively little power resident in their own bodies with the power inherent in the infinite Rule or Kingdom of God."[149] Christians throughout the history of the church have sought to do so by engaging in "spiritual disciplines," which Willard defines as "activities of mind and body purposefully undertaken, to bring our personality and total being into effective cooperation with the divine order."[150] Such practices are analogous to the "spiritual exercises" common within Greco-Roman philosophical schools (see above, p. 72).

Such an account clearly goes far beyond Aristotle's vision of human flourishing, in which the finite repository of independent bodily power is all that is needed to pursue *eudaimonia*, or human flourishing. Aristotle knows of no *spiritual* power dependent for its operation upon relationship with its divine source. Here, then, is where Paul's vision of the "good life" goes beyond that of the mainstream Greco-Roman tradition of virtue ethics. Not only is the *telos* different, but the power available to reach that goal is vastly increased.[151] And yet in the following respect, they share a common conviction: that conscious, deliberate effort is required to train the body to properly use the powers at its disposal.

Musonius Rufus, discussed earlier, indicates the manner in which both body and soul are affected by such training, or *askēsis*:

> For obviously the philosopher's body should be well prepared for physical activity, because often the virtues make use of this as a necessary instrument for the affairs of life. Now there are two kinds of training, one which is appropriate for the soul alone, and the other which is common to both soul and body. We use the training common to both when we discipline ourselves to cold, heat, thirst, hunger, meagre rations, hard beds, avoidance of pleasures, and patience under suffering. For by these things and others like them the body is strengthened and becomes capable of enduring hardship, sturdy and ready for any task; the soul too is strengthened since it is trained for courage by patience under hardship and for self-control by abstinence from pleasures. (*On Training* [*Peri Askēseōs*])[152]

These practices are clearly bodily, and may be understood to have a direct effect on the body itself. Yet Musonius' point appears to be that such practices also indirectly contribute to the shaping of character. Enduring hardship not only strengthens the body; it leads to the cultivation of courage.

The nature and purpose of the bodily practices described by Musonius cohere with Willard's definition of a "discipline": "any activity within our power that we engage in to enable us to do what we cannot do by direct effort."[153]

Although Paul did not endeavor to explicitly *teach* this principle elucidated by Musonius, he seems to have been well aware of it. Indeed, it appears that bodily disciplines lay at the heart of his own spiritual regimen. He writes in an earlier letter to the church in Corinth:

> Do you not know that in a race the runners all compete, but only one receives the prize? Run in such a way that you may win it. Athletes *exercise self-control* (*egkrateuetai*) in all things; they do it to receive a perishable wreath, but we an imperishable one. So I do not run aimlessly, nor do I box as though beating the air; *but I punish* (*hupōpiazō*) *my body and enslave* (*doulagōgō*) *it*, so that after proclaiming to others I myself should not be disqualified. (1 Cor 9:24–27; emphasis added)

Paul presents himself as engaging in a type of *askēsis*, or training.[154] The ascetic practices envisioned here may of course be dismissed as merely either metaphor or hyperbole. Or one might imagine that, although Paul may be describing certain actual bodily practices he himself undertakes, they are of little consequence to the gospel he proclaims. If such practices were somehow essential, one wonders, why does he not offer a programmatic account of them and their function?

The answer, I would suggest, is that spiritual disciplines function as a background concept in Paul's thinking. If, indeed, the value of such practices was widely acknowledged within Greco-Roman antiquity, Paul would have had little need to commend them to his readers.[155] In his former life as a Pharisee, Paul likely would have practiced such disciplines as fasting and prayer (cf. Phil 3:5; Luke 5:33).[156] His rhetorical question in the passage quoted above—"Do you not know?"—strongly suggests that his readers well understood the important place of *askēsis* within the framework of moral development.[157]

Although one does not find much explicit treatment of the practice of spiritual disciplines in Paul's letters, one can see their effect in the sort of person that Paul has become. Witness his remarkable boasting to the church in Corinth:

But whatever anyone dares to boast of—I am speaking as a fool—I also dare to boast of that. Are they Hebrews? So am I. Are they Israelites? So am I. Are they descendants of Abraham? So am I. Are they ministers of Christ? I am talking like a madman—I am a better one: with far greater labors, far more imprisonments, with countless floggings, and often near death. Five times I have received from the Jews the forty lashes minus one. Three times I was beaten with rods. Once I received a stoning. Three times I was shipwrecked; for a night and a day I was adrift at sea; on frequent journeys, in danger from rivers, danger from bandits, danger from my own people, danger from Gentiles, danger in the city, danger in the wilderness, danger at sea, danger from false brothers and sisters; in toil and hardship, through many a sleepless night, hungry and thirsty, often without food, cold and naked. And, besides other things, I am under daily pressure because of my anxiety for all the churches. Who is weak, and I am not weak? Who is made to stumble, and I am not indignant? If I must boast, I will boast of the things that show my weakness. (2 Cor 11:21–30)

Paul's boasting, of course, drips with irony and for good reason. False apostles—to whom Paul refers derisively as "super-apostles"—have been boasting to the church in Corinth of their conventional apostolic pedigrees (2 Cor 11:1–15). To great rhetorical effect, Paul counters their boasting by donning the mantle of the fool and boasting in his weakness.[158] He thereby aims to expose what he regards as the utter foolishness of his opponents, namely their false self-confidence and boasting "according to human standards" (2 Cor 11:17–20).

And yet Paul's foolish boasting is not merely a clever rhetorical ploy calculated to dress down his opponents.[159] At stake is far more than the question of Paul's own authority vis-à-vis that of his opponents. By rejecting Paul as the Lord's apostle, the Corinthian church would be failing to perceive the suffering character of Paul's apostleship, and by extension the way of suffering intentionally pursued by the king whom he represents. Paul boasts in his weakness—truthfully even if ironically—because he desperately desires his audience to correctly grasp the true nature of discipleship.

That Paul's boasting in weakness is genuine—rather than simply rhetorical—becomes ever more clear as he continues to boast of his own "visions and revelations" (2 Cor 12:1–8). He intends not to exult in some vaunted spiritual status that such experiences might be seen to confer. (Indeed, he is so reticent to boast about such things that he speaks of himself in the third person.) Rather, his point seems to be that one must *guard against* the natural human tendency to take such extraordinary experiences as the sign of spiritual status or strength. Thus he recounts that a "thorn in the flesh" was given to torment him, to keep him from becoming too elated (2 Cor 12:7). Although he had prayed for the Lord to remove the source of torment, Paul reports:

> [The Lord] said to me, "My grace is sufficient for you, for power is made perfect in weakness." So, I will boast all the more gladly of my weaknesses, so that the power of Christ may dwell in me. Therefore I am content with weaknesses, insults, hardships, persecutions, and calamities for the sake of Christ; for whenever I am weak, then I am strong. (2 Cor 12:9–10)

Paul boasts in weakness because it is the condition in which spiritual power—the power of Christ, to be precise—is made perfect. It may be asked how Paul came to acquire the character of one who is, as he says, "content" to experience the sort of undesirable circumstances that can be summed up as "weakness." One ought not assume that this settled state of character was instantly conferred upon Paul. Christ's power being made perfect in him appears to be a process.[160] While Paul does not reveal the mechanics, so to speak, of this process, his comments earlier in 1 Corinthians 9:24–27 strongly suggest that bodily practices—spiritual disciplines—played a decisive role.

Just as philosophers such as Seneca and Lucian practiced spiritual exercises aimed at bringing one into the transformative presence of the sage, so Paul, I suggest, practiced spiritual disciplines designed to bring him into the presence of Christ, the source of spiritual power that is made perfect in Paul's weakness.[161] The "transformation by vision" into the image of Jesus the philosopher-king, which Paul and the Corinthian believers alike are experiencing (2 Cor 3:18), depends both upon divine power and human efforts to dispose themselves to that power. My point is this: Paul's bodily training—punishing and enslaving his body—constitute the practices whereby he not only learns to be content with weakness, but furthermore is brought into the transformative presence of Jesus.

In all this, it must be stressed that Paul's aim is not self-justification but rather edification: "Have you been thinking all along that we have been defending ourselves before you? We are speaking in Christ before God (*katenanti theou en Christō laloumen*). Everything we do, beloved, is for the sake of building you up" (2 Cor 12:19). Indeed this has been his goal throughout the letter.[162] In other words, Paul hopes that the Corinthian church, in accepting him as the suffering ambassador of a suffering king, will not only accept his apostolic authority, but imitate him as he imitates Christ (cf. 1 Cor 11:1).[163]

It is vitally important that the Corinthian believers comprehend the basis of Paul's boasting in his weakness as they themselves endeavor to imitate Christ. To be transformed into the image of Christ the king requires a surprisingly nonintuitive grasp of the relationship between virtue and power. Within Hellenistic kingship treatises, the king is regarded as the quintessential human because he is both the paragon of virtue and the possessor of great power. Both of these goods—virtue and power—would naturally have appeared as desirable ends of moral transformation. Yet the distinction between coercive and justified power is notoriously difficult to perceive and maintain. To one who misuses power, even the virtues can be employed towards vicious ends. As Aristotle aptly observed, the shadow side of monarchy is tyranny (*Pol.* 3.1279a26–1279b10). Or, in the words of Shakespeare, "O! it is excellent to have a giant's strength; but it is tyrannous to use it like a giant" (*Measure for Measure* 2.2).

Paul, therefore, fittingly draws his letter to a close by imploring the church in Corinth to engage in sober self-reflection: "Examine yourselves to see whether you are living in the faith (*en tē pistei*). Test yourselves. Do you not realize that Jesus Christ is in you?—unless, indeed, you fail to meet the test" (2 Cor 13:5). The goal here is not anxious introspection but rather reasoned evaluation. Paul well knows the absurdity of his claim to be the suffering ambassador of a crucified king. His beaten and scarred body will appear, in the eyes of some, to reflect the absence of power.

And yet Paul has insisted that he and his partners in the gospel are "always carrying in the body the death of Jesus, so that the life of Jesus may also be made visible in our bodies. For while we live, we are always being given up to death for Jesus' sake, so that the life of Jesus may be made visible in our mortal flesh" (2 Cor 4:10–11).[164] To live a life of embodied allegiance (*en tē pistei*) to such a king requires disciplined effort to cultivate, as Paul does, contentment in weakness. Paradoxically, such weakness represents not the absence of power, but the condition for the perfection of Christ's power.

Up to this point, I have argued that Paul's christocentric vision of the "good life" entails both citizenship in the "heavenly commonwealth" over which Christ reigns, and transformation into the image of this utterly unconventional king. Such transformation, moreover, constitutes a restoration of the divine image in which the first human was created and hence a restoration of the human vocation.

We are nearly ready to explore the *telos* of this heavenly *politeuma*, the vocation to care for God's good creation in anticipation of its eschatological renewal, which Paul envisions in Romans 8. This will be taken up in chapter 5. But before we do so, we must address the question of unity within the church. If virtue is understood to be formed within the context of community, how does a virtue-forming community maintain a sense of unity amidst the wide diversity of human beings that inhabit it? Paul, I will argue, would offer two answers. The first draws upon the argument of the present chapter: unity in the church is one of the fruits of the inculcation of virtue itself. The second explores the way in which ritual forms character: unity in the church is one of the fruits of worship. To see how unity in the church is also the fruit of Christ's reign, let us examine Paul's two letters to churches in Asia Minor, Ephesians and Colossians.

CHAPTER 4

COMMUNITY

Worshiping the Peacemaking King in Ephesus and Colossae

1. Worship and Moral Formation

"When I observe the community drinking ceremony, I understand how gentle and easy the way of the true king can be."[1] With these words, the ancient Confucian philosopher Xunzi introduces a lengthy description of a traditional Chinese ritual aimed at the harmonious enjoyment of drinking, feasting, and music. Every fall when I ask students in my seminar class what might be the connection between a drinking ceremony and the way of the true king, I am met with puzzled stares. The puzzlement only deepens when I invite the seminar to reflect on particular community drinking ceremonies with which they are personally familiar. "*What* drinking ceremonies?" they wonder.

Tentatively and slightly nervously (all my students are under the legal drinking age) a student might ask if I am talking about fraternity or sorority parties (about which they officially know nothing). Not exactly, I tell them. Such opportunities for drinking are not what most would consider a ceremony, after all. Then I nudge them a bit, inviting them to ponder a problem common to all events at which alcohol is consumed, namely the possibility of immoderate consumption.

Can they think of a ceremony that is concerned in any way with the problem of drunkenness? If the class is still stumped, I read them the following sentence and ask if anyone knows where it comes from: "For when the time comes to eat, each of you goes ahead with your own supper, and one goes hungry and another becomes drunk." Eventually, someone will realize that I am quoting the Apostle Paul from a passage in 1 Corinthians in which he lambastes the church in that city for the ways in which they are abusing the practice of the Lord's Supper (1 Cor 11:17–22).

Now the class is *really* confused. For those of my students—quite a few, typically—who have some familiarity with Christianity, the questions arise immediately: What does the Lord's Supper, or Eucharist, have to do with the problem of drunkenness? What possible comparison could one draw between Xunzi's drinking ceremony (which does address the issue of immoderate drinking) and the Lord's Supper? What indeed? It does seem that these two rituals have almost nothing in common. My intent, I assure the class, is not to suggest, in the face of these obvious differences, that the two ceremonies are alike in some arcane way. Rather, my goal in setting these two rituals side by side is to help the class think about what all rituals *do* to us when we perform them.[2] The practice of ritual, I provocatively suggest to my students, would have been regarded as morally formative by both Xunzi and the Apostle Paul.[3] Moreover, both of these men would maintain that certain rituals seek to inculcate within those who practice them the "way of the true king."

This chapter explores the consequences of Jesus' reign for the goal of unity within the church, the heavenly commonwealth. Unity, that is, social harmony and solidarity, is one of the fruits of virtue. As individuals within the church are formed into the character of Jesus, unity within this social body results. As the previous chapter suggested, Paul regarded the practice of spiritual disciplines to be crucial to this task of transformation. The present chapter will explore the role of communal worship in the task—as Paul puts it—of "putting on" or "clothing oneself with" the virtuous character of Christ. Paul understands the church's ritual activity primarily to take place within the sphere of worship. This is not the case with Xunzi or the wider tradition of Confucian philosophy, which does not deal with the divine in the Western sense. What, then, do I hope to accomplish by bringing Paul and Xunzi into conversation, so to speak?

Recall Aristotle's memorable description of a human being as a "political animal," by which he means that only within the social context of the *polis* can one truly fulfill one's human function. Within the Christian tradition, the truly human function must be understood not merely within the *political* sphere but moreover within the *liturgical* sphere as well. That is, the human *telos* must be understood in relationship to the God whose image we bear. Worship is but one of the many ways in which humans relate to this God. The centrality of worship in the Christian understanding of the human *telos* has been articulated in numerous and diverse ways throughout the tradition. For example, the Westminster Shorter Catechism (a key doctrinal instrument for many Reformed Christians) asserts that the "chief end" of humankind is "to worship God and glorify him forever."

This understanding is not uniquely Christian, of course. It finds abundant support within the traditions of Israel's worship within which Paul was steeped. The psalmist declares, "All the nations you have made shall come and bow down before you, O Lord, and shall glorify your name" (Ps 86:9). Paul, therefore, would have understood the human to be more than (although surely not less than) a political animal, but furthermore, to borrow a phrase from philosopher James K. A. Smith, a *liturgical* animal.[4] In so describing the nature of a human being, Smith points not only towards the human *telos*, but also to the formative cultural *practices*, or "liturgies"—both secular and religious—that shape human identity.[5] To fully grasp the importance of worship in Paul's thinking, we must understand the function of ritual within worship, how it shapes the character and identity of the worshiper. It is in this effort to better understand the nature of ritual that we might find Xunzi's discussion of the drinking ceremony illuminating.

Xunzi lived during what is known as the Warring States period of Chinese history (ca. 403–221 BCE), a time of both political instability and intellectual ferment.[6] Precious few details are known about his life, but it is believed that in the mid-third century BCE, he spent time as a government-supported scholar in the court of the small Chinese state of Qi and also served as a magistrate in the state of Chu. Xunzi's writings betray a keen interest in both the practical and moral dimensions of education, the chief end of which, in those chaotic times, was effective government. Convinced that human nature and basic moral principles do not change over time, he looked to the half-legendary "sage kings" of the ancient and glorious Chinese past to inspire the rulers of the present. Although his teachings were little recognized in his own day, by the end of the second century BCE, Xunzi's philosophy had become the basis of the officially recognized Confucianism of the Han state that eventually unified all of China.

Xunzi's discussion of the drinking ceremony concludes his essay defending the morally formative dimension of music against the critique of his contemporary Mozi.[7] Music, Xunzi emphasizes, is not simply pleasant entertainment, but expresses powerful human emotions, which, if not properly guided, lead to disorder. Therefore, Xunzi explains, the former kings created music in order to "arouse the best in man's nature," filling its hearers with a sense of harmonious reverence, kinship, and obedience. By contrast, Xunzi warns that "seductive and depraved" music will produce a people that is "abandoned and mean-mannered."[8] Music clearly bears an astonishingly heavy load of freight in the task of moral pedagogy, as Xunzi concludes:

> Therefore, music is the means of guiding joy, and the metal, stone, stringed, and bamboo instruments are the means of guiding virtue. When music is performed, the people will set their faces toward the true direction. Hence music is the most effective means to govern men.[9]

Having defended the role of excellent music in moral formation, Xunzi turns next to the function of rites. In an essay exploring the essence of human nature, Xunzi grounds his understanding of ritual in a pessimistic anthropology. "Man's nature is evil," he repeatedly insists. "Goodness is the result of conscious activity."[10] Unlike his older contemporary Mencius, who optimistically believed that human nature inclines towards goodness, Xunzi insisted that disciplined, conscious activity was required for moral development. Human nature requires the instruction of a teacher, just as "a warped piece of wood must wait until it has been laid against the straightening board, steamed, and forced into shape before it can become straight."[11]

The proper application of ritual principles plays no small part in this moral education. "Rites," as Xunzi explains in another essay, "are a means of satisfaction." By this he means that ritual provides for the satisfaction of human desires while also preventing the natural consequences of pursuing such desires, namely wrangling, disorder, and exhaustion.[12] By providing external moral guidance that cannot be found internally due to one's inherent evil nature, rituals create an environment conducive to moral transformation. The repeated final two sentences of his essay on human nature make this point emphatically: "Environment is the important thing! Environment is the important thing!"[13]

The music and rites that comprise the drinking ceremony thus create an environment in which both unity and distinction find their proper place. The functions of music and ritual are integrally related in Xunzi's thought:

> Music embodies an unchanging harmony, while rites represent unalterable reason. Music unites that which is the same; rites distinguish that which is different; and through the combination of rites and music the human heart is governed."[14]

Within the ceremony, the ritualized behavior appropriate to the host, the honored guest, and other guests functions in various ways to ensure harmony. Distinctions in rank and age are preserved, while at the same time none are left out of the feasting. Moderation is ensured so that feasting can be enjoyed without disorder. The harmony thereby achieved in the drinking ceremony by the correct employment of music and ritual will naturally ripple outwards. Properly performed music and rituals, Xunzi concludes, "will be sufficient to insure moral training to the individual and peace to the state, and when the state is peaceful, the world will be peaceful. Therefore I say that when I observe the community drinking ceremony, I understand how gentle and easy the way of the true king can be."[15] The drinking ceremony provides proof, Xunzi believes, of his remarkable claim that music and rites can shape and govern the human heart and thereby lead to good government.

The function of ritual within Xunzi's worldview (and that of Confucianism more broadly) may help us think about the function of worship within the churches Paul helped to establish.[16] Let us begin this task by returning to Paul's admonitions to the church in Corinth regarding the celebration of the Lord's Supper. The tradition of this meal passed on by Paul goes back to Jesus' final meal with his disciples. It is perhaps one of most well-known passages of the New Testament, its very words constituting the heart of the weekly worship service for many churches over the past two millennia:

> For I received from the Lord what I also handed on to you, that the Lord Jesus on the night when he was betrayed took a loaf of bread, and when he had given thanks, he broke it and said, "This is my body that is for you. Do this in remembrance of me." In the same way he took the cup also, after supper, saying, "This cup is the new covenant in my blood. Do this, as often as you drink it, in remembrance of me." For as often as you eat this bread and drink the cup, you proclaim the Lord's death until he comes. (1 Cor 11:23–26)

Less well known, perhaps, is the context in which Paul transmits this tradition. Today, these words are most often spoken by the celebrant presiding over a ritual meal held within a church, a building whose primary function is to provide a space dedicated to Christian worship. In Paul's day, the "church" (Greek: *ekklēsia*) referred primarily to the community itself, the individuals gathered together in faithful allegiance to Jesus as king. The activity of worship took place not in a building constructed for that purpose, but rather in the home of one of the community's wealthier members. The central activity of this gathered community was an *actual* meal, rather than the purely ritual one at the center of most Christian worship today.[17]

Indeed, it is the problem of bad table manners that prompts Paul to recall this tradition. The Apostle sharply criticizes the church for its habitual way of celebrating the meal in a way that thoroughly undermines the meal's intent:

> Now in the following instructions I do not commend you, because when you come together it is not for the better but for the worse. . . . When you come together, it is not really to eat the Lord's supper. For when the time comes to eat, each of you goes ahead with your own supper, and one goes hungry and another becomes drunk. What! Do you not have homes to eat and drink in? Or do you show contempt for the church of God and humiliate those who have nothing? What should I say to you? Should I commend you? In this matter I do not commend you! (1 Cor 11:17–22)

In Greco-Roman society, one's social status normally determined one's place at table and the quality and amount of food one was served. The members of the Corinthian church, habituated to such distinctions, simply imported them into the practice of their communal meal: those of high status were served first and enjoyed the choicest food, while those of low status were served last and received the dregs.[18] As a result, the wealthy became drunk and the poor were humiliated. The meal thus habituated its participants in ways that were corrosive to individual character (unrestrained appetite) no less than to the character of the gathered Christian community (reinforcing divisions of status).

Paul responds to this community-destroying mealtime behavior by urging reflection and restraint. "Examine yourselves," he implores, "and only then eat of the bread and drink of the cup." To partake of the meal in a way that disregards the community's humbler members is to "eat and drink judgment against [oneself]" (1 Cor 11:28–29). Rather than indulging immoderately, the wealthy are to practice restraint by waiting for the poorer members before eating; if they are unable to do even this, they should eat at home before coming to the communal meal (1 Cor 11:33–34).

And yet these practical disciplines must be seen within the frame of the tradition itself that Paul provides for guiding the practice of the meal. As they share this meal, the Corinthian church is to recall and recite the words that Jesus spoke to his disciples, and it is precisely this ritual practice that is to shape their mealtime behavior. The disciplines of communal and self-reflection surely assist in the rehabilitation of the church's table fellowship, but the formative practice of the meal itself constitutes the heart of Paul's admonition. Recalling Jesus' final meal, the church is reminded of Jesus' obedience to the Father's will in being handed over to a redemptive death that inaugurated the new covenant.[19] Thus they are reminded that their common meal is not an opportunity for self-indulgence, much less for reifying divisive social distinctions. Rather the shared meal draws the community together in its unified proclamation of the Lord's death and of the hope of his coming again. It is therefore not simply that Paul hopes the Corinthian church can learn to behave well at the table *so that* they can enjoy the Lord's Supper in harmony. Rather, he hopes that the proper *practice* of the Lord's Supper—one guided by recollection of Jesus' final supper—will shape the communal life and public witness of the church and enhance its unity.[20]

What might one learn by setting side by side Paul's tradition of the Lord's Supper and Xunzi's description of the drinking ceremony? Initially, the significant differences between them might suggest that these ritual practices are not comparable in any meaningful way. The Lord's Supper takes place in the context of worship; the drinking ceremony does not. Xunzi strongly emphasizes the role of music in ritual ceremony; Paul does not, although hymns and music certainly played a role in early Christian worship (1 Cor 14:26; Eph 5:19; Col 3:16). The ritual behavior of the drinking ceremony seeks to ensure social harmony while at the same time explicitly preserving status distinctions; Paul believes the proper practice of the Lord's Supper will result in mutual welcome across the lines of social and economic stratification.[21] And yet, despite these differences, both Xunzi and Paul appear to agree that ritual possesses the capacity for moral formation.

I bring Paul and Xunzi into conversation here, as I do in my first-year seminar, not to answer questions so much as to raise them. My intent is not to suggest that the tradition of the Lord's Supper functions in a manner similar to the drinking ceremony. Much less am I proposing that Paul would agree with Xunzi that ritual and music are capable of bearing the heavy burden of moral formation attributed to them within Confucian philosophy. Rather, by drawing our attention to the way in which ritual is morally and socially formative in Xunzi's worldview, I am prompting us to consider how ritual functions in Paul's vision.

Since Paul himself, unlike Xunzi, offers no theoretical account of ritual, one must look elsewhere for help in understanding the ritual function of worship in his letters. To do so, I turn to the recent book by the contemporary philosopher James K. A. Smith, *Imagining the Kingdom: How Worship Works*. Smith asks how human beings are formed as moral agents. His answer begins with the intuition that our actions are driven more by what we love and less by what we think. We are more than mere "thinking things" or "brains on a stick"; we are creatures defined by "what we love."[22] The things we love, moreover, are shaped "below the radar of consciousness" by formative practices, which Smith refers to as "cultural liturgies."[23] We therefore need a "pedagogy of desire" that recognizes the nonconscious drivers of human action, takes into account the role of the body in forming our orientation to the world, and appreciates the centrality of story in moral formation. Smith offers the following concise account of how one is formed through worship:

> In short, the way to the heart is through the body, and the way into the body is through story. And this is how worship works: Christian formation is a *conversion of the imagination* effected by the Spirit, who recruits our most fundamental desires by a kind of narrative enchantment—by inviting us narrative animals into a story that seeps into our bones and becomes the orienting background of our being-in-the-world.[24]

The story Smith has in mind here is nothing less than "the true story of the whole world," the grand drama of God's creation and redemption.[25] Worship forms us not simply by narrating this story (for example, by preaching on biblical texts), but more so by *incorporating* worshipers into the story and into the body politic of the church.

To understand how worship does so, we must first grasp what anthropologist and sociologist Pierre Bourdieu calls *habitus*, "the system of structured, structuring dispositions . . . which is constituted in practice and is always oriented towards practical functions."[26] To say that *habitus* is "structured" means that it comes to us from outside ourselves; it is learned, not innate. To say that it is "structuring" means that *habitus* disposes us to constitute the world in certain ways. *Habitus* supplies us with dispositional inertia, inclining us to "lean into the world with a habituated momentum in certain directions."[27] One's particular *habitus*, for example, might incline one to construe a homeless person as either "a lazy leech on society or a sad testimony to the failure of mental health systems."[28] Importantly, *habitus* functions, without "conscious aiming" or "calculation," as a sort of "embodied history, internalized as a second nature and so forgotten as history."[29] Smith helpfully glosses *habitus* as "the visceral plausibility structure by which we make sense of our world and move within it."[30] *Habitus* enables one to acquire what Bourdieu terms "practical sense," what an athlete might call a "feel for the game," a know-how inscribed in the body.[31]

To ask how one *acquires* a *habitus* is to begin to grasp the formative capacity of worship. Consider how an individual body is incorporated into a larger social body or order. This process is achieved, according to Bourdieu,

> by the hidden persuasion of an implicit pedagogy which can instil a whole cosmology, through injunctions as insignificant as 'sit up straight' or 'don't hold your knife in your left hand,' and inscribe the most fundamental principles of the arbitrary content of a culture in seemingly innocuous details of bearing or physical and verbal manners, so putting them beyond the reach of consciousness and explicit statement. . . . The cunning of pedagogic reason lies precisely in the fact that it manages to extort what is essential while seeming to demand the insignificant.[32]

Through this embodied pedagogy, the larger social body slowly co-opts individual bodies "through the most mundane means: through bodily postures, repeated words, ritualized cadences."[33] The body thus comes to know things, and this knowledge spills over into the rest of life. Ritual, in other words, "is the way we (learn to) believe with our bodies."[34]

The formative power of ritual, then, its "cunning pedagogy," lies in its subtle ability to incorporate us within a narrative that lends meaning to human existence and orients our thoughts and actions. Liturgy, as Smith uses the term, "is the shorthand term for those rituals that are loaded with a Story about who and whose we are, inscribing in us a *habitus* by marshaling our aesthetic nature."[35] By co-opting us as inhabitants within a particular story, liturgy—whether secular or religious—creates a horizon of meaning, governing how we constitute the wider world. By immersion in a particular liturgical environment, we imbibe a metaphorical orientation; different operative metaphors make for different worlds. Certain operative metaphors dispose us, for example, to regard ourselves as existing at the center of the cosmos. Others lead us to inhabit the world as part of the community of creation.[36]

We can see more clearly the formative power of worship if we consider, for example, two rival accounts of sin. An intellectualist account might regard sinful action as merely the result of rational choices based upon faulty beliefs. The solution for sin, in this case, would be knowledge leading to right beliefs. But such an account, while it can explain discrete sinful actions, has difficulty registering a sinful way of life. Smith's account, which takes seriously the "incarnate significance" of human existence, regards sin as *also* the outcome of a disposition instilled within our bodies through *habitus*. He explains: "We absorb rival gospels as *habitus*, and thus act 'toward' them, as it were—pulled toward a different *telos* that rivals the coming kingdom of God."[37]

Worship is the antidote to liturgies that incorporate one into such rival gospels. Such a claim does not intend to diminish the importance of belief by implying that we are formed entirely at the subconscious level by habit and ritual. Much less does it aim to instrumentalize worship as merely a technique for spiritual formation. Rather, it recognizes that we are creatures defined by what we love, and that our loves are primed and directed by imagination. Worship sanctifies and restores the imagination, a process which is also a "re-story-ing" of the imagination. Worship addresses our need not merely to be convinced, but also "to be *moved*":[38]

> We need to be regularly immersed in the "true story of the whole world"; that is, our imaginations need to be restored, recalibrated, and realigned by an affective immersion in the story of God in Christ reconciling the world to himself.[39]

Smith's account of worship—a recalibration of the imagination—evokes that which Paul endeavors to do throughout his letters. Paul, as I have argued, aims to describe a new social imaginary—God's creation restored through the reign of Jesus—and to invite his audience to inhabit this new reality.

Paul, in other words, seeks to lead his audience into worship of Jesus as Lord. While his letters make rational arguments in favor of certain beliefs and behaviors, they also intend to lead those persuaded by such arguments into a posture of worship. This pastoral strategy can be seen throughout Paul's letters, but especially in Ephesians and Colossians. In the following exploration of these two letters, I will argue that worship plays a crucial role in the establishment and maintenance of unity in the church and is essential to Paul's vision of human flourishing. The practice of worship instills a new *habitus*, thereby enabling the church to inhabit the present-and-coming reign of Jesus. Worship aims to inculcate, as Xunzi might say, "the way of the true king."

2. The Puzzle of Unity: Divine Achievement or Human Effort?

Of all the letters attributed to Paul, none are more liturgical in character than Ephesians and Colossians. Especially in Ephesians, the very cadence of the prose seems to draw the audience into a posture of worship.[40] Indeed, the "liturgical" style of Ephesians, which is noticeably different than the style of many of Paul's other letters, has led numerous scholars to conclude that this letter was written not by Paul but by a later disciple of his. Increasingly, I have come to regard Pauline authorship of both letters as likely, even if by no means certain. Thus in the following argument I refer to the author of Ephesians and Colossians as simply Paul.[41] Related to the question of authorship—and of greater significance for the present argument—is the setting and purpose of both letters. I take both letters to be "efforts to shape Christian identity formation and growth within the context of the general cultural ethos of the early Roman imperial period."[42]

Ephesians is probably a circular letter intended for mostly Gentile congregations in the Roman province of Asia Minor (i.e., modern-day Turkey; see Eph 2:11). Colossians is directed to a particular Christian community in Colossae, a small city in southern Asia Minor; this community appears to have been more closely tied to its Jewish roots, an inference made on the basis of certain Jewish elements of the syncretistic "philosophy" Paul opposes in Colossians 2:8–23.[43] The letters are closely related to each other: both claim to be written by Paul in prison, both are delivered by a certain Tychicus, and both share similar contents, often appearing in the same order.[44] Because of the more general nature of

Ephesians, Paul's efforts in that letter to form the identity and character of his audience are more apparent. Therefore, the argument below will focus on Ephesians, drawing attention to parallels and differences in Colossians when salient.

Paul makes a rational argument in Ephesians that aims to shape the beliefs and behavior of his audience. Yet Paul's letter aims not merely to *convince*, but more so to *move*; not merely to narrate a particular story, but to incorporate its audience within that story. The letter achieves its goal of forming identity and character by appealing to both cognitive and affective dimensions through the language of worship. After a customary salutation (1:1–2), the first half of the letter consists of a series of prayers in which Paul blesses God for his many blessings (1:3–14); gives thanks for the readers' faith and love (1:15–16a); intercedes for both the readers' enlightenment (1:16b–19) and empowerment (3:14–19); and concludes with a doxology praising God for his power at work in the lives of believers (3:20–21). The second half of the letter consists in *paraenesis*, that is, ethical exhortation to live a life consistent with the identity formed in the first half of the letter (4:1–6:20).

The liturgically inflected prose in the first half employs a "cunning pedagogy": to read Paul's argument is to worship along with him.[45] The opening *berakah*, or blessing, enumerates three sequences of divine blessing, which result in a threefold response of praise.[46] In the first sequence, God is praised for blessings bestowed before the creation of the world:

> Blessed be the God and Father of our Lord Jesus Christ, who has blessed us in Christ with every spiritual blessing in the heavenly places, just as he chose us in Christ before the foundation of the world to be holy and blameless before him in love. He destined us for adoption as his children through Jesus Christ, according to the good pleasure of his will, *to the praise of his glorious grace (eis epainon doxēs tēs charitos autou)* that he freely bestowed on us in the Beloved. (Eph 1:3–6)

Here, God's blessing and election (or choosing) is accomplished *through* the agency of Christ. In the following sequence, Christ's agency is again central to God's plan of action within human history, which once more redounds in praise to God:

In him we have redemption through his blood, the forgiveness of our trespasses, according to the riches of his grace that he lavished on us. With all wisdom and insight he has made known to us the mystery of his will, according to his good pleasure that he set forth in Christ, as a plan for the fullness of time, *to gather up all things in him* (*anakephalaiōsasthai ta panta en tō Christō*), things in heaven and things on earth. In Christ we have also obtained an inheritance, having been destined according to the purpose of him who accomplishes all things according to his counsel and will, so that we, who were the first to set our hope on Christ, might live *for the praise of his glory* (*eis epainon doxēs autou*). (Eph 1:7–12)

In the final sequence, praise is called forth in response to God's redemption. This future act is partially experienced in the present through the Spirit, which is received through Christ:[47]

In him you also, when you had heard the word of truth, the gospel of your salvation, and had believed in him, were marked with the seal of the promised Holy Spirit; this is the pledge of our inheritance toward redemption as God's own people, *to the praise of his glory* (*eis epainon doxēs autou*). (Eph 1:13–14; emphasis added)

In beginning to consider the letter's larger goal of forming identity and character, it suffices to make the following observation. Paul is sketching a story whose arc extends backwards in time before the creation of the world and forwards to the consummation of God's plan to "gather up all things in Christ" (1:10). The verb Paul uses, *anakephalaioō*, literally means to "sum up," and was used to refer to the rhetorical summing up, or recapitulation, of an argument. Metaphorically, the expression envisions God's plan to restore a fractured cosmos through the death, resurrection, and heavenly enthronement of Christ. The audience is to see themselves as having been "written into" that story of God's gracious benefaction, enacted through Christ.[48] As Paul will presently explain, the result of this plan—calling forth the response of praise—is that God has already effected unity within the church through God's own action (2:11–22).

And yet the realization of unity within the church presents a genuine puzzle. Gentiles have been welcomed into God's covenant family, the commonwealth of Israel; thus Jews and Gentiles, previously alienated from each other, now constitute in Christ "one new humanity in place of the two" (2:15). On this account, unity in the church has been achieved by divine fiat. Yet later in the letter, Paul enjoins his audience to make "every effort to maintain the unity of the Spirit in the bond of peace" (4:3). Here, it would appear, unity in the church is achieved, or at the least maintained, through the church's own effort.

The same puzzle appears in Colossians, more obscurely, yet with greater urgency. In this letter, Paul again highlights Christ's cosmic significance, declaring that in Christ "God was pleased to reconcile to himself all things, whether on earth or in heaven, by making peace through the blood of his cross" (Col 1:20). The church is then reminded that it has "clothed [itself] with the new self, which is being renewed in knowledge according to the image of its creator," in which "there is no longer Greek and Jew, circumcised and uncircumcised, barbarian, Scythian, slave and free" (Col 3:10–11). And yet, it can be inferred that disunity persists in the church, revealed in Paul's admonitions not to fall prey to "philosophy and empty deceit" (Col 2:8) and to "bear with one another and . . . forgive each other" (Col 3:13).[49]

The puzzle is this: Is unity in the church a divine or human achievement? Has God in Christ already established unity in the church, or must the church by its own effort work to establish unity? Or is unity in the church the product of divine and human cooperation? And if so, can one say with clarity precisely what God has done and what remains for the church?

One could, of course, resolve this tension by discounting as merely hyperbolic Paul's declaration of peace as God's achievement in Christ. Or taking Paul at his word, one could explain the tension as the paradox of Paul's inaugurated eschatology. Paul believes that the resurrection of Jesus has inaugurated "the ends of the ages" (1 Cor 10:11); yet he also describes his current reality as "the present evil age" (Gal 1:4). Christ's cosmic reign has been inaugurated, yet not consummated; Paul can thus speak of Christ ruling in the heavenly places "not only in this age but also in the age to come" (Eph 1:21). One might, in other words, attribute the paradoxical achievement of unity in the church to the already-but-not-yet quality of Christ's reign.

This comes closer to Paul's meaning, but I think one may go even further in solving this puzzle by noting the ways in which Paul's portrayal of Christ in these letters reflects the portrait of the ideal king in Jewish and Greco-Roman antiquity.[50] Paul's argument with respect to unity in the church can best be understood by attending to three integrally related functions attributed to such a figure: the establishment of unity, the transmission of divine benefactions, and the inculcation of virtue. In order for unity to be achieved within the *polis*, virtue must first be inculcated within the citizenry. Both unity and virtue were furthermore considered the consequence of the good king's benefaction. These functions of the ideal king shed light on the relationship in Ephesians and Colossians between the moral effort required by the church in order to maintain unity within itself, and the divine benefaction that enables this effort.

3. Christ as Peacemaker

The primary theme uniting the argument of Ephesians is God's plan to reconcile the fractured cosmos through God's appointed agent, Jesus the Christ (Eph 1:10). As part of the plan to reconcile the fractured cosmos, God has welcomed Gentiles into the commonwealth of Israel, thus in effect reconciling the human family: "But now in Christ Jesus you who once were far off have been brought near by the blood of Christ. For he is our peace; in his flesh he has made both groups into one and has broken down the dividing wall, that is, the hostility between us" (Eph 2:13–14). We hear of a similar claim in Colossians, of a humanity renewed in the image of Christ,[51] in which "there is no longer Greek and Jew, circumcised and uncircumcised, barbarian, Scythian, slave and free; but Christ is all and in all" (Col 3:11). Such claims would have resonated loudly with both the Jewish and Greco-Roman portrayal of the good king as a peacemaker, one who establishes on earth the divine harmony and unity that exists in the heavens.

Across a wide array of texts drawn from biblical tradition, the reign of the ideal king was associated with the establishment of peace, harmony, and concord.[52] In Israel's prophetic tradition, the righteous king was hailed as the "prince of peace," under whose reign "there shall be endless peace for the throne of David and his kingdom" (Isa 9:6–7; cf. Isa 11:1–9). In similar fashion, the psalmist prayed for the reign of the just king: "In his days may righteousness flourish and peace abound, until the moon is no more" (Ps 72:7).

Similarly, in post-biblical Jewish thought, the *Sibylline Oracles* envisioned an eschatological kingdom characterized by the peaceful reign of prophet kings who "take away the sword, for they themselves are judges of men and righteous kings" (3.781–782).[53] Steeped in the Hellenistic traditions of kingship, the *Letter of Aristeas* placed on the lips of a Jewish elder the conviction that "the most important feature in a kingdom" is "to establish the subjects continually at peace" (291–292). The Hellenistic Jewish philosopher Philo praised the Roman Emperor Augustus as "the guardian of peace . . . the first and the greatest and the common benefactor" (*Legat.* 147, 149). The biblical character Joseph, while not technically a king, ruled as Pharaoh's vicegerent and was, in Philo's view, the quintessential statesman. Joseph's royal virtue was displayed in his ability to create "order in disorder and concord where all was naturally discordant" (*Joseph* 269).[54]

In Greco-Roman thought, the portrayal of the good king as one who establishes and maintains harmony within the *polis* stretches back at least as far as Classical Greece. Isocrates believed that kings, out of the abundance of devotion to humanity (*philanthrōpia*) "must try to preserve harmony, not only in the states over which they hold dominion, but also in their own households" (*Nicocles* 41). In the Hellenistic era, Neopythagorean political philosophers conceived of this harmony not merely as political in nature, but cosmic. The ideal king, the "living law" by which the *polis* was preserved in a state of justice and harmony, reflected and in some measure embodied divinity:[55]

> Now the king bears the same relation to the state as God to the world; and the state is in the same ratio to the world as the king is to God. For the state, made as it is by a harmonizing together of many different elements, is an imitation of the order and harmony of the world, while the king who has an absolute rulership, and is himself Animate Law (*nomos empsuchos*), has been metamorphosed into a deity among men. (Archytas, *Peri nomou kai dikaiosunēs* 4.7.61)[56]

In the Roman period, the Stoic philosopher Musonius Rufus employed the concept of the "living law" to capture the ideal king's godlike ability to effect harmony:

> In general it is of the greatest importance for the good king to be faultless and perfect in word and action, if, indeed, he is to be a "living law" (*nomon empsuchon*) as he seemed to the ancients, effecting good government and harmony, suppressing lawlessness and dissension, a true imitator of Zeus and, like him, a father of his people. (*That Kings Should Also Study Philosophy* 64.10–15)[57]

The Roman biographer Plutarch also believed that harmony and concord were the prerogatives of the good king, as seen in his encomiastic tribute to the virtues of Alexander the Great. Although ultimately unsuccessful, Alexander sought to bring together "into one body all men everywhere, uniting and mixing in one great loving-cup, as it were, men's lives, their characters, their marriages, their very habits of life" (*Alex. fort.* 329C). The emperor Augustus unabashedly praised himself for having established peace (*Res gest.* 13), as did his numerous admirers.[58] Panegyricists lauded any number of Roman emperors for allegedly having established a golden age of peace.[59] The notion that the ideal king creates peace and harmony was so widespread in both Jewish and Greco-Roman literature that one may safely assume the authorial audiences of Ephesians and Colossians would have been familiar with it.

How do the arguments of Ephesians and Colossians resonate with this particular aspect of the audience's cultural repertoire? In the opening *berakah* of Ephesians, God is praised for his plan to gather, or sum up (*anakephalaiōsasthai*), all things in heaven and on earth *through* the Christ (Eph 1:10).[60] Reconciliation between humanity and God (Eph 2:1–10) and within humanity itself (Eph 2:11–22), both effected through the agency of Christ, is understood as the working out of God's wider plan to restore a fractured cosmos. Acting thus as God's vicegerent to establish harmony, Christ fulfills the function of the ideal king in Mediterranean antiquity.[61] Looking closer, the political implications of Christ's peacemaking emerge. Gentiles, previously aliens from the commonwealth (*politeia*) of Israel, have now been included within God's covenant family, again through Christ (Eph 2:11–13).[62]

But the fact that the cosmic and political unity achieved through Christ resonated with the putative achievement of countless kings and emperors also creates a problem for the audience. Talk is cheap, and political talk is possibly the cheapest on the market. The imperial propaganda boasting of a golden age of peace—the *pax Romana* as *pax deorum*—was as ubiquitous as it was false. The *pax Romana* was an era of prosperity and concord for the elites within the Roman Empire, but not for those subjugated by Rome's military might. For conquered nations, the peace of Rome often meant severely limited freedom and even servitude.[63] Tacitus memorably expresses the view of the *pax Romana* from one of Rome's defeated enemies: "To robbery, slaughter, plunder, they give the lying name of empire; they make a solitude and call it peace" (*Agricola* 30).

Thus, what confidence could Paul's audience place in his claim that in fact Christ had actually achieved the peace of which many others had falsely boasted? After all, even in the church, it could hardly be claimed that distinctions of ethnic identity, gender, and status no longer divided. Could Paul's audience have understood God's reconciliation of the human family through Christ as more than empty propaganda?

To address this question, one must begin by recognizing that some modes of peacemaking are more effective than others. The Roman policy of peace won at the tip of the spear may have, for a time, achieved the cessation of hostility but did nothing to address its root causes. Indeed, it merely exacerbated them. Roman conquest of Palestine, for example, left the Jews oppressed and seething with resentment. Alexander the Great's dream of ethnic fusion through intermarriage at least recognized that peace depended upon social bonds such as those fostered within kinship groups. Yet Alexander's dream, of course, was never realized.[64] What, then, can one say about the way in which Christ is understood to have achieved genuine peace as well as the nature of the unity thereby established?

To begin with, the cost of peacemaking was borne by Christ himself. Whereas the Roman peace was achieved by the blood of slain enemies, the peace of the Christ is achieved through his own blood. Christ's own death, Paul declares, is the means by which strangers and aliens have been brought near the commonwealth from which they were previously estranged (Eph 2:13; cf. Col 1:21–22).[65] Proximity, however, is not the same as membership. Thus, Paul further says that in order actually to incorporate Gentiles into the commonwealth of Israel, Christ abolished the source of enmity between Gentiles and Jews by destroying the "dividing wall of partition" (*to mesotoichon tou fragmou*, Eph 2:14).

The "wall" here, I take it, refers to the actual partition in the Temple separating the court of the Gentiles from the court of Israel, referred to by Josephus (*Ant.* 15.417; *BJ* 5.194; cf. Acts 21:26–31). But metaphorically, the destruction of this wall denotes, as the next verse explains, Christ's abolition of the Mosaic law, with its commandments and ordinances, an act that removes the hostility between Jews and Gentiles and so welcomes outsiders into God's covenant family (Eph 2:13–15). I understand Paul to be talking here about Torah observance not merely as a practice that culturally distinguishes Jews from Gentiles, but more importantly as an important symbol of exclusion, and hence, a source of hostility.[66]

Christ's removal of this symbol is not, in Paul's view, merely an empty gesture, but rather a profound and decisive act that genuinely contributes to peace. Gentiles *qua* Gentiles have now been welcomed into the commonwealth of Israel. In sum, the mode of Christ's peacemaking is conducive to genuine unity both because it is noncoercive, and because it addresses the way in which cultural and religious difference had functioned as a source of hostility between Jews and Gentiles. And yet, there is still something incomplete about the peace established through Christ.

Although Christ's death has removed the source of hostility between Jew and Gentile (Eph 2:14) and put to death the hostility between humanity and God (Eph 2:16), one might well imagine that Jews and Gentiles would find it difficult to live peacefully with one another in view of the long history of cultural difference and hostility.[67] (Indeed, this difficulty can well be imagined *within* a cultural group as well as between different cultural groups.) The daily task of living together in peace requires effort: if a wall has been torn down, another structure—a holy temple, a dwelling place for God—is in the process of being built up (Eph 2:21–22).

The distinction between the peace already achieved through Christ and the present task of actually learning to live in peace is reflected by the shift in verb tense in Ephesians 2:11–22. The verbs and participles used to describe Christ's actions in vv. 11–17 are largely perfects, imperfects, and aorists; vv. 18–19 use present tense verbs to describe the current state of affairs resulting from Christ's actions; v. 20 can be seen as a transition, using an aorist passive participle to indicate that this new humanity has been established on the apostles and prophets; and vv. 21–22 use present tense verbs to indicate the present and ongoing work of growing and being built into a dwelling for God.[68]

To better grasp the ongoing need for maintaining the peace of Christ in the church, consider more closely the metaphor of the wall of hostility that Christ is understood to have broken down. Effective as symbols of division and as instruments of physical separation, walls can both symbolize and foster even deeper hostility. Several contemporary examples may serve to illustrate the point. The Berlin Wall was effective both in separating East and West Berlin and as a potent symbol of the broader animosity between East and West during the Cold War. More recently, consider the border wall being built by President Trump; even prior to its construction, the mere idea of the wall has become a divisive political symbol. And even closer to the topic at hand, the present-day security walls that enclose portions of the West Bank have proven effective, both symbolically and physically, in separating Palestinians from the State of Israel and Israeli settlements. While the removal of a physical wall can be accomplished in the span of days or weeks, the lingering effects of the hostility engendered by the wall last considerably longer.

Returning to Paul's metaphor, removing the "wall" of Torah observance for Gentiles creates the "space" for Gentiles within the commonwealth of Israel, providing them with the same "access in one Spirit to the Father" as God's covenant people Israel (Eph 2:18). Yet the removal of the wall by itself does not relieve both old and new "members of the household of God" from the task of learning to live in harmony together. The church is equipped for this task by means of Christ's benefaction, a function of the good king in antiquity, but it must fulfill the task by its own practices of common worship and peaceful living.

4. Christ as Benefactor of Divine Virtue

In fulfillment of God's plan to restore the fractured cosmos, Christ has united humanity into one body, and yet this body must make "every effort to maintain the unity of the Spirit in the bond of peace" (Eph 4:3). The means by which the church does so is through the benefaction of Christ: "Each of us was given grace according to the measure of Christ's gift" (Eph 4:7). Paul lends emphasis to the portrayal of Christ as benefactor through a *midrash* of Psalm 67:19 LXX: in the original, God *received* gifts, but in Paul's reshaping, Christ "*gave* gifts to his people" (Eph 4:8). Christ's activity resonates with the well-known function of the good king as benefactor in antiquity.

In both Jewish and Greco-Roman antiquity, the understanding of the good king as benefactor is rooted in the activity of the divine benefactor(s). The king imitates the benefactions of the god(s), thereby *transmitting* these divinely bestowed benefits upon the people. Thus, in the *Letter of Aristeas*, the Jewish elders address the king, "'As God showers blessings (*euergazetai*) upon all, you too in imitation of him are a benefactor (*euergeteis*) to your subjects'" (281).[69] The same sentiment is echoed by the Neopythagorean political philosopher, Diotogenes:

> A good king must extend assistance to those in need of it and be beneficent . . . Good kings, indeed, have dispositions similar to the Gods, especially resembling Zeus, the universal ruler, who is venerable and honorable through the magnanimous preeminence of virtue.

He is benign because he is beneficent (*euergetikos*) and the giver of good. (*Peri basileias* 4.7.62)

The king's benefaction bound his subjects in a relationship of reciprocity: "His friends he made subject to himself by his benefactions, the rest by his magnanimity he enslaved" (Isocrates, *Evag.* 45).[70] The actual benefits bestowed by the king varied widely, from the material—gifts of grain, reductions of taxes, financing of entertainments, patronage of temples—to the spiritual. In the latter category, the king was praised for bestowing upon the people the gift of his divine virtue.

The tradition of the good king's reign as integral to the acquisition of virtue has its roots in the political philosophy of Classical Greece. Preeminence in virtue was the requirement for rule, and the king's unique art, or *technē*, was the making of virtuous people.[71] These theoretical musings found currency in the era of Hellenistic monarchies among the Neopythagorean philosophers. Ecphantus, for example, extols the good king, whose benefaction inculcates virtue within his subjects through the divine *logos* within him:

[He] will beneficently endeavor to assimilate all his subjects to himself. . . . For without benevolence, no assimilation is possible. . . . The king alone is capable of putting this good into human nature so that by imitation of him, their Better, they will follow in the way they should go. But his logos, if it is accepted . . . restores what has been lost by sin. (*Peri basileias* 4.7.65)

These ideas became more widespread in the Roman era, as autocratic rule expanded its horizon beyond the small, self-contained Greek *polis* to the vast Mediterranean world. Plutarch recounts that the subjects of Rome's legendary king Numa were enabled to live virtuously and in harmony by merely beholding their king:

When they see with their own eyes a conspicuous and shining example of virtue in the life of their ruler, they will of their own accord walk in wisdom's ways, and unite with him in conforming themselves to a blameless life of friendship and mutual concord, attended by righteousness and temperance. (*Numa* 20.8).[72]

Christ's function as benefactor conforms to the portrait of the good king in antiquity. In the opening *berakah* of the letter, Paul writes that

God "has blessed us in Christ (*en tō Christō*) with every spiritual blessing in the heavenly places" (Eph 1:3). Taking the force of the prepositional phrase *en tō* instrumentally, Christ is the means by which God's blessing is transmitted to the church.[73] The church's reciprocal response to Christ's benefaction is "to lead a life worthy of the calling" to which they have been called (Eph 4:1).[74] Yet this response is itself enabled by the benefaction, the goal of which is the inculcation of Christ's character. Christ gave gifts, Paul continues, "for the building up of the body of Christ, until all of us come to . . . maturity, to the measure of the full stature of Christ" (Eph 4:12–13). Thus the church has "learned Christ" (Eph 4:20), that is, become transformed into the character of Christ.[75]

The same idea is conveyed in Colossians through the metaphor of clothing oneself with the new self, which is being renewed in the image of Christ (Col 3:10). Being transformed into the image of Christ entails the inculcation of virtue: this is seen in the parallelism in the way the Colossian believers are to "clothe themselves" with virtue as they "clothe themselves" with the new self, renewed in Christ's image (Col 3:12, 14). In light of Christ's having made peace (Col 1:20) and identification *as* "our peace" (Eph 2:14), it seems likely that these imperatives would have been interpreted as exhortations for the church to put on Christ's peacemaking, peaceful character. This possibility becomes even more likely when one considers two integrally related functions of the ideal king in antiquity: benefaction and the inculcation of virtue.

Finally, note that Christ's transformative benefaction is in turn distributed through the gift of apostles, prophets, evangelists, pastors, and teachers to the church (Eph 4:11). The divine benefaction is conveyed, it would appear, through human agency. Why might this be the case? One possibility is suggested by the importance of imitation in the process of human growth: "'We become like' what we imitate."[76] Becoming a mature person and believer, one who is attaining "the full stature of Christ," is an inescapably social process in which intention and effort is required to imitate human exemplars. The argument thus far has claimed that Christ has established peace within the church and given to the church the gifts required to maintain its unity. Both actions correspond with functions of the ideal king in antiquity. But now another question emerges: Why should the inculcation of virtue be a necessary condition for unity?

5. Clothed with Christ: Taking off Vice, Putting on Virtue

To understand the role of virtue in "maintain[ing] the unity of the Spirit in the bond of peace" (Eph 4:3), one must first understand the relationship between virtue and vice. Paul's argument in both Ephesians and Colossians reflects the belief in antiquity that the abolition of vice was the necessary precursor to unity.[77] Abolishing vice can also be understood as a necessary precursor to inculcating virtue. Both—taking off vice and putting on virtue—were the prerogative of the ideal king in antiquity. Virgil implies that it is the *scelus* ("wickedness," an offense meriting divine wrath) of the Roman people that is the root of civil war (*Georg.* 1.463–468). Augustus must therefore wipe out every trace of *scelus* in order to usher in the golden age.[78] The role of the good king in abolishing vice among the people can be seen in the writings of Seneca, Dio Chrysostom, and Suetonius, as well as in Jewish texts such as the *Psalms of Solomon* and the *Testaments of the Twelve Patriarchs*.[79]

The eradication of vice was not, however, an end in itself, but rather the means to a greater good, the establishment of harmony, another prerogative of the ideal king, as demonstrated above. This is implied perhaps already in Virgil, but comes to expression most potently with Dio Chrysostom. He emphasizes that "only by getting rid of the vices" that plague civic life within the *polis*, "only so . . . is it possible ever to breathe the breath of harmony" (*Or.* 34.19). For Dio, then, the abolition of vice is a necessary precursor to the establishment of harmony.

The structure of Paul's argument in Ephesians would seem to bear out Dio's intuition. In Ephesians 4:1–16, Christ bestows gifts upon the church that contribute to its unity. Paul picks up the topic of unity again in Ephesians 5:22–6:9, in which he argues for a traditional ordering of the household, albeit one in which the reciprocal relationships between husbands and wives, fathers and children, and masters and slaves have been reconfigured "in Christ" (cf. Col 3:18–4:1).[80] In between these two sections of the letter, one finds an extensive exhortation to cast off vice and put on virtue (Eph 4:17–5:21; cf. Col 3:5–17).[81] Paul's ethical instruction at this point in the letter might appear to be a digression until one considers Dio's remarks. If Paul, like Dio, regards putting off vice and putting on virtue as instrumental to unity, then his exhortations here—although formally a digression—appear rather as a vital plank in his larger argument. Christ's creation of unity in the church and in the household will only happen as the church puts on Christ's character, thereby acquiring a new bodily *habitus.*[82] When one looks more carefully at the vices and virtues that Paul discusses, one sees that unity is indeed in the forefront of his concerns.[83]

At first glance, the vices that are to be "put to death" or excised seem to have little to do with the unity of the church as a whole but concern sexual sin, which—from the perspective of much modern Western individualism—one might consider to be of a private nature: "fornication, impurity, passion, evil desire, and greed (which is idolatry)" (Col 3:5; cf. Eph 4:19, 22; 5:3, 5, 12). Yet Paul regards the unrestrained, greedy, and idolatrous pursuit of sexual gratification as corrosive to the trust that is foundational to community life.[84] The next set of vices, "anger, wrath, malice, slander, and abusive language from your mouth," describe a "discourse of violence" that not only is inimical to the flourishing of the community, but also can serve to justify and normalize the first set of community-destroying vices (Col 3:8; cf. Eph 4:25, 26, 29, 31).[85]

These vices which constitute the "old self" are to be stripped off, replaced with the virtues constitutive of the "new self" renewed in the image of Christ: "compassion, kindness, humility, meekness, and patience," forgiveness, and above all, love (Col 3:12–14; cf. Eph 4:24, 32; 5:1–2). These virtues are political, in that they envision a renewed *polis*, an alternative commonwealth to the surrounding Roman Empire.[86] The result, Paul insists, is that the peace of Christ will rule in their hearts (Col 3:15). The heart here does not indicate mere interiority, as though Paul envisioned simply a sense of mental or spiritual peacefulness. The heart is understood rather as the will, the locus of executive function.[87] The reigning of Christ's peace in the heart describes a community of individuals so transformed into Christ's peacemaking and peaceable character that their decisions habitually reflect this. Thus, the community that clothes itself with Christ's character, putting off vices and putting on virtues, will find that it is also the community in which the peace of Christ is established.

6. Spatialized Eschatology and the Hidden Realm of Divine Activity

If the church, through the benefaction of Christ, puts on the peacemaking character of Christ and so maintains unity within the church, to what extent does the church influence the larger world? How much does the unity within the church contribute to the unity of humankind outside the church? At first blush, the answer would seem to be "not much." Both Ephesians and Colossians display a markedly "sectarian" ethic, keen to preserve the character of the community against the threat of outside influence. And yet, this is not the whole picture. In thinking about the church's relationship to outsiders, it is instructive to reflect upon the "spatialized" eschatological perspective that frames the arguments of Ephesians and Colossians. Eschatology, derived from the Greek *eschaton* ("last"), is fundamentally a temporal concept, concerned with the "last things," the consummation of God's kingdom "on earth as in heaven." And yet, in these two letters, temporal eschatological expectation is often expressed in spatial terms.

In Ephesians, for example, the church is understood to be enthroned with Christ in the heavenly places (Eph 2:6). Similarly, in Colossians, the church must see its life as hidden with Christ, who is seated with God above (Col 3:1–3). The "hidden" quality of the church's life in Christ expresses spatially the eschatological reserve that Paul more commonly expresses temporally.[88] The future has invaded the present. Heaven has been brought to earth. The dimension of God's rule (heaven) has been brought into the sphere of human dominion (earth) but it is hidden from human perception. The church, however, can both see this reality, since baptism brings one into the realm of God's reign on earth (Eph 4:5; Col 2:12, 20; 3:1), and make it visible by its life together.

This task, to be sure, is fraught with tension. As mentioned above, Paul largely endorses the hierarchical organization of the household economy that prevailed within Greco-Roman society (Col 3:18–4:1; Eph 5:21–6:9). This acceptance of cultural norms, however, is framed by Paul's audacious claim that the distinctions between social groups no longer exist as a result of the renewal inaugurated by Christ's reign (Col 3:11; see also Gal 3:28; 1 Cor 12:13). Moreover, Paul insists that the traditional hierarchy of the household is to be observed "in Christ," or "in the Lord" (Eph 6:1; Col 3:18 and elsewhere). This qualification is not merely window dressing, a feeble gesture to encourage those at the top of the pyramid to exercise *noblesse oblige*. It bespeaks the fundamental nature of the hidden reality the church inhabits, one in which unjust and divisive structures of human society are even now being undone through the reign of Jesus.

Paul would thus seem to question the way in which divisions within the human family have been reified so as to appear part of the fabric of reality.[89] In pursuing unity across the lines of cultural difference and hostility, the church exposes these divisions as merely cultural products and points to the hidden truth that God through Christ has reconciled humanity to God and to itself. The task of the church with respect to outsiders is thus to interpret this hidden reality, to put flesh on the new humanity by putting on the character of Christ. In this task of interpretation, the congregation functions as the "hermeneutic of the gospel."[90]

7. "Learning Christ": Instilling a New *Habitus* through Worship

In order to take on this interpretive role, the church itself must first come to inhabit this transcendent, hidden dimension of reality where Christ is understood to reign. How is this to happen? The previous chapter suggested one likely answer: the practice of spiritual disciplines whereby one is brought into the transformative "presence" of Christ the king. Paul's liturgically inflected argument in Ephesians and Colossians suggests that the discipline of worship is particularly important in ushering the church into the hidden dimension of Christ's present-and-coming reign. Interpreters have long recognized, for example, the importance of baptism—the worship ritual whereby one is incorporated into this new humanity—in both letters. Ephesians, as noted earlier, has been interpreted as a baptismal homily, and much of the moral formation in Colossians stems from *remembering* baptism.[91]

Moving beyond this general observation, one can see evidence that the practice of worship aims to instill a new *habitus* that contributes to new behavior. Paul admonishes the church in Colossae: "But now you must get rid of all such things—anger, wrath, malice, slander, and abusive language from your mouth" (Col 3:8). He then provides a "powerful antidote" to these community-destroying vices, namely the communal activities of worship: "Let the word of Christ dwell in you richly; teach and admonish one another in all wisdom; and with gratitude in your hearts sing psalms, hymns, and spiritual songs to God" (Col 3:16).[92] Paul's argument at this point would seem to echo Xunzi's conviction, that "through the combination of rites and music the human heart is governed" (see above, p. 119). As the *habitus* of speech that breeds disunity is reformed by the practice of a different kind of speech in worship, a new life begins to emerge: "And whatever you do, in word or deed, *do everything in the name of the Lord Jesus*, giving thanks to God the Father through him" (Col 3:17).

Paul's injunction to *do everything in the name of the Lord Jesus* is neither hyperbole nor rhetorical flourish.[93] Rather, acting characteristically
in a way that embodies allegiance to Jesus is the expected outcome of worship. This is because worship, by recalibrating the imagination, instills a
new *habitus*, an embodied way of "learning Christ" (Eph 4:20; see n. 78
above). Through the practice of worship, in other words, Paul's prayer for
the church is realized: "that Christ may dwell in your hearts through faith"
(Eph 3:17).

To grasp the importance of a new *habitus* formed by worship, let us
return to the paradox introduced above: Paul believes that socially divisive
distinctions have been rendered inoperative in the new humanity established through Christ's reign, and yet approves of the household economy organized precisely along such lines. There are many plausible explanations for the obvious tensions within such an ethic.[94] Paul may have
been advocating a prudential accommodation to cultural norms on the
grounds that it would have been fruitless and harmful to the church to
challenge such entrenched practices. Alternatively, he may have intended his words to be read as a "hidden transcript," the subversive intent of
which was diametrically opposed to its plain meaning.

If we take seriously the formative capacity of worship, a third possibility emerges. Paul may have been content to let the status quo reign for the
time being, confident in the hope that the new *habitus* formed by worship
would have a ripple effect, spreading out further and further into every aspect of life.[95] As the church enters through worship into the hidden realm
of Christ's reign, it imbibes by degrees a new "visceral plausibility structure" by which it makes sense of the world in light of the gospel. This recalibration of the imagination effects a transformation of one's disposition
to the world, out of which flow characteristic actions.[96]

As an illustration of the way Paul expected worship to instill a *habitus*
that would in turn affect the rest of life, consider the example of the Lord's
Supper, with which we began this chapter. The church in Corinth, according
to Paul, had been celebrating this ritual meal in a way that reified and exacerbated divisions within the community. Paul's remedy is to reform their
practice of the meal itself. Michael Rhodes concludes his insightful study of
the morally formative aspect of the Lord's Supper in First Corinthians:

> Participants shaped by a Lord's Supper in which all were welcomed
> equally across lines of social hierarchy would be radically changed,

and *Paul expected that change to ripple out into every area of believ-ers' lives.* The result would be nothing short of a new people, a new humanity even, founded on Christ, formed by his eucharistic table, united across lines of status, class, gender, and ethnicity, faithfully engaged in sharing the gifts of the Spirit with one another, and par-ticipating in the mission of the crucified Christ until his return.[97]

The same conviction regarding the transformative capacity of worship helps to explain Paul's approach to the management of the household economy in Ephesians and Colossians. The ritual practices of worship co-opt, for example, both masters and slaves into a story in which both "have the same Master in heaven, and with him there is no partiality" (Eph 6:9; cf. Col 3:24). The disposition to treat one another as "in the Lord" or "in Christ" is the fruit, Paul hopes, of the new *habitus* instilled by worship.

Thinking about worship in such terms coheres well with the structure and logic of Paul's argument in Ephesians. Recall the *berakah* with which Paul begins the letter: a three-fold blessing for God's benefactions result-ing in a three-fold response of praise (Eph 1:3–14). Paul begins the letter in this manner with didactic intent, using the language of worship to re-inforce the enfolding argument concerning identity.[98] But what precisely does Paul aim to teach them? His audience would no doubt have recog-nized praise as the appropriate response to a divine benefactor; it is there-fore not likely that Paul feels the need to *convince* them to do so. Rather he hopes to *move* them to praise their benefactor, because it is in the very act of worship that they will be incorporated into this story of God's resto-ration of the fractured cosmos through the reign of Jesus.

This process of "re-story-ing," or recalibrating, their imagination is essential to the success of the letter's argument. Worship makes a bridge between indicative and imperative. It is the essential practice that rein-forces the connection between their newly constituted identity (Eph 1–3) and the behavior that is enabled as a result of this new identity (Eph 4–6). Observe that Paul does not actually enjoin them *to* render praise to God in response to God's benefaction. He does not exhort them, "Because you have received these blessings, therefore you *should* return praise." Rath-er he indicates that the state of affairs resulting from God's benefaction simply *is* praise. The story of God's beneficent activity on behalf of the church effects a new reality, one that in itself redounds "to God's glory" (*eis epainon doxēs autou*, 1:6, 12, 14).

The church is to see its own existence, its characteristic life together and towards outsiders, as wrapped up in this new praise-effecting reality. The NRSV translates Ephesians 1:11–12 in way that suggests that Paul is issuing a polite imperative: Through Christ, we have been brought into God's covenant family "so that we . . . *might live for the praise of his glory* (*eis to einai hēmas eis epainon doxēs autou*)."[99] The syntax of the sentence in Greek indicates not a *might* but an *is*.[100] Translated woodenly, the phrase means something like: "resulting in our existence being to the praise of his glory." For the church to see its very existence as constituting praise in response to God's benefaction is to be shaped by a profoundly world-changing operative metaphor.

To draw together the threads of the argument, I return to my original question: Is unity in the church in these two letters understood as a divine or human achievement? To say that it is a divine achievement that both enables and requires human effort may sound like nonsense unless this claim is framed within the cultural context of the reign of the ideal king. Such a figure was seen both to establish peace and through his benefaction to inculcate virtue, the latter being the necessary condition for the former. So when the church is enjoined to moral activity that results in unity—putting on the character of Christ—both activity and result must be understood as enabled by the reign of Christ.[101] Furthermore, it is through the practice of worship that the church's imagination is recalibrated such that it learns to live as faithful citizens of Jesus the king.

Thus far I have argued that Paul's vision of human flourishing entails citizenship in the heavenly commonwealth over which Christ reigns; transformation into the character and image of this king; and the unity which is the fruit of both character transformation and worship. It is appropriate to speak of this as a *vision* in the sense that, while this life has been inaugurated through Jesus' resurrection, it will not be consummated until his return. Even though the citizens of this heavenly commonwealth endeavor to live in faithful allegiance to their king in the present, they also look forward in eager anticipation of the day when Jesus' reign will be experienced in its fullness. How the church is to hope with patient endurance for this *telos* is the subject of the following chapter.

CHAPTER 5

CREATION

Anticipating the Glorified King in Rome

If you are a college student or spend enough time around college campuses, chances are high that you have frequently asked or heard this question: "So, what's your major?" Often this can be a throwaway question, the answer no sooner given than forgotten. Repeated *ad nauseum* in dorms, dining halls, and parties, the question is part of the well-worn ritual of introducing oneself to a stranger. (The post-college version is, "So, what do you do for a living?") Just below the surface of this slightly unimaginative question is something worthy of a further look: the way it takes for granted the *telos*—or one of them, at any rate—of a college education.

Unlike primary and secondary education, higher education aims to make us into specialists, or at least propels us in that direction. Educational specialization has great economic utility for society: it trains us to be doctors, engineers, primary school teachers, and the like. It also promises great economic advantage for us as individuals: it potentially enables us to achieve economic independence from our parents and become self-sufficient (even as this process becomes lengthier and more fraught with uncertainty). Such specialization is integral to our vision of personal and societal economic flourishing. But specialization comes at a cost. Before we get to that cost, I would like you to think for a moment about the range of answers you have heard to this question.

Have you ever asked, "So, what's your major?" and heard in reply, "Farming"? I doubt it. At the large public land-grant universities like Michigan State or Purdue, one can of course encounter students pursuing majors in the College of Agriculture, but such individuals are generally not preparing to become farmers but rather to enter the field of agribusiness.[1] I find myself both saddened and concerned by this observation. My sadness derives from the suspicion that the art and science of farming is not considered worthy of higher education, hence its absence from the college curriculum. There might well be other explanations, but I think it is safe to say that farming is held in low regard in America. As evidence of the widespread contempt for farming, I point to the mass exodus from the family farm: over the course of the twentieth century, the number of farmers has dropped precipitously from 40 percent of the work force to a mere 2 percent.[2] Young people who leave a family farm to go to college typically do not return, or if they do it is despite, not because of, their education. And anyone who desires to *start* a career in farming will face such economic obstacles as to render the goal impossible.[3]

My sadness over this state of affairs leads directly to my sense of grave concern. Competence in producing food is of course basic to human survival. As fewer and fewer people possess such competence, humankind, no less than the rest of creation, faces an existential threat. My intent in voicing my concern so nakedly is not to sound alarmist. "Fear," as Marilynne Robinson reminds us, "is not a Christian habit of mind."[4] The concern is nevertheless warranted, and to understand why, we must consider the costs of specialization.

A specialist, according to the old chestnut, is one who learns more and more about less and less, eventually coming to know everything about nothing. Although such a caricature is overdrawn, the specialization of knowledge constitutes a serious problem. An economy requiring an ever-greater degree of specialization among its labor force results in a population dependent upon experts for nearly every facet of existence. My father, although a highly trained surgeon, could not fix a leaky toilet to save his life. Most of us could not feed, clothe, and shelter ourselves if we needed to. As Wendell Berry observes,

> In living in the world by his own will and skill, the stupidest peasant or tribesman is more competent than the most intelligent worker or technician or intellectual in a society of specialists.[5]

Virtually all of us, in other words, are radically dependent upon a vast array of specialists for our basic sustenance. Perhaps your response to this observation is to roll your eyes and think, "Well, call a plumber!

Drive to the grocery store! Buy it on Amazon! Specialization isn't a *prob-lem*; it's the *solution!*"

Specialization obviously does solve the problem of a society depen-dent upon a body of technical knowledge too large and complex for a single individual to master. If we want to live in a society with doctors *and* plumbers (and all the panoply of trades and professions we depend upon), what other choice is there? I am inclined to agree with this sentiment to an extent, but what are the costs we incur in exchange for this benefit? Specialization involves a trade-off: we forgo knowledge or competence in a variety of fields in order to acquire mastery in one. For the most part this tradeoff appears advantageous to all (or at least those who have the economic advantages to participate in the system): as long as there are enough trained doctors and plumbers, everyone is happy. But imagine what might happen if not enough people decided to pursue training as plumbers? We can imagine a number of ways in which such a scenario might play out: the cost of fixing your toilet becomes astronomical; some people learn to fix their own toilets; and some people recognize the eco-nomic opportunity and train to become plumbers. Problem solved.

Now imagine that we decided to address the dearth of plumbers through technological innovation. Instead of fixing our own toilets or providing economic incentives to become a plumber, we invent plumbing robots. (Actually, if history is any guide, we would probably invent the plumbing robots *first*, driving most plumbers out of a job.) Aside from the multitude of unemployed plumbers, we would thereby seemed to have *permanently* solved the problem of supply and demand before it even be-gan. The cost for this solution, however, is that knowledge of plumbing would eventually fade entirely from the realm of human competence. I suspect that most would not find this cost too onerous, as long as we are thinking of plumbing in terms of leaky faucets and blocked toilets. Consider, however, the potential cost we would risk by the human loss of competence in administering the whole *system* of plumbing that supplies us with fresh water and carries away our waste. My concern, in any case, is not with plumbing, but with a field of knowledge more basic to the re-quirements of human life.

For the past decade or so, my wife and I (with the cheerful help of some good friends and the grudging help of our two sons) have endeavored to grow and produce as much of our own food as we can. This adventure has brought us profound delight and satisfaction and has taught us a great deal about the wonder and goodness of God's creation. It has also impressed upon us our woeful ignorance and the astonishing amount of hard work, care, and intelligence required to draw forth food from the earth. Our garden is considerable: at 5,625 square feet, it is larger than the footprint of our house. And yet, if we had to depend solely upon our garden for food, we would surely starve to death. I share my own story here because it is a microcosm of a much larger story.

When my wife first encouraged me to get my hands dirty in our backyard garden in Texas over a decade ago, I was fairly representative of the level of agrarian competence possessed by the average American. That is to say, I was almost entirely ignorant. I do not mean that I simply lacked the technical knowledge of how to grow food. I also lacked what I will refer to throughout this chapter as *agrarian virtues*, the excellences of character both required for, and fostered by, the proper care of the health of land and people, mindful of the integral relationship between the two. We have, as a culture, lost such virtues because we have entrusted the production of food to an increasingly small number of specialists who have become increasingly reliant upon methods of industrial farming that are, quite literally, destroying the earth.[6] Berry describes the consequences of this profound loss to our culture:

> We have given up the understanding—dropped it out of our language and so out of our thought—that we and our country create one another, depend on one another, are literally part of one another; that our land passes in and out of our bodies just as our bodies pass in and out of our land; that as we and our land are part of one another, so all who are living as neighbors here, human and plant and animal, are part of one another, and so cannot possibly flourish alone; that, therefore, our culture must be our response to our place, our culture and our place are images of each other and inseparable from each other, and so neither can be better than the other.[7]

Berry suggests, in other words, that we cannot flourish as humans apart from the flourishing of the entirety of God's creation.

This book has argued that Paul's vision of salvation entails not merely a blessed existence in God's presence after death, but also encompasses our flourishing in the present as disciples of Jesus. Eternal life is not divorced from our present existence, but is to a certain degree continuous with it. The good life for Paul is characterized by citizenship in the heavenly *politeuma*, by embodied allegiance to Jesus as king, by faithfully following him in the way of suffering (chapter 2). Membership within this community both requires and fosters the practices whereby citizens are transformed into the image of Jesus the king (chapter 3). Such transformation of character is furthermore crucial to the establishment and maintenance of unity within the community (chapter 4). The present chapter explores the *telos* of this community. Aristotle believed that one can arrive at the *telos* of a human being—*eudaimonia*—by deducing its special function, namely reason, which distinguishes the human from other animals. Paul, by contrast, would insist that the human *telos* is to "share in the glory of God" (Rom 5:2). This *telos* in turn shapes the virtues that characterize this community.

The virtues required and fostered by citizenship in the heavenly *politeuma* envisioned by Paul can be described as "agrarian."[8] Ellen Davis succinctly defines agrarianism as "a way of thinking and ordering life in community that is based on the health of the land and living creatures."[9] Within agrarian thinking, the land is understood "not as an inert object, but as a fellow creature that can justly expect something from us whose lives depend on it."[10] When Paul expresses the hope in Romans that "the creation itself will be set free from its bondage to decay and will obtain the freedom of the glory of the children of God" (8:21), he is thinking of the flourishing of land and humans as inextricably intertwined. Seen from the perspective of Romans 5–8, the *telos* anticipated by the heavenly *politeuma* is nothing less than the eschatological renewal of creation under the reign of the Messiah. The virtues of this community are thus agrarian in the sense that they help the church to envision and work towards the eschatological restoration of humans to their proper and original vocation as stewards of God's creation (Gen 1:26–28; 2:15). In particular, Romans 5–8 presents hope and endurance as agrarian virtues essential to the church's task of eschatological anticipation, virtues that are acquired and practiced in the midst of suffering.

1. Reading Romans in Its Cultural, Economic, and Theological Contexts

Before examining Paul's argument in Romans, we must establish its cultural, economic, and theological contexts. Paul writes within a culture shaped by Roman imperial ideology, which boasted that the emperor's virtues had ushered in a golden age of righteousness, peace, prosperity, and agricultural bounty. Yet economic realities on the ground told a different story, of agricultural practices that damaged the land and the communities that cultivated it, resulting in the diminution of agrarian virtues. Paul's thinking, moreover, is shaped theologically by the biblical narrative, which understood fertile soil to be God's gift to be held in trust by God's covenant people.

1.1. Rome's Agricultural Golden Age

Roman fascination with a return to a golden age,[11] to be imminently ushered in by the reign of Augustus, derives from the writings of the Roman poet, Publius Vergilius Maro (70–19 BCE), commonly known as Virgil.[12] Virgil's fourth *Eclogue*, a poem drawing on Hesiod's myth of the "Ages of Metal" (*Op.* 106–201) and the "Life under Cronus" myth (Aratus, *Phaenomena* 114–43),[13] depicts a return to an age of peace, justice, and virtue (*Ecl.* 4.15–17), brought about by the reign of the "sweet child of the gods, great increment of Jove" (*Ecl.* 4.49).[14] The created order's voluntary submission to this "child" (*Ecl.* 4.18–25)[15] results in such agricultural bounty that the land does not even need to be tilled, and sheep give purple and crimson wool (*Ecl.* 4.28–45). It is an age when all creation rejoices (*Ecl.* 4.52).

Virgil takes up the theme of a similar return to plenty and prosperity in his great epic poem the *Aeneid*, in which Jupiter prophesies to Venus that the golden age will come when a "Trojan Caesar" named Julius shall arise. His empire will be bounded only by the ocean, his fame by the stars, and the gates of war will be shut (*Aen.* 1.286–294).[16] Aeneas' deceased father Anchises, whom he encounters in the underworld, makes clear that this new golden age will be ushered in by Augustus:

> This, this is he . . . Augustus Caesar, son of a god, who shall again set up the Golden Age amid the fields where Saturn once reigned, and shall spread his empire past Garamant and Indian, to a land that lies beyond the stars, beyond the paths of the year and the sun. (*Aen.* 6.791–797)

Virgil imagines the Augustan golden age to be one in which Rome rules the world in peace (*Aen.* 6.850–854). It will be a return to the reign of Saturn, in which the people are "righteous, not by bond or laws, but self-controlled of their own free will and by the custom of their ancient god" (*Aen.* 7.202–704).[17] Augustus, inheriting the divine reign of Saturn, is viewed by Virgil as the earthly Jupiter, that is, Jupiter's vicegerent on earth.[18] The social implications of such a return are significant. The ideology functions to put the emperor, as the sole hope for the abolition of *scelus*, an offense incurring the wrath of the gods, at the center of the return, and urges subjection of all to him in service of this ideal order.[19] For Virgil and his contemporaries,

> The Return of the Golden Age theme . . . belongs to a complex of ideas the effect of which was to provide Augustus with a role that made him essential for the preservation of Roman society. . . . Only through voluntary submission to the great mediator Augustus can they recapture innocence and Paradise.[20]

Virgil's favorable estimation of kingship at a time when the term *rex* (king) was out of fashion contrasts with what scholars of the Augustan era have called the official view—namely that Augustus represented the restoration of the virtuous Roman Republic, the *princeps* being nothing more than a magistrate, or at most the first among equals. In Virgil, however, there is evidence for the existence of an emerging "unofficial" view: "the rule of one man as a permanent necessity; that man was a god-to-be, if not a god on earth, as well as a king."[21]

Indeed, Augustus himself betrays this developing understanding of his cosmic as well as political significance in his self-congratulatory *Res gestae divi Augusti*. In this encomium to himself, the emperor presents himself as preeminent in virtue, a generous benefactor, and the one who has brought peace to the Roman people. Although he was loath to take on the formal mantle of absolute monarch, Augustus' encomiastic rehearsal of his achievements uses categories of evaluation suggestive of the ideal Hellenistic king.[22]

By asserting his own preeminence in virtue as a feature of his reign, the emperor evokes the commonplace that the "best man" in society should rule. Indeed, towards the conclusion of the *Res gestae*, Augustus recounts the bestowal by the senate of a golden shield "on account of my courage, clemency, justice and piety" (34.2). These four exemplary qualities comprised a canon of imperial virtues that soon became part of Roman imperial propaganda designed to convince the masses that the emperor not only had the requisite qualities for his position as supreme ruler but also embodied transcendent strengths.[23]

The elevation of Augustus' virtues to greater heights, by himself and others, must be further understood in the context of the Roman Cult of Virtues, through which the emperor came to be regarded not merely as a model of divine virtues, but moreover as the source of divine benefits and the means by which divine order was established in the common-wealth (see earlier discussion in chapter 2).[24] Rome's "theology of victory," denoting the complex political mythology whereby the stability and harmony of the cosmic order was made dependent upon the emperor, placed particular emphasis on the emperor's Victory (*Victoria*). His pos-session of this virtue resulted in his divinely enabled military victory and the tangible benefits it realized for the Roman citizenry. The objective of imperial propaganda was thus not simply to persuade the public that the emperor possessed the needed virtues of the ideal king, but rather that he had access to and actually conveyed in his person the divine power needed to rule, "the power to conquer, to save, to bring harmony and stability, and to distribute benefits."[25]

In sum, the soon-triumphant Roman imperial propaganda rejoiced in the arrival of a golden age, allegedly characterized by agricultural abundance, achieved on the merits of the emperor's divinely blessed vir-tue. It must be stressed that this glorious state of affairs was believed—or at least claimed—to exist as a benefit brought about by the emperor's virtue *in the present*. In this respect, we can describe the eschatology of the imperial cult as presentist, that is, it brought before current witness-es an ideal condition normally ascribed to a mythical past or a distant hoped-for future.[26] Yet the presentist eschatology baked into the notion of a restored golden age as a *fait accompli* inevitably stirred a degree of cognitive dissonance and potential political discontent. Steven J. Friesen describes the problem thus:

> Space was centered on Rome and time was organized around Augus-tus and the accomplishments of empire. These cosmological inter-ests were so strong that they produced an eschatological absurdity: the best one could hope for was the eternal continuation of Roman rule.[27]

For present purposes, the latent contradiction arises in the relationship of the supposed cosmic imperial virtues to the actual agrarian life visible to those of the time. Any thoughtful attention to actual first-century Ro-man agricultural practices must lead one not merely to question whether a golden age had truly arrived, but furthermore to question whether such practices could even be said to contribute toward the health of the land and the communities that cultivated it.

1.2. Rome's Economic Practices: Slavery and Tenant Farming

Most citizens of Rome's capital in the first century would not merely have read or heard imperial propaganda boasting of the present golden age of agricultural fecundity; they would have seen daily evidence of it.[28] On any given day of the month, some seven thousand men could be seen throughout the city carrying home their monthly grain allotment, approximately thirty-three kilograms. Since the time of the Republic, Roman authorities had been enhancing the city's food supply to hedge against food shortages and price fluctuations. By the early principate, these interventions had evolved into the *frumentum publicum*, the government's free distribution of the "public wheat" each month to some two hundred thousand adult male Roman citizens.[29] This daily sight of the emperor's benefaction constituted a powerful ritual of political and social inclusion, tangible proof that the land itself had brought forth its bounty in response to the emperor's divine virtue.

Doubtless many of Rome's citizens were recipients of this imperial largesse, but would they have been inclined to accept the propaganda claims it was intended to illustrate? Surely they would have known that this massive amount of grain—two hundred thousand tons consumed annually, by conservative estimate—did not appear magically, but was grown, harvested, collected, and shipped from all over Italy and from provinces throughout the empire.[30] To the extent that they were aware of the agricultural practices by which this grain arrived at the port of Ostia to be distributed throughout the city, Rome's hungry masses would have had cause not for rejoicing, but rather for lamenting the poor health of the land and the communities of people who cultivated it. When we look at the larger picture of first-century Roman agriculture, the public supply of grain to Rome (*annona civica*) provides us with evidence not of a golden age of agricultural fecundity but rather of a disconcerting loss of agrarian virtues.

1.2.1. Overview of Roman Agriculture

Agriculture was the backbone of the Roman economy, supplying the surplus upon which the wealth of Rome's elites was founded.[31] Indeed, land was conventionally regarded as the only stable and respectable form of investment.[32] Thanks to a number of extant treatises dating from the late Republic through the early empire, we are well informed of Roman agricultural practices, the economic aspects of farming, and Roman concerns about the state of agriculture.[33]

Farming in the Mediterranean climate faced the challenges of long, hot summers and cool, wet winters, as well as a great deal of annual and seasonal variability in rainfall. Several bad years in a row were not uncommon, nor were the food shortages that resulted. Grain yields were typically modest, on the order of 500 kg/ha. To minimize risk under these conditions, farmers favored polyculture, the intercultivation of sown and planted crops. Often, wheat or barley, rotated with beans and lupines, was grown among olive trees or vines. Olive oil and wine were more profitable, but cereal grains constituted the lion's share of the diet for most Romans.[34] This sort of farming, aided with limited but appropriate technology, required the "constant, devoted attention" of small-scale subsistence farmers, of whom there are numerous accounts in ancient literature.[35]

Yet independent, peasant farmers were by no means the only sort of agricultural labor in antiquity; in fact, their existence was increasingly threatened by the two largest sources of farm labor, slaves and tenant farmers. This movement—from small-scale, independent, subsistence farming to large-scale, dependent, profit-driven farming—played a decisive role in the loss of Roman agrarian virtues.

As illustrated by the Roman historian Livy's account of the patriotic hero Cincinnatus (ca. 458 BCE), who was summoned from the plough on his modest farm of seven *iugera* to become temporary dictator (*History of Rome* 3.26.8), early Roman farming was traditionally the province of small, independent farmers.[36] But through the course of Roman conquest and expansion over the third and second centuries BCE, many farmers were forced to abandon their farms to fight in the army. Moreover, during the Second Punic War, fought largely on Italian soil (218–202 BCE), both farms and farmers alike suffered violence.[37] Although Rome was greatly enriched by this conquest, the wealth was not evenly distributed:

> Rich men had money to invest and poor men, their farms laid waste and neglected through years of campaigning, had land to sell. The great holdings thus accumulated could now be worked by slaves, who had become plentiful as a result of the wars, and were frequently converted to stock-raising as part of the same process. The

dispossessed peasantry moved to the towns, and became the urban mob that we know from contemporary orators and historians.[38]

The tradition of small allocations continued through the Gracchan land reforms of the late second century, after which farms in excess of 100 *iugera* (62.5 acres), operated by slaves, begin to appear. Slave labor by this point was already widespread; during the years 297–167 BCE, some 700,000 persons had been enslaved as a result of military campaigns.[39] The use of agricultural slave labor, often in chain gangs, became increasingly prevalent, since it enabled larger surpluses and greater returns on investments. This in turn fueled the conspicuous consumption and grand public building projects of Rome's "consumer city" economy.[40] Columella, writing towards the end of the first century CE, assumes that his audience consists nearly exclusively of wealthy Romans farming for profit on estates operated either by tenant farmers or slaves (*De Re Rustica* 1.7.11).[41] Yet despite the ubiquity of slave and tenant labor, Columella laments the carelessness and greed inherent in this manner of cultivation, observing that because of it, "the land pretty often gets a bad name" (1.7.7), referring to the common complaint in his day that Italian soil had become exhausted and unfruitful (1.pref.1). By the early principate, both slave and tenant labor, with their attendant problems, had become institutionalized in what is often referred to as the villa system of agriculture.

1.2.2. From the Villa System to *Latifundia*

Although it is difficult to define precisely what a villa actually was, literary sources give us a picture of "a place in the country, normally (but not always) associated with farming, sometimes with connotations of luxury or relaxation, and in most cases a single house rather than a group of them."[42] The term, moreover, seems to describe a country place from a townsperson's point of view; most villas were owned by townspeople as sources of investment and were rarely inhabited by their owners. While some villas were used primarily as luxury retreats for the wealthy, the typical villa was a working farm run for profit, described memorably by historian Michael Rostovtzeff as "an agricultural factory run by slaves."[43] When historians speak of the villa *system* of agriculture, they intend to describe a social and economic institution resulting from capital inflow to Rome, allowing absentee landlords to invest in land, "the capital being available, not to the farming community itself, but to the wealthy senators and businessmen, who needed for various reasons to invest in landed property, but were tied by status or occupation to Rome and the other Italian cities."[44] This system expanded in the late Republic, fueled by the increasingly ample supply of slaves and indeed creating further demand for slaves.[45] Of course not all villas were cultivated by slave labor; both small- and large-scale tenants, including sharecroppers, were employed, but it is important to note that tenants were often economically dependent upon their landlords and in some cases were more economically vulnerable than slaves.[46]

On the whole, then, the villa system that predominated in the first century of the principate was organized in such a way that absentee landowners were not closely involved in the actual cultivation of the land, while those who labored on the land—slaves and tenants for the most part—were largely deprived of the fruits of their labor.

Over the course of the second century, possibly due in part to increased agricultural competition from the provinces, the villa system was gradually replaced by *latifundia*, which were not unified or contiguous estates, but rather "agglomerations of individual farms pieced together over the course of time through bequest or purchase."[47] The term *latifundia* does not appear in any extant Latin text prior to the first century CE and is nowhere defined, yet the context of its usage suggests both the great size of *latifundia* and their undercultivation.[48] For example, in southern Italy and Sicily, vast tracts of arable land were converted to pasturage, resulting in the loss of both small farms and the market towns that had previously depended upon farming.[49] Pliny the Elder famously remarks,

> In old times it was thought that to observe moderation in the size of a farm was of primary importance, inasmuch as the view was held that it was more satisfactory to sow less land and plough it better; and I observe Virgil was of this opinion. And if the truth be confessed, large estates have been the ruin of Italy [*latifundia perdidere Italiam*], and are now proving the ruin of the provinces too—half of Africa was owned by six landlords when the Emperor Nero put them to death. (*Nat. Hist.* 18.35 [Rackham])[50]

Pliny does not explain why he believes that *latifundia* are ruining Italy, although the larger context of book 18 suggests that he is concerned with the poor quality of work that was characteristic of the slave labor required to cultivate large estates. Recalling a number of well-known Roman nobles who were also farmers (including Cincinnatus), he poses the rhetorical question "whether everything prospers better under honourable hands because the work is done with greater attention" (*Nat. Hist.* 18.19). He laments, by contrast, that

> nowadays those agricultural operations are performed by slaves with fettered ankles and by the hands of malefactors with branded faces! ... And we forsooth are surprised that we do not get the same profits from the labour of slave-gangs as used to be obtained from that of generals! (*Nat. Hist.* 18.21)

Scholars are inclined to view Pliny's appraisal of *latifundia* as nothing more than "emotional exaggeration," a pining for a romanticized agrarian past that did not actually exist.[51] Granted that some level of rhetorical amplification is probable, Pliny's comments here should nevertheless be taken seriously as an indication that Italian agriculture towards the end of the first century CE "was in a far from flourishing condition," and that this state was due in large part due to labor practices and land use.[52]

1.2.3. Effects of Roman Agricultural Practices

It is therefore clear that the Roman *annona civica* likely served not only a practical economic function but also as a powerful symbol reinforcing the propaganda that Rome had ushered in an age of agricultural bounty. Given this account of the agricultural practices that enabled the Roman distribution of grain to its citizens, there were several important effects of these practices.

First, these practices threatened the subsistence and self-sufficiency of many of Italy's small farms. Subsistence farming had historically constituted the backbone of the Roman economy, and self-sufficiency had long been not only a practical, but also a moral ideal.[53] Yet the growth of the villa system and then that system's subsequent eclipse in the second century CE by *latifundia* came at the expense of the majority of Italy's subsistence farmers, who were forced to become tenant farmers, day laborers, or slaves.[54]

Second, the decline in small farms contributed directly to growing economic inequality, with over half the population of the Roman Empire living at or below the subsistence level.[55] Increasingly, the elite came to "enjoy almost the entire surplus of the economy."[56]

Third, the loss of economic self-sufficiency resulted unsurprisingly in widespread malnutrition, the evidence of which can be found in the cash benefits (*alimenta*) distributed to children in towns throughout Italy in order to help families purchase food.[57]

Fourth and finally, although the issue of ecological degradation in Mediterranean history is contested among scholars, it seems likely that large-scale agriculture and pasturage had a grievous effect on the land itself, contributing to deforestation and soil erosion.[58]

It is reasonable to suppose that many, if not all, of these effects would have been perceived and understood by most residents of Rome in the first century. Indeed, given that over half of the urban population in the Roman world was living at or below subsistence, it is likely that a good many of Rome's inhabitants were *personally* acquainted with the economic deprivation resulting from Roman agricultural practices. To be clear, I am not suggesting that these practices were the sole cause of poverty in the Roman world—only that they substantially contributed to people's inability to provide for themselves through their own agricultural labor, and that this would have been well-known in the city of Rome.

With this critical historical and social context in mind, is it likely that the recipients of Paul's letter to the church in Rome—some of whom would presumably have been beneficiaries of the *annona civica*—would have taken the free distribution of grain as evidence of agricultural fecundity brought about through the emperor's virtue? This question is not intended to invite speculation into the thought processes of individual first-century Romans, but rather to subject the contemporaneous imperial propaganda regarding the emperor's divinely inspired bounty to critical scrutiny on the basis of what we know about the actual socioeconomic conditions within the empire. What, further, does the *annona civica* tell us about the health of the land and those who cultivated it?

In the first place, it is clear that grain distributions in Rome had increasingly become a political *necessity* since their inception in 123 BCE.[59] This was the case due to two related factors: the steady movement of rural poor into Rome, and the consequent growth in Rome's population, such that the city could not be sustained by the produce of its immediately surrounding regions. Grain shortages or price fluctuations could lead quickly to angry mobs, a serious threat to stability. Thus Rome soon became deeply dependent upon shipments of grain from throughout Italy as well as Sicily, Sardinia, Spain, Africa, Gaul, and Egypt, requiring growing imperial administrative oversight of its collection, transportation, and distribution.[60]

Moreover, the vast amount of grain flowing into Rome was paid for largely through the taxes and rents on producers, which further served to widen the inequality gap, putting enormous economic pressure on small farms.[61] This cost was borne disproportionately by the provinces. While Italy was exempt from tax on agricultural land, census documents from Palestine during the time of the Bar Kochba revolt (ca. 132 CE) indicate that as much as half the crop was owed in taxes.[62] Thus, while the *annona civica* may well have theoretically supported Virgil's illusory boast of the land producing all its needs without the aid of human cultivation (*Ecl.* 4.39–40), the practices that enabled Rome's free distribution of grain told a very different story: of a city unable to support its own population, dependent instead upon the exploitation of the labors of the most vulnerable populations—day laborers, tenants, and slaves—across its vast empire.

1.2.4. Slavery and the Loss of Agrarian Virtues

Imperial propaganda claimed that the return to a golden age had been achieved by the merits of the emperor's virtues. The above survey of Roman agricultural practices suggests, however, that this boast was hardly consistent with the actual state of agrarian practices within the Roman Empire. The result is a paradox: In the face of claims that divinely ordained imperial virtue had resulted in agricultural fecundity, the actual agrarian virtues required to bring about and sustain the health of the land were in decline. The agrarian commentator Columella repudiates the oft-repeated criticism made by "leading men of our state" that the soil had become unfruitful as a result of an inclement climate or exhaustion due to overproduction in the past. Rather, he claims:

> I do not believe that such misfortunes come upon us as a result of the fury of the elements, but rather because of our own fault; for the matter of husbandry, which all the best of our ancestors had treated with the best of care, we have delivered over to all the worst of our slaves, as if to a hangman for punishment. (*On Agriculture* 1.pref.3 [Ash])

Columella, then, correlates the increasing practice of slavery, the degrading labor system that fueled the Roman economy, with a decline in practices necessary for sustained land health. This decline is furthermore reflected in—and possibly the result of—the low esteem in which genuine agrarian virtues had come to be commonly held. Columella continues, "everyone summons from the company of the wise a man to mould his intellect and instruct him in the precepts of virtue; but agriculture alone, which is without doubt most closely related and, as it were, own sister to wisdom, is as destitute of learners as of teachers" (*On Agriculture* 1.pref.4).

The agrarian social critic is bewildered that the art most necessary to human existence "should be looked upon with scorn" (*On Agriculture* 1.pref.8). How did this lamentable state of affairs come to pass? The root of the problem, Columella suggests, begins with large-scale urbanization: "All of us who are heads of families have quit the sickle and the plough and have crept within the city-walls" (*On Agriculture* 1.pref.15). This demographic change leads to the further problem that those who own the land do not cultivate it, while those who work the land have no stake in its fruitfulness. Sweat equity by landowners would atone for a multitude of sins, even ignorance, he insists,

> for the diligence that goes with proprietorship would compensate in large measure the losses occasioned by lack of knowledge; and men whose interests were at stake would not wish to appear forever ignorant of their own affairs, and for that reason more zealous to learn, they would gain a thorough knowledge of husbandry. As it is we think it beneath us to till our lands with our own hands. (*On Agriculture* 1.pref.11)

The result of the common belief that "farming is a mean employment and a business which has no need of direction or of precept"—in other words, a widespread decline in agrarian virtues—is the "importation of grain from our provinces beyond the sea, that we may not suffer hunger" (*On Agriculture* 1.pref.20). We may take Columella, then, as articulating the view—present already in the middle of the first century—that the *annona civica* was not an indication of Roman agrarian virtues, but rather their lack.

Columella provides us with first-century literary evidence that Roman agriculture was in a state of decline, but he does not offer a robust account of the process by which this state came to be. Nor is this his goal; indeed, it is clear that the above comments merely constitute the rationale for his treatise in agronomy, namely the need to recover the capacious intelligence and wisdom—"the greatest mental acuteness" in his own words—so necessary for the restoration of "rural discipline" (*On Agriculture* 1.pref.21–33).

Nevertheless, to the extent that Columella accurately reflects the practices and attitudes of his day, he does provide us with some valuable insights on the relationships between agrarian practices and the moral character of his society. One, agricultural work is held in contempt as a pursuit requiring little intelligence and possessing little dignity. Two, agricultural work is therefore considered fit only for slaves. Three, agrarian virtues—the excellences necessary to cultivate and preserve the health of the land—are held in disrepute and suffer neglect.

These critiques of ancient Roman agricultural economics (even if not called that) bear a striking resemblance to those of the contemporary American agrarian writer, Wendell Berry, whose corpus of fiction, poetry, and essays spanning over fifty years focuses on human communities and their relationship to the land that sustains them. Berry is not a student of Mediterranean antiquity, but he conveys with singular force the social factors underlying the loss of agrarian virtues in the Roman Empire. Berry elucidates certain parallels between our own North American context and the Greco-Roman world, sometimes explicitly. For example, in making the case for a return to "our old agrarian ideal . . . of a countryside populated by settled families and stable communities earning a decent livelihood from their work and their goods," he emphatically declares:

> The people who do the land's work should own the land. It should *not* be owned in great monopolistic estates by a class of absentee landlords, as in the latter days of the Roman Empire, and as increasingly now, with us, in the time of our own decadence.[63]

Here, Berry directly echoes the lament of Pliny the Elder, that such monopolistic estates were proving to be the ruin of Italy: *latifundia perdidere Italiam*. Whereas Pliny is frustratingly vague regarding the reasons for his claim, however, Berry explains that latifundialization (or its modern equivalent) contributes to creating an inevitably precarious and unsustainable imbalance of city and countryside. The only sustainable city, he writes, "is a city in balance with its countryside . . . paying as it goes all its ecological and human debts." Yet both Rome and the vast majority of modern American cities have destroyed this balance: "Rome destroyed the balance with slave labor; we have destroyed it with machines and 'cheap' fossil fuel."[64] Here, then, Berry reveals the essential problem behind the loss of agrarian virtues: Rome's reliance on agricultural slave labor.

To understand why this is the case, Berry's extended essay, *The Hidden Wound*, provides a trenchant analysis of the devastating legacy of slavery and racism in America. Born in Kentucky in 1934, Berry grew up in a society that was rapidly becoming more urban, a society moreover in which "farming was looked down upon as a hard and generally unremunerative way of life," both of which could be said equally of Greco-Roman society in the first century CE.[65]

Although slavery in the United States had been abolished some seventy years before Berry's birth, the racism that had supported and enabled slavery, as well as attitudes toward agricultural labor that had arisen during slavery, remained entrenched.[66] While not in the least denying the brutality and injustice suffered by blacks under slavery, Berry insists that whites also suffered grievously from its legacy of racism, as though from a mortal disease:

> the white man's experience of this continent has so far been incomplete, partly, perhaps mostly, because he has assigned certain critical aspects of the American experience to people he has considered his racial or social inferiors. . . . As the white man has withheld from the black man the positions of responsibility toward the land, and consequently the sense of a legally permanent relationship to it, so he has assigned to him as his proper role the labor, the thousands of menial small acts by which the land is maintained, and by which men develop a closeness to the land and the wisdom of that closeness. . . . racism, by dividing the two races has made them not separate but in a fundamental way inseparable, not independent but dependent on each other, incomplete without each other . . . and the division between us is the disease of one body, not of two.[67]

As a consequence of relegating the care of the land to blacks, whites came ineluctably to regard agricultural work, in Berry's words, as "nigger work" unworthy of themselves.[68] Unsurprisingly, whites failed to develop "the emotional resilience and equilibrium and the culture necessary to endure and even enjoy hard manual labor wholly aside from the dynamics of ambition. . . . What we should have learned willingly ourselves we *forced* the blacks to learn, and so prevented ourselves from learning it."[69]

A social and economic system in which those who own the land fail to develop the virtues to care for it results in cultural, agricultural, and ecological disaster. Thus Berry draws his essay to a close:

The white man, preoccupied with the abstractions of the economic exploitation and ownership of the land, necessarily has lived on
the country as a destructive force, an ecological catastrophe, because
he assigned the hand labor, and in that the possibility of intimate
knowledge of the land, to a people he considered racially inferior;
in thus debasing labor, he destroyed the possibility of a meaningful
contact with the earth.[70]

Berry's essay helps us analyze the relationship between contempt for agricultural work, slavery, and the loss of agrarian virtues, the three closely
connected components of Columella's critique of Rome's actual practice as
distinct from its lofty rhetoric.

There are, of course, significant differences between the Greco-
Roman world of the first century and the modern world presupposed by
Berry's argument. Rome's pre-industrial economy was largely dependent
upon agriculture, which meant that a large portion of the population
was involved in some way with agricultural production. In the modern
world, farming has increasingly become industrialized, resulting in fewer and fewer people having any meaningful relationship to the land that
sustains us.

Slavery in antiquity was, moreover, not based upon race as it was in
the United States; thus Berry's argument concerning the legacy of racism
vis-à-vis agricultural labor does not neatly apply to the Roman context.
Drawing selectively upon Berry's analysis, however, does illumine what
ancient sources such as Pliny and Columella suggest without argument,
namely, that a system of agriculture dependent upon slave labor necessarily results in contempt for agriculture and a concomitant loss of the
agrarian virtues necessary for the sustained health of the land and the
communities that depend upon it.[71]

If this analysis is correct, then we can say that first-century Rome
was a society whose cultural context and elevated rhetoric was deeply
at odds with its economic context and actual practice, especially insofar as agriculture is concerned. The Greco-Roman cultural ideal of the
good king—embodied in Rome's emperor—was a figure through whose
divinely sanctioned virtue the golden age had been restored, and who
moreover was able to transmit and inculcate this virtue among his subjects. Thus the agricultural fecundity represented tangibly by the *annona civica* would have been touted by the purveyors of Roman political

mythology as the achievement of the emperor's virtues, which in his role as benefactor he transmitted to his subjects. Yet the economic reality told a different story, of the exploitation of both land and people resulting in the steady decline in the health of the land and the virtues required to sustain it. It was into such a society, laden with contradictions and *de facto* if largely unrecognized hypocrisies, that the Apostle Paul's religiously charged letter would land.

1.3. Israel's Scriptures and the Agrarian Vocation

Besides the Roman cultural and social context, however, Paul's letter to the church in Rome was deeply formed by a theological perspective quite different from that of the general worldview of the day. Having been trained within the Jewish party of the Pharisees, Paul's worldview was profoundly shaped by the theological tradition of Israel's Scriptures.[72] As Ellen Davis has persuasively demonstrated, that tradition was agrarian in essence, and even if Paul cannot rightly be considered a classic ancient agrarian on the basis of his literary corpus, that essence is nonetheless detectable in his thinking.[73]

This is evident at the most fundamental level in how Paul views material reality—not simply as nature but rather creation, "a single, covenanted unity" in which every creature "is connected to every other creature by the great web of life that Isaiah and other biblical writers call *běrît ʿōlām*, a reality that is comprehensive in space and time."[74] Thus Paul attributes agency to creation itself, an entity which is capable of eager longing and groaning, of being subject to, and liberated from, futility (Rom 8:19–23). Paul's argument thus reveals an awareness of what Davis calls "the Bible's distinctly *theological* land ethic," the basic elements of which are the following:

> that humans and land exist in a biotic unity before God, that their unity has identifiable moral dimensions (faithful action, truth, righteousness), that the moral restoration of God's people elicits God's gracious response in the form of agricultural productivity, and further . . . that human righteousness is the one condition that invites and even makes possible God's continued presence in the land.[75]

Several important features of the biblical metanarrative reflect what might be called this "theological land ethic": the uniquely human challenge, as God's image-bearers, to care for creation; the economic implications for

God's covenant people as stewards of God's creation; and the prophetic summons to repentance as crucial to the restoration of creation.[76] This narrative tradition, and the theological commentaries on it, provide the resources to foster the agrarian virtues required by the health of the land and the communities that live upon it.

The metanarrative of Scripture begins with a poetic account of creation that portrays the complex interrelationship between God, humans, and the rest of creation. To put it thus is already to acknowledge the distinction between humans and the creation of which they are also a part. Humans alone are created in the image of God and tasked with ruling over the non-human creation:

> Then God said, "Let us make humankind in our image, according to our likeness; and let them have dominion [rdh] over the fish of the sea, and over the birds of the air, and over the cattle, and over all the wild animals of the earth, and over every creeping thing that creeps upon the earth." So God created humankind in his image, in the image of God he created them; male and female he created them. God blessed them, and God said to them, "Be fruitful and multiply, and fill the earth and subdue it [kbš]; and have dominion over [rdh] the fish of the sea and over the birds of the air and over every living thing that moves upon the earth." (Gen 1:26–28)

This passage has been read as constituting the basis of an anthropocentric view of reality responsible for the present ecological crisis.[77] Context, however, argues against interpreting the Hebrew verbs rdh and kbš as condoning humans' violent exploitation of creation. Davis argues that the verb rdh connotes the exercise of *communal* power and should be translated "have mastery among" the creatures, indicating the nature of conformity to God's image. The verb kbš indicates the exercise of mastery, but the command must be heard in the particular historical context in which this text most likely received its written form, Israel's exile from the land as a consequence of disobedience to YHWH. The command to conquer is therefore not triumphalistic but ironic, moving those shaped by the biblical story to reevaluate their present circumstances and exercise moral judgment, realizing both that humans have a role in maintaining the order established by God, and that land can be lost as a result of disobedience to God.[78]

Furthermore, if we respect the canonical shape of Scripture, we are led to read the complementary accounts of creation in Genesis 1 and

Genesis 2 as comprising a theological unity, despite their disparate details and composition histories.[79] In Genesis 2:15, the first human (*adam*) made from humus (*adamah*) is set in the garden of Eden "to till and keep it" (*lĕ 'obĕdāh ûlĕšomĕrāh*), a phrase Davis translates, "to work and serve it, to preserve and observe it."[80] Thus the divine command for humans to exercise mastery among creation must also reflect the divine command to serve the land, learning from it and respecting its limits.

The sharp narrative turn in Genesis 3 suggests something of the nature of those limits as well as the limits of what it means for humans uniquely to be created in God's image, an expression that connotes both functional and intrinsic aspects of human nature. Functionally, humans are commanded to rule over creation in God's stead, serving as God's vicegerents; yet humans also intrinsically bear God's image, extending God's presence into the whole of creation. This distinct aspect of human nature surely also tells us something about God, who, by creating humans in the *imago Dei*, enters into a unique, and limited, power-sharing relationship with them.[81] "Godlikeness" is not a status to be achieved, but rather bespeaks a commitment on the part of both humans and God to a life together.[82] In Genesis 3, humans fail to take their appropriate place in the world because of a failure to perceive the proper way to be like God. By contrast, the seventh day depicted in Genesis 2:2–3 shows the proper way, "the paradigmatic exercise of God's own dominion of delight."[83]

If humans, in the function of representing God's image in the world, are tasked with working and serving the land even as we observe and learn from it (Gen 2:15), what potential economic implications follow? Reflecting on the etymology of the word *economics*, it is appropriate to ask: If creation is God's household (*oikos*), by what principle (*nomos*) should humans steward that household? Ellen Davis makes the case that the biblical vision for proper land use is predicated upon the existence of local economies measured by the standards of self-sufficiency and permanence.[84] The biblical idea of a local economy is captured in the complex of ideas behind the Hebrew word *naḥălâ*, referring to land held in trust for successive generations on the condition of obedience to YHWH, a term expressing the "spirituality" of the Israelite village.[85] Only by means of "kindly use" and the "economics of permanence," in contrast to the economics of exploitation and extraction, could farmers gain intimate knowledge of their land and so make it prosper and hand it on to successive generations.[86]

These same agrarian values presupposed in the concept of *naḥălâ* are reflected in the law codes in Exodus 21–23, in which land care is presented as a dimension of covenant life. The first concern expressed within these codes, setting limits upon slavery, points to the economic fragility of the small holder and ensures that the vulnerable are bound to the community (Exod 21:1–11).[87] The command to observe a sabbatical year reminds Israel that land is God's domain, placing an ethical obligation upon the people to recognize God's ultimate ownership, thus reinforcing the idea of stewardship (Exod 23:10–13). Elsewhere in the Torah we observe that even the land itself cares how it is used and can "vomit out" people for misuse (Lev 18:25–28).

When Israel fails in its vocation to care for the land—largely through the failure of its leaders to exercise faithfulness to the covenant with YHWH—the agrarian poetry of prophets such as Amos and Hosea fuels the call for social and economic change entailed in a return to covenant fidelity. Their challenge to royal authority is so radical as to "envision the end of kingship and even of Israel's tenure in the land."[88] In their prophetic poetry one finds the convictions that soil is God's gift, Israel's relationship to soil is fundamental, and that Israel's misuse of the gift of land ultimately results in the undoing of political structures.[89]

These searing critiques were rooted in historical realities. Prior to the eighth century, Israelite agriculture consisted of diversified, self-sustaining small farms on marginal lands in upland villages connected by cooperative trade networks. The expansionist regimes of Jeroboam II of Israel (ca. 786–746 BCE) and Uzziah of Judah (ca. 785–733 BCE) saw the large-scale transformation of land and the rural economy. Small-scale subsistence farming was replaced by commodity agriculture controlled by the crown, designed to maximize production of grain to feed the cities, and of wine and oil for both export revenue and luxury consumption.[90] These changes required increased taxation-in-kind, conscripted labor, and appropriation of valuable metals for military use—quite literally the turning of plowshares into swords, the reverse of the prophetic call (Isa 2:4; Mic 4:3; but cf. Joel 3:10).

These developments in turn resulted in growing latifundialization and absentee landowners, as the crown gained the land of failing farmers. Families no longer self-sufficient found themselves forced to buy staples such as grain on the market, yet without the ethical constraints previously known by trading within a kinship network. In response to these changes, Amos' "soil-centered" prophecy critiques Israel's political leaders for "centralizing power and extracting wealth from people who are treated as subjects, not citizens" (Amos 9:14–15).[91] Amos calls for a return to the constitutional ideal that all Israel had a right to participate in the soil, reinforcing the belief that "Israel's political disorder is a disturbance of creation itself" (Amos 4:13; 5:8–9; 9:5–6).[92]

Hosea, using the literary convention of seeing the female body as a representation of the social body in its vulnerability, employs the trope of fornication to criticize the way in which "the religious establishment lends respectability to the market economy, which sets the state's interests over those of the people" (Hos 1:2; 4:12–13).[93] He also criticizes the use of sanctuaries as warehouses in commodity agriculture, whereby priests as state employees issued loans to farmers and collected grain taxes in kind that were then stored, redistributed, processed, or exported (Hos 4:10–11; 7:14). Finding a parallel between humans' behavior towards each other and towards the earth, Hosea "envisions renewal in the form of a divinely initiated covenant, a bond of affection and responsibility, which here explicitly links Israel with every living creature" (Hos 2:18–19a, 21–22; cf. Jer 31:31; Mark 14:24).[94] For Hosea, it is thus the renewal of the covenant that brings forth the bounty of the land. His prophecy does not end with destruction but holds forth hope in repentance,

> a change of thought and action rooted in love, which includes, but extends far beyond, the personal sphere. The highest agrarian priority, then, is the cultivation of affectionate minds . . . when affection is fully developed, it becomes an *economic* disposition, orienting our desires to the Source of life.[95]

The agrarian poetry of Israel's prophets thus reminds its audience of the economic implications of repentance and the call to return to its covenant vocation, the responsible stewardship of God's creation. As Paul read these prophets, he would have seen in their critique of Israel a critique that could be equally applied to first-century Rome—a failure to exercise communal power among God's creatures in a way that appropriately bears God's image throughout creation. He would have been skeptical, however, of the sunny optimism of imperial propaganda proclaiming the fiction of a return to a golden age. The theological context in which Paul makes his argument to the church in Rome is thus based not on an optimistic assessment of present conditions or dominant political rhetoric, but rather on a distinctive eschatological hope.

2. Suffering, Endurance, Hope, and the Inculcation of Virtue in Romans 5–8

Three key contexts for the Epistle to the Romans have thus been established. First, Roman imperial propaganda lauded the arrival of a golden age of agricultural fecundity, established on the merits of the emperor's divinely channeled virtues. Second, Roman agricultural practices, especially slavery and tenant farming, imperiled and diminished the agrarian virtues required to sustain the health of the land and the communities that tended the land. Paul's intended audience thus would have experienced cognitive dissonance as they sought to reconcile the gap between high Roman propaganda and unsavory practice. Third, Israel's Scriptures provided both Paul and his audience with a critical counternarrative to that of Rome, one that could both espouse agrarian virtues and look to the future rather than fulfillment and triumph in the present.

The difference between Paul's theological/eschatological perspective and that of Roman "golden age" imperial propaganda is crucial. In contrast to the thoroughgoing, triumphalist, presentist eschatology of Rome, Paul looked forward to an eschatological fulfillment that lay in the future. Nevertheless, the future had at least partially arrived for Paul as a consequence of the Messiah's resurrection and heavenly reign.[96] To be part of the church, the heavenly *politeuma*, is to live in the Messiah's unfolding reign, in anticipation of the *parousia*, the Messiah's appearing at the *eschaton*. To live in anticipation of this eschatological fulfillment is to put on—to "clothe oneself" with, as Paul says elsewhere—the virtues that properly characterize life in God's kingdom (Eph 4:24; Col 3:10–14). Paul can also refer to this process as "clothing oneself" with the Messiah himself (Gal 3:27). In Romans, Paul describes this as being glorified with the Messiah (8:17). This task of eschatological anticipation, of transformation into the character of the Messiah, of glorification, even in the present when his kingdom has not fully arrived, requires the virtues of hope and endurance.

The way these two virtues—hope and endurance—relate to each other in Paul's mind emerges in a simple, yet revealing, analysis of his language. Paul's use of *hypomonē* (patient endurance) and *elpis* (hope) and cognate terms throughout the argument of Romans are often correlated, appearing together four times: Romans 5:2–5; 8:20–25; 12:12; 15:4–5.[97] Additionally, terms denoting suffering are also frequently correlated with *hypomonē* and *elpis*: *thlipsis* in Romans 2:9; 5:3; 8:35; 12:12; and *pathēma* in Romans 8:18. This pattern suggests at the outset that the virtues of patient endurance and hope are virtually inseparable in Paul's thinking, and furthermore that these virtues are acquired or practiced in the context of suffering. Moreover, these three terms, tightly grouped together, serve as bookends for Paul's argument in Romans 5–8:

> we boast in our hope (*ep' elpidi*) of sharing the glory of God. And not only that, but we also boast in our sufferings (*en tais thlipsesin*), knowing that suffering (*thlipsis*) produces endurance (*hypomonēn*), and endurance (*hypomonē*) produces character, and character produces hope (*elpida*), and hope (*elpis*) does not disappoint us, because God's love has been poured into our hearts through the Holy Spirit that has been given to us. (Rom 5:2b–5).

> I consider that the sufferings (*pathēmata*) of this present time are not worth comparing with the glory about to be revealed to us. . . . For in hope (*elpidi*) we were saved. Now hope (*elpis*) that is seen is not hope (*elpis*). For who hopes (*elpizei*) for what is seen? But if we hope (*elpizomen*) for what we do not see, we wait for it with patience (*di' hypomonēs*). (Rom 8:18, 24–25)

Understanding more deeply the profound relationship between endurance and hope within the argument of Romans 5–8, then, is integral to grasping the church's central task of living in eschatological anticipation.

In Romans 1–4, the beginnings of the letter, Paul is concerned with justification, and in Romans 5–8 with glorification. The relationship between these two terms and the two sections of Romans is the following: if one has been justified—brought into right covenant standing—through the faithfulness of the Messiah Jesus (Rom 1–4), then one may confidently hope to be glorified—transformed into the very character of the Messiah (Rom 5–8).[98] To grasp the role of hope in Romans 5–8, then, we must look back to Romans 4, in which Paul first introduces the theme of hope as it applies to the covenant's original recipient, Abraham. Paul recalls that God promised that Abraham would inherit the world (4:13). This promise was made, not on the basis of law, but on the basis of faith, so that it would encompass all who are children of Abraham by faith. Abraham's faith is demonstrated in that he believed, "hoping against hope" (*par' elpida ep' elpidi*, 4:18) in God's promise to provide him a family despite his old age and Sarah's barrenness. Therefore, on account of his faith, it was reckoned to him as righteousness (*eis dikaiosunēn*, 4:22), right standing in the covenant.[99]

Like Abraham, the adherents of the new covenant have been justified on the basis of faith and thus, Paul claims at the beginning of Romans 5, we are at peace with God and hope to share in God's future glory (5:1–2). Yet Paul is keen to make plain that this hope is not, as in Roman imperial propaganda, merely a sunny fictionalized version of present reality. Paul is not, in other words, attempting to tell his readers that they should ignore the suffering all around them and pretend that they are living in the present golden age. Rather, he foregrounds the reality of suffering; it is something to be celebrated, not because it is a good in itself, but because it leads to the virtues of patience, character, and ultimately hope (5:3–5). And hope, again in contrast with imperial propaganda, is essential because it provides the vision that guides action in the present reality. Yet surely Paul must realize that he has made a claim that, on the face of it, is nearly absurd. As in his letter to the church in Philippi, Paul must address the conventional wisdom that suffering is normally taken not as grounds for hope but rather as cause for despair.[100] So Paul is now at pains to demonstrate why his claim that hope can only be grounded in suffering is reasonable. This he does in the course of chapters 5–8.

To that end, Paul begins by clarifying the nature of the kind of hope he is urging on his readers. He argues from the lesser to the greater: if believers have been justified by the Messiah's death, how much more will they be saved by his life (5:9–10)? This future salvation, for which believers hope, consists in "reigning" in life through the one man, Jesus (*en zōē basileusousin dia tou henos Iēsou Christou*, 5:17), in blatant contrast to the reign of death resulting from Adam's transgression (5:12–14). This stark comparison between Adam and the Messiah in this passage identifies the future reigning in the Messiah with the regaining of what was lost through Adam's sin. Indeed, for Paul, Adam is a type of the one who would come, namely the Messiah (5:14). This comparison also strongly suggests—but stops just short of clearly declaring—that the glory of God referred to in 5:2 consists in reigning over creation in the Messiah exactly as Adam, and from him all humanity, were originally created to do. Thus, what has occurred as a result of the Messiah's obedience is a change in status, from the dominion of death brought on by sin to reigning in life. This dramatic transformation then raises an important question for the reader: does this change in status necessarily entail a change in behavior?

Paul responds to this implicit question in chapter 6 by outlining a process whereby humans come to live differently in light of the radically altered condition. The process begins with baptism, which confers the new status that Paul has just described. Baptism is the reason one need not, indeed cannot, live as though still under the dominion of sin. Using the analogy of the likeness between a seed and the plant that grows from it, Paul implies that sharing in the Messiah's death through baptism leads to sharing in the resurrection (6:5). New status ineluctably leads to new behavior, not as a matter of choice but of nature—just as the plant inevitably grows from the seed.

The next step in the process entails reckoning, or calculating, that one is dead to sin and alive to God in the Messiah (6:11). Paul does not elaborate this point, but it appears he envisions the reasoned evaluation of possibilities newly available to one—or no longer available—by virtue of one's changed status. Finally, one must engage in bodily disciplines: refraining from presenting "limbs and organs" (*ta melē humōn*) to sin, but rather turning them to God (6:13, 19; cf. 7:5). The end result is sanctification (*hagiasmos*, 6:22), that is, receiving, or experiencing, the life of the ages (*to de telos zōēn aiōnion*, 6:23).[101] This is the "hope of the glory of God" of which Paul spoke earlier (5:2), namely the coming age of the Messiah's reign, in which the present hope of glory will be finally realized.

And yet, as Paul clarifies in chapters 7–8, this life, promised but not delivered by Torah, is already partially realized in the present through the Spirit. Former enslavement to sin (6:17–18) has been replaced by "enslavement" to the new life of the Spirit (7:6).[102] Indeed, it is the law of the Spirit of life in the Messiah Jesus that has freed his followers from the law of sin and death (8:2).[103] Recalling his argument in chapter 6, Paul now makes clear that it is the Spirit that puts to death the deeds of the body and enables life (8:13). Thus, it is the Spirit that enables the process of moral transformation. The Spirit also bears witness that the Messiah's adherents are God's children and hence, heirs (8:14).

And with this claim, Paul now returns at last to his surprising claim in Romans 5:3, that suffering is not to be avoided or despised but rather celebrated as a true means to hope. Here he states, equally surprisingly, that glorification with the Messiah is actually dependent upon suffering with him (8:17). Yet such suffering is incomparable with the scale of the glory to be revealed unto (or possibly "in") those who believe (*eis hēmas*, 8:18). The prepositional phrase *eis hēmas* indicates that the glory will actually appear embodied in these persons, that is, with their transformation into the character of the Messiah, they can properly undertake the divinely bestowed task of stewarding creation. Suffering, in other words, is to be celebrated because it is the means by which the human vocation is realized.

The hoped-for result is that "creation itself will be set free from its bondage to decay and will obtain the freedom of the glory of the children of God" (8:21). By way of explanation of the certainty of this result—"for we know" (*oidamen gar*)—Paul introduces the metaphor of labor pains to remind his audience of something they apparently already—or perhaps merely should—know: that any "new birth" comes only after pain and suffering. So, in exactly the same way, it is evident "that the whole creation has been groaning in labor pains until now" (8:22).

What is Paul hoping to explain with this crucial metaphor? Each of the three previous sentences (8:18, 19, 20) begins with the explanatory particle *gar*, suggesting that in these verses Paul is endeavoring to explain his startling claim in 8:17, namely that suffering is *necessary* for glorification. If so, then by the logic of the metaphor of labor pains, suffering is necessarily entailed because something new—something cosmically new—is being brought to birth. One form of existence (the gestating fetus) must painfully be brought to an end, and a new form (the baby) is violently brought forth.

It is indeed fitting that Paul concludes his argument regarding glorification in Romans 5–8 with the help of this metaphor, as the idea of pregnancy and childbirth appears to have been on his mind since the conclusion of his argument regarding justification in Romans 1–4. There, Abraham serves as a pivotal transition figure. As the quintessential example of faith, he serves as the father for all those who are justified by faith, thus bringing to conclusion Paul's argument that one is brought into right covenantal standing through the faithfulness of the Messiah. Yet as one who "hoped against hope" in Yhwh's promise for a child in the face of Sarah's barrenness, Abraham also serves to introduce Paul's argument that those who have been justified through the Messiah can indeed confidently hope to be glorified—as confidently as Abraham and Sarah now hoped for the promised child.

The use of childbirth imagery as bookends for the argument in Romans 5–8—hope for pregnancy at one end, the pangs of labor pain at the other—encourages us to look more broadly at the metaphor of childbirth in order to understand the relationship between suffering, hope, and endurance in this section of Romans. Consider first the imagery of labor pains.[104] The suffering of labor pains requires both endurance—the ability to persevere in the midst of persistent pain—and hope—a confident vision of the new life that lies on the other side of pain. Just as suffering is intrinsic to the process of giving birth, Paul suggests that the future glorification and the liberation of creation necessarily entails suffering.[105]

This would explain why the suffering entailed in glorification *requires* endurance and hope, but it does not go far towards explaining why suffering is required *so that* (*hina*) believers may be glorified with the Messiah (8:17). Therefore, to understand this aspect of suffering, consider the following question: How is it that a woman acquires the virtues of hope and endurance that enable her to persevere through the hours (and sometimes days) of labor? The answer surely is to be found somewhere in the nine months preceding labor, as the mother-to-be learns to hope and endure through the daily trials and discomforts of pregnancy. This is the notion of suffering Paul has in mind in Romans 5:2–5, the catalyst for acquiring virtues of character. Thus, in order to endure with hope the pangs of labor, one must have already cultivated the virtues of hope and endurance through pregnancy, aware of the real pain that is to come.

Suffering, then, is necessary because it is intrinsic to the process of giving birth. But suffering, because it cultivates hope and endurance, is *also* necessary because it cultivates the virtues needed for giving birth. In other words, we can say both that suffering *requires* hope and endurance and that the cultivation of hope and endurance *requires* suffering. This is not to valorize suffering for its own sake, but simply to acknowledge that the virtues of hope and endurance cannot be cultivated except through suffering. This is so by definition: we can only hope for that which we suffer the absence, and we can only endure that through which we suffer pain.[106]

Looking at suffering, hope, and endurance from the perspective of childbirth—as Paul's use of childbirth imagery prompts us to do—explains why celebrating in the midst of suffering, his surprising claim in Romans 5:3, is indeed rational—and not simply masochistic or delusional, as some would claim.[107] Hope and endurance are the virtues required to live in anticipation of the eschatological fulfillment of the Messiah's reign, of the glorification of the children of God and the attendant liberation of all creation.

3. Hope and Endurance as Agrarian Virtues

But how can these virtues be considered "agrarian" in any meaningful sense? To describe the virtues of hope and endurance as agrarian is to say that they are fundamentally concerned with the proper relationship of people to land and with the health of both. This can be understood by attending to Paul's distinctive already-inaugurated eschatological perspective, a vision that contrasts sharply with the superficially similar presentist eschatology of the Roman Empire. Rome boasted the present reality of a golden age of agricultural fecundity secured by the emperor's virtues. Because the golden age was understood to already exist in the present, it required neither hope nor endurance. One neither hopes for, nor endures the privation of, that which one already possesses. Yet, Roman agricultural practices like slavery and tenant farming both betrayed the falsity of this boast while at the same time actually eroding the agrarian virtues that truly foster land health.

By contrast, Paul's already-inaugurated but yet-unrealized eschatology looks to the future for the restoration of creation while at the same time understanding that the church has a crucial task in the present of anticipating that eschatological fulfillment, which has been telescoped partially into the present through the Messiah's resurrection and heavenly reign.[108] Inaugurated eschatology thus requires the virtue of hope in order to see a possible future that is radically different than the present, and it requires the virtue of endurance in order to patiently live out a life that anticipates the new age that God will bring into existence even amidst contrary present realities.

This liberation of creation from its "bondage to decay" (Rom 8:21) therefore necessarily entails a re-envisioning of humankind's relationship to land, which in turn requires a re-envisioning of economics. This is so because land was the backbone of the Roman economy: it was the source not only of basic human sustenance, but also of the surplus that fueled Rome's vast economic, political, and cultural activity. Thus the human relationship to land was inescapably economic. But what is the true subject matter of economics? Aristotle distinguished between two closely related terms, "*oikonomia*" and "*chrematistics*," the former concerning the ordering of a household, the latter concerning the accumulation of wealth (*Pol.* 1257a–1258a).[109] Herman E. Daly describes the distinction thus:

> Oikonomia is the science or art of efficiently producing, distributing, and maintaining concrete use values for the household and

community over the long run. Chrematistics is the art of maximiz-
ing the accumulation by individuals of abstract exchange value in
the form of money in the short run.[110]

Using this distinction, the Roman relationship to land was over-
whelmingly "chrematistic"—aimed at the acquisition of monetary wealth
through the exploitation of human labor through practices (slavery and
tenant farming) that deprived those who cultivated the land of a share in
its bounty. This is not surprising given Rome's presentist eschatological
perspective: if the present is the best one can hope for, it makes perfect
sense to exploit the land and one's fellow human beings for financial gain.
Therefore, first and foremost, the virtue of hope entails a re-envisioning
of human relationship to land, measured not according to the standard
of chrematistic exploitation, but according to the standard of economic
stewardship.

If Paul is not thinking directly about the economic implications of the
liberation of creation, such concerns may be seen hovering in the background, visible in the way Paul casts his argument in Romans 6–8 in terms
of Israel's liberation from slavery in Egypt. N. T. Wright has argued exten-
sively that the "new-exodus" theme lies behind the entire exposition of
this portion of the letter:

> In Romans 6, those who are 'in the Messiah' are brought from slavery
> to freedom; in Romans 7, the story takes us to Mount Sinai; then
> in Romans 8 . . . the Messiah's people are 'led', not by the cloud and
> fire, but by the spirit, and, assured of that 'sonship' which is itself an
> exodus-blessing, they are on the way to the 'inheritance'.[111]

Wright's interpretation of Romans 6 is particularly apposite: he finds in
Paul's presentation of baptism an echo of Israel crossing the Red Sea in
their flight from Egypt. "[T]he Messiah's people [believers in the new
covenant] are therefore the new-exodus people, the freed former slaves,
who have to learn new habits of heart and body commensurate with their
freedom."[112] With the exodus story in the background, these "new habits
of heart and body" appear in direct opposition to the ways the economic
system of slavery forms (or deforms) the human person.

This dramatic contrast between Israel's newly found freedom and its
former life of slavery in Egypt is on display in the manna narrative in Exodus 16. Yhwh's provision of food for Israel in the wilderness seeks to heal

Israel from "Egypt's disease" by both gift and test, providing radically different economic principles to separate Israel from Egypt, a totalitarian regime in which the land was worked by slaves, the grain belonged to royal granaries, and the surplus went to the elites. Israel must thus learn a "new moral economy of food production and distribution" characterized by restraint rather than hoarding, and Sabbath rather than slave-production.[113] Ellen Davis concludes, "Because food procurement and consumption constitute the most essential economic act within every culture, they may be seen as the first and best test of such a healthful conformity; that is the logic underlying this first story of the people Israel in freedom."[114]

Egypt and Rome, the closest approximations in the ancient world to the modern industrial society, bore many resemblances to each other: both possessed a dominant military, extracted forced labor, were characterized by extreme economic inequality, and practiced industrial agriculture. So as Paul reflected upon Israel's need to unlearn the habits they acquired as slaves in Egypt, he may well have been led to consider the ways in which the church had been shaped by the economic practices of the dominant superpower of his own day.

Paul's hope that "the creation itself will be set free from its bondage to decay" as it obtains "the freedom of the glory of the children of God" (8:21) reflects his awareness that the Roman fiction of the present golden age was unsustainable. This was the case not only because it was built upon a falsehood, but more importantly because it was sustained by economic practices—slavery and tenant farming—that perpetuated creation's bondage to decay. An unsustainable system will eventually reach the point of collapse. Wendell Berry's remarks on the unsustainability of the present economic order pertain equally to that of ancient Rome:

> We must be aware too of the certainty that the present way of things will eventually fail. If it fails quickly, by any of several predicted causes, then we will have no need, being absent, to worry about what to do next. If it fails slowly, and if we have been careful to preserve the most necessary and valuable things, then it may fail into a restoration of community life—that is, into understanding of our need to help and comfort each other.[115]

Paul's admonitions in Romans 13 to obey civil authority indicate that he did not anticipate the precipitous collapse of the Roman Empire. Rather, his ubiquitous exhortations to the church to form themselves into a radically alternative community—in Romans 12 and throughout his other letters—suggest that he envisioned the slow collapse of the Roman order. Thus he exhorts the church in Rome to cultivate hope and endurance, the virtues that enable a community to both perceive and continue steadfastly in "the most necessary and valuable things" in the midst of a ruinous economic system. Insofar as these virtues are directed toward the liberation of creation from the ruinous agricultural and economic practices of Rome, hope and endurance can be described as agrarian virtues.

CHAPTER 6

PAUL AND THE GOOD LIFE

Contemporary Conversations

1. Incompatible Narratives

The African church father Tertullian (ca. 160–225) was well acquainted with the suffering of the church. In its early days, the church was regarded by Rome as a sect within Judaism and thus initially enjoyed the religious toleration generally extended toward that religion. However, as Christians and Jews gradually parted ways over the first two centuries of the common era, Christians came increasingly under persecution. Initially, the persecution was sporadic and localized, but eventually the church suffered periods of intense state-sanctioned persecution for their allegiance to Jesus as king, which they had come to regard as incompatible with allegiance to Rome's emperor.[1]

In the final chapter of his *Apology* (ca. 197), written in the context of increasing (although not yet empire-wide) persecution, Tertullian likens the Christian's attitude toward suffering to the soldier's desire for war. Neither would willingly choose to suffer, but like the soldier, the Christian fights willingly, "and when victorious, rejoices in the battle" (*Apol.* 50).[2] Yet unlike soldiers, who wage war with the sword, the Christians "battle for the truth" before the tribunal, making a rational defense, an *apology*, for their embodied allegiance to Jesus. Yet victory in such a battle is paradoxical in nature:

> But the day is won when the object of the struggle is gained. This
> victory of ours gives us the glory of pleasing God, and the spoil of

life eternal. But we are overcome. Yes, when we have obtained our
wishes. Therefore we conquer in dying; we go forth victorious at the
very time we are subdued. (*Apol.* 50)

Likening the Christian willingness to suffer to a "victory robe" and a "triumphal car," Tertullian insists that persecution will not destroy the church. On
the contrary, he presciently declares: "The oftener we are mown down by you,
the more in number we grow; the blood of Christians is seed" (*Apol.* 50).

Less than half a century later, the situation had changed dramatically.
On October 28, 312, Constantine marched with an army towards Rome
to face his rival Maxentius. The night prior he had experienced a vision
in which he was instructed to fight under the sign of the cross, which he
did. Attributing his victory over Maxentius at the Battle of the Milvian
Bridge to the Christian God, Constantine converted to Christianity. In
his position as senior ruler over the Roman Empire, Constantine quickly
extended imperial favor to this erstwhile persecuted religion. Through the
so-called Edict of Milan in 313, Christians were officially granted freedom
to worship, and previously confiscated church property was returned. By
325, when Constantine summoned the Council of Nicaea to resolve the
Arian controversy, it had become clear that Christianity was henceforth
to enjoy the closest of relations with the Roman empire. "Victory" for the
church would no longer be axiomatically equated with suffering.

This shift can be seen in Eusebius' "Tricennial Oration," written by
the fourth-century church historian in celebration of the thirtieth year of
Emperor Constantine's reign. Redolent with the language of victory and
virtue, this panegyric resonates with the Roman "theology of victory." Eusebius portrays Christ as the true cosmic king, the victor *par excellence*,
who has triumphed over every power arrayed against him:

> Who else has power to make war after death, to triumph over every
> enemy, to subjugate each barbarous and civilized nation and city,
> and to subdue his adversaries with an invisible and secret hand?
> (*Laud. Const.* 17.11)[3]

Moreover, through his victory, Eusebius claims, Christ has established a
golden age, "that universal peace . . . established by his power throughout
all the world . . . the mutual concord and harmony of all nations" (*Laud.
Const.* 17.12). This king is, moreover, as virtuous as he is victorious. Indeed, Eusebius takes Christ's virtue to be the proof of his divine power:

The day itself would fail me, gracious emperor, should I attempt to exhibit in a single view those cogent proofs of our Saviour's Divine power which even now are visible in their effects; for no human being, in civilized or barbarous nations, has ever yet exhibited such power of Divine virtue as our Saviour. (*Laud. Const.* 17.12)

Eusebius, however, is not interested merely in asserting the cosmic lordship of Christ; he further claims that Constantine's own victorious and virtuous reign mirrors that of Christ. Constantine's victory over his foes is the result of divine enablement:

Such were the dealings of the Supreme Sovereign, who ordained an invincible champion to be the minister of his heaven-sent vengeance (for our emperor's surpassing piety delights in the title of Servant of God), and him he has proved victorious over all that opposed him, having raised him up, an individual against many foes. (*Laud. Const.* 7.12)

This victorious and now Christian Roman emperor is portrayed, as we might expect, as a paragon of divinely bestowed virtue, "gifted as he is by God with native virtues, and having received into his soul the outflowings of his favor" (*Laud. Const.* 5.1). There is, finally, a correlation between Constantine's virtue and his imperial power. Unlike vicious men who obtain power "through despotic violence," Constantine's reign is the just reward for virtue: "And truly may he deserve the imperial title, who has formed his soul to royal virtues, according to the standard of that celestial kingdom" (*Laud. Const.* 5.2).

Just as Christ's victorious and virtuous reign has resulted in a golden age of concord and harmony, in Eusebius' view, so too has Constantine's:

Thus speedily, according to the counsel of the mighty God, and through our emperor's agency, was every enemy, whether visible or unseen, utterly removed: and henceforward peace, the happy nurse of youth, extended her reign throughout the world. (*Laud. Const.* 8.9)

The ultimate effect is the spread of divine virtue throughout the empire:

Such are the blessings resulting to mankind from this great and wondrous Sign, by virtue of which the evils which once existed are now no more, and virtues heretofore unknown shine everywhere resplendent with the light of true godliness. (*Laud. Const.* 10.3)[4]

In so portraying both Christ and Constantine as rulers whose victory and virtue are inextricably bound, Eusebius is adopting and "christianizing" the very same "theology of victory" that Rome had used for centuries to legitimize imperial rule. This move is both understandable and problematic.

On the one hand, how could the church have refused the opportunity to join hands with the political order and take responsibility for the good government of society? Lesslie Newbigin insists: "It could not do so if it was to be faithful to its origins in Israel and in the ministry of Jesus."[5] It was entirely appropriate, in other words, for the church that saw itself as the "heavenly *politeuma*" (Phil 3:20) to take an active role in the governance of the earthly *polis* in view of Christ's inauguration of God's heavenly kingdom on earth. Even if it can be justly said that the cause of the gospel has suffered as a result of the Constantinian synthesis of church and state, nevertheless the impulse accords with Paul's vision of human flourishing under the present-and-coming reign of Christ.

One can thus understand Eusebius' overly eager correlation between Constantine's reign and the fullness of Christ's coming reign. And yet, Eusebius' appropriation of the Roman theology of victory is misguided for at least two reasons. In the first place, Eusebius would seem guilty of the same eschatological miscalculation observable in Roman imperial ideology—too much emphasis on the *already* and insufficient recognition of the *not yet*. Second, like some of the recipients of Paul's letters, Eusebius appears to have lost sight of Jesus as a *suffering* king.

Although Christians were no longer dying for their allegiance to Jesus as they had a half-century earlier, Eusebius would have done well to recall Tertullian's assertion—"we conquer in dying" (*Apol.* 50). Tertullian's insight was true not merely in reference to the persecution and suffering of Christians at that particular time, but rather captured the essence of Christ's paradoxical kingship. To give one's embodied allegiance—*pistis*, or faith—to Jesus meant, to Tertullian as it had to Paul, to follow Jesus in the way of suffering. To identify the Messiah's victory over death and evil with the political and military victories of a human leader represented, therefore, a false turn for the church.[6] In thus lauding Constantine for inaugurating a new golden age through his victory and virtue, Eusebius betrays a grievous failure of imagination. By this I mean a failure to perceive that Rome's theology of victory and Paul's theology of suffering reflect radically incompatible narratives.

The incompatibility between these narratives—in our day no less than in Paul's—gives rise to numerous challenges to those intent on pursuing the life of flourishing under the present-and-coming reign of Jesus. In what follows I explore and respond to some of these challenges with a view to contextualizing Paul's christological vision of the good life for our own time and place.

2. Suffering Citizens: The Antidote to a Theology of Victory

Paul introduces his hymnic narration of Jesus' self-emptying descent with an exhortation to the church in Philippi to "let the same mind be in you that was in Christ Jesus" (Phil 2:5). To think thus is to allow Jesus' narrative to shape their own identity as citizens of a heavenly *politeuma* loyal to a suffering king. Moreover, Paul's intent here is to form his audience missionally, to enable them to function as the "hermeneutic of the gospel."[7] To consider the implications of this missional formation for our own time and place, I will first sketch the way in which our own society provides us with an identity-shaping narrative analogous to Rome's theology of victory, a narrative that is incompatible with the gospel.[8] And second, I will suggest how the "public virtue" of suffering, cultivated within the heavenly *politeuma*, might serve as an antidote to the idolatry of victory cultivated within the wider *polis*.

Paul's invitation to participate in the suffering of the Messiah flew in the face of Rome's boast on behalf of its citizens, namely that it had ushered in "on the wings of victory" a golden age of peace and prosperity. Where might we hear echoes of this Roman theology of victory within our own context, and how ought the church counterculturally and indeed subversively to proclaim the good news of the Messiah Jesus in response?

In present-day North America, we do not deify our political leaders for having ushered in a golden age of peace and prosperity.[9] Rather we demand that at least every four years they make exuberant (and often unfulfilled) promises to do so. When Governor Bill Clinton ran for President in 1992, a widely celebrated sign in his campaign headquarters concisely captured the spirit of a pervasive and profoundly influential American narrative: "It's about the Economy, stupid."[10]

Just as Roman citizenship was shaped by the theology of victory, so our identity as citizens of the United States is shaped by the marriage of a capitalist economy and a liberal democratic society. Within a capitalist economy, the human *telos* is to produce and consume goods. This particular human function requires, above all, the limitless *growth* of the economy. Yet the consumption and eventual exhaustion of limited resources within a closed system (the earth) inevitably creates winners and losers.[11] As some economies continue growing, others shrink or even fail. Even within a growing economy, the relentless law of competition often results in individuals and entire communities losing their livelihood.[12] This is accepted as normal, even if unfortunate. Whereas the medieval view of economics was tied to ethics and hence theology, the modern view is of a science whose primary law is covetousness.[13] Thus, as Newbigin observes, "The free market is a good way of balancing supply and demand. If it is absolutized and allowed to rule economic life, it becomes an evil power."[14]

The *telos* of capitalism would therefore, at first blush, appear to be in tension with the ideals of liberal democratic society. Capitalism envisions prosperity for those few who possess or control economic capital. Liberal democratic society's vision is decidedly more universal, founded upon the eighteenth- and nineteenth-century aspiration that the enlightened use of reason will result in the limitless progress of the *entire* society.[15] Yet the concept of citizenship circumscribes the lofty ideals of liberal society by limiting their scope to the citizens of a *particular* nation state. Clinton's 1992 slogans—and the promises of American politicians before and since—assuredly envision prosperity and progress for *American citizens*, not for the world at large. As our fraught national conversation regarding immigration clearly illustrates, citizenship within the United States is regarded as an unalloyed good, a highly esteemed privilege that opens the door to economic opportunity and security, to a "standard of living" envied throughout the world.

It is revealing to reflect upon what is meant by this ubiquitous phrase, "standard of living." When we express a wish for a "higher standard of living," we do not indicate an intention to live according to a higher ethical standard. We merely desire the economic ability to consume more goods and services. That this is unarguably (and unreflectively) the case suggests that the church in North America lives in the tension between two incompatible narratives, each of which seeks to form our identity and demands our allegiance. Citizenship within the terrestrial *polis* (the nation state) holds out the promise of a higher level of consumption to those who share the privilege of citizenship. Citizenship within the heavenly *politeuma* (the church) offers participation in the suffering of Jesus the Messiah, whose death and resurrection has inaugurated on earth God's kingdom, to which is invited the entire human family.

A fundamental tension, if not contradiction, thus follows. Fellowship (*koinōnia*) in suffering is the fundamental virtue (*aretē*) shared within the heavenly *politeuma*, yet it is anathema to citizenship within the modern nation state. Indeed, much of our consumption is aimed at avoiding or alleviating many different sorts of suffering. The pharmaceutical industry offers us freedom from physical pain and suffering, although often at ruinous cost and at the risk of addiction. A vast panoply of technologies spares us from the suffering of physical labor, yet often estranges us from one another and from creation. Staggering sums spent on military defense protect us against the threat of suffering at the hand of enemies, yet frequently result in an equally staggering cost in human lives.

In short, sharing in the sufferings of a crucified Messiah sounds like nonsense within the plausibility structure of a twenty-first-century superpower, much as it did to the citizens of a first-century superpower. First-century Romans looked to a victorious emperor as the guarantor of prosperity; twenty-first-century Americans place our hope rather in a victorious economy.[16] The idolatrous hope placed in victory—whether military, economic, or otherwise—is incompatible with citizenship in the heavenly *politeuma*.

In light of the tension between these two incompatible narratives, I ask: How might we in the church today conduct ourselves as citizens (*politeuein*) worthy of the gospel in such a way as to both unmask this idolatry and bear witness to the public truth of the gospel, namely that even now God's authority is being exercised (if only partially) in the heavenly, or transcendent, realm through the resurrected Messiah?

If Paul, after writing to the church in Philippi, could have traveled through time and space to my own church (St. Andrew's Episcopal Church of Valparaiso, Indiana), he would have observed numerous differences, large and small, between the congregation he found listening to his letter in the present day and the congregation to whom he had originally written.[17] One difference in particular is worthy of comment. Paul wrote to a church that most likely was largely poor, and was suffering economic hardship as a result of their allegiance to Jesus.[18] St. Andrew's is largely, although not exclusively, middle- and upper-middle class. As an aggregate, we suffer comparatively little economic hardship, and what we do is rarely (if at all) attributable to our loyalty to Jesus. This would not describe every church in North America (and certainly not worldwide), yet affluent, un-persecuted churches such as this are hardly unique in our context.

This marked difference in our social location profoundly impacts how we hear Paul's exhortation to sharing in the Messiah's suffering (Phil 1:29; 3:10). For Paul's original audience, this would have been heard as a call to stay the course, to remain faithful *in the midst of present suffering*. For many of us today, we must hear in Paul's letter a challenge *not to avoid the possibility of suffering*. Listening carefully to Paul's "master story," we are not to consider our economic and social status as "something to be exploited" (Phil 2:6). And we must remember that Paul is not enjoining us to pursue a path of individual moral behavior, but rather to behave as cit-izens (*politeuein*) of a heavenly *politeuma*. In practical terms, how might the church's willingness to suffer, viewed as a political act of citizenship, bear witness to the public truth of the gospel?

I have suggested already that we in North America live in a society engineered to insulate us from suffering. This is not necessarily a bad thing, and indeed Paul urges his audience to have regard for the suffer-ings of *others*: "In humility regard others as better than yourselves. Let each of you look not to your own interests, but to the interests of others" (Phil 2:3–4). Yet when it comes to avoiding one's *own* suffering, we must realize that any relative good can be absolutized and turned into an idol. If we in the church in North America were cheerfully to renounce our status and share in the sufferings of the Messiah, we would thereby un-mask our society's idolatry of victory and vividly symbolize the coming of God's kingdom under the rule of the Messiah Jesus. Let me offer one illustration from my own experience of what this might look like in the local congregation.

Over the past half century at least, there has been a steady exodus of wealth from America's urban centers.[19] Many downtown churches, real-izing with dismay that their members must now commute into the city center every Sunday, make the pragmatic decision to relocate to the sub-urbs.[20] The congregation of Calvary Baptist Church, located in the Sanger Heights neighborhood of Waco, Texas, found itself contemplating just such a decision in the early 1990s, but ultimately decided to remain on the corner of 18th and Bosque.[21]

To stay put entailed the possibility of various types of suffering, real and imagined: the loss of members (and their tithing) who wished to worship in a church that was newer, closer to where they lived, and more representative of life in the suburbs; the awkwardness and discomfort of ministering among, and welcoming to worship, a population that was culturally, socially, and economically remarkably different than Calvary's congregation up to that point in time; and the eventual decision faced by not a few of Calvary's members, whether to relocate back into the church's neighborhood. As a consequence of its decision to share in the sufferings of the Messiah by sharing in the sufferings of its own neighborhood, the congregation of Calvary Baptist has become a compelling symbol of the reconciliation now made possible through the Messiah.[22]

What has the story of Calvary Baptist Church to do with the Apostle Paul, missional formation, and citizenship in the heavenly *politeuma*? Let me conclude with the following three points. First, as Aristotle contended and our own experience confirms, citizenship forms identity. The *polis* to which we pledge our allegiance forms, and deforms, our characters in ways both overt and subtle.[23] By choosing to become citizens of the heavenly *politeuma*, we choose to be formed not by an idolatrous theology of victory but rather through sharing in the sufferings of the Messiah.

Second, cultivating the public virtue of suffering bears witness to the public truth of the gospel. While the church is indeed called to proclaim the gospel in both word and deed, it is not likely that our verbal announcement of the worldwide reign of God's crucified and resurrected Messiah will sound remotely plausible in our present cultural context. Yet the *fact* of a people conformed to the image of that Messiah provides a clue to this present reality that cannot so easily be ignored.

And third, as citizens within the heavenly *politeuma* are formed into people who can obediently and cheerfully share in the sufferings of the Messiah and of their neighborhoods, the church will find, with God's grace, that it is also forming a people who can inhabit God's coming kingdom, a people who can wisely and lovingly reign over God's creation, in the power of, and under the leadership of Jesus the king. The church will produce the sort of people who are equipped to solve a host of practical problems that currently appear intractable within our nation and throughout the world.[24] In short, the eschatological fulfillment of the heavenly *politeuma* will probably entail the "suffering" of many who enjoy the privileges of western citizenship, even as it will equally result in the blessing of many who are not citizens of our *polis*.

3. Forming Character When the House Is on Fire

Paul asserts to the church in Corinth that "all of us, with unveiled faces, seeing the glory of the Lord as though reflected in a mirror, are being transformed into the same image" (2 Cor 3:18). As I have argued, Paul believes that in order properly to inhabit the heavenly commonwealth over which Christ rules, the church must be formed into the character of this suffering philosopher-king. This vision of human flourishing depends upon, even as it significantly modifies, the framework of virtue ethics articulated by Aristotle. A number of critiques can and have been leveled against Aristotle's moral theory, and this is not the place to mount a robust defense of virtue ethics.[25] Nevertheless, there is at least one criticism requiring a response, because it fundamentally casts doubt upon whether Paul even thought about ethics in the same way as Aristotle.

We can think about this objection in terms of the perceived propriety of solutions to problems. The problem that all ethical theories address is how to be or become a moral agent. Virtue ethics presents a solution to this problem that takes a great length of time to implement, a lifetime in fact. But what if the proper moral action is called for immediately? What if one simply does not have a lifetime to engage in the slow, deliberate process of forming character? What if, so to speak, the house is on fire?

Actually, virtue ethics has a compelling answer to that question: In order to respond appropriately in a crisis, one must have developed the sort of character that knows automatically the proper thing to do and is able to do it.[26] And yet, I take the force of this criticism to be that the *perception* of being in an acute crisis casts doubt upon the effectiveness of virtue ethics as a guide for moral action. Might it be the case that Paul saw himself as inhabiting a crisis calling for a radical reconsideration of conventional moral wisdom and ultimately a rejection of the framework of virtue ethics?

A number of Pauline scholars have in fact argued this to be the case, claiming that Paul's thought was profoundly influenced by the first-century Jewish "apocalyptic" worldview. Within this worldview, the true nature of reality was disclosed by divine revelation—hence the term "apocalyptic," which derives from the Greek verb *apokaluptō*, "to reveal." Such divine revelation made known that the present created order was soon coming to an end. God's final judgment of the wicked and vindication of the righteous would presently usher in a new blessed age. While the hope for this imminent divine invasion was not uncommon among first-century Jews,

Christians were unique in their belief that the new age had *already* been inaugurated by Christ's death, resurrection, and ascension. Paul clearly believed that he was living in this overlap between two ages and that the church, as recipient of this revelation, was the community "on whom the ends of the ages have come" (1 Cor 10:11).

According to this school of interpretation, Paul understood himself to be living in a house on fire, a crisis requiring a radically new way of thinking about ethics. Paul, it is claimed, held a thoroughly negative view of conventional conceptions of human flourishing because, as he makes plain, "the present form of this world is passing away" (1 Cor 7:31).[27] In light of the advent of Jesus—a truly apocalyptic event, in Paul's perception—radical doubt is cast upon all previous human traditions.[28] Moreover, the imminent return of Jesus to consummate God's kingdom would further render irrelevant any efforts to pursue human flourishing in the present age.

But the problem with virtue ethics from an apocalyptic frame of reference is not merely, as Paul acknowledges, that "the night is far gone, the day is near" (Rom 13:12). It is not simply that time has run out for the lifelong process of forming character. The issue is also whether humans possess the sort of moral agency that character formation requires. In apocalyptic thought, humankind in the present age cannot hope to make genuine moral progress, since all humanity is in the grip of the cosmic power of sin. Paul reflects this view in Romans 5:12–21, in which he speaks of sin and death "as inimical powers or beings that victimize and enslave human beings, and that do so contrary to God's intention for the world."[29] The influence of the malevolent power of Sin (capital S) habituates us ineluctably in the wrong way, making us complicit by our own human acts of sin (small s).[30]

The cosmic invasion of divine grace through the Christ-event changes this state of affairs, of course, but not in a way (it is alleged) that makes moral formation (at least in the way I have described it) any more of a real possibility. The *irruption* of divine grace in human history is regarded fundamentally as an *interruption* to the patterns of human thought and behavior. Christ, therefore, is seen as having rescued humankind both from the tyranny of sin and from the wrong-headed and ineffectual endeavor to rescue ourselves through our efforts at moral formation.

This reading correctly grasps Paul's self-understanding as standing at the overlap between two ages, inhabiting a situation of crisis disclosed by divine revelation in Jesus. Moreover, this view helpfully draws our attention to the cosmic power of sin; Paul does indeed believe that, because humankind is enslaved to this power, moral progress is impossible without Jesus. Yet, I believe, this view misunderstands the *nature* of the crisis Paul inhabited in the following ways.

First, despite the urgency of Paul's rhetoric, I do not find in his letters evidence of a belief in the imminent, cataclysmic end to the world. If he in fact held such a belief, it may only be inferred on the basis of his affinity with an apocalyptic worldview. However, I am also not convinced that apocalyptic texts actually envision such a world-ending cataclysm. Apocalyptic literature *does*, of course, commonly present the imminent divine judgment in language that evokes cosmic catastrophe. Witness Jesus' remarks concerning the destruction of the Temple:

> "But in those days, after that suffering, the sun will be darkened, and the moon will not give its light, and the stars will be falling from heaven, and the powers in the heavens will be shaken. Then they will see 'the Son of Man coming in clouds' with great power and glory. Then he will send out the angels, and gather his elect from the four winds, from the ends of the earth to the ends of heaven." (Mark 13:24–27)

Such language has sometimes been taken as evidence that first-century Christians expected the imminent cataclysmic destruction of the cosmos. Yet such language is better understood as aiming to invest the events of human history with cosmic significance. Taken this way, apocalyptic literature—and the larger worldview it gives voice to—does not necessarily envision the destruction of the material world and the end of human history. Rather it can be seen as articulating the conviction that God will act decisively (or has in fact already done so) to defeat those powers arrayed against him and bring to fruition his purposes for his creation.

Second, while there is indeed discontinuity between the present evil age and the blessed age to come in Paul's thinking, this discontinuity is not total.[31] Paul emphatically insists that, in Christ, "everything old has passed away; see everything has become new" (2 Cor 5:21)! Properly understood, however, this newness implies *renewal* rather than *replacement*. Paul, in other words, conceives of divine grace renewing our capacity as moral agents. Human moral wisdom is to be transformed rather than categorically rejected.[32]

In my reading of Paul, then, the true nature of the crisis revealed in the life, death, resurrection, and ascension of Christ is that God has, in an unexpected and unprecedented way, entered into our story as a human in order to restore the wholeness of creation and to restore humankind to our proper place within in it.[33] This state of affairs is indeed a *crisis* in that it calls for a radically changed way of imagining both the world in which we live and the nature of the life of human flourishing under the reign of Jesus. But this new state of affairs implies neither a rejection of the inherent goodness of God's creation, nor a wholesale rejection of human wisdom such as one finds in the ancient tradition of virtue ethics.[34]

Paul, I am arguing, envisioned the good life as one in which humans are restored to our divinely bestowed vocation to exercise dominion over the earth as we are transformed into the character of Christ. Is such a vision still compelling? Or do we perceive ourselves today as living in a house on fire, a crisis whose nature renders null and void Paul's conception of the good life?

Niccolò Machiavelli might seem to think so. *The Prince*, completed in 1513 while Machiavelli was under house arrest for suspicion of conspiring against the powerful de' Medici family of Florence, presents a breathtakingly fresh take on political wisdom. Half a millennium later, this slender tome still inspires—and horrifies—its readers. Political theorists continue to disagree sharply regarding Machiavelli's intentions in writing it. Did he merely intend to curry favor with Lorenzo de' Medici through flattery, in the hope of being released from house arrest and regaining his position in society? Did he conceive it as a clever and ironic joke? An impassioned plea to restore to the Italian people, by any means necessary, the glory of the Roman empire? A dispassionate and scientific examination of political theory?

One thing seems certain: Machiavelli did not think much of the classical tradition of virtue ethics. Within this tradition, as we have seen, political leaders were exhorted to both cultivate virtue and inculcate virtue among their people. Machiavelli, by contrast, urges the prince to view virtue instrumentally, as a means to an end. What that ultimate end was for Machiavelli remains a matter of debate, but the penultimate end was clearly the acquisition and maintenance of power. Sometimes a prince is wise to practice the classical virtues, if that is what the circumstances call for. But if political expediency requires him to jettison the virtues, then that is what he must unhesitatingly do:

And furthermore one should not care about incurring the fame of those vices without which it is difficult to save one's state; for if one considers everything well, one will find something appears to be virtue, which if pursued would be one's ruin, and something else appears to be vice, which if pursued results in one's security and well-being.[35]

A particularly chilling example of the lengths to which the prince must pursue vice in order to obtain "security and well-being" is found in Machiavelli's account of Cesare Borgia's campaign in Romagna.[36] To reduce this territory to obedience, Borgia had appointed Messer Remirro de Orco, described as a "cruel and ready man," in whom he vested the "fullest power" to quash civil unrest. De Orco's harsh methods were effective, but Borgia became worried that his henchman had now inspired hatred among the people, a condition rendering Borgia's maintenance of power extremely tenuous if that hatred had turned toward him. Machiavelli approvingly recounts Borgia's remedy to this looming political problem:

He had him [de Orco] placed one morning in the piazza at Cesena in two pieces, with a piece of wood and a bloody knife beside him. The ferocity of this spectacle left the people at once satisfied and stupefied.[37]

Like the residents of Cesena, my students and I are stupefied when we come to this passage. But unlike those who witnessed this bloody spectacle firsthand, we find ourselves profoundly troubled rather than satisfied.

While perhaps no politician today would (publicly) endorse Cesare Borgia's barbarous methods, Machiavelli's maxim that it is "much safer to be feared than loved" still holds currency among those who hold political office, as evidenced by Jonathan Powell's 2010 book, *The New Machiavelli: How to Wield Power in the Modern World*.[38] Setting aside his seeming endorsement of immoral behavior by politicians, Machiavelli raises an important question that cannot so easily be dismissed: Why bother with character formation when what really matters is *power*? For some, the final word of this sentence would not be *power* but rather *effective policy*, or *technological solutions*, or *social change*. In all these iterations of the question, the fundamental challenge to my reading of the Apostle Paul is essentially the same: Character transformation is an inadequate solution to the various crises besetting the world in the present day. Why bother with character when the house is on fire?

Paul's insistence that the church be transformed into the image of Jesus might even suggest to some a quietist strategy, a retreat "out of the world into a safe religious enclave" in which the messy world of politics is forgotten.[39] Piously endeavoring to be more like Jesus may conjure for some a "holy huddle" sequestering itself from the perceived malign influences of "worldly" people and things. Nothing could be further from Paul's intentions, in my view. To see why character formation is relevant—or rather, *essential*—to the innumerable crises we face in society, recall for a moment the relationship between Aristotle's *Nicomachean Ethics* and *Politics*. The former serves the ultimate end of the latter. That is, Aristotle offers a plan to reliably form virtuous individuals in service of the larger goal of forming a flourishing *polis*. The *polis* flourishes only to the extent that its citizens possess the sort of character that enables them to live together in harmony.[40] This relationship is, of course, reciprocal: for Aristotle, good character can only be shaped within a good *polis*. To properly attend to the problems besetting the *polis*, then, we must paradoxically attend to our own character.

Our failure to lean into this paradox may be due to the common assumption that big problems require big solutions. This assumption leads us to look for solutions "at the top": the politicians we elect to public office, the policies they enact, the systemic change thereby effected. I am not for a moment trivializing or denigrating the civic responsibility required of citizens in a democracy.[41] Nor do I deny the existence of systemic problems calling for wisely chosen and enacted policies.[42] Good government can have a beneficial effect upon society; we should therefore give careful thought to those whom we elect and hold them accountable.[43] But the tendency to focus upon big solutions is also dangerous for several reasons.

In the first place, this tendency may sometimes lead to the hubristic conviction that the kingdom of God can be achieved through the implementation of a particular political agenda. To travel down this road is to risk repeating the many well-intentioned but misguided attempts to establish by human effort the "kingdom of God" on earth. Recall Eusebius' misplaced enthusiasm for Constantine's political and military victories, which he regarded as evidence of his divinely sanctioned reign. Newbigin rightly warns that "the sacralizing of politics, the total identification of a political goal with the will of God, always unleashes demonic powers."[44] Granted, the strong form of this conviction—a desire to return to the church-state synthesis under Christendom—is rarely articulated in the public square. Yet in its weaker forms—the assumption that one's own political and moral judgments align perfectly with God's will—it is often noisily and rancorously attested in contemporary political discourse.

Second, big solutions unhelpfully tend to simplify the complexity of problems at the local level. Wendell Berry distinguishes between *big* solutions and *good* solutions. He is concerned primarily "with the irony of agricultural methods that destroy, first, the health of the soil and, finally, the health of human communities." And yet, he insists, the predilection for solutions that fail to solve problems—and indeed worsen them—is "characteristic not of our agriculture but of our time."[45] Observing that many big solutions either immediately worsen the problem or result in a ramifying set of new problems, Berry argues for the sort of solution that "causes a ramifying set of solutions—as when meat animals are fed on the farm where the feed is raised, and where the feed is raised to be fed to the animals that are on the farm."[46] Such a solution

> implies a concern for pattern, for quality . . . for balance or symmetry, a reciprocating connection in the pattern of the farm that is biological, not industrial, and that involves solutions to problems of fertility, soil husbandry, economics, sanitation—the whole complex of problems whose proper solutions add up to *health*: the health of the soil, of plants and animals, of farm and farmer, of farm family and farm community, all involved in the same internested, interlocking pattern—or pattern of patterns.[47]

While a good solution leading to health and preserving patterns of biology and human community may be described as "organic," it nevertheless requires human intervention. Our ability to so intervene "depends on virtues that are specifically human: accurate memory, observation, insight, imagination, inventiveness, reverence, devotion, fidelity, restraint." Berry therefore concludes: "A good solution, then, must be in harmony with good *character*, cultural value, and moral law."[48]

Berry's conclusion nicely brings me to my third reason for regarding big solutions with suspicion: the effectiveness of any solution ultimately depends upon the *character* of the persons involved in it. Democracy, for instance, presents a balanced solution to the interrelated problems of the need for wise governance, respect for individual liberty, and human ignorance and sinfulness. And yet this form of government, no less than the institutions that support it, depend for their success upon the characters of individual human beings—upon office-holders who cleave to integrity and shun corruption, as well as a public that seeks the common good above short-sighted self-interest. A flourishing society must do more than protect its citizens from harm; it must moreover produce people capable of inhabiting the vision of the good to which it aspires. Dallas Willard makes this point with clarity and force:

> From the practical point of view, then, the radical problem concerning the power structures of this world is how to transform *normal* human character away from its usual high level of readiness to disregard God and harm others for the sake of our own fear, pride, lust, greed, envy and indifference. . . . Individual change *is* the answer, even though many believe strongly the answer lies in social change.[49]

In responding to the question, "Is character formation relevant when the house is on fire?", I answer—as I believe Paul would—with a resounding *yes*. This is true, as I have been arguing, principally because only a properly formed character allows one to respond prudently and courageously in the midst of a crisis, to know the good as well as do it. Paul would agree with Aristotle on this, but I think he would further add that being transformed into the image of the Lord results in a substantially different character than the one envisioned by Aristotle. This difference depends on many factors, not least of which is a difference in the *telos* towards which we are aiming. Crucially, Paul insists that we inhabit the good creation of a loving God who will not abandon creation, but rather already is at work to restore it. We are even now living in, and indeed part of, this new creation. The slow work of being transformed into the character of Jesus is necessary, Paul might say, because after all the house is *not* on fire.[50]

4. Does Worship Really Work?

Paul admonishes the churches in Ephesus and Asia Minor to live no longer as do the Gentiles, "alienated from the life of God because of their ignorance and hardness of heart." Perhaps with a note of exasperation, he then reminds them, "That is not the way you learned Christ" (Eph 4:18, 20)! Although one must be wary of the dangers of "mirror-reading," the presence of so much moral exhortation in Paul's letters suggests, at the very least, that it was warranted by the behavior of the churches to whom he wrote.

Paul, I have argued, believes that the reign of Jesus effects unity in the church as that body is formed into the character of its king Jesus. This formation is achieved, in part, through the inculcation of a new *habitus* that takes place in worship. But we may well presume that Paul was not introducing these churches to the practice of worship for the first time in his letters. If these churches were *already* worshipping communities, and if worship instills a *habitus* that leads to unity, why is it that Paul so often needs to address community-destroying behavior? In other words, the evidence of disunity in Paul's churches raises the question: Does worship really work?

Disunity was not simply a problem for the churches founded by Paul. The story of the church over the past two millennia has been characterized by schism far more than ecumenism. The historical evidence of Christian disunity is as abundant as it is sorrowful: the schism dividing the Eastern and Western church in the eleventh century; the Reformation that divided Protestants from Catholics in the sixteenth century; and the innumerable divisions giving rise to "denominations" within Protestantism within the modern era. Even within the ostensible theological unity represented by a given ecclesial body, one still finds deep and painful social divisions. Addressing the disfiguring divide of racism within American Christianity, Martin Luther King, Jr. observed that the most segregated hour in the United States was "eleven o'clock on Sunday morning," the hour when Christians gathered weekly for worship.[51]

Thinking about the transformation into the character of Jesus that undergirds unity, the church again seems to be failing. By any metric of moral behavior, the church appears largely indistinguishable from the surrounding culture. If worship is the spiritual discipline intended to recalibrate the imagination, thereby enabling one authentically to inhabit the gospel story, why are so many Christians seemingly impervious to the transformative capacity of this practice?

These questions do not imply the total failure of the church. To be sure, many faithful Christians *are* steadily and quietly growing into the likeness of their king Jesus. Rather, my questions aim to take seriously the observations of those—both within and outside the church—that Christian worship does not *reliably* effect the moral transformation that the Apostle Paul seems to think it should.[52] Why is this?

Two interrelated answers can be given. First, as Dallas Willard has observed, many churches neither *envision*, nor *intend*, nor provide the *means* for their members to be transformed into the character of Jesus. Vision, intention, and means constitute the three essential components of any realistic practical plan to form disciples of Jesus. Absent any one of them, the project of discipleship, like a three-legged stool, cannot stand.[53] In order to have its transformative effect, worship must take place within a realistically conceived plan of holistic discipleship.

Second, the transformative capacity of worship is greatly affected by what James K. A. Smith terms the "angle of entry."[54] The posture with which one enters worship determines the quality of the experience and, to an extent, the outcome. Jesus tells a parable that aptly demonstrates this point:

> "Two men went up to the temple to pray, one a Pharisee and the other a tax collector. The Pharisee, standing by himself, was praying thus, 'God, I thank you that I am not like other people: thieves, rogues, adulterers, or even like this tax collector. I fast twice a week; I give a tenth of all my income.' But the tax collector, standing far off, would not even look up to heaven, but was beating his breast and saying, 'God, be merciful to me, a sinner!' I tell you, this man went down to his home justified rather than the other; for all who exalt themselves will be humbled, but all who humble themselves will be exalted." (Luke 18:10–14)

The two men clearly approach worship with different expectations of what it means to pray to a merciful God to whom "all hearts are open, all desires known, and from [whom] no secrets are hid."[55] The Pharisee's self-righteousness and self-exaltation make him seemingly impervious to the fact that, in the eyes of God, he is no different than the man whom he holds in contempt. By contrast, the tax collector's sober assessment of his sinful condition, no less than the humility before God that it elicits, leads to a transformative experience in prayer.

Worship is not magic, a ritual performed in an attempt to harness supernatural power. To regard it as such merely reduces it to "dead ritual," an ersatz form of worship in which the words of one's mouth are far from the condition of one's heart (see Isa 29:13). God's rejection of empty ritual observance is well known in Scripture. Through the prophet Amos, the LORD makes known to Israel that worship is odious when divorced from fidelity to the covenant: "I hate, I despise your festivals, and I take no delight in your solemn assemblies" (Amos 5:21; cf. Micah 6:6–8). Although the formation of *habitus* through worship occurs largely at the subconscious level, worship itself is a conscious act requiring the participation of the whole person. Liturgical formation plays an important—even indispensable—role in shaping one as a moral agent, but only within the context of a realistic plan of discipleship (vision, intention, and means).

I have described these two answers as interrelated. In fact, they are different ways of saying the same thing. The "angle of entry" into worship is determined by the larger constellation of spiritual disciplines practiced—or ignored—within the church. The practice of worship, if it is to realize its transformative potential, cannot be removed from the other spiritual disciplines that aim to place one in the presence of Jesus. This principle applies also to the argument of this book. The four elements that comprise Paul's christological vision of the good life—citizenship, character, community, creation—cannot be pursued in isolation from one another. One cannot, for example, hope to be a citizen of the heavenly commonwealth without intending to be transformed into the image of its king, and vice-versa. True health implies wholeness, both of the individual and of the social body.[56]

Equally important as the posture with which one enters worship is the nature of worship itself. If worship aims to "re-story" us, to recalibrate our imagination such that we can inhabit God's story, then it greatly matters whether or not worship gets that story right.[57] To explain, let me contrast two rival versions of the same story frequently encountered in Christian worship.

In what we might call the "fall–redemption" version, the story begins with the problem of human sin, the consequence of which is alienation from God.[58] Jesus' atoning death provides the solution to the problem of sin, such that sinners who accept the pardon for sin offered by this death may enjoy eternal union with God in heaven after death. This version tends to marginalize, if not outright ignore, the significance of God's creation. Imagining this story as a play, we might think of creation as merely the stage on which the unfolding action takes place. By the end of the play—union with God in a heaven far away from earth—creation has been long since forgotten.

How might one be formed by such a story? By diminishing the importance of creation—eliminating it from both beginning and ending—this story aims to direct our desires elsewhere. What we should really love, the story implies, is God, and the place where God dwells, namely heaven. What it means to live within and to care for God's creation recedes into the background. The question of how *I* live in relationship to plants, animals, people, and places—and the use of *I* is quite deliberate here—pales in comparison to the question of whether or not *I* am going to heaven.

The problem with this story is not so much that it is wrong as that it is incomplete. It begins and ends in the wrong place. We can see this clearly by comparing it to another version, which we can call the "creation—fall—new creation" story.[59] This version begins with God's good creation, of which humans constitute a part, and over which they have been given the vocation to bear God's image through their wise and loving care. In this story, sin results not only in alienation from God but also in futility with respect to the human vocation. Christ's atoning death effects a new creation in which humanity is both reconciled with God and (ultimately) restored to our vocation to care for a creation that will itself be restored through the return of Jesus to reign in fullness.

This story directs our desires not away from creation but rather toward creation's inherent goodness and its ultimate renewal. To be formed by such a story is to become a person who shares God's concern and care for all aspects of creation—not only what God has made, but what humans make, the wide diversity of human culture.[60] To inhabit this story is to be formed *politically*, that is, oriented towards the flourishing of both the heavenly *politeuma* and the wider *polis*.

In order for worship to "work," to form us as citizens of the heavenly commonwealth, it must be *political*. By this I certainly do not mean that pastors and priests should tell their parishioners whom to vote for. That would constitute egregious pastoral malpractice (and land you in serious trouble with the IRS to boot). Nor do I mean simply that churches ought to encourage their members to vote and in other ways be civically engaged, although this is appropriate and good. Nor am I suggesting that all churches ought to pursue an agenda of political activism. Rather, I mean that worship must remind us of the political nature of the church itself. James K. A. Smith puts it this way:

> The body of Christ is a kind of republic of the imagination, a body politic composed of those whose citizenship is in heaven (Phil. 3:20). The practices of the body of Christ inculcate in us a social imaginary,

> orienting us to a *telos* that is nothing less than the kingdom of God. Worship is the "civics" of the city of God, habituating us as a people to desire the shalom that God desires for creation.[61]

Worship, which constitutes the "rites of citizens of the heavenly city," ought to bathe the imagination in the acts of God in history "in order to discern what is kingdom-like in the continued providence by which God *still* acts in history."[62] This "re-storied" imagination in turn enables one to properly envision the *telos* of history, the restoration of creation accomplished through the return of Jesus the king.

Only when worship tells the whole story, rather than a truncated version of it, does it instill within us a *habitus* that primes our desires, thoughts, and actions towards the proper *telos*. Worship that begins and ends with the goodness of God's creation forms us for engagement with the world, not for retreat from it. This kind of worship not only implants within us a longing for God's rule over creation, but also teaches us what that sort of rule is like: "not an antinatural tyranny but more like the authority of the gardener who husbands creation to its fullness."[63]

Thinking about God as a gardener leads to my final reflection on the sort of practice that helps us to endure hopefully as we eagerly anticipate the renewal of creation.

5. "Plant Gardens and Eat What They Produce"

Paul boldly articulates to the church in Rome a hope "that the creation itself will be set free from its bondage to decay and will obtain the freedom of the glory of the children of God" (Rom 8:21). In order to live properly in eschatological anticipation of this *telos*, Paul believes that the church must foster what I have argued are the agrarian virtues of hope and endurance. How might we envision and cultivate such virtues in our own context?

To address this question, we must begin by acknowledging the many salient differences between Paul's context and our own. Unlike the readers of Paul's letters, most readers of this book, I suspect, have little meaningful connection to agrarian culture. Unlike the Roman economy of Paul's day, modern western economies are not powered by the engine of slave labor. And unlike first-century imperial propaganda, our governments no longer assure us that our political leaders have ushered in a golden age by means of their divine virtue.

Yet behind these noteworthy differences are hidden some surprising similarities. While our political rhetoric has largely abandoned the quasi-religious notion of a return to a golden age, politicians nevertheless run for office on platforms promising a return to seemingly lost prosperity and economic dominance. The slogan "Make America Great Again" seeks to capture, as most slogans do, a vast panoply of diverse hopes for a better future, in this case grounded in a sense of current discontent. Certainly one of these hopes was for a revitalized economy brought about by the policies and willpower of a political party, or a single "heroic" individual.

Such rhetoric is similar to Roman imperial propaganda in its presentist eschatological perspective. The promised economic revitalization is occurring not only within current lifetimes, but within four years! Such promises, or declarations, require little from the public beyond a commitment to optimism and increased consumption. No one is asked to hope, or endure, or suffer. Whatever the actual lives of Americans may be—and certainly many suffer greatly—politicians assure them that they are now—or shortly will be—living in the greatest nation on earth.

And while this nation has long abandoned (although not honestly addressed) its shameful legacy of slavery, its economy still depends upon goods and services provided by persons (largely overseas) whose economic condition is profoundly dehumanizing. Although America's agrarian virtues are no longer eroded by the institution of slavery, the meteoric rise of industrial farming robs most people of these virtues. The prevalent attitude towards agriculture is thus worryingly similar to that of first-century Rome: while still fundamentally dependent upon the health of both the land and the communities that care for it, the great mass of citizens has largely lost the virtues of knowledge and affection that the land requires of us.

How then can the agrarian virtues of hope and endurance be relevant to the present context, in which "creation waits with eager longing for the revealing of the children of God" (Rom 8:19) just as surely as it did—albeit now with far greater urgency—in Paul's day? First, we must cultivate a hope which can serve as the antidote to the scourge of resigning ourselves to the inevitable. Those who bemoan the sacrifice of traditional agrarian virtues to the ascendancy of industrial agriculture will likely be dismissed as Luddites with some confident assertion the likes of, "there is no going back on progress" or "technological innovation is simply inevitable." Granted, any technological innovation—the steel plough, for example—cannot simply be "forgotten." But we should nevertheless give careful consideration to the appropriateness of whatever technology—agricultural or otherwise—we adopt.[64] To that end, we do well to recall Aldo Leopold's "land ethic": "A thing is right when it tends to preserve the integrity, stability, and beauty of the biotic community. It is wrong when it tends otherwise."[65] In particular, we should insist, as the Luddites did, upon "the precedence of community needs over technological innovation and monetary profit."[66]

While it is true that we cannot "un-invent" technological inventions, it is equally true that we cannot "turn back the clock" on our ecological degradation. There is simply no way to recover clear-cut old growth forests, strip-mined mountain tops, poisoned streams and rivers, or eroded topsoil. Such losses are permanent. Furthermore, it may well be the case that this degradation of the biotic community will result, inevitably, in further degradation. Beyond a certain point, a diseased body may not recover.

Yet in a more profound sense, the assertion of inevitability is both false and morally crippling. The first step towards a future different than the one claimed by some to be inevitable is to *imagine* that future as possible, even if only dimly so. Hope is the virtue that enables us to imagine the eschatological liberation of creation from bondage to decay in the face of present circumstances that, by human standards, make such hope seem rather foolish. Once again, Paul's letter calls for a recalibration of our imaginations.

The second step towards that future is to work—with humility, intelligence, and perseverance—towards it, confident that the outcome is not up to us but rather to God. We can think of such work as preserving—or in many cases, seeking to recover—what Berry refers to as "the most necessary and valuable things" upon which the health of the land and those who care for it depend.[67] To cultivate such virtues—neighborliness, thrift, affection for place and community—we must first possess the virtue of endurance, the ability to persevere in a countercultural pattern of living amidst suffering.

This of course raises a practical question: By what means are these virtues cultivated? To answer this question we must, first of all, think of virtues and practices as integrally related to one another. To engage in a given practice requires certain virtues; in turn, those very virtues are fostered through engaging in the practice itself.[68] Thus if we wish to cultivate the virtues of hope and endurance, we must attend to the sort of practice that both requires and fosters those virtues. Second, we might helpfully conceive of the church as a "virtue-forming community," an alternative *polis* both requiring and fostering a set of virtues that frequently run counter to those of the surrounding culture.[69] Thus we must ask: What are the practices of the church—the heavenly *politeuma*—that will foster the agrarian virtues of hope and endurance? I would suggest the practice of gardening as an ideal candidate for consideration.

When the prophet Jeremiah encouraged the exiles in Babylon to "plant gardens and eat what they produce" (Jer 29:5), he assuredly intended himself to be taken literally. To plant a garden can certainly be understood in metaphorical terms to reflect the intention to reside in a certain place for an extended period of time. In that sense, the prophet's words clearly intend to extinguish false hope for a speedy return to Israel. Yet this advice is also eminently practical. The practice of gardening enables one to receive sustenance from the land as a divine gift, encouraging a way of life reliant upon the grace of God rather than other sources.[70]

Gardening, moreover, is a practice that both fosters and requires the virtues of hope and endurance. To plant a seed into soil is quintessentially an act of hope—an act that envisions a vast and mysterious process by which this tiny seed will receive life from sources beyond our comprehension and control, finally bringing nourishment and life to oneself and family. To cultivate that seed in its long journey to bearing fruit furthermore requires endurance—patiently submitting through the long, hot months of summer to what my wife aptly describes as the "tyranny of the garden." Of course many practices require and foster hope and endurance, but gardening is a practice that cultivates these virtues in an agrarian register, directing them to anticipate the eschatological fulfillment of creation's liberation from bondage to decay. As Berry observes, "A person who undertakes to grow a garden at home, by practices that will preserve rather than exploit the economy of the soil, has set his mind decisively against what is wrong with us."[71]

What should be the role of the church in all this? In the first place, the church must become the primary place where the agrarian virtues of hope and endurance are called forth.[72] I doubt that I am an anomaly in having never heard a sermon on Jeremiah 29:5, whose application was the literal exhortation to plant a garden. In my experience, this command of the prophet is understood solely in its metaphorical sense, as indeed are most aspects of the Bible's agrarian vision of life. An agrarian way of life was well-suited in iron-age Israel, we might think, but incomprehensible in twenty-first-century urban or suburban America.[73] The decline of agrarian culture was ushered in by the industrial revolution; its demise, we presume, is now inevitable.

But to claim that something is inevitable is surely a defect in our ability to imagine other possibilities and to anticipate those possibilities in the patterns of daily living. Put differently, to believe in the inevitable demise of agrarian culture is a failure of hope and endurance. Thus the church as heavenly *politeuma* must become the place where these countercultural agrarian virtues are called into being. In the second place, there is now in most communities a vital need for some institution other than the household to provide physical space for and basic instruction in the practice of gardening. Jeremiah's audience would assuredly have had the know-how to plant a garden; many in our own culture do not. This practical assistance is not uniquely the purview of the church—the community gardening movement has been going on for quite some time now—but it is uniquely the church's role to make space for the practice of gardening as a *spiritual discipline*.

By that I mean, to borrow Paul's words, a bodily practice that trains us to "present [ourselves] to God as those who have been brought from death to life, and present [our] members to God as instruments of righteousness" (Rom 6:13).[74] Just as the Israelites were given the daily practice of gathering manna in order to unlearn their former enslaved way of life in Egypt, so Paul's letter directs us to bodily practices that teach us to hope for and endure in the practices that anticipate the eschatological liberation of creation from bondage to decay and its sharing in the freedom of the glory of the children of God (Rom 8:21). God intended humans and land to exist in a relationship of *mutual* flourishing, but as Wendell Berry observes, "things that belong together have been taken apart."[75] The church is called to facilitate the mending of that which has been torn asunder.

CONCLUSION

IN THE IMAGE OF THE KING

The Journey Ahead

On the campus of the university where I teach, there are two striking visual representations of Jesus. The fifteen-foot bronze and steel sculpture of "Christus Rex" (Christ the King), situated behind the altar of the Chapel of the Resurrection, is larger than life in every respect. Although it is affixed to a twenty-four-foot wooden cross, from the front aspect it appears to be floating in the air in front of the cross. Its gilded finish shines brightly in the light of the east-facing stained-glass windows behind it. A crown on his head, hands lifted to the heavens—not nailed to the cross—this is clearly the *risen* Christ, resplendent in royal glory.[1]

Outside the chapel, lying on a bench by a walking path, lies "Homeless Jesus." This sculpture is life-sized; indeed, it only takes up about two-thirds of the bench, inviting passersby to come and sit a while at Jesus' feet. Inspired by a homeless man sleeping on a park bench in Toronto, Canadian sculptor Timothy P. Schmalz created a work of art evoking Jesus' comparison of himself to the hungry, thirsty, strangers, naked, and imprisoned (Matt 25:31–46). Covered by a blanket with only his nail-pierced hands and feet visible, this sculpture portrays the *crucified* Jesus. Unlike the sublime and glorious sculpture dominating the Chapel of the Resurrection, "Homeless Jesus" is "a man of suffering and acquainted with infirmity" (Isa 53:3).[2]

These two images of Jesus—the risen and the crucified, the glorious and the suffering—have often been torn asunder in the Christian imagination. This book has sought to mend this rift in our imagination, presenting Jesus as the suffering king. Although Jesus will indeed return in glory to consummate his reign, we now live in the "in-between" time in which having the mind of Christ entails following Jesus in the way of suffering (Phil 2:5–8).

The challenge of living in this in-between time brings me to another rift in the Christian imagination, namely how we think about the nature of salvation. Recall, from the introduction, the two ways we might consider being saved—*from* a life-threatening peril, or *to* a life of flourishing. There has been a tendency within the church to see these two concepts of salvation as constituting an "either/or" choice. Mending this rift in our imagination constitutes the central bind of this book: Jesus both rescues us *from* the tyrannical power of sin and by his reign over us restores us *to* a life of flourishing.

When this book was about halfway done, I approached Carey Newman, then the director of Baylor University Press, to see if he might be interested in this project. To get a better sense of the book's argument, Carey gave me what seemed at the time a rather whimsical task: to sketch out the book's argument in the form of a fairy-tale, such as one might read to a child at bedtime. To my surprise, this thought experiment proved enormously helpful in bringing to light the central bind the book endeavors to resolve—how to live in the in-between time, in which the kingdom of God has been inaugurated but not consummated.

As I have stressed throughout, Paul's aim is to recalibrate our imagination, to "re-story" it within the narrative of God's dealings with humankind and the rest of creation. In the spirit of this effort to re-story our imagination, I offer, as a kind of summary of my argument, the fairy-tale version of this book.

"The Herald and the King"

Once upon a time there was a city ruled over by an evil king, a tyrant who kept his people in thrall to fear. Although the people hated their king, they nevertheless followed in his wicked ways, fighting and quarreling constantly among themselves. Night and day, the people—and even the land itself—cried out to heaven for justice. At long last, heaven's king appeared, defeating the evil king and liberating his people. "Hurrah!" the people cried. "We are saved!" Children danced in the streets. Elders wept for joy. Strangers embraced.

With shouts of "Long live the heavenly king!", the people lifted up the conquering savior and brought him to the palace. "Stay and rule over us," they pleaded. "Be our king and we will be your people." The king replied, "Indeed I shall be your king, and as many as pledge their loyalty to me this day shall be my people." Many bowed and gave their allegiance to the king. But some who had prospered under the old tyrant refused to bow the knee, harboring hopes that the wicked king might return.

What happened next surprised everybody.

"I must leave you," said the king, "for there are other cities I must save." In the shocked silence that followed, the king reached inside his tunic and brought forth a small image of himself, stunning in its likeness. Handing it to the people, he reassured them, "I will always be with you and one day I shall return in royal glory. Until then, remain faithful to me." And with those words the good king left.

Some time later, a herald of the good king arrived in the city. At least he *claimed* to be the king's herald, for the shabby little fellow certainly did not look the part, and many dismissed him with scornful laughter. What the herald found in the city greatly dismayed him: many of those who had sworn allegiance to the good king had not kept their word, allying themselves to one or another of the petty tyrants constantly vying for the throne. And yet, some remained faithful in their oath of allegiance to the departed king.

In truth, however, those loyal to the good king had quite nearly lost all hope, for they suffered dearly as the price for their allegiance. Moreover, it was difficult to see that life under the reign of their departed king was much different than before, since petty tyrants still held sway. Indeed, some loyal to the good king found that they had returned to their old wicked ways, or nearly so. The people—and the land itself—languished in despair. And so the herald gave them strength and hope with these four words.

First, he told them, in your suffering, remember that you are subjects of a suffering king, and you must follow your king in the way of suffering. You are citizens of the heavenly kingdom, and by living worthily of your suffering king, you show that he indeed reigns. *Second*, he reminded them, your king is indeed present among you. Did he not leave you with his image? Recall that you bore the image of the wicked king when he reigned over you. So now, fix your eyes daily on the image of the good king and be transformed into his likeness. *Third*, it grieves me greatly to see that you fight and quarrel among each other, for that is not how you learned the way of the true king! The peace of heaven has already been established among you; therefore, clothe yourselves with the peacemaking character of your true king, and make every effort to live in peace. *Finally*, see how the land itself cries out for justice, the trees and the fields alike groaning under the weight of human wickedness. The whole of creation belongs to heaven's king, and when he returns, he will bring freedom to all that he loves—field and forest, beast and bird, no less than you who faithfully bear his image. Persevere in hope of the king's return.

Although many years have passed, those loyal to heaven's king still faithfully await his return, strengthening their hope with these four words.

May it be said also of us.

NOTES

Introduction

1   Most scholars believe Galatians or 1 Thessalonians to be Paul's earliest letter, written around 50 CE.

2   The task of determining the nature and extent of Paul's influence on later gospel writers is complex; see the nuanced argument of Joel Marcus, "Mark—Interpreter of Paul," *NTS* 46 (2000): 473–87. On the historical process by which the New Testament was formed, see Bruce M. Metzger, *The Canon of the New Testament: Its Origin, Development, and Significance* (Oxford: Clarendon, 1987). A less technical account is provided by Arthur G. Patzia, *The Making of the New Testament: Origin, Collection, Text and Canon* (Downers Grove, Ill.: InterVarsity, 1995).

3   The second semester reading list includes: Martin Luther, Immanuel Kant, John Stuart Mill, Jane Austen, Virginia Woolf, Lu Xun, Ryonosuke Akutagawa, James Baldwin, and Flannery O'Connor.

4   The question is posed by Tertullian in *Prescription Against Heretics* 7 (*Tertullian*, ed. Alexander Roberts and James Donaldson, vol. 3 of *The Ante-Nicene Fathers*, rev. A. Cleveland Coxe [Buffalo, N.Y.: Christian Literature Co., 1885–1896], 246). Tertullian's answer essentially amounts to "not much": Christian faith and philosophy were antithetical in his eyes, the latter being closely correlated to heresy. While I am indebted to Tertullian for raising the question, it should be apparent that we part company in our answers.

5   Among the numerous introductions to Paul's letters, I have found the following particularly helpful: Michael J. Gorman, *Apostle of the Crucified Lord: A Theological Introduction to Paul and His Letters*, 2nd ed. (Grand Rapids: Eerdmans, 2017). For systematic treatments of Paul's theology, see James D. G. Dunn, *The Theology of Paul the Apostle* (Grand Rapids: Eerdmans, 1998); Udo Schnelle, *Apostle Paul: His Life and Theology*, trans. M. Eugene Boring (Grand Rapids: Baker Academic, 2005); Michael Wolter, *Paul: An Outline of His Theology*, trans. Robert L. Brawley (Waco, Tex.: Baylor University Press, 2015).

6   My thinking in this area has been profoundly shaped by N. T. Wright, *After You Believe: Why Christian Character Matters* (New York: HarperOne, 2010). See also Daniel J. Harrington and James F. Keenan, *Paul and Virtue Ethics: Building Bridges Between New Testament Studies and Moral Theology* (Lanham, Md.: Rowman & Littlefield, 2010; Jonathan T. Pennington, *The Sermon on the Mount and Human Flourishing: A Theological Commentary* (Grand Rapids: Baker Academic, 2018).

7   A number of scholars would disagree that Paul can meaningfully be placed into conversation with Aristotelian virtue ethics, with its notions of "this-worldly" flourishing and a relatively stable concept of human character. Such scholars insist that Paul was an "apocalyptic" thinker who understood God's sudden and unexpected incursion of grace as that which alone liberates one from the powers of sin and death. I respond to this criticism in ch. 6 of this book (see the section entitled "Forming Character When the House Is on Fire"). At present, it suffices to say that, along with other interpreters of Paul such as N. T. Wright and Michael Gorman, I find the idea of character formation to be compatible with the incursion of divine grace that profoundly shaped Paul's thinking. For readers unfamiliar with the apocalyptic reading of Paul, I recommend the concise introduction by Michael J. Gorman, "Pauline Theology: *Perspectives, Perennial Topics, and Prospects*," in *The State of New Testament Studies: A Survey of Recent Research*, ed. Scot McKnight and Nijay K. Gupta (Grand Rapids: Baker Academic, 2019), 202–3. N. T. Wright offers a concise introduction to the scholarly debate in *The Paul Debate: Critical Questions for Understanding the Apostle* (Waco, Tex.: Baylor University Press, 2015), 41–64; see also his extensive treatment in *Paul and His Recent Interpreters: Some Contemporary Debates* (Minneapolis: Fortress, 2015), 132–218. For a diverse array of scholarly perspectives, see Ben C. Blackwell, John K. Goodrich, and Jason Maston, eds., *Paul and the Apocalyptic Imagination* (Minneapolis: Fortress, 2016).

8   Throughout the book, I generally use the term "political" in the sense Aristotle intended, describing the functioning of the *polis*, a union of persons directed to the common purpose of human flourishing.

9   Thus, for example, we might say that the *aretē*, or virtue, of a knife is its sharpness; that of an eye is its visual acuity, and so forth.

10   Francis Watson, "In the Beginning: Irenaeus, Creation and the Environment," in *Ecological Hermeneutics: Biblical, Historical and Theological Perspectives*, ed. David G. Horrell et al. (London: T&T Clark, 2010), 130, referring to the Valentinians' flawed rendering of the biblical story. On the biblical vision of humankind as members of the "community of creation," see Richard Bauckham, *The Bible and Ecology: Rediscovering the Community of Creation*, Sarum Theological Lectures (Waco, Tex.: Baylor University Press, 2010).

11   On the importance of place within Christian theology and human existence more broadly, see the wide-ranging discussion in Craig G. Bartholomew, *Where Mortals Dwell: A Christian View of Place for Today* (Grand Rapids: Baker Academic, 2011).

12   On the importance of the distinction (for both Paul and contemporary readers of Paul) between nature and creation, see Norman Wirzba, *From Nature to Creation: A Christian Vision for Understanding and Loving Our World*, The Church and Postmodern Culture (Grand Rapids: Baker Academic, 2015). Wirzba explains that the Greek word *physis*, which is often translated as "nature" in English, "referred to the principle whereby a thing is what it is or the powers and processes by which it achieves its end" (33). The concept gave rise to the ethical implication that one should strive to live one's life in accordance with the power or reason at work in the natural world.

1 Salvation and the Good Life

1   Book 1 of Aristotle's *Nicomachean Ethics* (1094a–1103a) raises and answers this question. Aristotle begins by establishing that the highest and best good is political, that is, having the good of the *polis* as its aim (1094a20–1094b15). He then poses the question, "Since every sort of knowledge and decision pursues some

good, what is the good that we say political science seeks? What, [in other words,] is the highest of all the goods achievable in action?" (1095a14–16). This good he calls *eudaimonia*, a term often translated as "happiness." However, this English word, in contemporary parlance, often suggests the subjective experience of some kind of pleasure. Aristotle's concept implies the more objective sense of a being fully obtaining or activating its potential, and is thus more accurately rendered as "flourishing." English translations of this text are from Aristotle, *Nicomachean Ethics*, 2nd ed., trans. Terence Irwin (Indianapolis: Hackett, 1999). Unless otherwise noted, English translations of other Greek and Roman texts are from the editions of the Loeb Classical Library. See further T. H. Irwin, "Conceptions of Happiness in the *Nicomachean Ethics*," in *The Oxford Handbook of Aristotle*, ed. Christopher Shields (New York: Oxford University Press, 2012), 495–528; Richard Kraut, "Aristotle on Becoming Good: Habituation, Reflection, and Perception," in *The Oxford Handbook of Aristotle*, ed. Christopher Shields (New York: Oxford University Press, 2012), 529–57.

2   For the prevalence of this understanding within the contemporary church, see Wright, *After You Believe*, 1–26. But note the answer Jesus himself gives to the man: "'You lack one thing; go, sell what you own, and give the money to the poor, and you will have treasure in heaven; then come, follow me'" (v. 21). This understanding of salvation suggests that eternal life is to be found in a life of following Jesus.

3   Aristotle conceived of the good life in teleological terms, achieving the unique human *telos* or function, namely the "activity of the soul in accord with virtue" (*Nic. Eth.* 1098a17).

4   The tensions between these two different soteriologies, and the anthropologies that lie beneath them, can be seen clearly in the conflict between Pelagius and Augustine. The former contended that humans possess the ability to take the initial critical steps toward salvation; the latter insisted that any movement towards salvation is impossible without divine grace. An introduction to this debate as well as relevant primary texts can be found in J. Patout Burns, trans. and ed., *Theological Anthropology*, Sources of Early Christian Thought (Philadelphia: Fortress, 1981).

5   Many scholars argue that a later disciple of Paul wrote Ephesians, claiming that the letter does not directly reflect Paul's own thinking, but rather a later development of it. Although I myself was once persuaded by such arguments, I now find arguments for Pauline authorship of both Ephesians and Colossians more convincing. In any event, Paul makes a similar claim in Rom 10:9; in Rom 3:26 he makes nearly the same point, using there the language of justification rather than salvation.

6   The genesis of this misreading of Paul is complex, but can be traced in part to Augustine's polemically motivated retrieval of Paul from Manichaean interpretation; see J. Albert Harrill, *Paul the Apostle: His Life and Legacy in Their Roman Context* (Cambridge: Cambridge University Press, 2012), 138–62. See further the landmark essay, Krister Stendahl, "The Apostle Paul and the Introspective Conscience of the West," *HTR* 56, no. 3 (July 1963): 199–215.

7   To see how "rescue from" and "rescue to" are often bound together, we might helpfully extend the analogy of addiction to consider the twelve steps of Alcoholics Anonymous. Although the ultimate *telos* of this practice is the restoration of an addicted person *to* a life of wholeness, the immediate interventions are concerned with a rescue operation *from* the ravages of addiction. For example, one must make a rigorous moral inventory (step 4); confess wrongdoing (step 5); and ask forgiveness and make restitution where possible (steps 7 and 8). These steps, while immediately concerned with the guilt of sin and its forgiveness, are also oriented to

the larger *telos* of flourishing. I am grateful to my friend Michael Rhodes for this observation.

8   On the confusion regarding ultimate human hope that pervades the church and the world, see N. T. Wright, *Surprised by Hope: Rethinking Heaven, the Resurrection, and the Mission of the Church* (New York: HarperOne, 2008), 3–30.

9   The story itself does not speak of sin, a concept that only makes sense within a theistic framework. In supplying this concept, I am admittedly offering a theological interpretation of this story. This is warranted, I believe, because the story itself is offering a nontheistic critique of what may be loosely regarded as the Christian view of salvation.

10   This might feel like a trick question. Although you could clearly view one answer as true and the other as false, you might well think that *both* answers are true in different ways. You might personally believe that we live in a world in which sin is a reality, but you might also perceive that much of the world around you rejects that view (or vice versa). If you answered the question this way, you have grasped what it means to live in a *secular age* in the sense laid out by contemporary philosopher Charles Taylor. This does not mean that the world consists entirely of atheists; rather, it describes a world of contested beliefs, a world in which belief in God is no longer axiomatic (Charles Taylor, *A Secular Age* [Cambridge, Mass.: Belknap, 2007], 3).

11   The television adaptations are often radically different from the original short stories, now collected in the volume Philip K. Dick, *Philip K. Dick's Electric Dreams* (New York: Houghton Mifflin Harcourt, 2017). These differences reveal much about the contemporary *Zeitgeist*, at least as perceived through the sensibilities of purveyors of cinematic entertainment. In many cases, the stories are not merely updated; they are fundamentally changed. In some cases the plot itself is radically altered. In many cases some fundamental truth about the world we live in has been inserted, removed, or replaced. In the original story "Exhibit Piece," we are only ever dealing with one character who passes between two worlds but maintains his own identity. There is no question, moreover, whether we live in a world in which sin and guilt are real or illusory. It is not merely that the original story provides a different answer; it doesn't even ask the question. Times have changed.

12   The late missiologist Lesslie Newbigin makes this point with even greater force, claiming that the gospel itself violates what he calls the "plausibility structure" of modern Western society (*Foolishness to the Greeks: The Gospel and Western Culture* [Grand Rapids: Eerdmans, 1986], 10). Newbigin borrows the term "plausibility structure" from the work of Peter Berger (*The Heretical Imperative*, 1979), defining the term as follows: "a social structure of ideas and practices that create the conditions determining what beliefs are plausible within the society in question." Within the plausibility structure of the modern (and postmodern) world, Newbigin explains, facts are to be distinguished from values. The former belong in the public sphere, the latter in the private. The claims of religion are regarded as privately held values, not publicly shared facts. In claiming to articulate a public truth, the gospel violates this plausibility structure.

13   Stanley Hauerwas and William H. Willimon capture this idea when they speak of salvation as "(1) placing us within an adventure that is nothing less than God's purpose for the whole world, and (2) communally training us to fashion our lives in accordance with what is true rather than what is false" (*Resident Aliens: Life in the Christian Colony*, expanded 25th anniversary ed. [Nashville: Abingdon, 2014], 52–53). Hauerwas and Willimon cite Paul (Rom 6:5–11) as the biblical

warrant for the claim that we are brought into this adventure through baptism into the death and resurrection of Christ. Similar arguments that the New Testament picture of salvation encompasses both "eternal life" and the "good life" can be found in Dallas Willard, *The Spirit of the Disciplines: Understanding How God Changes Lives* (San Francisco: Harper, 1988), 2–43; C. S. Lewis, *Mere Christianity* (New York: HarperOne, 2001), 153–227.

14   Isocrates, *Evag.* 51–57; Musonius Rufus 60.8–12; Martial, *Epig.* 5.1.7–8; *Ps. Sol.* 17:3; *Sib. Or.* 3:652–656; Philo, *Legat.* 22; *T. Sim.* 7.1–2. See Francis Dvornik, *Early Christian and Byzantine Political Philosophy: Origins and Background*, 2 vols., DOS 9 (Washington, D. C.: Dumbarton Oaks Center for Byzantine Studies, 1966), 1:266. Dvornik notes that the eastern provinces of the Roman Empire hailed Augustus as *sōtēr* for having ended civil strife (2:491–494). For the use of this epithet applied to Roman emperors, see M. P. Charlesworth, *Documents Illustrating the Reigns of Claudius Collected by M. P. Charlesworth* (Cambridge: Cambridge University Press, 1939), 3–5; Adolf Deissmann, *Light from the Ancient East: The New Testament Illustrated by Recently Discovered Texts of the Graeco-Roman World*, trans. Lionel Richard Mortimer Strachan (London: Hodder & Stoughton, 1910), 353–61, 368–69.

15   English translation from *Dio Chrysostom*, 5 vols., trans. J. W. Cohoon and H. L. Crosby, LCL (Cambridge, Mass.: Harvard University Press, 1932–1951).

16   Peter J. Rabinowitz, "Truth in Fiction: A Reexamination of Audiences," *Critical Inquiry* 4 (1977): 121–41, describes the "authorial audience" as the hypothetical audience possessing the necessary cultural literacy to understand an author's communication.

17   In 1 Tim 1:17; 6:15, God is referred to as *basileus*, but not Jesus. Paul's authorship of this letter, moreover, is disputed. On the issue of authorship for the pastoral letters—1–2 Timothy and Titus—see Raymond F. Collins, *I and II Timothy and Titus: A Commentary*, NTL (Louisville: Westminster John Knox, 2002), 3–9.

18   Paul uses that expression, or a comparable one, in Rom 14:17; 1 Cor 4:20; 6:9, 10; 15:24, 50; Gal 5:21; Col 4:11; 1 Thess 2:12—a total of nine times. By contrast, the Synoptic Gospels contain 76 kingdom sayings, or 103 if parallel sayings are included.

19   Matthew V. Novenson, *Christ among the Messiahs: Christ Language in Paul and Messiah Language in Ancient Judaism* (New York: Oxford University Press, 2012), 5–6.

20   Joshua W. Jipp, *Christ Is King: Paul's Royal Ideology* (Minneapolis: Fortress, 2015), 1–42.

21   A paradox, in G. K. Chesterton's memorable phrase, is "truth standing on her head to attract attention" (from the short story, "When Doctors Agree," collected in *The Paradoxes of Mr. Pond* [Cornwall: Stratus Books, 2008], 41). A paradox is counter-intuitive and thus apparently contradictory, but may, upon further investigation, prove to be true.

22   See the discussion in Erwin R. Goodenough, "The Political Philosophy of Hellenistic Kingship," *Yale Classical Studies* 1 (1928): 55–102; Dvornik, *Political Philosophy*, 1:205–77. Ultimately, the relevance of Paul's monarchic portrayal of Jesus to our own context can only be demonstrated through the course of this book's argument.

23   The question of Paul's relevance is reflected in the frank comment one of my students made in the margins to a draft of this book: "OK, great. Why is this important

to me though? Is it important in a scholarly conversation, out of curiosity? Is it important for me as a young person?"

24   The particular shape of this book has grown out of my own dissatisfaction at the stumbling responses I have offered to students who want to put Paul in conversation with contemporary issues about which they care deeply.

25   I borrow the strategy of placing Paul "in conversation" from Susan Grove Eastman, *Paul and the Person: Reframing Paul's Anthropology* (Grand Rapids: Eerdmans, 2017).

26   Julien C. H. Smith, *Christ the Ideal King: Cultural Context, Rhetorical Strategy, and the Power of Divine Monarchy in Ephesians*, WUNT 2/313 (Tübingen: Mohr Siebeck, 2011). See also Jipp, *Christ Is King*; Pennington, *Sermon on the Mount*.

27   A noteworthy exception in this regard is Patrick Gray, *Paul as a Problem in History and Culture: The Apostle and His Critics through the Centuries* (Grand Rapids: Baker Academic, 2016), especially chs. 5–7 and 10. See also Sarah Ruden, *Paul among the People: The Apostle Reinterpreted and Reimagined in His Own Time* (New York: Pantheon, 2010). Ruden, a classical philologist, endeavors to interpret Paul's writings from the perspective of Greco-Roman culture, although she is sensitive as well to contemporary questions.

28   Given our particular social location at a private, church-related university, this sense of transgression is muted. I suspect that this sort of discussion would be frowned upon at a public university. It would probably be illegal in a public high school.

29   Newbigin makes this argument in a variety of ways across a number of his published works, in particular the following: *Foolishness*; *The Gospel in a Pluralist Society* (Grand Rapids: Eerdmans, 1989); *Truth to Tell: The Gospel as Public Truth* (London: SPCK, 1991); *The Open Secret: An Introduction to the Theology of Mission*, rev. ed. (Grand Rapids: Eerdmans, 1995); *Truth and Authority in Modernity*, Christian Mission and Modern Culture (Valley Forge, Pa.: Trinity Press International, 1996). For a critical assessment of Newbigin's contributions, see Scott W. Sunquist and Amos Yong, eds., *The Gospel and Pluralism Today: Reassessing Lesslie Newbigin in the 21st Century*, Missiological Engagements (Downers Grove, Ill.: InterVarsity, 2015).

30   Newbigin, *Truth to Tell*, 56.

31   Newbigin, *Truth to Tell*, 56–57. This vision of knowledge is based upon the efforts of British-Hungarian polymath and philosopher Michael Polanyi to, in Newbigin's words, "reform the epistemological basis of science" (51).

32   Newbigin, *Gospel*, 222–33.

33   The task of interpreting Paul's letters (hermeneutics) cannot be separated from the task of living out the life to which they call us (ethics). Thus N. T. Wright, *Paul in Fresh Perspective* (Minneapolis: Fortress, 2005), 174, contends that the church is called "to the dangerous and exhilarating task of being, knowing, and telling. The question of Pauline hermeneutics in the twenty-first century may well turn out to be a matter not so much of comprehension, but of courage."

34   Matthew W. Bates, *Salvation by Allegiance Alone: Rethinking Faith, Works, and the Gospel of Jesus the King* (Grand Rapids: Baker Academic, 2017), argues that *pistis* is best translated "allegiance" in a number of key places in the NT, and that this greatly affects how one understands "salvation by faith alone." One is not saved by faith understood as cognitive assent to a proposition, namely that "Jesus died to save me from my sins so that I'll go to heaven when I die." Rather, one is saved by embodied allegiance to Jesus as the enthroned king. Salvation here is understood as a present

embodied life in Jesus' kingdom on earth, as opposed to a future disembodied existence in a heaven divorced from earth. The importance of this translational choice will be seen throughout the following chapter.

35   Newbigin's work has inspired a number of biblical scholars to take up the task of missional hermeneutics, reading the Bible in a way that foregrounds the importance of the *Missio Dei*. For a concise and helpful overview of this approach, see George R. Hunsberger, "Proposals for a Missional Hermeneutic: Mapping a Conversation," *Missiology: An International Review* 39 (2011): 309–21. The work of scholars associated with the Gospel and Our Culture Network has been exemplary in developing and applying this hermeneutic. See, for example, Michael J. Gorman, *Becoming the Gospel: Paul, Participation, and Mission*, The Gospel and Our Culture Series (Grand Rapids: Eerdmans, 2015); Michael W. Goheen, ed., *Reading the Bible Missionally*, The Gospel and Our Culture Series (Grand Rapids: Eerdmans, 2016); Michael Barram, *Missional Economics: Biblical Justice and Character Formation*, The Gospel and Our Culture Series (Grand Rapids: Eerdmans, 2018).

36   Willard, *Spirit of the Disciplines*, 14–17.

37   Part of the problem here, as Bates, *Salvation by Allegiance Alone*, 2–5, argues, is reducing "salvation by faith" to "salvation by belief."

38   Willard, *Spirit of the Disciplines*, 95–129. On the place of spiritual exercises in ancient philosophy, see Pierre Hadot, *Philosophy as a Way of Life: Spiritual Exercises from Socrates to Foucault*, ed. Arnold I. Davidson, trans. Michael Chase (Malden, Mass.: Blackwell, 1995).

39   The historical reasons for the diminution of such practices are complex and stem from the Reformation era response to the gradual perversion of asceticism within the monastic movement. Observe Martin Luther's stinging condemnation of monks in "The Pagan Servitude of the Church": "Nowhere is there less of faith, or of the true church, than among the priests, monks, and bishops" (*Martin Luther: Selections from His Writings.*, ed. John Dillenberger [Garden City, N.Y.: Doubleday, 1962], 311). See further Willard, *Spirit of the Disciplines*, 139–48. An exception to this aversion to traditional spiritual disciplines among Reformers can be found in Calvin's emphasis on regeneration and sanctification. See Matthew Myer Boulton, *Life in God: John Calvin, Practical Formation, and the Future of Protestant Theology* (Grand Rapids: Eerdmans, 2011), 222–28.

40   Dallas Willard systematically addresses this problem in *Renovation of the Heart: Putting on the Character of Christ* (Colorado Springs: NavPress, 2002).

41   Willard, *Spirit of the Disciplines*, 110–18.

42   James K. A. Smith, *Desiring the Kingdom: Worship, Worldview, and Cultural Formation*, Cultural Liturgies 1 (Grand Rapids: Baker Academic, 2009). Willard, *Spirit of the Disciplines*, 177–79, would have no argument with Smith on this point. Indeed, for Willard, communal (as well as individual) worship is to be seen as one of the core spiritual disciplines. Willard and Smith present thus complementary arguments for the task of moral formation: we are shaped both by individual disciplines and by communal liturgies.

43   James K. A. Smith, *Desiring the Kingdom*, 155–214. As N. T. Wright and others have argued, the Christian Scriptures address the task of moral action by presenting us with a story and inviting us to imaginatively see ourselves as characters within it. See N. T. Wright, *Scripture and the Authority of God: How to Read the Bible Today* (San Francisco: HarperOne, 2005); Craig G. Bartholomew and Michael W. Goheen, *The Drama of Scripture: Finding Our Place in the Biblical Story* (Grand

Rapids: Baker Academic, 2004); Richard Bauckham, "Reading Scripture as a Coherent Story," in *The Art of Reading Scripture*, ed. Ellen F. Davis and Richard B.
Hays (Grand Rapids: Eerdmans, 2003), 38–54.

44   James K. A. Smith, *Imagining the Kingdom: How Worship Works*, Cultural Liturgies
2 (Grand Rapids: Baker Academic, 2013), 101–50.

45   James K. A. Smith, *Imagining the Kingdom*, 151–91.

46   James K. A. Smith, *Awaiting the King: Reforming Public Theology*, Cultural Liturgies
3 (Grand Rapids: Baker Academic, 2017), 114–22.

47   Some recent studies of Paul could be strengthened by the insights of Willard and
Smith. For example, Gorman, *Becoming the Gospel*, argues that Paul's gospel is not
merely about cognitive assent to a rational proposition, but rather about *becoming*
the good news, that is, being transformed into the image of Christ. Gorman's focus
is squarely upon Paul in his first-century context, although he points along the way
to contemporary images of how this might play out. His argument, persuasive in
my estimation, would be further strengthened by a more systematic understanding, such as Willard and Smith provide, of how we are transformed, individually
and communally.

48   Laura Dunn, *Look and See: A Portrait of Wendell Berry*, documentary (Two Birds
Film, 2016).

49   Wendell Berry, "Christianity and the Survival of Creation," in *Sex, Economy, Freedom and Community: Eight Essays* (New York: Pantheon Books, 1993), 93–99.

50   Berry, "Survival of Creation," 114–15.

51   See his comments in Harold K. Bush, "Hunting for Reasons to Hope: A Conversation with Wendell Berry," *Christianity & Literature* 56 (2007): 230.

52   I don't think Paul would have used the adjective "religious" to describe his writing
either, but the term is conventionally applied to Paul and other biblical writers. See
Jeffrey Bilbro, "When Did Wendell Berry Start Talking Like a Christian," *Christianity & Literature* 68 (2019): 272–96, for the development in Berry's thought and
language from a pagan to a sacramental vision.

53   Berry, "Survival of Creation," 96.

54   Berry, "Survival of Creation," 104–5, insists that the holiness of creation calls us to
honor God with good work, and that failing to do so is nothing short of blasphemy.

55   By engaging our moral imagination through story, Berry's fiction aims to do something similar to what Smith sees as the function of worship; namely, it "stories" us
within a more capacious reality.

56   The "exercise of skillful mastery" is the way Ellen F. Davis renders the Hebrew
verb *radah* in Gen 1:28 (*Scripture, Culture, and Agriculture: An Agrarian Reading
of the Bible* [New York: Cambridge University Press, 2009], 53–59.) The NRSV,
by contrast, translates this way: "Be fruitful and multiply, and fill the earth and
subdue it; and have dominion [Heb: *radah*] over the fish of the sea and over the
birds of the air and over every living thing that moves upon the earth." See further ch. 5 of this book.

57   As far as I know, Berry never writes about the "reign of Christ" as being significant in our task of caring for creation. Nevertheless, in a discussion of the goodness of creation, he claims that "belief in Christ" is dependent upon the "inherent
goodness—the lovability—of the world." He continues to assert that creation, of
which humans are a part, consists in "the constant participation of all creatures
in the being of God" ("Survival of Creation," 97). Moreover, Berry plainly believes
that the Gospels must be taken "as seriously as possible," in particular Jesus' challenge that "the way to more abundant life is the way of love," a way that resists

"desecrating the world and . . . destroying creation." Yet this challenge must be borne humbly as a burden, rather than with the air of self-confidence he finds all too common in the church ("The Burden of the Gospels," *Christian Century* 122, no. 19 [September 2005]: 22–27).

58   To borrow a strategy from James K. A. Smith, *Awaiting the King*, 98–100, I shall attempt in what follows to provide a genealogy that links these four thinkers to Paul.

59   James K. A. Smith, *Imagining the Kingdom*, 17, speaks of imagination "as a quasi-faculty whereby we construe the world on a precognitive level."

60   Charles Taylor, *Modern Social Imaginaries*, Public Planet Books (Durham: Duke University Press, 2004).

61   Of course, one might respond to this observation with exasperation: We *are* too busy to eat! This is not a matter of imagination, but fact! This is no doubt true, but does not invalidate my point. We arrived at this state of affairs by imagining that being too busy to eat would be a good (or at least acceptable) way to live.

62   This headline first ran on *The Onion* on May 27, 2014 (https://www.theonion.com/no-way-to-prevent-this-says-only-nation-where-this-r-1819576527). The article has since been reposted eleven times (through November 8, 2018) in response to mass shootings in which a total of 177 people have been killed (https://kottke.org/18/11/no-way-to-prevent-this-says-only-nation-where-this-regularly-happens).

63   The inspiration for this sort of discussion, if not for its form, comes from G. B. Caird, *New Testament Theology*, ed. L. D. Hurst (Oxford: Clarendon, 1994).

64   Johan Christiaan Beker, *Paul the Apostle: The Triumph of God in Life and Thought* (Philadelphia: Fortress, 1980), 23–26.

65   Wright, *Paul in Fresh Perspective*, 154–74.

66   To be clear, I am not trying to play one off against the other. We obviously need both.

2 Citizenship

1   Bates, *Salvation by Allegiance Alone*, 77–100. The definition is found on p. 92.

2   Scholars have doubted the truth of Luke's claim on the grounds that it is unlikely that someone of Paul's pedigree would possess such uncommon privilege. Although there is no way to validate Paul's Roman citizenship (he never mentions it in his letters), it seems plausible to believe Luke's claim. See the discussion in Schnelle, *Apostle Paul*, 60–62.

3   The following discussion takes Luke's account of Paul's ministry to be generally reliable, according to the canons of first-century historiography. On the difficulties of using Acts as a source for Paul's biography, and on the tensions between Acts and Paul's letters, see Schnelle, *Apostle Paul*, 48, 51–54.

4   Given that Paul was born in Tarsus, his words obviously do not mean that he was born in the city of Rome. Rather, his claim indicates that he received the privilege of Roman citizenship by virtue of his birth, implying that his father was also a Roman citizen.

5   Why didn't Paul inform the magistrates in Philippi of his Roman citizenship *before* his flogging as he did later in Jerusalem? Perhaps it was the earlier imprisonment in Philippi that taught Paul what the mention of this privilege could do for him. Mary Beard observes that simply claiming Roman citizenship did not always save one from an illegal beating. She notes that the "most famous ancient use" of the phrase *Civis Romanus sum* (I am a Roman citizen) "was as the unsuccessful plea of

an innocent victim [Publius Gavius] under a sentence of death imposed by a rogue Roman governor [Gaius Verres]" (Mary Beard, *SPQR: A History of Ancient Rome* [New York: W. W. Norton, 2015], 254).

6   For this interpretation of *pisteuson*, see Bates, *Salvation by Allegiance Alone*, 88–89. On the meaning of salvation in the context of this episode, see N. T. Wright, *Paul: A Biography* (San Francisco: HarperOne, 2018), 182–83.

7   Scholars debate whether these charges in Acts accurately reflect the perceived threat posed by the Christian mission. C. Kavin Rowe, *World Upside Down: Reading Acts in the Graeco-Roman Age* (Oxford: Oxford University Press, 2010), 17–89, argues that the Christian mission indeed posed a genuine threat in that it challenged pagan culture, but that Christians did not intend to launch a coup against the Roman government. Rowe clarifies that, in Acts, "the kingdom of which Jesus is King is not simply 'spiritual' but also material and social, which is to say that it takes up space in public" (101). Christians engaged in three core practices, "confessing Jesus as Lord, engaging in mission to the ends of the earth, forming publicly identifiable communities of Jews and Gentiles," which indeed had the effect of "turning the world upside down" and making the charges in Thessalonica politically plausible (135). Mikeal C. Parsons, *Acts*, Paideia (Grand Rapids: Baker Academic, 2008), 237, further adds that if the authorial audience of Acts were familiar with Paul's anti-imperial rhetoric in 1 Thess 4:15–17; 5:3, it would not have been surprised to read of the charges of sedition in Paul's first visit to Thessalonica.

8   The significance of the king as living law will be further explored in chs. 3 and 4 of this book.

9   See Wayne A. Meeks, *The Moral World of the First Christians* (Philadelphia: Westminster Press, 1986); Willard, *Spirit of the Disciplines*, 95–129; Abraham J. Malherbe, *Paul and the Popular Philosophers* (Minneapolis: Fortress, 1989); Troels Engberg-Pedersen, *Paul and the Stoics* (Louisville: Westminster John Knox, 2000); N. T. Wright, *Paul and the Faithfulness of God*, Christian Origins and the Question of God 4 (Minneapolis: Fortress, 2013), 197–245, 1354–407. Meeks, Willard, Malherbe, and Wright seek to understand aspects of Paul's theology by placing him in a larger philosophical discourse. Engberg-Pedersen goes further, by attempting a reading of Paul that is "'naturalistic' *and not* 'theological.'" Paul, he claims, drew freely upon Stoic ethics and his thinking can be understood largely within that ethical system (*Paul and the Stoics*, 1–44, here 2). For a critique of Engberg-Pedersen's project, see Wright, *Paul and the Faithfulness of God*, 2:1386–406.

10   Hadot, *Philosophy as a Way of Life*, 82–83.

11   Hadot, *Philosophy as a Way of Life*, 274.

12   Willard, *Spirit of the Disciplines*, 127.

13   It is important to point out that neither Paul nor his audience likely read Aristotle, Plato, or one of the many Hellenistic treatises on kingship. On the other hand, it is likely that the ideas articulated within this literary tradition—principally the relationships between *polis*, king, and virtue—were so foundational and widespread in antiquity that they were "in the air," so to speak. Engberg-Pedersen, *Paul and the Stoics*, 47–53, observes, for example, that the Stoics of Paul's day continued to be influenced by Aristotle's basic claim that the *telos* of the good life was *eudaimonia*. By analogy, one need not have read John Stuart Mill's *On Liberty* to be aware of its seminal concept of the "harm principle" because its influence has been so pervasive within western liberal society. Attending to the cultural repertoire reflected in this kingship discourse, especially as it was filtered through Roman imperial

ideology, provides us with the proper contextual "echo chamber" within which to hear the argument of Philippians.

14   Scholars debate whether the best life for Aristotle consists purely in theoretical contemplation (as book 10 suggests) or in morally virtuous action (as books 1–9 suggest). Following Irwin, "Conceptions," I am persuaded of the latter interpretation. So also Dorothea Frede, "The Political Character of Aristotle's *Ethics*," in *The Cambridge Companion to Aristotle's* Politics, ed. Marguerite Deslauriers and Pierre Destrée (Cambridge: Cambridge University Press, 2013), 33, who concludes that the life of moral action is more typically human than the "superhuman" theoretical life, and thus an appropriate pursuit for the citizens of the *polis*.

15   Aristotle offers the following definition: "Virtue, then, is a state that decides, consisting in a mean, the mean relative to us, which is defined by reference to reason, that is to say, to the reason by reference to which the prudent person would define it. It is a mean between two vices, one of excess and one of deficiency" (*Nic. Eth.* 1107a1–4).

16   Aristotle explains the connection between these similar Greek terms: "Virtue of character [i.e., of *ēthos*] results from habit [*ethos*]; hence its name 'ethical', slightly varied from 'ethos'" (*Nic. Eth.* 1103a15–20).

17   Growth in virtue is, moreover, not merely a matter of mindless repetition. Reflection on what one is doing is required so that the proper affective response may be acquired. Such thoughtful repetition also leads to growth in *phronēsis* (practical wisdom), a crucial virtue of thought (book 6, 1140a25–1145a12). *Phronēsis* is necessary in order to judge the particulars relevant to the practice of a virtue. For example: To whom should one be generous? In what amount? In which circumstances? See Kraut, "Habituation," 536–40; Frede, "Political Character," 22–25.

18   See in particular his comments with respect to moral education, which function as a segue from the *Ethics* to the *Politics* (*Nic. Eth.* 1179a34–1181b25). Moreover, the communal context is doubtless in view for Aristotle because society rather than the individual was the focus of political thought in Classical Greece. See Paul Cartledge, "Greek Political Thought: The Historical Context," in *The Cambridge History of Greek and Roman Political Thought*, ed. Christopher Rowe and Malcolm Schofield (Cambridge: Cambridge University Press, 2005), 12–13.

19   For Aristotle, the best life, the life of virtue, is characterized by *prohairesis*, or "thoughtful choice." Yet the achievement of such a life entails the following difficulty, as Stephen Salkever, "Reading Aristotle's *Nicomachean Ethics* and *Politics* as a Single Course of Lectures: Rhetoric, Politics, and Philosophy," in *The Cambridge Companion to Ancient Greek Political Thought*, ed. Stephen Salkever (New York: Cambridge University Press, 2009), 234, explains: "Political activity is an essential component of the prohairetic life; political activity always and necessarily compromises and limits the prohairetic life."

20   Pierre Pellegrin, "Aristotle's *Politics*," in *The Oxford Handbook of Aristotle*, ed. Christopher Shields (New York: Oxford University Press, 2012), 582, observes that Aristotle's *Politics* had "almost no posterity in antiquity," for the simple reason that the *polis*, conceived along Greek lines as an autonomous city-state, did not last long as a political entity. Nevertheless, as Meeks, *Moral World*, 23–28, demonstrates, the *polis* (understood as not as an independent state but merely as a city) remained the basic social setting of moral formation in the Roman period.

21   Charles Norris Cochrane, *Christianity and Classical Culture: A Study of Thought and Action from Augustus to Augustine* (New York: Oxford University Press, 1944), 82, explains that for Aristotle "the *polis* constitutes a response to

the specifically human demand for a specifically human order." In that sense it is "natural" but that does not imply that the *polis* occurs naturally in the course of human history.

22 The implied contrast in *Politics* between Athens and Sparta illustrates this point. Aristotle disparages a "vulgar decline into the cultivation of qualities supposed to be useful and of a more profitable character," namely the martial virtues characteristic of Sparta. In that *polis* the legislator directs "the whole of his legislation to the goal of conquest and war." Aristotle concludes, "we can all see for ourselves that they were not a happy community and their legislator was not right . . . here is a people which has stuck to his laws and never been hindered in carrying them out, and yet it has lost all that makes life worth living" (*Pol.* 1333b; English translation from Ernest Barker, trans., *The Politics of Aristotle* [New York: Oxford University Press, 1962]). On Aristotle's disagreement with Spartan values, see further *Pol.* 1271b2–10; 1324b5–9. See the discussion in Jean Roberts, *Aristotle and the* Politics, Routledge Philosophy Guidebooks (London: Routledge, 2009), 79–80.

23 In *Nic. Eth.* 10.9, Aristotle argues that habituation is insufficient for the acquisition of virtue; one must also be taught. Moral education is thus facilitated by good laws, which requires a flourishing *polis* (*Nic. Eth.* 1179b20–37; *Pol.* 1253a29–33). See R. C. Mulgan, *Aristotle's Political Theory* (Oxford: Clarendon, 1977), 25–28.

24 So Mulgan, *Aristotle's Political Theory*, 57: "The virtue of the citizen is therefore relative to the virtue of the constitution of which he is a member and may, if the constitution is a bad one, involve the pursuit of undesirable aims."

25 Malcolm Schofield, "Aristotle: An Introduction," in *The Cambridge History of Greek and Roman Political Thought*, ed. Christopher Rowe and Malcolm Schofield (Cambridge: Cambridge University Press, 2005), 312.

26 J. Rufus Fears, "The Theology of Victory at Rome: Approaches and Problems," *ANRW* 2.17.2 (1981): 759. Victor Goldschmidt, *Les dialogues de Platon: Structure et méthode dialectique*, 4th ed. (1947; repr., Paris: Presses Universitaires de France, 1988), 68 n. 20, observes that *aretē* in Plato conforms to a general formula, the administration of the *oikos* and *polis*; see, e.g., Plato, *Gorgias* 520e; *Meno* 71e, 73a. See further Aristotle, *Nic. Eth.* 1144a; 1107a; 1106b.

27 Whether Plato or Aristotle thought this possibility likely is doubtful. See the discussion of Plato's *Politicus* (*The Statesman*) 291a–303a in Christopher Rowe, "The *Politicus* and Other Dialogues," in *The Cambridge History of Greek and Roman Political Thought*, ed. Christopher Rowe and Malcolm Schofield (Cambridge: Cambridge University Press, 2005), 244–51. The significance of the philosopher-king for Paul's Christology is further discussed in ch. 3 of this book.

28 The term "principate" (Latin *principatus*) derives from the Latin *princeps*, meaning "first" or "first man." *Princeps* emerged as an informal way of recognizing the preeminence of Octavian, Rome's first emperor. *Principatus* was used by Romans to describe "both the period of leadership of an individual (what we could call a 'reign') and the system of government established by the early emperors." The English terminology of "empire" (e.g., emperor, imperial) derives from the Latin *imperator*, a term of military acclamation given to a victorious general (Richard Alston, *Rome's Revolution: Death of the Republic and Birth of the Empire*, Ancient Warfare and Civilization [Oxford: Oxford University Press, 2015], 225–26).

29 Indeed, beholding the glorious figure of the king was often thought to be instrumental to the process of moral formation, a phenomenon I and others have referred to as "transformation by vision." This phenomenon is discussed in ch. 3

of this book. See further Charles H. Talbert, *Reading the Sermon on the Mount: Character Formation and Decision Making in Matthew 5–7* (Columbia: University of South Carolina Press, 2004); Julien C. H. Smith, *Christ the Ideal King*; Jipp, *Christ Is King*.

30 Talbert, *Sermon*, 39.

31 Talbert, *Sermon*, 38–39. In addition to Plato and Aristotle mentioned above, see Musuonius Rufus, Plutarch, and Philo.

32 The significance of the king's role of benefactor vis-à-vis moral transformation is further discussed in ch. 4 of this book.

33 Aristotle distinguished between the virtues of generosity and magnificence, the former applying to the spending and giving of the typical person, the latter confined to those whose wealth could and should benefit the entire *polis* (*Nic. Eth.* 1119b23–1123a34).

34 For Aristotle, magnanimity (*megalopsuchia* means "greatness of soul") does not merely indicate, as it does today, a generosity of spirit: "The magnanimous person, then, seems to be the one who thinks himself worthy of great things and *is really worthy of them*" (*Nic. Eth.* 1123b3; emphasis added). Aristotle concedes that the magnanimous person will often *seem* arrogant, given that he is disdainful of small honors not worthy of his greatness (*Nic. Eth.* 1124a20). My students often remark that the magnanimous person actually *is* arrogant.

35 The relationship between benefactor and beneficiary is a particular iteration of what is often referred to as the patron-client relationship. For an overview of patronage in the Roman period, see Richard Saller, "Status and Patronage," in *The High Empire, A.D. 70–192*, ed. Alan K. Bowman, Peter Garnsey, and Dominique Rathbone, vol. 11 of *The Cambridge Ancient History* (Cambridge: Cambridge University Press, 2000), 817–54. For discussion of the patron-client relationship within the larger dynamic of honor and shame, see Bruce J. Malina, *The New Testament World: Insights from Cultural Anthropology*, rev. ed. (Louisville: Westminster John Knox, 1993), 28–60, 99–112. Numerous scholars have found this approach illuminating of NT texts. David deSilva, for example, concludes that apostasy in Hebrews must be understood as an affront to the loyalty required in the divine-human patron-client relationship ("Exchanging Favor for Wrath: Apostasy in Hebrews and Patron-Client Relationships," *JBL* 115 [Spring 1996]: 115–16).

36 Klaus Bringmann, "The King as Benefactor: Some Remarks on Ideal Kingship in the Age of Hellenism," in *Images and Ideologies: Self-Definition in the Hellenistic World*, ed. A. W. Bulloch et al., Hellenistic Culture and Society (Berkeley: University of California Press, 1993), 17.

37 English translation from *Isocrates*, 3 vols, trans. George Norlin and Larue van Hook, LCL (Cambridge, Mass.: Harvard University Press, 1954). Bringmann, "King as Benefactor," 18, argues that in the Hellenistic era, "beneficence became a device of policy establishing strong moral ties between kings and cities."

38 Saller, "Status and Patronage," 842: "Subjects expressed their gratitude in several standard ways, above all through loyalty." Alston argues that imperial benefaction was "the key to the regime's stability" (*Rome's Revolution*, 278–83, here 278).

39 In addition to the literature discussed here, see Polybius' *Hist.* 2.61, in which the author praises the Megalopolitan refugees for preserving *pistis* with the Achaean League in 233 BCE. They chose to suffer great hardships "for the sake of not betraying their good faith (*pistin*) towards their allies." Here, *pistis* denotes loyalty reciprocated between political agents. See the discussion in Benjamin Gray, "Scepticism About Community: Polybius on Peloponnesian Exiles, Good Faith ('Pistis') and

the Achaian League," *Historia: Zeitschrift für Alte Geschicthe* 62 (2013): 323–60; the translation of Polybius is from p. 330. Herodotus uses the term *pistis* to denote the exchange of guarantees of mutual assistance between allied Greek states during the invasion of Xerxes in 480 BCE (*Hist.* 7.145). See also Jörg-Dieter Gauger, "Antiochos III. und Artaxerxes: Der Fremdherrscher als Wohltäter," *JSJ* 38 (2007): 197–98, 213, who demonstrates that *pistis* often conveys the sense of political loyalty in the writings of Josephus. The Latin term *fides*, which can be translated as "faithfulness," also conveys the idea of "good faith" expressed between political allies; see Thomas Wiedemann, "Reflections of Roman Political Thought in Latin Historical Writing," in *The Cambridge History of Greek and Roman Political Thought*, ed. Christopher Rowe and Malcolm Schofield (Cambridge: Cambridge University Press, 2005), 524.

40   The Maccabean literature consists of four separate texts, 1–4 Maccabees. They were composed at different times by different authors between the second century BCE and the first century CE. They were written in Greek, although 1 Maccabees may be a translation of an original Hebrew text.

41   Some time after Demetrius I's death, his son Demetrius II undertakes negotiations with Jonathan, fulfilling much of what his father had promised earlier. Erich S. Gruen, *Heritage and Hellenism: The Reinvention of Jewish Tradition*, Hellenistic Culture and Society 30 (Berkeley: University of California Press, 1998), 17, observes that the son is portrayed as benefactor like the father, offering gifts in exchange for loyalty. Demetrius II writes, "We have determined to do good to the nation of the Jews, who are our friends and fulfill their obligations to us, because of the goodwill (*eunoias*) they show toward us" (1 Macc 11:33). Like *pistis*, the term *eunoia* was part of the vocabulary of the reciprocal exchange of benefaction and loyalty; see John Ma, "Kings," in *A Companion to the Hellenistic World*, ed. Andrew Erskine, Blackwell Companions to the Ancient World (Oxford: Blackwell, 2003), 103.

42   Similar usage of this terminology to convey political loyalty is found elsewhere in 1 Maccabees. Demetrius is advised to choose a delegate to subdue Judaea: "'Now then send a man whom you trust (*pisteueis*)" (7:7); the king appoints Bacchides, who was "a great man in the kingdom and was faithful (*piston*) to the king." In 1 Macc 8:16, the Roman system of government is described in this manner: "They trust (*pisteuousin*) one man each year to rule over them and to control all their land." Implicit in the notion of trust here is the reciprocal expression of allegiance in response to rule.

43   This account, whose aim is to show that reason, guided by Torah, is sovereign over the passions, is derived from the account in 2 Macc 6–7.

44   F. W. Walbank, "Monarchies and Monarchic Ideas," in *Cambridge Ancient History*, vol. 7.2, ed. F. W. Walbank et al. (Cambridge: Cambridge University Press, 1984), 69–70.

45   The loyalty (*pistis*) demanded by the Seleucid king is contrasted with the martyrs' loyalty (*pistis*) owed to God, their divine benefactor. See David A. deSilva, *Introducing the Apocrypha: Message, Context, and Significance* (Grand Rapids: Baker Academic, 2002), 370–71.

46   For a helpful introduction to the historical and social context of the Maccabean literature, see deSilva, *Introducing the Apocrypha*, 42–62.

47   Third Maccabees, a historical romance, provides a colorful narrative of events that transpired during the reign of the Egyptian king Ptolemy Philopator, some 150 years before the Maccabean revolt. Having been rebuffed in his attempt to

enter the Holy of Holies in the Jerusalem Temple, Philopator exacts revenge by enacting a series of hostile decrees against the Jews of Egypt. But those who become initiates into the mystery cult of Dionysus (to which the king was devoted) would be granted citizenship in Alexandria (2:25–31). When the majority of Jews reject the king's offer, he becomes enraged and devises a plan to put the Jews to death. Nevertheless, the Jews remain blameless of these calumnies, as the narrator insists that "The Jews, however, continued to maintain goodwill and unswerving loyalty (*pistin*) toward the dynasty" (3:3). The king has the Jews throughout Egypt rounded up and deported to Alexandria, yet his plans to execute them are thwarted twice. Upon the second occasion, the king actually forgets his hatred of the Jews and instead praises them, "'who give me no ground for complaint and have exhibited to an extraordinary degree a full and firm loyalty (*pistin*) to my ancestors" (5:31). When the king is eventually persuaded by two angels to abandon his violence, he blames his advisors for having led him astray, observing that the Jews had "faithfully (*en pistei*) kept our country's fortresses" (6:25), a reference to their loyal military service. So also the king's earlier reference to "myriad affairs liberally entrusted (*pepisteumena*) to them" refers to the Jews' loyal military service, in exchange for which they were offered Alexandrian citizenship (3:21).

48   See especially ch. 3 of Teresa Morgan, *Roman Faith and Christian Faith*: Pistis *and* Fides *in the Early Roman Empire and Early Churches* (Oxford: Oxford University Press, 2015), 77–122. The political nuance of the term is often ignored *a priori* as having little relevance to its usage in the NT. Consider the comment of Rudolf Bultmann in his article "πιστεύω κτλ." in Gerhard Kittel and Gerhard Friedrich, eds., *Theological Dictionary of the New Testament*, 10 vols., trans. Geoffrey William Bromiley (Grand Rapids: Eerdmans, 1964), 7:145. In a footnote to his discussion of the Greek usage, he notes that the article "deals only with the main uses of πίστις etc. in the Gk. world which are of importance in the history of the bibl. concept or in comparison with this."

49   The Stoics, for example, contended that *eudaimonia* consisted in nothing more than moral virtue, whereas Aristotle thought some modicum of external goods was also necessary (Engberg-Pedersen, *Paul and the Stoics*, 53). I agree with Wright, *After You Believe*, that Paul's christologically shaped understanding of the human *telos* is intended to upstage the eudaimonism of Aristotle. As Stanley Hauerwas, "The Difference of Virtue and the Difference It Makes: Courage Exemplified," *Modern Theology* 9 (1993): 249–64, contends, there is no general theory of virtue. Aristotle and Aquinas articulate strikingly different understandings of courage—what it looks like and what it is good for. This difference, moreover, is more than idiosyncratic, but has to do with the differences that characterize the communities these two men belong to. Hauerwas observes, "the characterizations of the virtues, their content, how they interrelate, will differ from one community and tradition to another" (260). Aristotle would agree with Hauerwas on this point: Sparta and Athens, he believed, were characterized by markedly different understandings of virtue.

50   The transition from republic to the new form of government that emerged under Augustus—what I term "constitutional monarchy"—was politically complex. In January of 27 BCE, Octavian returned to the Senate the extraordinary powers he had been given, thus appearing to restore the republic. Yet as it turned out, this gesture led rather to a "refiguring of Octavian's power. . . . There was never any intention that the newly named Augustus would step aside and retire from the political fray. He remained the dominant figure in Roman politics" (Alston, *Rome's Revolution*, 213–36, here 235–36).

51   Nicholas Purcell, "Romans in the Roman World," in *The Cambridge Companion to the Age of Augustus*, ed. Karl Galinsky (Cambridge: Cambridge University Press, 2005), 90–91. "Roman political culture's extraordinary openness and willingness to incorporate outsiders," as Mary Beard shows, can be traced back to the myth of the city's founding (Beard, *SPQR*, 66–69, here 67).

52   Roman *imperium* was the supreme power to interpret and execute law, up to and including the death penalty, vested in the magistrate.

53   Eventually, the Emperor Caracalla (r. 198–217) granted Roman citizenship to all free persons in the Empire.

54   Greg Woolf, "Provincial Perspectives," in *The Cambridge Companion to the Age of Augustus*, ed. Karl Galinsky (Cambridge: Cambridge University Press, 2005), 122. Thus, for example, cities vied for the title "*neokoros*," which indicated that the city possessed a temple of the Imperial Cult. The city of Pergamum boasted that it was the first to be "thrice *neokoros*," that is, possess three such temples. Ephesus boasted in return that it was the only city *neokoros* four times over. On this, see A. N. Sherwin-White, *The Roman Citizenship* (Oxford: Clarendon, 1939), 237–38.

55   Sherwin-White, *The Roman Citizenship*, 168.

56   Witness Augustus' effusive self-praise in the *Res gestae*.

57   The term "cult" as used in this sense refers neutrally to the activity of religious veneration. It does not imply anything sinister or aberrant, as the term does in modern parlance. The Cult of Virtues functioned as a vehicle for the appropriation and modification of Hellenistic political and religious concepts widespread in the eastern Mediterranean world that the Romans gradually conquered. This phenomenon had been developing for some time. According to J. Rufus Fears, "The Cult of Virtues and Roman Imperial Ideology," *ANRW* 2.17.2 (1981): 848–49, it was established during the early period of Roman imperialism stretching from the Samnite Wars (343–290 BCE) to the defeat of Antiochus III (190 BCE). However, Duncan Fishwick, *The Imperial Cult in the Latin West: Studies in the Ruler Cult of the Western Provinces of the Roman Empire*, 7 vols. (Leiden: Brill, 1991–2004), 2.1:456, places the inception of the cult earlier, in 367 BCE, with the founding of a temple to Concordia on the eastern slope of Capitol. The following discussion is indebted to the treatment found in both Fears and Fishwick.

58   Fears, "Theology of Victory," 740. See Symmachus, *Relationes* 3.8; Cicero, *Nat. d.* 2.61.

59   The expression comes from Varro's lost work, *De gente populi Romani libri*, preserved in part in Augustine's *City of God* 6.5. On the tendency of Roman religion to turn abstract concepts into concrete realities (i.e., gods), see Andrew Wallace-Hadrill, "The Emperor and His Virtues," *Historia* 30 (1981): 314–17.

60   In addition to what we might typically think of as the Roman pantheon of gods and goddesses—Jupiter, Juno, Neptune, Minerva, and the like—Romans also venerated these virtues—Concordia, Pax, Victory, and so forth—*as* actual gods and goddesses.

61   In both the Roman and Greek worlds, the deification of abstract ideas was common. The objects of worship in the Roman Cult of Virtues, however, were not merely personified abstract ideas, but rather concrete conditions brought about by divine power. Cicero called them *utilitates*, since each one brought a particular benefit (*utilitas*). Stoics designated such divine beings as *pragmata*. Fears, "Cult of Virtues," 828–33, renders them "Virtues," following Milton's translation of *utilitates*. A Virtue in this sense is understood as "the power or operative influence inherent in a supernatural being."

62   The Greek word *aretē* could also denote "manliness," although this concept was more normally evoked by the word *andreia*, the quintessential "manly" virtue often translated as "bravery." See the discussion in Fears, "Theology of Victory," 747–48.

63   In this regard, note Suetonius' frank appraisal of imperial wickedness, particularly in the lives of Tiberius, Gaius Caligula, Claudius, and Nero (Suetonius, *Lives of the Caesars*, trans. J. C. Rolfe, LCL [Cambridge, Mass.: Harvard University Press, 1914]).

64   Fears, "Cult of Virtues," 875. The emperor referred to himself as the *princeps inter pares*, "the first among equals," thus preserving the semblance of a constitutional republic. Scholars thus commonly refer to this form of government as the "principate."

65   Fears, "Cult of Virtues," 887.

66   Fears, "Cult of Virtues," 889.

67   See the discussion in the following chapter of the Roman victory parade, the *pompa triomphalis* or "triumph" as it is commonly called, one of the most spectacular means by which Roman victory was celebrated and emphasized. For thorough discussion of the triumph in Roman culture, see Mary Beard, *The Roman Triumph* (Cambridge, Mass.: Belknap, 2007). Although such spectacles celebrated the military victories of numerous generals, Augustus' military dominance was regarded as unparalleled. As Andrew Wallace-Hadrill observes, "Victory was an imperial specialty" (*Augustan Rome*, 2nd ed., Classical World Series 10 [London: Bloomsbury Academic, 2018], 89).

68   Fears, "Theology of Victory," 739–40. The theology of victory was comprised of three central elements: "the justification and legitimization of absolute power; defeat as the proof of tyranny and falsehood; the conqueror as invincible and clement inaugurator of a new and eternal era of prosperity" (752). For the ways in which religion functions to legitimate social structures, see Peter L. Berger and Thomas Luckmann, *The Social Construction of Reality: A Treatise in the Sociology of Knowledge* (Garden City, N.Y.: Doubleday, 1966), 86–96.

69   In 17 BCE, the Secular Games were held in Rome to mark the end of an age (*saeculum*) and the beginning of a new one. The tradition of such games dates back to 249, at which funereal rites were celebrated to appease the offended gods whose favor was presumed to have been lost. Under Augustus, the rites associated with the Secular Games were decidedly celebratory rather than funereal. Augustus, so the games proclaimed, had ushered in a golden age of peace and prosperity. The games were a triumph of Roman propaganda, as Alston concludes: "The Secular Games were a performance of the regime's ideology. They linked key ideas: military success, peace, prosperity of the land, childbirth, divine blessings, and the disciplining of the Roman people through legislation" (*Rome's Revolution*, 291–97, here 293–94). Rome's "golden age" propaganda is further discussed in ch. 5.

70   Fears, "Theology of Victory," 815: "Thus in the Roman empire, as in Egypt and in the ancient Near East, the image of victory conveyed far more than the mere fact of military triumph. It rather characterized a conception of the social order in which the well-being of the body politic was seen to reside entirely in the figure of a charismatic monarch." Andrew Wallace-Hadrill describes the reshaping of the Roman Forum throughout the reign of Augustus, including the rebuilding of the senate house—renamed the Curia Julia—which had burned down after the death of Julius Caesar. Each session of the Senate began with worship, the focus of which were the statue of Victory commemorating Augustus' victory in the civil wars and a golden shield proclaiming his virtues (*Augustan Rome*, 79–80).

71   Fears, "Theology of Victory," 749; emphasis added. See also Wallace-Hadrill, "Virtues," 318–19.

72   Richard Alston observes that the unprecedented celebrations of Octavian's victories at Actium and Alexandria were in part born out of fear, motivated by the desire to show loyalty to Octavian lest he be inclined to "launch a fresh purge on his return, as others had done before him. The voting of lavish honors was not so much a mark of thanks to the victor as a sign of insecurity" (*Rome's Revolution*, 227).

73   As Alston notes, the Augustan practice of colonization was "one of the most direct ways in which the rewards of empire were distributed to the people." Thereby, ensuring the well-being of soldiers, he continues, "was a political and financial priority" (*Rome's Revolution*, 278–79).

74   Chaido Koukouli-Chrysantaki, "Colonia Iulia Augusta Philippensis," in *Philippi at the Time of Paul and After His Death*, ed. Charalambos Bakirtzis and Helmut Koester (1998; repr., Eugene, Ore.: Wipf and Stock, 2009), 23: "a large number of veterans" were settled in Philippi. Peter Oakes, *Philippians: From People to Letter*, Society for New Testament Studies Monograph Series (Cambridge: Cambridge University Press, 2001): veterans constituted a minority of the overall population.

75   Peter Garnsey, *Social Status and Legal Privilege in the Roman Empire* (Oxford: Clarendon, 1970), 221–23, 245–51. Such privilege was also accorded by virtue of their Roman citizenship, although the practical advantages of Roman citizenship were declining over the course of the first two centuries of the principate (260–71).

76   Oakes, *Philippians: From People to Letter*, 1–76.

77   Gorman, *Becoming the Gospel*, 125–29.

78   Oakes, *Philippians: From People to Letter*, 77–96.

79   This scene remains etched in my memory to this day. For decades, in fact, whenever I had to distinguish my left from right, I instinctively positioned myself in that classroom, mentally (and sometimes even physically!) placing my hand over my heart. Maybe this just means that I am especially spatially challenged. But I think it also bears witness to the indelible impression this solemn ritual made on my young person, one that has to this day not departed.

80   The U.S. Pledge of Allegiance was first widely promoted in the 1890s, during a period of great concern about the loyalty—or perhaps dual loyalties—of new immigrants. It was never actually a requirement for citizenship, although most states eventually mandated it in schools; and of course the Supreme Court specifically allowed the Jehovah's Witnesses and others who object on religious grounds to be exempt from the Pledge. I am grateful to my colleague Mel Piehl for this historical note.

81   The potentially deformative effects of giving allegiance to persons, institutions, and symbols will be taken up in ch. 6 of this book. To anticipate that discussion we might briefly consider the problematic aspect of pledging allegiance to a symbol such as the flag of a nation state. In the Pledge of Allegiance, the flag may be seen to symbolize a common project of human flourishing in which liberty and justice is promised for all. Yet symbols such as flags are often co-opted and employed towards the more sinister end of subservience to the state or the unquestioning acceptance of a national mythos. We might dwell on these paradoxical imperatives found in one of Wendell Berry's poems: "Denounce the government and embrace the flag. Hope to live in that free republic for which it stands" ("Manifesto: The Mad Farmer Liberation Front," in *The Country of Marriage* [New York: Harcourt Brace Jovanovich, 1973], 16–17).

82   In terms of epistolary genre, Philippians has been described variously as a letter of thanks, a letter of consolation, or a family letter. For a useful introduction to ancient letters, see Patrick Gray, *Opening Paul's Letters: A Reader's Guide to Genre and Interpretation* (Grand Rapids: Baker Academic, 2012). More technical discussion can be found in Hans-Josef Klauck, *Ancient Letters and the New Testament: A Guide to Context and Exegesis* (Waco, Tex.: Baylor University Press, 2006); for Philippians, see especially 317–20. See further the introductory sections in the following commentaries: Bonnie B. Thurston and Judith Ryan, *Philippians and Philemon*, SP 10 (Collegeville, Minn.: Liturgical, 2005), 24–37; Markus Bockmuehl, *The Epistle to the Philippians*, BNTC (London: A & C Black, 1997), 20–42; Charles B. Cousar, *Philippians and Philemon: A Commentary*, NTL (Louisville: Westminster John Knox, 2009), 11–12.

83   As noted above, the church in Philippi was most likely of modest means (see 2 Cor 8:1–5), and may have been experiencing economic persecution as a result of their faith.

84   See Stephen E. Fowl, "Know Your Context: Giving and Receiving Money in Philippians," *Int* 56 (2002): 45–58.

85   Thurston and Ryan, *Philippians and Philemon*, 49–50. See also 1:5, where Paul speaks of their "sharing (*koinōnia*) in the gospel"; and 4:15: "No church shared (*ekoinōnēsen*) with me in the matter of giving and receiving, except you alone." Of course, Paul's use of the term does not imply a contractual, legal relationship with the Philippian believers; see John Reumann, *Philippians: A New Translation with Introduction and Commentary*, AB 33B (New Haven: Yale University Press, 2008), 119, 146.

86   Paul describes their sacrificial generosity in a later letter to the church in Corinth this way: "For, as I can testify, they voluntarily gave according to their means, and even beyond their means, begging us earnestly for the privilege of sharing (*koinōnian*) in this ministry to the saints—and this, not merely as we expected; they gave themselves first to the Lord and, by the will of God, to us" (2 Cor 8:3–5).

87   See Phil 1:20–21; it is possible that Paul has been imprisoned on a capital charge.

88   NIV, NASB, NET: "conduct yourselves"; KJV: "let your conversation be"; LEB: "lead your lives"; RSV, ESV: "let your manner of life"; TEV: "your way of life"; NCV: "live in a way".

89   The semantic domain is wider than this meaning. In some instances it means to live in accordance with the precepts of a religion. But in no instance does it merely mean to live morally. See R. R. Brewer, "The Meaning of Politeuesthe in Philippians 1:27," *JBL* 73 (1954): 76–83; Ernest C. Miller, "Πολιτεύεσθε In Philippians 1.27: Some Philological and Thematic Observations," *JSNT* 15 (1982): 86–96. Commentators frequently translate the verb in a way that captures the political nuance. See, e.g., Bockmuehl, *Philippians*, 96–98; Thurston and Ryan, *Philippians and Philemon*, 68.

90   For example, Paul uses the verb *peripatein* (to walk) some thirty-two times to describe a way of living according to a moral standard. His usage in Rom 13:13 is typical: "Let us live (*peripatēsōmen*) honorably as in the day, not in reveling and drunkenness, not in debauchery and licentiousness, not in quarreling and jealousy."

91   It is worth noting that this is the single instance in which Paul uses the verb. It is used only one other time in the NT, in Acts 23:1. There, Luke narrates Paul's defense before the Sanhedrin: "Brothers, up to this day I have lived my life (*pepoliteumai*) with a clear conscience before God." The Sanhedrin's authority was both

religious and political, and it is thus reasonable to think that Luke's choice of the verb intends to capture its political nuance.

92 Bates, *Salvation by Allegiance Alone*, 44, concludes that, for Paul, the gospel is a "power-releasing story about Jesus, the one who is now ruling as the allegiance-demanding Lord of heaven and earth. The gospel centers on Jesus as king."

93 For an explanation of the dative of advantage and the dative of cause, see Daniel B. Wallace, *Greek Grammar Beyond the Basics: An Exegetical Syntax of the New Testament* (Grand Rapids: Zondervan, 1996), 142–44, 167–68.

94 Paul is not referring to individuals in the church in Philippi, but rather to certain persons he has become acquainted with during his current imprisonment. Their motivation to proclaim the gospel—self-promotion—does, however parallel the "selfish ambition" that characterizes some in the Philippian congregation (Phil 2:3); see Bockmuehl, *Philippians*, 76–81; Cousar, *Philippians and Philemon*, 35–37.

95 This approach was common among Stoic philosophers, who sought to cultivate an attitude of indifference to all things outside of one's control (Pierre Hadot, *What Is Ancient Philosophy?* trans. Michael Chase [Cambridge, Mass.: Belknap, 2002], 222).

96 Fears, "Theology of Victory," 747.

97 Paul S. Minear, "Singing and Suffering in Philippi," in *The Conversation Continues: Studies in Paul and John in Honor of J. Louis Martyn*, ed. Robert Tomson Fortna and Beverly Roberts Gaventa (Nashville: Abingdon, 1990), 202–19, suggests that Paul, by focalizing the hymn within the letter's argument, is deliberately recalling the hymn's original liturgical context in the Philippian church. This rhetorical strategy assumes that doxology and theology are closely linked. That is to say, worship forms thinking.

98 The markers of the parallel structure—A, A' and so forth—are my own.

99 Gorman, *Apostle of the Crucified Lord*, 488–91, documents the many echoes of the hymn throughout the letter.

100 Gorman, *Becoming the Gospel*, 115–25.

101 Gorman, *Apostle of the Crucified Lord*, 507–10.

102 Such persons, it is important to note, are not enemies of Christ himself, but rather of the cruciform pattern of his life—renunciation of status, suffering, and eventual exaltation—to which Paul is exhorting his audience to conform.

103 I am indebted to Gorman, *Apostle of the Crucified Lord*, 496–518, for this reading of the letter. Although not much can be known with confidence about the identities of these two women, it is clear that Paul holds them in high regard and considers them valued partners in the gospel. They are not to be identified with the "enemies of the cross of Christ" (3:18–19). Paul is aware of a dispute between them, but it does not therefore follow that this interpersonal friction is the sole locus of disunity Paul addresses. See Robert F. Hull Jr., "Constructing Euodia and Syntyche: Philippians 4:2–3 and the Informed Imagination," *Priscilla Papers* 30, no. 2 (2016): 3–7; Francis X. Malinowski, "The Brave Women of Philippi," *BTB* 15 (1985): 60–64; Veronica Koperski, "Feminist Concerns and the Authorial Readers in Philippians," *Louvain Studies* 17 (1992): 269–92.

104 I disagree with Elizabeth A. Castelli that the call to imitate Paul is intended to "[reinscribe] Paul's privileged position within the hierarchy as the mediating figure through whom the community might gain access to salvation" (*Imitating Paul: A Discourse of Power*, Literary Currents in Biblical Interpretation [Louisville: Westminster John Knox, 1991], 96). Rather, I understand the practice of imitation within the philosophical tradition of virtue ethics as the practice whereby one is

habituated into virtuous behavior. While I find much of Castelli's discussion of the background of mimesis in antiquity helpful (59–87), I am not persuaded that Paul's mimetic discourse is a "coercive move" that "masks the will to power which one finds in Pauline discourse" (87).

105   A wooden translation that follows the Greek syntax might be: "this think among yourselves, which also in Christ Jesus" (*touto phroneite en humin ho kai en Christō Iēsou*). The meaning is either taken to be: (a) "have the mind that Christ had"; or (b) "have the mind which is yours in Christ." See the discussion in Bockmuehl, *Philippians*, 121–22. Gorman, *Becoming the Gospel*, 118, argues that the *ho kai* ("which also") links the two phrases *en humin* and *en Christō Iēsou*. His translation runs, "Cultivate this mindset within your community (*en humin*), which is in fact (*ho kai*) a community in Christ Jesus (*en Christō Iēsou*)."

106   My claim finds support in the argument of Stephen E. Fowl, "Christology and Ethics in Philippians 2:5–11," in *Where Christology Began: Essays on Philippians 2*, ed. Ralph P. Martin and Brian J. Dodd (Louisville: Westminster John Knox, 1998), 145–48. For the description of *phronēsis* as "moral insight," see Engberg-Pedersen, *Paul and the Stoics*, 51.

107   Aristotle distinguishes *phronēsis* from other intellectual virtues such as *epistēmē* (scientific knowledge), *technē* (craft knowledge), *nous* (understanding), and *sophia* (wisdom). Unlike scientific knowledge, which can be taught, practical wisdom must be acquired experientially. This is the case because it requires not merely knowledge of universals, but also of particulars. For example, one might know the universal principle that bodily health is good, but not the particular foods that promote health. *Phronēsis* thus requires both universal and particular knowledge. See *Nic. Eth.* 6 (1139b15–1141b23).

108   See the discussion of ancient Mediterranean honor-shame culture in Malina, *New Testament World*, 28–62.

109   In addition to giving money, Augustus assists the treasury (17), gives grain (18), builds and restores public buildings (19, 20), builds and restores temples (21, 24), and gives gladiatorial games (22, 23). P. A. Brunt and J. M. Moore, eds., *Res Gestae Divi Augusti: The Achievements of the Divine Augustus* (Oxford: Oxford University Press, 1967), 58, comment that all of these benefactions "must have had an incalculable effect in winning the 'universal consent' of which he boasts in 34.1. . . . His largesses seem usually to have a particular political explanation."

110   Bringmann, "King as Benefactor," 16, notes that benefaction was frequently motivated by the love of honor, which was also its reward.

111   English translation from Carnes Lord, trans., *Aristotle's Politics* (1984; repr., Chicago: University of Chicago Press, 2013), here and below.

112   See the comprehensive review of evidence from classical literature, inscriptions, and papyri in W. Ruppel, "Politeuma: Bedeutungsgeschichte eines staatsrechtlichen Terminus," *Phil* 82 (1927): 268–312, 433–54, as well as the helpful summary and discussion in Andrew T. Lincoln, *Paradise Now and Not Yet: Studies in the Role of the Heavenly Dimension in Paul's Thought with Special Reference to His Eschatology*, Society for New Testament Studies Monograph Series 43 (Cambridge: Cambridge University Press, 1981), 97–101. Recently, some of Ruppel's conclusions have been challenged by Gert Lüderitz, "What is the Politeuma?" in *Studies in Early Jewish Epigraphy*, ed. Jan Willem van Henten and Pieter Willem van der Horst, AGJU 21 (Leiden: Brill, 1994), 183–225.

113   So Lincoln, *Paradise Now and Not Yet*, 99. It is also unlikely that Paul was encouraging the church to think of themselves as a private club or voluntary organization

(e.g., a club of soldiers, a festival association, or cult society), another possible meaning for *politeuma*. Elsewhere in the letter, Paul expresses fervent hope that they are "holding fast (*epechontes*) to the word of life" (Phil 2:16), an expression that implies some kind of public proclamation of the gospel, for which they appear to be suffering. Whether the verb *epechō* means "to hold fast" or "to hold forth" is debated. Likely it implies both. See the helpful discussion in Gorman, *Becoming the Gospel*, 125–29. It is further unlikely that Paul has in view a *politeuma* as a public organization with special legal rights, such as an ethnic community living in a foreign city. Although Paul no doubt envisions the church as a public body, nowhere does he imply that the church should be accorded special legal rights, as was (allegedly) the *politeuma* of Jews in Alexandria. Lüderitz, "What is the Politeuma?" challenges the historical evidence thought to support this meaning. Finally, as Newbigin, *Gospel*, 223, observes, the church of the first three centuries was a martyr church, refusing the "protection offered by Roman law to the private exercise of religion as a way of personal salvation."

114 Polybius, *Hist.* 3.2.6; 8.2–3; 6.3.11; 10.6f; 12.9; 14.12; 43.1; 46.9; 50.4; 51.1 Josephus, *C. Ap.* 2.184; *Ant.* 1.5.13; Plutarch, *Solon* 9.2; *Romulus* 20.2; *Theseus* 35.4; 2 Macc 12:7.

115 Aristotle, *Pol.* 3.6.1278b: "A constitution (*politeia*) is the arrangement of magistracies in a state (*poleōs*), especially of the highest of all. The government (*politeuma*) is everywhere sovereign in the state (*poleōs*), and the constitution is in fact the government (*politeuma d'estin hē politeia*)." See further 3.6.1278b; 7.1279a; 3.13.1283b; 4.6.1293a; 13.1297b; Mulgan, *Aristotle's Political Theory*, 57.

116 My argument follows Lincoln, *Paradise Now and Not Yet*, 101–9, against that of Helmut Koester, "The Purpose of the Polemic of a Pauline Fragment," *NTS* 8 (1962): 317–32, who sees only a future temporal referent in "the heavens."

117 Paul's confident hope in the future, and indeed the way this hope thoroughly transformed his view of the present, stands in marked contrast with the views of Stoics and Epicureans. As Hadot, *Philosophy as a Way of Life*, 268, observes, the spiritual exercises of these schools aimed to bring one's focus resolutely upon the *present* moment.

118 See ch. 1.

119 Bockmuehl, *Philippians*, 230.

120 Wright, *Paul and the Faithfulness of God*, 2:1400.

121 Note that citizenship is a present reality: "Our citizenship *is* (*huparchei*) in heaven." The verb, which means "to exist," is in the present tense. Yet Jesus "*will* transform (*metaschēmatisei*) the body of our humiliation that it may be conformed to the body of his glory." Here the verb is in the future tense. Although this transformation will not be completely effected until the *eschaton*, it nevertheless begins in the present. See further Bockmuehl, *Philippians*, 234–35; Cousar, *Philippians and Philemon*, 80–81. This present dimension of transformation into the image of Jesus is discussed in the following chapter.

122 This can be seen in the way that the end of Phil 3:21 ("by the power that also enables him to make all things subject to himself") echoes Ps 8:6 ("You have given them dominion over the works of your hands; you have put all things under their feet"), and also Paul's earlier letter (1 Cor 15:27). Psalm 8 recalls the vocation of the first humans, to rule over creation as God's vicegerents. Philippians 3:21 echoes the original human vocation and predicates it of Christ's reign. The eschatological transformation of humans, "being conformed to the body of his glory," thus amounts to restoring humanity to its pristine vocation. See Wright, *After You Believe*, 73–100; Wright, *Paul and the Faithfulness of God*, 2:821–22; cf. Reumann, *Philippians*, 600.

123 Newbigin, *Gospel*, 232.

124 The quotations are from Acts 17:6–7, following the argument of C. Kavin Rowe, *World Upside Down*. Whether or not Paul sees the Roman empire as a threat to the gospel is debated. John M. G. Barclay, *Pauline Churches and Diaspora Jews* (Grand Rapids: Eerdmans, 2016), 363–87, argues that the Roman empire was insignificant to Paul. Wright, *Paul and the Faithfulness of God*, 2:1271–319, contends rather that Paul's announcement that "Jesus is Lord" implied at once that "Caesar is not." However this debate is adjudicated, it is clear that Paul is not concerned with *Realpolitik* in Philippians 3:20; so Bockmuehl, *Philippians*, 234.

125 The Stoic tradition comes closest, insisting that suffering must be endured with equanimity, which testified to one's moral character.

126 Hadot, *Philosophy as a Way of Life*, describes the spiritual exercises practiced by various philosophical schools (e.g., Stoics, Epicureans), which intend to cultivate an appropriate response to suffering.

127 On the ubiquity and centrality of spiritual exercises within ancient philosophical schools, see Hadot, *Philosophy as a Way of Life*, 81–125; Willard, *Spirit of the Disciplines*, 98–100. In a similar vein, Stephen E. Fowl, "Christology and Ethics," 148, explains that the Philippian Christians are not to imitate Paul and his associates with a "wooden sort of identical repetition" but rather to develop the virtue of practical reasoning (*phronēsis*), a process which involves habituation and practice.

128 Willard, *Spirit of the Disciplines*, 44–55; J. Richard Middleton, *The Liberating Image: The Imago Dei in Genesis 1* (Grand Rapids: Brazos, 2005). See note 122 above.

129 It is, at least in part, the church's failure to resist the allure of coercive power that has led many to reject the public truth claims of the gospel. For this reason, Newbigin insists, it is vitally important that the church formulate a doctrine of freedom, whereby it acknowledges the truth of the gospel while making room for other truth claims (*Foolishness*, 137–41).

130 Newbigin, *Gospel*, 108, contends that the church is called to be a witness to the veiled reality of God's kingdom. It is the "hiddenness" of the kingdom that makes conversion, the free acceptance of the gospel, possible. Thus the church must witness to the public truth of the gospel in a way that invites, but does not demand, acceptance.

3 Character

1 See https://www.reportlinker.com/insight/smartphone-connection.html; accessed June 17, 2019. The basis for this data consists of "536 online respondents representative of the general US population." Interviews were conducted January 12–13, 2017 by ReportLinker. Some of the other statistics are eye-opening. Thirty-one percent open up a mail app first thing, while another 31 percent check social media first. Seventy-five percent do not completely switch off their phones every day (83 percent of millennials). In answer to the question, "Which situation best describes the last time you usually consult your smartphone on a typical day?" 53 percent answered "before going to bed"; 13 percent—"when I fall asleep"; 13 percent—"never." Ten percent of respondents admit that they wake up at night to check their smartphones.

2 Cecilie Schou Andreassen et al., "The Relationship Between Addictive Use of Social Media and Video Games and Symptoms of Psychiatric Disorders: A Large-Scale Cross-Sectional Study," *Psychology of Addictive Behaviors* 30, no. 2 (2016): 252–62; Mai-Ly N. Steers et al., "I Want You to Like Me: Extraversion, Need for Approval, and Time on Facebook as Predictors of Anxiety," *Translational Issues*

in Psychological Science 2, no. 3 (2016): 283–93; Mary Sherlock and Danielle L. Wagstaff, "Exploring the Relationship Between Frequency of Instagram Use, Exposure to Idealized Images, and Psychological Well-Being in Women," *Psychology of Popular Media Culture* 8, no. 4 (2019): 482–90.

3   Tim Wu, *The Attention Merchants: The Epic Scramble to Get Inside Our Heads* (New York: Vintage, 2017), 12. Across the Atlantic, Jules Chéret's colorful and arresting posters began to vie for the attention of Parisians in the 1860s (18–23). Although these commercially (and subsequent politically) motivated attempts to harvest the attention of the populace were novel, the monopolization of attention had been around for centuries. Wu contends that prior to the twentieth century, "the Church was the one institution whose mission depended on galvanizing attention; and through its daily and weekly offices, as well as its sometimes central role in education, that is exactly what it managed to do" (27).

4   Wu, *Attention Merchants*, 123–43. The objective of the intrusion was to turn the American home of the 1950s into the locus of consumerism: "For the first time, to be at home and awake was, for most Americans, to be sold something" (142).

5   Statistics from https://instagram-press.com/our-story/; accessed June 25, 2019. See also Wu, *Attention Merchants*, 311–17.

6   Wu observes that in contrast to the candid nature of many Facebook photos, "Instagram's photos would generally be more dramatic, glamorous, and often edgier, for the simple reason that they were posted with the calculated intent to seize attention and to elicit a reaction" (*Attention Merchants*, 312). The highly curated, even contrived nature of reality presented in many Instagram accounts is betrayed by the contrast between "Rinstagram" and "Finstagram" accounts. A "Rinstagram" account is a supposedly "real" account in which one's artfully crafted public persona is maintained. Confusingly, or perhaps merely ironically, one's "Finstagram" or "fake" account would be the one in which one presents a more authentic version of oneself for a smaller circle of followers.

7   Wu, *Attention Merchants*, 314.

8   Wu, *Attention Merchants*, 314–15.

9   James K. A. Smith, "Alternative Liturgy: Social Media as Ritual," *Christian Century*, March 6, 2013, 33. In this "competitive world of self-display and self-consciousness" we might hear echoes of the agonistic pursuit of "ruling virtues" that characterized the behavior of Roman elites.

10   Wu, *Attention Merchants*, 317.

11   H. S. Versnel, "What Did Ancient Man See When He Saw a God? Some Reflections on Greco-Roman Epiphany," in Effigies Dei: *Essays on the History of Religions*, ed. Dirk van der Plas (Leiden: Brill, 1987), 46–47. Versnel provides a number of vivid examples such as the following: "Sapor I, while planning to attack the temple of Apollo Bryaxis at Daphni near Antiochia, was 'converted' by the mere look of the statue of the god and withdrew his troops." Versnel further observes, "One widespread custom in oracular practice was to carry around the statue of the god and to read for its (=his) movements the divine answers to oracular questions."

12   The letter known as Second Corinthians is most likely Paul's third letter to the church in Corinth. The story of Paul's relationship with this church is difficult to reconstruct, in part because of uncertainty regarding the literary integrity of Paul's correspondence; see discussion below on p. 88. Many scholars dispute the literary integrity of 2 Corinthians, claiming that the canonical versions of 1 and 2 Corinthians together represent a composite of anywhere between two and nine letters. For an overview of these issues, see Ralph P. Martin, *2 Corinthians*, WBC (Nashville:

Thomas Nelson, 1986), xxxviii–xlvi; Victor Paul Furnish, *II Corinthians*, AB 32A (Garden City, N.Y.: Doubleday, 1984), 29–54. Among the numerous arguments supporting partition theories, see in particular Laurence L. Welborn, who argues that Paul's larger apostolic defense in 2 Cor 2:14–7:4 should be regarded as an independent fragment ("Like Broken Pieces of a Ring: 2 Cor 1.1–2.3; 7.5–16 and Ancient Theories of Literary Unity," *NTS* 42 [1996]: 559–83). For arguments in favor of literary unity, see, e.g., J. D. H. Amador, "Revisiting 2 Corinthians: Rhetoric and the Case for Unity," *NTS* 46 (2000): 92–111; Fredrick J. Long, *Ancient Rhetoric and Paul's Apology: The Compositional Unity of 2 Corinthians*, Society for New Testament Studies Monograph Series 131 (Cambridge: Cambridge University Press, 2004); Thomas Schmeller, "No Bridge Over Troubled Water? The Gap Between 2 Corinthians 1–9 and 10–13 Revisited," *JSNT* 36 (2013): 73–84. The present argument depends neither upon the supposed literary integrity of the entire letter, nor upon a particular partition theory. However, in view of both the failure of any single partition theory to win widespread acceptance and the cogency of arguments for literary integrity, I am inclined to view the latter position as providing at least as viable an explanation of the entire letter's argument and composition history as the former.

13   I am indebted to Charles H. Talbert for this turn of phrase. In his book *Reading the Sermon on the Mount*, he coins the phrase to describe the way that Jesus' disciples were formed through their association with him. Talbert contends that this concept, the transformative power of association, was operative within Greco-Roman moral discourse, particularly within philosophical schools.

14   Aristotle discusses bravery at great length in *Nic. Eth.* 3.6. The four cardinal virtues are bravery, temperance, justice, and prudence. Aristotle himself does not speak of these as "cardinal" virtues; that description emerged from later interpreters. "Cardinal" comes from the Latin word for door: *cardo*. These four virtues are "cardinal" in the sense that they function as the hinges upon which the entire "door" of virtue formation swings. "Pivotal" would be an equally apposite description of these virtues within Aristotle's theory.

15   For Aristotle, bravery was the quintessential "manly" virtue. This cultural bias was encoded even at the lexical level: the Greek term for bravery, *andreia*, is derived from the word for man, *anēr*. Aristotle's prejudice notwithstanding, it goes without saying that men and women equally possess the capacity to acquire this virtue.

16   This three-step process of character formation is discussed at length by Dallas Willard; see his *Spirit of the Disciplines*; *Renovation of the Heart*.

17   In Hebrew, the imagery is more graphic: one sharpens the *face* of another.

18   Recently, missiologist William R. Burrows has put his finger on a *lacuna* in Newbigin's work, namely the challenge of "*how to form the agents who will bring the gospel to the nations*" ("Newbigin's Theology of Mission and Culture After Twenty-Five Years: Attending to the 'Subject' of Mission," in *The Gospel and Pluralism Today: Reassessing Lesslie Newbigin in the 21st Century*, ed. Scott W. Sunquist and Amos Yong, Missiological Engagements [Downers Grove, Ill.: InterVarsity, 2015], 66; emphasis original). The present chapter takes a step towards filling this hole.

19   Hans Windisch, in his landmark 1924 commentary, claimed that 2 Cor 3:7–18 fit so uneasily in its literary context that it could be excised from the letter without any damage to the surrounding argument (*Der Zweite Korintherbrief*, 9th ed., ed. Georg Strecker, KEK [Göttingen: Vandenhoeck & Ruprecht, 1924], 112). Since Windisch, scholars have been keen to explain the appearance of this passage not by recourse to Paul's argument but to a supposed conflict with opponents in Corinth. Of note among those responding to Windisch's implicit challenge is the highly influential

and widely debated study of Dieter Georgi, *The Opponents of Paul in Second Corinthians* (Philadelphia: Fortress, 1986). Georgi concludes that Paul implicitly argues against the "super apostles" whom he explicitly names in chs. 10–13 of the letter (315–17). On the difficulties of identifying Paul's unnamed opponents with the precision required by an argument such as this, see Jerry L. Sumney, *Identifying Paul's Opponents: The Question of Method in 2 Corinthians*, JSNTSup 40 (Sheffield: Sheffield Academic Press, 1990). My own approach assumes that this passage is integral to the overall structure of Paul's argument regarding his apostolic legitimacy. On the lasting influence of Windisch's commentary, see Scott J. Hafemann, *Paul, Moses, and History of Israel: The Letter/Spirit Contrast and the Argument from Scripture in 2 Corinthians 3*, Paternoster Biblical Monographs (Milton Keynes: Paternoster, 2005), 255–63. `

20   Convinced that philosophical intelligence should serve political power, Plato responded to the summons of his disciple Dion, minister to the tyrant Dionysius of Syracuse, who implored him to come and convert his master to the way of philosophy. In this task Plato was ultimately unsuccessful. His motivations for the attempt reveal his conviction that philosophy properly aims to guide political action: "I set out from home—not in the spirit which some have supposed, but dreading self-reproach most of all, lest haply I should seem to myself to be utterly and absolutely nothing more than a mere voice and never to undertake willingly any action" (*Epistle* 7.328C).

21   The king's happiness, Plato reckons, is 729 times greater than that of the tyrant (*Rep.* 587E). The mode of calculation—admittedly "overwhelming and baffling"— is not to be taken seriously, although the general point certainly is.

22   Rosamond Kent Sprague, *Plato's Philosopher-King: A Study of the Theoretical Background* (Columbia: University of South Carolina Press, 1976), 115.

23   The comparison of the good king to a shepherd was quite common in antiquity; see Xenophon, *Cyr.* 8.1.2; Ecphantus 4.7.64; Dio Chrysostom, *Or.* 1.12–13, 15–20; 2.6; 4.33–34. Dio often uses the image of the shepherd to contrast the good king with the tyrant, who is nothing but a butcher. This contrast is also found in the biblical tradition: the prophet Ezekiel distinguishes between King David, the good shepherd, and the multitude of false shepherds who prey upon God's people (Ezek 34, 37). The image of the good king as Davidic shepherd is echoed in *Psalms of Solomon* 17, a Jewish text from the mid-first century BCE.

24   A helpful overview of these schools and movements may be found in Hadot, *What Is Ancient Philosophy?* 55–145. My discussion of philosophy in antiquity is deeply indebted to Hadot's expertise in this area.

25   Hadot, *What Is Ancient Philosophy?* 65; emphasis added. Hadot demonstrates that concern for inculcating a way of life was at the heart of the other philosophical schools as well. On Aristotle's school, see 77–90; on the Epicureans, see 113–26; on the Stoics, see 126–39; on the Cynics, see 108–13; on the Skeptics, see 142–45.

26   Hadot argues that for Plato, knowledge is not merely a theoretical, abstract concept, but rather "the knowledge which chooses and wants the good—in other words, an inner disposition in which thought, will, and desire are one" (*What Is Ancient Philosophy?* 65).

27   The adjective "spiritual" in this sense refers to the will (the faculty of choosing) as distinct from thoughts and feelings. Insofar as one's "character" describes the ability to reliably make decisions (whether good or bad), character formation and spiritual formation may be seen as roughly equivalent concepts. To conceive of a spiritual dimension resists a strictly materialist account of a human person,

although it does not require a Christian, or even religiously inspired, one. I have found Dallas Willard's discussion of the six dimensions of the person (thought, feeling, will [or spirit], body, social context, soul) to be helpful (*Renovation of the Heart*, 30–39).

28   Hadot, *What Is Ancient Philosophy?* 177. The importance of *habitus*, and the means by which it is formed, is further discussed in the following chapter. Plutarch insists that the goal of philosophical discourse is moral action. He rebukes those who "have taken a false notion of philosophy (*ho tēs philosophias logos*; lit. "the discourse of philosophy"), they make it much like the art of statuary, whose business it is to carve out a lifeless image in the most exact figure and proportions, and then to raise it upon its pedestal, where it is to continue for ever. The true philosophy is of a quite different nature; it is a spring and principle of motion wherever it comes; it makes men active and industrious, it sets every wheel and faculty a going, it stores our minds with axioms and rules by which to make a sound judgment, it determines the will to the choice of what is honorable and just; and it wings all our faculties to the swiftest prosecution of it" ("That a Philosopher Ought to Converse Especially with Men in Power," *Moralia* 776C–D).

29   Hadot, *What Is Ancient Philosophy?* 177, 179–80; see further 179–220.

30   The English word "asceticism" is derived from the Greek word *askēsis* (training), but the way in which asceticism is understood in common parlance sometimes obscures the connection. Asceticism connotes rigorous self-discipline, austerity, and self-denial. Often these characteristics are misunderstood to be the actual goods of asceticism (sometimes even by those who practice this lifestyle). Properly understood, ascetic practices aim at some other good (e.g., the virtue of self-control), to which end self-denial is merely a means. Within the Christian monastic tradition, ascetic practices typically aimed at *mystical* union with God. The classical concept of *askēsis*, however, aimed at a far more *practical* end, as Dallas Willard contends: "Asceticism rightly understood is so far from the 'mystical' as to be just good sense about life and, ultimately, about spiritual life" (*Spirit of the Disciplines*, 130–55, here 150).

31   Cora E. Lutz, "M. Rufus, 'The Roman Socrates,'" *YCS* 10 (1947): 52–57.

32   The letter is preserved in Diogenes Laertius, *Lives of Eminent Philosophers* 10.133: "Exercise thyself in these and kindred precepts day and night, both by thyself and with him who is like unto thee; then never, either in waking or in dream, wilt thou be disturbed, but wilt live as a god among men. For man loses all semblance of mortality by living in the midst of immortal blessings." See further Martha Nussbaum's discussion of "Lucretius' Epicurean therapy," which aimed to release one from the fear of death (*The Therapy of Desire: Theory and Practice in Hellenistic Ethics*, Martin Classical Lectures [Princeton: Princeton University Press, 1994], 192–238).

33   See further Hadot, *What Is Ancient Philosophy?* 135–39.

34   Hadot, *Philosophy as a Way of Life*, 81–125, here 83. See also Nussbaum, *Therapy of Desire*, who describes Hellenistic philosophical schools as intending to create a "therapeutic community" aimed at the removal of the passions (40–41).

35   Victor Goldschmidt insists that, despite the obvious doctrinal freight conveyed by Plato's dialogues, "The dialogue intends to form rather than inform" (*Le dialogue veut former plutôt qu'informer*) (*Platon*, 3; translation mine). So-called philosophical discourse that is not commensurate with the philosophic way of life is merely sophistry. In Plato's *Apology*, Socrates contends that his accusers are mere sophists who construct rhetorically brilliant arguments that are nevertheless false (17A). Socrates, by contrast, claims to be rhetorically unpolished (17C–18A), while his

life, characterized by integrity of speech and action, represents the philosophic ideal (33A).

36   It should be noted that philosophical discourse itself can be considered such a spiritual exercise, since "discourse always has, directly or indirectly, a function which is formative, educative, psychagogic, and therapeutic. It is always intended to produce an effect, to create a *habitus* within the soul, or to provoke a transformation of the self" (Hadot, *What Is Ancient Philosophy?* 176).

37   See the use of the adjective *aristos* in the quotation from Plato, *Rep.* 580B–C above, p. 69.

38   See further *Nic. Eth.* 5.1132a22, where Aristotle speaks of the magistrate as a "living righteousness" (*dikaion empsuchon*). Roman culture also recognized the importance of legislation in forming public morals. Alston notes the ways in which the Secular Games of 17 BCE bear witness to this notion (*Rome's Revolution*, 291–97).

39   In Plato's *Crito* 50A–51C, Socrates refuses to escape from Athens following his death sentence, for such an act would unjustly violate the laws of the *polis*. The laws, he argues, are like parents, nurturing and educating the citizens of Athens. One must therefore honor the laws for their central role in moral education.

40   Salkever, "Rhetoric, Politics, and Philosophy," 234, observes that Aristotle would have regarded this possibility as extremely unlikely. See further Dvornik, *Political Philosophy*, 1:183–86.

41   See further the discussion in ch. 5.

42   The following discussion draws upon my earlier treatment in *Christ the Ideal King*, 43–46, 54, 61–63, 75–76, 87–88, 98–99, 147, 150, 152–53. See also the excellent and concise discussion in Jipp, *Christ Is King*, 46–60. For further exploration, see especially Goodenough, "Political Philosophy"; Erwin R. Goodenough, "Kingship in Early Israel," *JBL* 48 (1929): 169–205; Dvornik, *Political Philosophy*; Glenn F. Chesnut, "The Ruler and the Logos in Neopythagorean, Middle Platonic, and Late Stoic Political Philosophy," *ANRW* 2.16.2 (1978): 1310–32.

43   The roots of this concept can be traced back to Classical Greece. Xenophon (ca. 429–357 BCE), a contemporary of Plato, provides a portrait of the Persian King Cyrus in *Cyropaedia* (the "education of Cyrus"). There he remarks that Cyrus "believed that he could in no way more effectively inspire a desire for the beautiful and the good than by endeavouring, as their sovereign, to set before his subjects a perfect model of virtue in his own person. For he thought he perceived that men are made better through even the written law, while the good ruler he regarded as a law with eyes for men, because he is able not only to give commandments but also to see the transgressor and punish him" (*Cyr.* 8.1.21–22).

44   For the Neopythagoreans, see Diotogenes (4.7.61–62); Archytas (4.1.135); Ecphantus (4.7.64). For the concept expressed more broadly in Hellenistic political philosophy, see further Ps-Aristotle, *Rhet. Alex.* 1420b; Hans Volkmann, "Ἔνδοξος δουλεία als ehrenvoller Knechtsdienst gegenüber dem Gesetz," *Phil* 16 (1956): 52–55. In the Roman period, see Musonius Rufus, *That Kings Also Should Study Philosophy* 64.10–15 and the discussion below in ch. 4; on Plutarch and Philo, see below.

45   The reference to Pindar is from Plato, *Gorgias* 784B; *Laws* 690B.

46   On the difficulty of dating the Neopythagorean kingship treatises, see Julien C. H. Smith, *Christ the Ideal King*, 36–37.

47   For more examples from Neopythagorean literature, see Julien C. H. Smith, *Christ the Ideal King*, 41–43.

48   Analogously, the physical presence of a charismatic leader was also considered crucial for success in battle. J. Rufus Fears claims that "The physical presence of the
charismatic figure ensured success, bringing the intervention of the gods and re-
sultant victory." Victory was dependent upon the leader's *eutychia* (good luck, fortune), "a numinous and almost tangible force which radiated from the charismatic
leader and was essential to his practical success, endowing him with supernatural
powers over the forces of nature and rendering his troops victorious" ("Theology
of Victory," 762).

49   Chesnut, "Ruler and Logos," 1310-12.

50   On the king as descendent of the gods, see Xenophon, *Cyr.* 4.1.24; 7.2.24; Virgil,
Aen. 6.791-797. Dio Chrysostom viewed the ideal king as an imitator of Zeus (*Or.*
1.41, 45; 4.27-39). The Roman panegyricist Martial goes even further, explicitly identifying the Roman emperor Domitian as a god (*Spec.* 16B.3-4; *Epig.* 5.8.1;
7.5.3). Martial even implies that Domitian is superior to the god Jove (*Epig.* 9.3;
9.20; 9.36.2). Martial's contemporary Statius likewise insists that Domitian is superior to the gods of Olympus because he is a present god (*Sylv.* 5.2.168-70), a
god on earth (*Sylv.* 1.1.61-62; 1.6.46-47). For further discussion of Martial and
Statius, see John Garthwaite, "The Panegyrics of Domitian in Martial Book 9," *Ramus* 22 (1993): 78-102; Kenneth Scott, "Statius' Adulation of Domitian," *AJP* 54
(1933): 247-59.

51   Compare Seneca's description of Nero's radiant face: "Such is the present Caesar;
such our ruler Nero on whom Rome will gaze. His shining face glitters, while on
his neck his flowing hair falls" (*Apoc.* 4; cf. *Clem.* 1.8.4-5; Virgil, *Aen.* 6.791-94;
Ecphantus 4.7.64). On the widespread use of astral symbolism in Hellenistic and
imperial encomia, see further: J. Rufus Fears, "The Solar Monarchy of Nero and the
Imperial Panegyric of Q. Curtius Rufus," *Historia* 25 (1976): 494-96.

52   See, e.g., Seneca, *Clem.* 1.1.2; Martial, *Epig.* 9.20.9-10; 9.36.9; Statius, *Sylv.*
4.3.124-29; Dio Chrysostom, *Or.* 2.75-76; Pliny, *Pan.* 5.1; *Ps. Sol.* 17:21, 32, 34, 46;
Let. Arist. 224.

53   Bréhier contends that the happiness of the sage is not acquired progressively but
immediately and totally (*Chrysippe*, Les grands philosophes [Paris: Félix Alcan,
1910], 218); however, he is speaking here only of the way in which the sage himself
is thought to be transformed, not the students within the school.

54   Hadot, *What Is Ancient Philosophy?* 220; see further Hadot's description of the
sage's identity (220-23).

55   Bréhier, *Chrysippe*, 217-18.

56   Hadot, *What Is Ancient Philosophy?* 224-29, here 224.

57   Chrysippus, who became head of the Stoic school in 232 BCE, figured prominently
in the moral education of the students under his direction. Émile Bréhier describes
this figure as seeking to achieve "an intimate transformation of the soul" (*une
transformation intime de l'âme*) (*Chrysippe*, 217).

58   The significance of this facial focus is germane to Paul's *synkrisis* of Moses and
Jesus, in which the faces of Moses, Jesus, and the Corinthians play a vital role in his
argument.

59   The dialogue is prefaced by a letter to Nigrinus, in which Lucian indicates his intent, namely to reveal his state of mind to the philosopher. His exclamation, "how
deeply I have been moved by your discourse (*pros tōn sōn logōn*)," demonstrates the
point made above, that philosophical discourse itself was a transformative exercise.

60   Nothing is known about the person of Nigrinus save what Lucian relates in
this dialogue. The account that follows seems related to Lucian's conversion

to philosophy around the age of 40. The magnitude of the transformation is apparent. He exclaims, "Don't you think it wonderful, in the name of Zeus, that once a slave, I am now free! 'Once poor, now rich indeed'; once witless and befogged, now saner?" (*Nigr.* 1).

61   Lucian's comments here support the point made in the previous paragraph about the transformative aspect of philosophical discourse. The adjective *entheos* literally means "full of the god" or "inspired by the god"—a lofty way of speaking about his philosophical conversion, but also a profoundly meaningful one.

62   The *Letter of Aristeas* and Dio Chrysostom's kingship orations are excellent examples of this genre.

63   This characterization of Moses' function is, of course, not exclusive, but incorporates his other vital roles as priest, prophet, and lawgiver, as noted below. On the importance of Moses' priestly function for Philo, see Michael Cover, *Lifting the Veil: 2 Corinthians 3:7–18 in Light of Jewish Homiletic and Commentary Traditions*, BZNW 210 (Berlin: De Gruyter, 2015), 280–86. The Hellenistic ideal of kingship commonly incorporated the role of high priest; see Ulrich Busse, "Metaphorik und Rhetorik im Johannesevangelium: Das Bildfeld vom König," in *Imagery in the Gospel of John: Terms, Forms, Themes, and Theology of Johannine Figurative Language*, ed. Jörg Frey et al., WUNT 200 (Tübingen: Mohr Siebeck, 2006), 279–318.

64   That the two objects compared in a *synkrisis* should be of comparable value is clear from the *progymnasmata* of Aelius Theon, who observes that "someone wondering whether Achilles or Thersites was braver would be laughable" (*Prog.* 112 in George Alexander Kennedy, ed. and trans., *Progymnasmata: Greek Textbooks of Prose Composition and Rhetoric*, WGRW 10 [Atlanta: Society of Biblical Literature, 2003], 52–55, here 53). This feature of the *synkrisis* helps one realize that Paul is probably not mounting a secessionist argument in 2 Cor 3:7–18 in favor of "Christianity" over "Judaism" (which moreover constitutes an anachronism). This interpretation had nevertheless been influential in the mid-twentieth century; see the review of scholarship in Hafemann, *Paul, Moses*, 255–63.

65   Erwin R. Goodenough, "Philo's Exposition of the Law and His De Vita Mosis," *HTR* 26 (1933): 109–25; Wayne A. Meeks, *The Prophet-King: Moses Traditions and the Johannine Christology*, NovTSup 14 (Leiden: Brill, 1967), 102–3; Louis H. Feldman, *Philo's Portrayal of Moses in the Context of Ancient Judaism*, CJAS 15 (Notre Dame, Ind.: University of Notre Dame Press, 2007), 11–16. The present discussion is indebted to my earlier presentation of kingship in Philo's corpus in *Christ the Ideal King*, 141–55. See also Jipp, *Christ Is King*, 51–52.

66   Philo echoes Plato, *Rep.* 473D (see above, p. 69). Meeks notes that of these four faculties, kingship is the only one whose attribution to Moses Philo feels no need to explain, suggesting that Moses' kingship was widely accepted in Philo's circle (*Prophet-King*, 108).

67   See further the expansive discussion of Moses' virtues in Feldman, *Philo's Portrayal*, 235–357.

68   According to Wayne A. Meeks, this mystical ascent whereby Moses is enthroned constitutes a unique element in Philo's portrait of the ideal king ("Moses as God and King," in *Religions in Antiquity: Essays in Memory of Erwin Ramsdell Goodenough*, ed. Jacob Neusner [Leiden: Brill, 1968], 371). Meeks is followed by Peder Borgen, "Moses, Jesus, and the Roman Emperor: Observations in Philo's Writings and the Revelation of John," *NovT* 38 (1996): 151–52; Joachim Kügler, "Spuren ägyptisch-hellenistischer Königstheologie bei Philo von Alexandria," in *Ägypten und der östliche Mittelmeerraum im 1. Jahrtausend v. Chr.*, ed. Manfred Görg and

Günther Hölbl, ÄAT 44 (Wiesbaden: Harrassowitz, 2000), 234. See further Meeks, *Prophet-King*, 122–25, 130.

69   As Burton L. Mack observes, "the visual moment itself, the imaging of the γραφή [*graphē*], the reception of the impressions of the paradigm, is the moment of transition itself for Philo" ("Imitatio Mosis: Patterns of Cosmology and Soteriology in the Hellenistic Synagogue," *SPhilo* 1 [1972]: 39). Similarly, Walther Völker, *Fortschritt und Vollendung bei Philo von Alexandrien: Eine Studie zur Geschichte der Frömmigkeit*, TUGAL 49.1 (Leipzig: Hinrichs, 1938), 283: "Diese Schau Gottes erreicht der Vollkommene, sie ist das Ziel all seines Strebens" (*Det.* 89, 158; *Conf.* 97; *Contempl.* 11). The transformative effect of vision can be seen even more clearly in Philo's life of Joseph, who also conforms to the type of ideal king. Philo thus describes the transformation of Joseph's fellow-prisoners: "For by setting before them his life of temperance and every virtue, like an original picture of skilled workmanship, he [Joseph] converted even those who seemed to be quite incurable, who as the long-standing distempers of the soul abated reproached themselves for their past and repented with such utterances as these: 'Ah, where in old days was this great blessing which at first we failed to find? See, when it shines on us we behold as in a mirror our misbehaviour and are ashamed'" (*Joseph* 86–87).

70   The dates, a matter of scholarly debate, are approximate. See the discussion in Wright, *Paul*, 209–338; Martin, *2 Corinthians*, xlvi–lii.

71   Some scholars argue that this tearful letter, a rebuke to the one (or ones) who had offended Paul, is preserved in fragmentary form in 2 Cor 10–13; see, e.g., Laurence L. Welborn, "The Identification of 2 Corinthians 10–13 with the 'Letter of Tears,'" *NovT* 37 (1995): 138–53.

72   There is broad (although not universal) consensus, even among scholars who dispute the literary integrity of Second Corinthians, about the subject of Paul's argument within these three sections of the letter. Those arguing for various partition theories would, however, dispute both the internal connections between these arguments and their chronological arrangement. For example, if chs. 10–13 are a fragment of an earlier "tearful letter" (or some other prior letter), then it concerns not "lingering" opposition, but rather opposition that has already been dealt with by the time Paul composes chs. 1–9.

73   Paul resumes the contrast in 4:2, this time identifying false apostles as those who adulterate or falsify (*dolountes*) God's word.

74   Paul's argument also evokes the contrast between the heart of stone and the heart of flesh in Ezek 36:26–27 (cf. 11:19–20). The latter condition is furthermore associated with the implanting of God's spirit, which enables fidelity to Torah.

75   Paul Brooks Duff insists that in vv. 7–10 Paul draws a comparison not between two covenants, but rather between two ministries (*Moses in Corinth: The Apologetic Context of 2 Corinthians 3*, NovTSup 159 [Leiden: Brill, 2015], 133). His point is well taken, although Paul's reference to the "old" (3:14) and "new" (3:6) covenants appears calculated to evoke Jeremiah's discussion of the same. In agreement with Scott J. Hafemann, I see the point of the contrast as highlighting the functional difference of two ministries—the former cannot effect transformation, while the latter can (*Paul, Moses*, 156–73).

76   The last sentence contains a phrase repeated verbatim in 12:19—"before God in Christ we speak" (*katenanti theou en Christō laloumen*). The phrase is unusual, occurring only in these two locations in Paul's corpus. Significantly, at 12:19, Paul uses the phrase to respond to a rhetorical question he has raised: "Have you been thinking all along that we have been defending ourselves (*apologoumetha*) before

you? We are speaking in Christ before God. Everything we do, beloved, is for the sake of building you up." Paul appears both to be echoing his earlier claim in 2:17 and to be reframing the argument of the entire letter, not as an act of self-defense but an act of love. Hearing this echo both presupposes literary unity and serves as evidence for it. For the argument, on the basis of rhetorical analysis, that Second Corinthians constitutes a unified letter of apology, see Long, *Ancient Rhetoric and Paul's Apology*.

77   For detailed discussion of every aspect of the Roman triumph, from the fate of victims to the honor accrued to the victorious general, as well as the multifarious ways the triumph influenced Roman culture, see Beard, *Roman Triumph*. See also the discussion of literary and artistic descriptions of the *pompa triumphalis* in Cilliers Breytenbach, "Paul's Proclamation and God's 'Thriambos': (Notes on 2 Corinthians 2:14–16b)," *Neot* 24 (1990): 265–69. For the most comprehensive discussion of the numerous interpretive possibilities of this verse, see the recent monograph, Christoph Heilig, *Paul's Triumph: Reassessing 2 Corinthians 2:14 in Its Literary and Historical Context*, BTS (Leuven: Peeters, 2017).

78   The role of the triumph in emphasizing Rome's victory cannot be underestimated. Mary Beard puts it well: "The triumph, in other words, re-presented and re-enacted the victory. It brought the margins of the Empire to its center, and in so doing celebrated the new geopolitics that victory had brought about" (*Roman Triumph*, 32). The *Fasti Capitolini* (the Capitoline Chronology or Calendar) was erected on the Roman Forum during the reign of Augustus as a monument to the victorious generals who had celebrated triumphs up to that point in history (hence sometimes referred to as the *Fasti Triumphales*). Although its accuracy is disputed, it clearly demonstrates the prominence of victory in the imagination of Augustan Rome (61–67, 72–106).

79   This "triumphalistic" interpretation can be traced back as far as the fourth century exegete John Chrysostom and is taken up by leading Reformers John Calvin and Martin Luther. For the history of interpretation, see Lamar Williamson Jr., "Led in Triumph: Paul's Use of Thriambeuō," *Int* 22 (1968): 327–32.

80   For a thorough discussion of the lexical options, see Heilig, *Paul's Triumph*, 25–116.

81   See the discussion of lexical evidence in Williamson, "Led in Triumph," 318–22; Breytenbach, "Paul's Proclamation," 259–65.

82   Scott J. Hafemann, *Suffering and Ministry in the Spirit: Paul's Defense of His Ministry in II Corinthians 2:14–3:3* (Grand Rapids: Eerdmans, 1990), 19–34. As the example of Vercingetorix shows, even humiliated kings could be among the eminent captives paraded through Rome and destined for execution. Vercingetorix, acclaimed king of the Alverni, revolted against Julius Caesar in 52 BCE, was defeated, held captive for five years, then led in triumph and executed. See the accounts in Plutarch, *Caes.* 25–27; Caesar, *Bell. gall.* 7.88. However, not all prominent captives were executed; Octavian notably showed clemency to captives after his victories at Actium and Alexandria (Alston, *Rome's Revolution*, 226). As Beard notes, some captives were ultimately "integrated" into Roman society, albeit at the very bottom of the social hierarchy. Some captives even went on to receive Roman citizenship, and in at least one case, an infant captive, Publius Ventidius Bassus, became a successful general, ultimately celebrating his own triumph against the Parthians in 38 BCE (*Roman Triumph*, 128–41).

83   The description comes from O'Connor's sparkling gem of an essay, "The Fiction Writer and His Country," in *Mystery and Manners*, ed. Sally Fitzgerald and Robert Fitzgerald (New York: Farrar, Straus & Giroux, 1957), 25–35, here 34. Granted,

O'Connor is addressing the concerns of a Christian novelist writing to a modern, increasingly secular audience. One might thus question the relevance of her remark to this letter of Paul, who is neither a novelist nor modern, and whose audience is far from secular. Yet Paul, in my view, shares the following basic dilemma with regard to audience that the modern novelist faces. O'Connor describes the problem thus: "The novelist with Christian concerns will find in modern life distortions which are repugnant to him, and his problem will be to make these appear as distortions to an audience which is used to seeing them as natural" (33). For Paul, the natural tendency to regard victory as the trappings of discipleship would have constituted such a dangerous distortion.

84   Luke notes Apollos' rhetorical eloquence (Acts 18:24) and the fact that Apollos visited Corinth while Paul was in Ephesus (Acts 19:1). Paul addresses these divisions in 1 Cor 1–4, asserting that Christ sent him to proclaim the gospel "not with eloquent wisdom, so that the cross of Christ might not be emptied of its power" (1 Cor 1:17; see also 2:4). Paul is not categorically against rhetoric, understood as the faculty of persuasion. Indeed, he is without a doubt the "greatest wordsmith of the first Christian generation," albeit employing an "anti-rhetorical rhetoric" in 1 Cor 1–4 (Margaret M. Mitchell, *Paul, the Corinthians and the Birth of Christian Hermeneutics* [Cambridge: Cambridge University Press, 2010], 4). However, it may have been the case that he was perceived as lacking *oratorical* eloquence, which Paul himself acknowledges (2 Cor 10:10). According to orators and sophists, such deftness with the spoken word was the mark of wisdom and virtue (Adam G. White, *Where Is the Wise Man? Graeco-Roman Education as a Background to the Divisions in 1 Corinthians 1–4* [London: Bloomsbury T&T Clark, 2015], 83–106). Paul, on the other hand, much like Socrates in Plato's *Apology*, is skeptical of the use to which such verbal sophistication is employed (see above n. 35, and Plato's critique of the rhetoric of sophists in *Gorgias*). Mark T. Finney further observes that rhetorical prowess was intimately bound up in the competitive pursuit of honor (*philotimia*) ("Honor, Rhetoric and Factionalism in the Ancient World: 1 Corinthians 1–4 and Its Social Context," *BTB* 40 [2010]: 27–36). Bruce W. Winter argues that in the church at Corinth, this agonistic disposition was characteristic of the factions, each claiming a fierce loyalty to their perceived "teacher" (*After Paul Left Corinth: The Influence of Secular Ethics and Social Change* [Grand Rapids: Eerdmans, 2001], 31–43). Paul's concern rather is with the way that rhetoric had been "weaponized," so to speak, in a way that led to division.

85   Peter Marshall, "A Metaphor of Social Shame: ΘΡΙΑΜΒΕΥΕΙΝ IN 2 Cor 2:14," *NovT* 25 (1983): 302–17, argues that Paul is using the image of the triumph metaphorically to indicate social shame. Although Marshall admits he cannot find ancient literary evidence that the verb *thriambeuō* was used metaphorically, it is obvious that Paul himself is doing so. Whether "social shame" is the precise referent of the metaphor is, of course, debatable.

86   Hafemann, *Suffering and Ministry in the Spirit*, 37–45, argues that the terms "fragrance" (*osmē*, 2:14, 16) and "aroma" (*euōdia*, 2:15) are technical terms connoting cultic sacrifice within Israelite worship. Understood in this fashion, the imagery conveys Paul's self-understanding as the cultic sacrifice by which Christ is made known. It makes better sense, in my view, to understand the olfactory imagery within the context of the Roman triumph, since this is the metaphor Paul himself provides. Nevertheless, it is possible that the imagery functions on multiple levels in Paul's mind.

87   Breytenbach, "Paul's Proclamation," 266–69. George H. Guthrie argues that Paul is likening himself and his mission to the incense bearers, those who are sharing in

and celebrating the general's victory ("Paul's Triumphal Procession Imagery [2 Cor 2.14–16a]: Neglected Points of Background," *NTS* 61 [2015]: 79–91). The major objection to Guthrie's interpretation, as Ludvig Svensson points out, is that when the verb *thriambeuō* takes a direct personal object, as it does here, that person is always a defeated enemy, not a co-celebrant ("Paul in the Roman Triumph: Possibilities in the Interpretation of θριαμβεύω [2 Cor 2:14]," *SEÅ* 83 [2018]: 91–96).

88   The way in which prisoners were displayed in a triumph is, as Beard admits, "a matter of guesswork," although ancient sources commonly describe their place in the procession: *ante currum*, "in front of the chariot" (*Roman Triumph*, 124–25). The actual configuration of a triumph, suggested by the triumphal frieze on the Arch of Trajan at Beneventum, was complex and varied. Literary representations of triumphs, however, exploited the potential interplay between captives and generals suggested by this proximity (107–42).

89   The appearance of captives presented a dilemma. If they appeared overly weak and bedraggled, it might suggest that the general's victory was less than impressive. Yet if high-status captives were paraded in regal finery or in impressive martial attire, as they sometimes were, they could "steal the show" (Beard, *Roman Triumph*, 133–39).

90   Heilig concludes his summary of exegetical options with the suggestion that Paul's intent in deploying the metaphor of the triumph is rhetorically complex: "Thus, *the complex move to encourage the Corinthians to identify themselves with the watching crowd only to find themselves challenged in their simplistic perception of Paul's ministry is not as far-fetched as one might think at first*" (*Paul's Triumph*, 259; emphasis original).

91   George H. van Kooten helpfully highlights the anti-sophistic setting of 2 Corinthians ("Why Did Paul Include an Exegesis of Moses' Shining Face [Exod 34] in 2 Cor 3?: Moses' Strength, Well-Being and [Transitory] Glory, According to Philo, Josephus, Paul, and the Corinthian Sophists," in *Significance of Sinai* [Leiden: Brill, 2008], 154–57).

92   This claim resonates with Paul's earlier self-description as one who both speaks in Christ and stands before the presence of God; for the rhetorical significance of this, see above, n. 76.

93   Duff, *Moses in Corinth*, 93–95, suggests that Paul is being deliberately ambivalent by introducing a triumphal metaphor that can be read in two divergent ways: as depicting a captive led to death or as portraying an epiphany procession revealing the mighty deeds of the deity. Duff further argues that Paul employed such a plastic metaphor because he implicitly wished to prompt his audience to consider how they viewed his ministry. I am in agreement with Duff's larger point, although whether or not Paul had in mind an epiphany procession is doubtful, given that the immediate context of 2:14–17 does not seem to support such a reading. For Duff's detailed argument, see his earlier article: "Metaphor, Motif, and Meaning: The Rhetorical Strategy Behind the Image 'Led in Triumph' in 2 Corinthians 2:14," *CBQ* 53 (1991): 79–92. See the measured critique by Jan Lambrecht, "The Defeated Paul, Aroma of Christ: An Exegetical Study of 2 Corinthians 2:14–16b," *Louvain Studies* 20 (1995): 182–83.

94   For the interpretation that Paul seeks to present his apostolic identity as manifested not in strength but in weakness, see: Maurice Carrez, "Odeur de mort, odeur de vie (à propos de 2 Cor 2:16)," *RHPR* 64 (1984): 136; Furnish, *II Corinthians*, 174–75; Margaret E. Thrall, *A Critical and Exegetical Commentary on the Second Epistle of the Corinthians*, 2 vols., ICC (London: T&T Clark International, 2004), 1:191–95.

95   On the function of commendatory letters, see Klauck, *Ancient Letters and the New Testament*, 72–77.

96   Indeed, an early textual variant substituting *humōn* ("your") for *hēmōn* ("our") in 3:2 bears witness to such a reading. The variant *humōn* is attested in the fourth century uncial manuscript Sinaiticus, as well as a handful of late minuscule manuscripts and Greek lectionary texts.

97   Quintilian refers to this figure of speech in *Inst.* 9.3.68. See also Ps-Cicero, *Rhet. Her.* 4.14.21. I am grateful to Peter Kanelos, my former dean, for bringing to my attention this figure of speech.

98   If imputing this rhetorical strategy to Paul makes him appear overly clever, note that it conforms well with what Pseudo-Cicero calls the "subtle approach" (*insinuatio*) of introducing an argument, called for when "the hearer has apparently been won over by the previous speakers of the opposition" (*Rhetorica ad Herrenium* 1.6.9).

99   Klaus Scholtissek understands the function of the letter metaphor analogously: insofar as the Corinthians commend Christ, they also commend Paul ("'Ihr seid ein Brief Christi' [2 Kor 3,3]," *BZ* 44 [2000]: 201).

100 As throughout this book, I have quoted here the NRSV, a translation of a particular version of the Hebrew Bible known as the Masoretic Text (MT). Paul, however, read and quoted from a Greek translation of the Hebrew Bible known as the Septuagint (LXX). The LXX of Jeremiah differs from the MT in numerous places: it is approximately one-eighth shorter than the MT, and after Jer 25:13, the order of material differs (thus accounting for the difference in chapter locations of the quoted text). In this particular passage, however, the MT and LXX cohere closely. Compare the English translation of the LXX found in Albert Pietersma and Benjamin G. Wright, eds., *A New English Translation of the Septuagint* (Oxford: Oxford University Press, 2007).

101 "A new heart I will give you, and a new spirit I will put within you; and I will remove from your body the heart of stone and give you a heart of flesh. I will put my spirit within you, and make you follow my statutes and be careful to observe my ordinances" (Ezek 36:26–27).

102 See Jipp, *Christ Is King*, 43–76, who argues that the concept of the king as a living law illuminates Paul's claims about Christ in Gal 5:14; 6:2.

103 See the conclusion reached by Paul Brooks Duff, "Transformed 'from Glory to Glory': Paul's Appeal to the Experience of His Readers in 2 Corinthians 3:18," *JBL* 127 (2008): 779–80. Although our readings of this text differ in many respects, we both understand Paul's *apologia* to rest upon the Corinthians recognizing that they have been transformed through the spirit as a result of Paul's ministry.

104 The former term is used and described by Meir Sternberg, *The Poetics of Biblical Narrative: Ideological Literature and the Drama of Reading*, ILBS (Bloomington: Indiana University Press, 1985), 365–440. The latter is preferred by Ronald D. Witherup, "Functional Redundancy in the Acts of the Apostles: A Case Study," *JSNT* 48 (1992): 68–70.

105 So Duff, *Moses in Corinth*, 134.

106 See n. 52.

107 The argument that *kurios* in 3:16 (and in the following two verses) refers to God rather than Jesus derives support from the context of Exod 34:34, which is echoed here. Thus Furnish, *II Corinthians*, 211–12, 235. Yet note the clear attribution of the title "lord" to Jesus in 4:5: "For we do not proclaim ourselves but Jesus Christ, the lord (*Iēsoun Christon kurion*)." Note further the other correlations within the letter

between Jesus and the spirit: 1:21–22; 11:4. Finally, Paul elsewhere commonly identifies Jesus with God's spirit: Rom 8:9–11; 1 Cor 15:45; Gal 4:6; cf. Eph 3:14–19. C.
Kavin Rowe draws attention to the overlap in referents for the term *kurios* in Luke's
Gospel (*Early Narrative Christology: The Lord in the Gospel of Luke*, BZNW 139
[Berlin: De Gruyter, 2006], 40–45). Wesley Hill argues that this so-called "kyriotic
overlap" characterizes Paul's writing as well (*Paul and the Trinity: Persons, Relations, and the Pauline Letters* [Grand Rapids: Eerdmans, 2015], 114, 146, 149).

108   *Contra* William Walker, "2 Corinthians 3:7–18 as a Non-Pauline Interpolation,"
JSPL 3 (2013): 198–202.

109   The extant *progymnasmata*, preliminary composition exercises, from the Greco-
Roman world demonstrate that students exercised some latitude with respect to
the "headings" of a *synkrisis*. Thus, although there were conventional headings for
comparison—birth, education, offspring, office, condition of body, external goods,
virtues of character, and so forth—one need not provide an exhaustive comparison
of all these headings. It was universally expected, however, that *all* the evaluative
topics employed in a *synkrisis* must be compared with respect to each of the subjects. Aphthonius the Sophist (fourth c. CE) demonstrates the point in the example
he provides of a *synkrisis* between Achilles and Hector. Each topic of comparison
(land of birth, ancestry, bravery, prestige gained from war, manner of death) requires an evaluative comment pertaining to both heroes. See *Prog.* 43–44 in Kennedy, *Progymnasmata*, 114–15.

110   E.g., Plutarch, *Mor.* 539B–547F ("On Praising Oneself Inoffensively").

111   Although Duff acknowledges that Paul's implicit self-comparison with Moses is
"extraordinarily bold," he nevertheless sees no reason to question the aptness of
the comparison (*Moses in Corinth*, 101). Duff rightly contends that the comparison functions to legitimate Paul's fitness for ministry. The present argument,
however, goes further by recognizing that in certain respects Paul and Moses are
incommensurate.

112   That the fundamental comparison in this passage is between Moses and Christ is
recognized by Robin Scroggs, *The Last Adam: A Study in Pauline Anthropology*
(Philadelphia: Fortress, 1966), 96.

113   Many other interpreters have documented the fascination with the shining face of
Moses in ancient texts. See, e.g., Duff, *Moses in Corinth*, 147–50. None, however,
observe that radiant faces in antiquity were frequently ascribed to kings. Note, for
example, Seneca's description of Nero: "Such is the present Caesar; such our ruler
Nero on whom Rome will gaze. His shining face glitters, while on his neck his flowing hair falls" (*Apoc.* 4 [Athanassakis]; cf. *Clem.* 1.8.4–5; Virgil, *Aen.* 6.791–794).
See further Fears, "Solar Monarchy," 495.

114   Taking the verb *katargeō* to mean "to abolish, set aside, nullify" rather than "to
fade," along with Frank J. Matera, *II Corinthians: A Commentary*, NTL (Louisville:
Westminster John Knox, 2003), 83; Furnish, *II Corinthians*, 203; Hafemann, *Paul,
Moses*, 301–9.

115   Hafemann argues that the veil symbolizes God's mercy in light of Israel's disobedience; that is, Moses veils his face to shield Israel from God's judgment (*Paul,
Moses*, 310–13). Hafemann commendably attempts to read 2 Cor 3 as Paul's own
attempt to read Exod 34 in its own literary context rather than supplying an alien,
Christian context. My own reading of Paul attempts to do the same, albeit seeing
Jeremiah's critique of the incapacity of the first covenant as part of the wider (but
not alien) literary context.

116 Taking the participle *katoptrizomenoi* in 3:18 to mean "beholding" rather than "reflecting" as in a mirror; so Furnish, *II Corinthians*, 214; Martin, *2 Corinthians*, 71; Thrall, *Second Corinthians*, 1:282–90; *contra* Jacques Dupont, "Le Chrétien, miroir de la gloire divine d'après II Cor., III, 18," *RB* 56 (1949): 407–8. However, M. David Litwa is correct to observe that the story of Moses unites both seeing and reflecting divine glory ("Transformation Through a Mirror: Moses in 2 Cor. 3.18," *JSNT* 34 [2012]: 294). Reading 3:18 in the light of ancient kingship ideology provides a solution to the puzzle of this verb's conceptual background; see the discussion in Thrall, *Second Corinthians*, 1:291–97. Thrall concludes that the most likely source for the metaphor of the mirror is the deuterocanonical book, the Wisdom of Solomon. There, the persona of King Solomon likens wisdom to "a spotless mirror of the working of God, and an image of his goodness" (Wis 7:26). The association between Solomon and the philosophical pursuit of wisdom may provide indirect support for the importance of kingship with respect to moral transformation. Solomon's transformative pursuit of wisdom in the Wisdom of Solomon is described using categories borrowed from Hellenistic philosophical discourse (David Winston, *The Wisdom of Solomon: A New Translation with Introduction and Commentary*, AB 43 [Garden City, N.Y.: Doubleday, 1979], 25–63). In this pursuit, Solomon embodies the ethos of the quintessential king and sage (James M. Reese, *Hellenistic Influence on the Book of Wisdom and Its Consequences*, AnBib 41 [Rome: Biblical Institute Press, 1970], 71–87; John S. Kloppenborg, "Isis and Sophia in the Book of Wisdom," *HTR* 75 [1982]: 73–78). Josephus (37/38–ca. 100 CE), for example, likens Solomon to a Hellenistic philosopher-king (*Ant.* 8.42–44) who possesses the wisdom "of a rational and philosophical king and judge" (Louis H. Feldman, "Josephus' Portrait of Solomon," *HUCA* 66 [1995]: 103–67, here 103).

117 I provide my own translation of the Greek Septuagint (LXX) rather than the Hebrew Masoretic Text (MT) because it is important to see the precise lexical allusion. The Greek *anthropos* here translates the Hebrew *adam*. On the Septuagint, see n. 100. For discussion of detecting "echoes" of Scripture in Paul's letters, see Richard B. Hays, *Echoes of Scripture in the Letters of Paul* (New Haven: Yale University Press, 1989), 25–33. For discussion of the possibility that "image" in 3:18 and 4:4 is intended to evoke the *imago Dei*, see Furnish, *II Corinthians*, 215–22; Paul Barnett, *The Second Epistle to the Corinthians*, NICNT (Grand Rapids: Eerdmans, 1997), 207; Thrall, *Second Corinthians*, 1:309–11.

118 Here Paul is citing the complementary creation account in Gen 2:7 (LXX); see Richard B. Hays, *First Corinthians*, Int (Louisville: John Knox, 1997), 272.

119 In ch. 5, I return to the significance of Rom 5:14 for the way in which Paul sees the human vocation restored through the reign of Christ.

120 Matthew Black contends that "the Second Adam doctrine provided St. Paul with the scaffolding, if not the basic structure, for his redemption and resurrection Christology" ("The Pauline Doctrine of the Second Adam," *SJT* 7 [1954]: 173). Paul doubtless formulates this doctrine in familiarity with contemporary Jewish speculation concerning the glorious nature of Adam prior to the fall; see W. D. Davies, *Paul and Rabbinic Judaism: Some Rabbinic Elements in Pauline Theology*, 2nd ed. (London: SPCK, 1955), 44–47.

121 Scroggs, *The Last Adam*, 97–99. Both within the symbolic world of Gen 1 and within the ancient Near Eastern context, the creation of the human in the image of God implies the human's vocation to rule as God's vicegerent; see Middleton, *Liberating Image*, 43–145. As J. Gordon McConville argues, however, the ruling function of the human does not exhaust the meaning of the *imago Dei*; "image" also carries both relational and representational aspects (*Being Human in God's*

World: An Old Testament Theology of Humanity [Grand Rapids: Baker Academic, 2016], 11–29).

122 See Joseph A. Fitzmyer, who argues for a Palestinian Jewish background to the notion of transfiguration by vision, albeit not a royal one ("Glory Reflected on the Face of Christ [2 Cor 3:7–4:6] and a Palestinian Jewish Motif," *TS* 42 [1981]: 630–44).

123 Dupont, "Miroir de la Gloire," 403–4. Dupont contends that Paul characteristically conceives of transformation into the glorious image of Christ as an eschatological event effected by divine power. In two passages, Col 3:10 and Rom 12:2, internal renewal is required in order to know Christ, but Dupont argues that this is the inverse of what seems to be happening according to 2 Cor 3:18.

124 Georgi, *Opponents*, 271–77; Kooten, "Moses' Shining Face," 177.

125 Jane M. F. Heath provides a succinct account of the *religionsgeschichtlicht* approach associated with R. Reitzenstein (*Paul's Visual Piety: The Metamorphosis of the Beholder* [Oxford: Oxford University Press, 2013], 176–81).

126 Thus I disagree with the conclusion of Paul Barnett, that in 4:4, "'seeing' of 'the light . . . of the glory' is, of course, metaphorical for *hearing*" (*Second Corinthians*, 220; emphasis original).

127 Interestingly, Paul's remarks in 2 Cor 10:1–6 concern the waging of divinely empowered war. The portrayal of the ideal king as victorious in war was common in ancient political discourse. The importance of the visual encounter is found also in Paul's insistence that "it was before your eyes that Jesus Christ was publicly exhibited as crucified" (Gal 3:1). See the treatment of this verse in Jipp, *Christ Is King*, 66–67. Jipp contends that the Galatians' transformation is dependent upon their beholding Christ.

128 The grammatical construction of the verb to learn (*manthanō*) followed by a personal direct object is exceedingly rare. I argue that this expression evokes the inculcation of moral virtue through the presence of Christ, a philosopher-king. See the discussion in the following chapter, which borrows from my argument in *Christ the Ideal King*, 226–33.

129 The arrangement of Paul's argument in 2:14–4:6 betrays evidence of a concentric, or chiastic, structure. This can be observed in the repetition of the following key terms and concepts. A (2:14)—the knowledge of God (*tēs gnōseōs autou*) is being revealed through Paul's life; B (2:15–16)—those being saved are contrasted with those who are perishing (*en tois apollumenois*); C (2:17)—Paul refuses to peddle the word of God (*kapēleuontes ton logon tou theou*); D (3:1–6)—a letter written on hearts (*en tais kardiais*), not of the letter (*ou grammatos*) but of the spirit (*alla pneumatos*); E: (3:7–14)—setting aside (indicated by the verb *katargeō* in a variety of inflected forms) of the glory (3:7), the covenant or administration (3:11), the goal or end (*telos*, 3:13), and the veil (3:14) associated with Moses; D' (3:15–18)—the veil over the heart (*kalumma epi tēn kardian*) is contrasted with the spirit of the Lord (*to pneuma kuriou*); C' (4:1–2)—Paul refuses to distort the word of God (*dolountes ton logon tou theou*); B' (4:3–5)—Paul's gospel is perceived as veiled by those who are perishing (*en tois apollumenois*); A' (4:6)—the knowledge of God's glory (*tēs gnōseōs tēs doxēs tou theou*) in the face of Christ is being revealed to the heart.

130 W. Bauer et al., *A Greek-English Lexicon of the New Testament and Other Early Christian Literature*, 3rd ed., rev. F. W. Danker (Chicago: University of Chicago Press, 2000), 342, 530.

131 Long finds in 2:17 and 12:19 evidence of what he describes as Paul's incarnational rhetoric: "Christ is *incarnated* through Paul in his speech" (*Ancient Rhetoric and Paul's Apology*, 240; emphasis original).

132   The NRSV translates the singular *kardia* in the final sentence with the plural "minds." While this is an acceptable translation, I have rendered *kardia* with the singular "heart" to make clear its primary lexical meaning and to highlight the fact that Paul is using a different word than *noēma* (thought, or intellect) in the first sentence. In Greek, the heart can be used to denote the more limited faculty of thought, but often conveys the more expansive notion of the entirety of the interior life, especially the faculty of volition. See Bauer et al., *Greek-English Lexicon*, 508, 675; Kittel and Friedrich, *TDNT*, 3:608–12, 4:960; Robert Jewett, *Paul's Anthropological Terms: A Study of Their Use in Conflict Settings*, AGJU 10 (Leiden: Brill, 1971), 313, 328–29.

133   Hafemann concludes, "The problem signified by the veil is thus not a *cognitive* inability due to the lack of a special spiritual endowment, but an inescapable *volitional* inability as a result of a hardened heart untouched by the Spirit's transforming power" (*Paul, Moses*, 363–86, here 374; emphasis original).

134   For this understanding of the intent of Torah, see Talbert, *Sermon*, 59–66; Pennington, *Sermon on the Mount*, 172–74, 290–94.

135   All the other instances of *apistos* within the Corinthian correspondence refer to those outside the church: 1 Cor 6:6; 7:12–16; 10:27; 14:22–25. Commentators therefore take this to be the referent here; so, e.g., Barnett, *Second Corinthians*, 218–20; Furnish, *II Corinthians*, 220–21; Thrall, *Second Corinthians*, 1:306.

136   See Derk William Oostendorp, *Another Jesus: A Gospel of Jewish-Christian Superiority in II Corinthians* (Kampen: Kok, 1967), 47: in 4:3–4, "Paul is not thinking about all those who are not saved, but specifically about the members of the churches which he has founded who have not been obedient to the gospel. Paul's answer to the opponents' charge is that the presence of such sinners at Corinth does not prove that his gospel is faulty but that the 'god of this world' has power over their minds." Oostendorp adds that such a reading also helps to solve a thorny problem of translation. The verb *augasai* most commonly means "to show forth," but most translators and commentators conclude that in 4:4 the verb must mean "to see," a rarer, more poetic meaning of the verb. Paul's point, it is claimed, is that unbelievers cannot *see* the light of the gospel. But Oostendorp points out that if the *apistoi* are not "unbelievers" but rather disobedient believers, Paul's point could very well be that such individuals fail to *show forth* the light of the gospel. This reading garners support from N. T. Wright's interpretation of the participle *katoptrizomenoi* ("beholding as in a mirror") in 3:18—although it is Christ's glory that believers behold, this glory can also be seen when beholding fellow believers (*The Climax of the Covenant: Christ and the Law in Pauline Theology* [Minneapolis: Fortress, 1992], 185–89).

137   Wright, *Climax*, 190.

138   Although Paul does not explicitly exhort the Corinthians to imitate him in this letter, the discourse of mimesis, or imitation, is present elsewhere in his letters (1 Thess 1:6–7; 2:14; Phil 3:17; 1 Cor 4:16; 11:1) and thus appears to be a mainstay in his efforts to form believers into the image of Christ. In disagreement with Elizabeth A. Castelli, however, I do not find that "Paul's discourse of mimesis uses rhetoric to rationalize and shore up a particular set of social relations or power relations within the early Christian movement. . . . Participating positively in the mimetic relationship with Paul, the early communities are to be rewarded with salvation. Resisting the mimetic relationship, by contrast, has dire consequences" (*Imitating Paul*, 116). Paul's concern is not primarily that his position of apostolic power be restored, but rather that the Corinthian believers see Christ. As he says

towards the end of the letter, "Have you been thinking all along that we have been defending ourselves before you? We are speaking in Christ before God. Everything we do, beloved, is for the sake of building you up" (2 Cor 12:19). For this reason, I also disagree with Harrill, *Paul the Apostle*, 80–88, who argues that Paul's rhetoric of *auctoritas* (Latin: "clout" or "influence") "advances, participates in, and colludes with particularly Roman ways of exercising power" (88).

139   Willard, *Spirit of the Disciplines*, 121.

140   The following understanding of the human body's capacity for spiritual power is indebted to Willard, *Spirit of the Disciplines*, 44–55.

141   J. Richard Middleton, *A New Heaven and a New Earth: Reclaiming Biblical Eschatology* (Grand Rapids: Baker Academic, 2014), 41–55, argues that creation in God's image further implies that human creation of culture ought to mirror God's creation. On the theologically charged vocabulary of Gen 2:15, see ch. 5.

142   The word "being" in the NRSV renders the Hebrew *nephesh*, which is translated in the LXX as *psychē*. In the earlier King James Version (KJV), the word "soul" is used.

143   Wendell Berry contends that this verse resists a dualistic conception of the person: "The formula given in Genesis 2:7 is not man = body + soul; the formula there is soul = dust + breath. According to this verse, God did not make a body and put a soul into it, like a letter into an envelope. He formed man of dust; then, by breathing His breath into it, He made the dust live. The dust, formed as man and made to live, did not *embody* a soul; it *became* a soul. 'Soul' here refers to the whole creature. Humanity is thus presented to us, in Adam, not as a creature of two discrete parts temporarily glued together but as a single mystery" ("Survival of Creation," 106; emphasis original).

144   Willard, *Spirit of the Disciplines*, 52.

145   Willard, *Spirit of the Disciplines*, 53; emphasis added.

146   Willard further defines spirit as "*unembodied personal power*" in contrast to unembodied *impersonal* power, such as electricity, magnetism, and gravity (*Spirit of the Disciplines*, 64).

147   Willard suggests that the first humans exercised this spiritual power in a way that truly reflected, and was enabled by, divine power. Just as God speaks the created world into being, so Adam exercises his governing power over the animal kingdom through speech, naming the animals God brings before him (*Spirit of the Disciplines*, 49–52).

148   Willard, *Spirit of the Disciplines*, 54; emphasis added.

149   Willard, *Spirit of the Disciplines*, 54.

150   Willard, *Spirit of the Disciplines*, 68. Willard helpfully groups such practices into two categories. "Disciplines of abstinence" aim to curb sins of commission and include practices such as: solitude, silence, fasting, frugality, chastity, secrecy, and sacrifice. "Disciplines of engagement," on the other hand, aim to curb sins of omission: study, worship, celebration, service, prayer, fellowship, confession, and submission (156–92). An excellent guide to practicing such disciplines is found in Richard J. Foster, *Celebration of Discipline: The Path to Spiritual Growth* (San Francisco: Harper & Row, 1978).

151   Despite these significant differences, I agree with N. T. Wright, that "what Paul is arguing for is a Christian form of the ancient pagan theory of virtue." And yet, he clarifies, "it isn't a case of Aristotle being topped up by Paul." Rather, ancient virtue ethics "has indeed been thoroughly Christianized. It has . . . been put to death and brought to new life" (*After You Believe*, 240).

152   Lutz, "Roman Socrates," 54–55. See the earlier discussion above, p. 72.

153   Dallas Willard, *The Divine Conspiracy: Rediscovering Our Hidden Life in God* (San Francisco: HarperSanFrancisco, 1998), 353.

154   The verbs he uses are common to the Greco-Roman philosophical discourse of *askēsis* (Victor C. Pfitzner, *Paul and the Agon Motif: Traditional Athletic Imagery in the Pauline Literature*, NovTSup 16 [Leiden: Brill, 1967], 23–35). See further the articles in Kittel and Friedrich, *TDNT*: ἐγκράτεια κτλ. (2:339–42); ὑπωπιάζω (8:590). Interestingly, the author of the latter article "rules out comparison with philosophical and religious ascetics of every kind" as a conceptual background for 1 Cor 9:27. Nevertheless, whether or not this judgment is warranted, it clearly indicates that the verb *hupōpiazō* in fact *was* used to describe ascetical practices in the Greco-Roman world.

155   Willard, *Spirit of the Disciplines*, 98–102. See also Calvin Roetzel's discussion of Paul as "the model ascetic" (*Paul: The Man and the Myth* [1997; repr., Minneapolis: Fortress, 1999], 134–51).

156   It is difficult to reconstruct the beliefs and practices of the Pharisees from the extant sources. See the essays in Jacob Neusner and Bruce D. Chilton, eds., *In Quest of the Historical Pharisees* (Waco, Tex.: Baylor University Press, 2007). Their practices of prayer and fasting, however, seem well attested.

157   Willard argues that Paul's own self-control belies his practice of spiritual disciplines (*Spirit of the Disciplines*, 102–7). NT scholars have not often attended to the importance of ascetic practices in Paul's life. Witness the collected articles in Vincent L. Wimbush, ed., *Semeia* 58 (1992). In this two-volume issue of the journal, entitled "Discursive Formations, Ascetic Piety and the Interpretation of Early Christian Literature," the mere possibility that Paul's ascetic practices may be in view in 1 Cor 9:24–27 does not rate even a mention. This *lacuna* in NT scholarship may be due to the prejudice against what Willard describes as the "consuming asceticism" characteristic of certain strains of medieval monasticism. Luther's criticism of this perversion of ascetic practices is well known and has been influential within Protestantism; see the discussion in *Spirit of the Disciplines*, 130–55.

158   Jennifer A. Glancy argues against the interpretation that Paul boasts of his beatings in the same way that soldiers boasted of battle wounds. There is an important "semiotic distinction between a battle-scarred body and a flogged body. In boasting of beatings, Paul does what he says he does: he boasts of things that show his weakness" ("Boasting of Beatings [2 Corinthians 11:23–25]," *JBL* 123 [2004]: 134).

159   Even Calvin Roetzel, who claims that Paul's rhetoric "intends to hurt, to silence speech and to eliminate opposition," admits that Paul's larger approach is a complex blending of "emancipatory" and "disciplinary" models of rhetoric ("The Language of War [2 Cor. 10:1–6] and the Language of Weakness [2 Cor. 11:21b–13:10]," in *Violence, Scripture, and Textual Practice in Early Judaism and Christianity*, ed. Ra'anan S. Boustan, Alex P. Jassen, and Calvin J. Roetzel [Leiden: Brill, 2009], 96).

160   The verb *teleitai* ("is made perfect") is in the present tense, which in *koinē* Greek often, although not always, conveys a present, ongoing process; see Friedrich Blass, Albert Debrunner, and Robert Walter Funk, *A Greek Grammar of the New Testament and Other Early Christian Literature*, ed. Robert Walter Funk (Chicago: University of Chicago Press, 1961), 166–67. This reading is found in Barnett, *Second Corinthians*, 573: "is being made perfect." Consider also the comments of Thrall, *Second Corinthians*, 2:821: "This power is not a static possession, but rather something continually appropriated and experienced afresh on each occasion of struggle with weakness."

161 See above, p. 81, for the discussion of such spiritual exercises described by Seneca and Lucian.

162 Recall that in 2:17, Paul uses the same phrase—*katenanti theou en Christō laloumen*—to contrast himself against those who peddle God's word. See above, n. 76.

163 Paul's injunctions to imitate him, and by extension Christ and even God, are frequent: 1 Cor 4:6; 11:1; Eph 5:1; Phil 3:17; 1 Thess 1:6; 2:14; 2 Thess 3:7; 9.

164 Thrall, *Second Corinthians*, 1:284–85, observes that, in the Corinthian correspondence, Christ is made visible both in Paul's ministry and in the Eucharist. This observation anticipates the argument of the following chapter.

4 Community

1 Burton Watson, trans., *Xunzi: Basic Writings*, Translations from the Asian Classics (New York: Columbia University Press, 2003), 121.

2 See the discussion of ritual in Wayne A. Meeks, *The First Urban Christians: The Social World of the Apostle Paul* (New Haven: Yale University Press, 1983), 140–63. Meeks thinks of rituals as a kind of performative speech: "The appropriate question, as we undertake to describe the rituals mentioned in the Pauline letters, is 'What do they *do*?'" (142; emphasis original). Richard E. DeMaris contends that, more than text, belief, or experience, ritual brings one closer to the life of the early church (*The New Testament in Its Ritual World* [London: Routledge, 2008], 9). DeMaris challenges the assumption that rituals are derivative and dependent upon some deeper theological significance. Rather, he understands rites "as generative and creative—as having a life of their own" (8). Important for the discussion below are his observations that rites "engender an idealized situation that may not match—and hence stand in tension with—reality" (30) and that, while "writing and reading engage the mind . . . ritual engages the body" (34). For a wide-ranging theoretical grounding to ritual studies and their application to study of early Christianity, see the essays in Part One of Risto Uro et al., eds., *The Oxford Handbook of Early Christian Ritual* (Oxford: Oxford University Press, 2019), 3–133.

3 See Aaron Stalnaker, *Overcoming Our Evil: Human Nature and Spiritual Exercises in Xunzi and Augustine* (Washington, D.C.: Georgetown University Press, 2006); Michael J. Rhodes, "Formative Feasting: Practices and Economic Ethics in Deuteronomy's Tithe Meal and the Corinthian Lord's Supper" (PhD diss., University of Aberdeen, 2019).

4 James K. A. Smith, *Desiring the Kingdom*, 39–73.

5 James K. A. Smith, *Desiring the Kingdom*, 75–129. Smith further defines "liturgies" as "rituals of ultimate concern," by which he means rituals that "inculcate particular visions of the good life, and do so in a way that means to trump other rituals" (85–89). See also Klyne R. Snodgrass, *Who God Says You Are: A Christian Understanding of Identity* (Grand Rapids: Eerdmans, 2018), 163: "Rituals in worship are habits we practice that maintain and shape our identity."

6 See Burton Watson's introduction in *Xunzi*, 1–14.

7 "A Discussion of Music," in Burton Watson, *Xunzi*, 115–23.

8 Burton Watson, *Xunzi*, 116–18.

9 Burton Watson, *Xunzi*, 120.

10 "Man's Nature is Evil," in Burton Watson, *Xunzi*, 161–74.

11 Burton Watson, *Xunzi*, 162. Mencius, by contrast, likens virtue to four sprouts that all humans possess "just as they have four limbs. . . . When we know how to enlarge

and bring to fulfillment these four sprouts that are within us, it will be like a fire beginning to burn or a spring finding an outlet" (2A6) (Irene Bloom, trans., *Mencius*, ed. Philip J. Ivanhoe, Translations from the Asian Classics [New York: Columbia University Press, 2009], 35). Xunzi's philosophy of moral education seems closer to that of Confucius: "Duke Ai asked, 'What can I do to induce the common people to be obedient?' Confucius replied, 'Raise up the straight and apply them to the crooked, and the people will submit to you. If you raise up the crooked and apply them to the straight, the people will never submit" (2.19) (Edward Slingerland, trans., *Confucius: The Essential Analects* [Indianapolis: Hackett, 2003], 5).

12   Burton Watson, *Xunzi*, 93.

13   Burton Watson, *Xunzi*, 174.

14   Burton Watson, *Xunzi*, 120.

15   Burton Watson, *Xunzi*, 123. Note how Xunzi's exclamations regarding the way of the true king function as *inclusios* that interpret the significance of the ceremony within his larger argument.

16   Ritual practice is culturally specific, and I am not suggesting that *particular* rituals of the Warring States period in China might shed light on *particular* rituals that emerged in the early church. Rather, the following discussion presumes that, beneath the layer of cultural particularity, humans across cultures relate to ritual practices in ways that are similar.

17   Although it was an actual meal, it was also a *ritual* meal as well (DeMaris, *Ritual World*, 32, 34, 69). See further Soham Al-Suadi, "The Meal in 1 Corinthians 11," in *T&T Clark Handbook to Early Christian Meals in the Greco-Roman World*, ed. Soham Al-Suadi and Peter-Ben Smit (London: T&T Clark, 2019), 227–39, who argues that Paul is refiguring a typical Hellenistic meal by introducing Jesus as the symposiarch, or presider, over the meal.

18   There are, of course, alternative historical reconstructions of the social setting of this meal; see Anthony C. Thiselton, *The First Epistle to the Corinthians: A Commentary on the Greek Text*, New International Greek Testament Commentary (Grand Rapids: Eerdmans, 2000), 848–99.

19   Hays, *First Corinthians*, 199.

20   See especially Rhodes, "Formative Feasting," 244–301. Rhodes concludes, "This eucharistic practice, which served as a compressed narrative of Christ's self-sacrificial death on behalf of his church, should orient the community toward a common *telos* and foster virtues of hospitality, care for others, and solidarity with the 'have nots.' It should also shape the community's public character, or politics, to 'fit' the apocalyptic inbreaking of God's mysterious plan to bring to naught existing social hierarchies by calling to himself a people primarily comprised of the 'have nots'" (300). Rhodes insists that Paul aimed to reform more than the practice of the Lord's Supper itself: "Paul expected that change to ripple out into every area of believers' lives" (301).

21   Rhodes, "Formative Feasting," 287–91.

22   It is important to note that, although James K. A. Smith strenuously resists an intellectualist account of the person, his argument is not *anti*-intellectualist. Rather, he aims to place reflection, or intellectual activity, within a broader framework of what phenomenologist Maurice Merleau-Ponty calls "perception," the body's unconscious way of "knowing" or "taking in" the world (*Imagining the Kingdom*, 31–73).

23   James K. A. Smith, *Imagining the Kingdom*, 31–38. Smith offers a perceptive exegesis of familiar secular cultural liturgies such as the experience of shopping at a mall,

attending a football game at a stadium, or matriculating at a university (*Desiring the Kingdom*, 19–27, 89–118).

24   James K. A. Smith, *Imagining the Kingdom*, 12–15, here 14–15; emphasis added. Smith conceives of imagination "as a quasi-faculty whereby we construe the world on a precognitive level, on a register that is fundamentally *aesthetic* precisely because it is so closely tied to the body" (19; emphasis original). Smith's use of the term "imagination" parallels Merleau-Ponty's *praktognosia*, an embodied "know-how." It is this faculty, for example, that enables one to understand stories as more than merely the stringing together of events (58–69). See also Maurice Merleau-Ponty, *Phenomenology of Perception*, trans. Donald A. Landes (1945; repr., London: Routledge, 2012), 105–41. Finally, it is worth noting that, according to Richard Hays, Paul's use of Scripture (i.e., the Old Testament) aims to effect a similar "conversion of the imagination" (*The Conversion of the Imagination: Paul as Interpreter of Israel's Scripture* [Grand Rapids: Eerdmans, 2005], 1–24).

25   James K. A. Smith, *Imagining the Kingdom*, 153–54. Smith is drawing on N. T. Wright, *The New Testament and the People of God,* Christian Origins and the Question of God 1 (Minneapolis: Fortress, 1992), 41–42: "But in principle the whole point of Christianity is that it offers a story which is the story of the whole world. It is public truth." For an interpretation of the Bible understood as a "grand narrative" along the lines envisioned by Wright, see Bartholomew and Goheen, *Drama of Scripture.*

26   Pierre Bourdieu, *The Logic of Practice*, trans. Richard Nice (1980; repr., Stanford: Stanford University Press, 1990), 52–65, here 52.

27   James K. A. Smith, *Imagining the Kingdom*, 79.

28   James K. A. Smith, *Imagining the Kingdom*, 51.

29   Bourdieu, *The Logic of Practice*, 53, 56.

30   James K. A. Smith, *Imagining the Kingdom*, 92.

31   Bourdieu, *The Logic of Practice*, 66–67.

32   Bourdieu, *The Logic of Practice*, 69. Bourdieu describes, for example, the numerous small ways in which manners teach the body to recognize the social construction of sexual difference (70–79).

33   James K. A. Smith, *Imagining the Kingdom*, 95.

34   James K. A. Smith, *Imagining the Kingdom*, 92.

35   James K. A. Smith, *Imagining the Kingdom*, 139.

36   James K. A. Smith, *Imagining the Kingdom*, 110–24. Smith formulates this argument in conversation with the work of philosopher Mark Johnson, whose work *The Meaning of the Body: Aesthetics of Human Understanding* (Chicago: University of Chicago Press, 2007) explores aspects of embodied meaning and cognition. Smith explains the importance of metaphor for understanding both cognition and action: "For finite, embodied creatures like us, meaning is fundamentally rooted in metaphor because that is the inferential 'logic' of the body" (*Imagining the Kingdom*, 124).

37   James K. A. Smith, *Imagining the Kingdom*, 141.

38   James K. A. Smith, *Imagining the Kingdom*, 157; emphasis original.

39   James K. A. Smith, *Imagining the Kingdom*, 163.

40   A number of scholars have thus argued that Ephesians was written as a baptismal homily: Nils Alstrup Dahl, "Adresse und Proömium des Epheserbriefes," *TZ* 7 (1951): 263–264; John Coutts, "Ephesians 1:3–14 and 1 Peter 1:3–12," *NTS* 3 (1957): 125–127; cf. J. C. Kirby, *Ephesians: Baptism and Pentecost: An Inquiry*

into the Structure and Purpose of the Epistle to the Ephesians (London: SPCK, 1968), 144–61 (a homily associated with the renewal of baptismal vows at the Feast of Pentecost).

41   The question of authorship of these two letters, no less than the relationship between them, continues to be debated. Arguments for deutero-Pauline authorship can be found in Andrew T. Lincoln, *Ephesians*, WBC 42 (Dallas: Word, 1990), lix–lxxiii; for Pauline authorship, Harold W. Hoehner, *Ephesians: An Exegetical Commentary* (Grand Rapids: Baker Academic, 2002), 2–61. My previous study adopted the view that Ephesians was written by a disciple of Paul towards the end of the first century; see *Christ the Ideal King*, 9.

42   Talbert, *Ephesians and Colossians*, 12–15, here 15.

43   For discussion of these opponents—whether real or merely anticipated by Paul—see Margaret Y. MacDonald, *Colossians and Ephesians*, SP 17 (Collegeville, Minn.: Liturgical, 2000), 10–13, 96–126.

44   Some scholars therefore posit literary dependence, usually arguing for the priority of Colossians. The evidence, however, does not permit confidence in concluding whether, and in which direction, literary dependence exists. See Talbert, *Ephesians and Colossians*, 1–5.

45   Augustine's *Confessions* employs the same strategy, inviting the reader to follow Augustine along his journey to faith by praying along with him.

46   Talbert, *Ephesians and Colossians*, 42–49.

47   The prepositional phrase *en Christō* is often translated "in Christ," yet the force of the preposition is frequently instrumental, especially as Paul uses it in Ephesians. Thus the phrase *en hō* ("in him") in 1:13 denotes Christ as the agent *through* whom the church is sealed with the Spirit. See the discussion in Julien C. H. Smith, *Christ the Ideal King*, 182–85.

48   Paul himself has been similarly written into that story and his relationship to the church constitutes part of their own story. For further discussion of the narrative world created by this letter, see Julien C. H. Smith, *Christ the Ideal King*, 195–203.

49   Identifying the opponents behind the so-called "Colossian heresy" has been notoriously difficult. Yet if one cannot confidently know much about it, one can at least say that some members of the congregation were persuaded by it. Note that Paul uses the present tense in 2:20: "why do you live . . . why do you submit?" This would indicate that some have been persuaded by this heresy and have changed their behavior. It seems reasonable to assume that this has resulted in some level of disunity.

50   The following argument draws upon my earlier monograph, *Christ the Ideal King*, in which I argue that Paul's portrayal of the Christ in Ephesians as a type of ideal king unites many of that letter's central themes and sharpens its rhetorical strategy. See also Joshua W. Jipp, "Sharing in the Heavenly Rule of Christ the King: Paul's Royal Participatory Language in Ephesians," in *"In Christ" in Paul: Explorations in Paul's Theology of Union and Participation*, ed. Michael J. Thate, Kevin J. Vanhoozer, and Constantine R. Campbell, WUNT 2/384 (Tübingen: Mohr Siebeck, 2014), 251–79.

51   Paul writes in Col 3:10 of the "image of its creator," but it is clear from 1:15 that this image can also be identified with Christ; so Jerry L. Sumney, *Colossians: A Commentary*, NTL (Louisville: Westminster John Knox, 2008), 202.

52   The following summary borrows from chs. 2 and 3 of my earlier work, *Christ the Ideal King*. See the summaries on 86–89, 170–73.

53   John J. Collins, *The Sibylline Oracles of Egyptian Judaism*, SBLDS 13 (Missoula, Mont.: Scholars' Press, 1974), 35, describes the perspective of book 3 of the Sibylline Oracles as "royal eschatology—the expectation of radical and decisive change to be brought about by a king or kingdom." English translations of Jewish pseudepigrapha are from James H. Charlesworth, ed., *The Old Testament Pseudepigrapha*, 2 vols., ABRL (Garden City, N.Y.: Doubleday, 1983–85).

54   I treat all of these texts in greater detail in ch. 3 of *Christ the Ideal King*.

55   The understanding of a king as "living law" was widespread: For Philo, the philosopher-king *par excellence* was Moses, who reigned by virtue of the "living law" (*nomos empsuchos*) within him (*Mos.* 1.162; 2.4). Plutarch used similar terms to describe the good king's ability to rule as originating from "reason endowed with life within him" (*empsuchos ōn en autō logos*) (*Princ. iner.* 780D).

56   English translations of the Neopythagorean philosophers are taken from Kenneth Sylvan Guthrie, trans. *The Pythagorean Sourcebook and Library: An Anthology of Ancient Writings Which Relate to Pythagoras and Pythagorean Philosophy*, ed. David R. Fideler (Grand Rapids: Phanes, 1987). For helpful discussion along with translation of selected Neopythagorean kingship treatises, see Goodenough, "Political Philosophy."

57   English translation from Lutz, "Roman Socrates."

58   Virgil, *Aen.* 1.286–294; 6.791–797; Seneca, *Apoc.* 10; cf. *Clem.* 2.1.3–2.2 on his hope for a golden age to be ushered in by Nero.

59   Martial, *Epig.* 5.19.1–2, 6; Statius, *Sylv.* 1.6.39–50; Pliny, *Pan.* 94.2; Suetonius, *Aug.* 22; cf. *Tib.* 37.

60   The dative phrase *en tō Christo* is understood to have instrumental force here and in many instances throughout the letter. See John A. Allan, "The 'In Christ' Formula in Ephesians," *NTS* 5 (1958): 54–61.

61   Smith, *Christ the Ideal King*, 88, 171, 206–7.

62   Taking *en tō haimati tou Christou* instrumentally.

63   Klaus Wengst, *Pax Romana and the Peace of Jesus Christ*, trans. John Bowden (Philadelphia: Fortress, 1987), 7–13, 21–24.

64   Diodorus of Sicily records Alexander as having left instructions to Craterus to unite Europe and Asia through intermarriage (*Hist.* 18.4.4). This policy of ethnic fusion, though admired by his successors, was never implemented (*Hist.* 18.4.6).

65   The passage in Colossians is actually referring to reconciliation with God, which Paul discusses in Eph 2:1–10. Reconciliation of humanity to God and within humanity itself are both aspects of God's plan to reconcile the cosmos. This can be seen in the parallelism in Eph 2:15b and 2:16a; see Gerhard Sellin, *Der Brief an die Epheser*, 9th ed., KEK 8 (Göttingen: Vandenhoeck & Ruprecht, 2008), 217.

66   It does not follow, however, that Paul is abolishing Torah observance for Jewish Christians. The argument in this letter is directed towards a Gentile audience. See the forthcoming article, Andrew Remington Rillera, "*Tertium Genus* or Dyadic Unity? Investigating Socio-Political Salvation in Ephesians," *BR* 65 (2020).

67   Miriam Pucci Ben Zeev, "Jews among Greeks and Romans," in *The Eerdmans Dictionary of Early Judaism*, ed. John J. Collins and Daniel C. Harlow (Grand Rapids: Eerdmans, 2010), 237–55.

68   *ēte, apēllotriōmenoi* (v. 12); *egenēthēte* (v. 13); *poiēsas, lusas* (v. 14); *katargēsas, ktisē* (v. 15); *apokatallaxē, apokteinas* (v. 16); *elthōn, euēggelisato* (v. 17); *exomen* (v. 18); *este* 2x (v. 19); *epoikodomēthentes* (v. 20); *sunarmologoumenē, auxei* (v. 21); *sunoikodomeisthe* (v. 22).

69 The psalmist chides an ungrateful Israel for forgetting the benefactions (*euergesiōn*) of the LORD (Psalm 77:11; cf. Psalm 12:6; Wis 16:11 LXX).

70 See the discussion of reciprocity characteristic of the Greco-Roman culture of benefaction in John M. G. Barclay, *Paul and the Gift* (Grand Rapids: Eerdmans, 2015), 24–51; Talbert, *Ephesians and Colossians*, 20–25.

71 Plato believed that the ideal king should be a philosopher in order to attain virtue (*Rep.* 473D). Plato's student, Aristotle, similarly believed that the goal of the state should be to inculcate virtue in its citizenry (*Nic. Eth.* 1179b–81b). Although Aristotle primarily looked to laws to train people in the habits of virtue, he conceded that this task could be accomplished by a person supreme in virtue, who would indeed be a god among men (*Pol.* 1284a.3–11).

72 Philo's writings suggest that these ideas were known among first-century Jews as well (*Joseph* 86–87, 157, 174; cf. 164; *Moses* 2.4, 36, 43, 189).

73 Julien C. H. Smith, *Christ the Ideal King*, 186; Allan, "'In Christ,'" 57–58.

74 Talbert, *Ephesians and Colossians*, 23–24, claims that Paul's language here—"I . . . beg you (*parakalō*)"—reflects the technical terminology used to call forth the reciprocal response to benefaction.

75 Of course at this point in the argument, Paul is warning his audience against living "as the Gentiles live" (4:17), *as though* they had not learned Christ. For the argument that "learning Christ" functions as a metaphor for character transformation, see my *Christ the Ideal King*, 226–31.

76 Eastman, *Paul and the Person*, 141. Here, Eastman is commenting upon the insight of Plato, *Phaedrus* 253a–b on participating in God by becoming like God, and *Thaetetus* 176e, 177a on becoming like what we imitate. Earlier in the book, drawing upon work in the philosophy of mind and developmental psychology, she observes that "mimetic interaction" is fundamental for human development. Imitation, or rather *being* imitated, is crucial for intimacy (65–68).

77 The following summation of ancient textual evidence is borrowed from my earlier work, *Christ the Ideal King*, 234.

78 Andrew Wallace-Hadrill, "The Golden Age and Sin in Augustan Ideology," *Past and Present* 95 (1982): 19–36; see also Virgil, *Ecl.* 4.11–14; *Georg.* 1.466–514.

79 Seneca, *De clementia* 1.1.1; 1.6.3; 1.22.2–3; 2.1.3–2.2; Dio Chrysostom, *Or.* 2.55–56, 77; 34.19; Suetonius, *Vespasian* 11; *Pss. Sol* 17:27; *T. Levi* 18:9c.

80 Paul's assumption of the normative nature of these hierarchical relationships will strike many modern readers as *detracting from*, and even *corrosive to* harmony, rather than contributing to it. The cultural gap between us and Paul is so wide at this point because Paul does not share our cultural expectation for radical social equality. Furthermore, Paul's remarks here must be understood within the context of conventional Greco-Roman wisdom concerning the "household," which was more akin to a family business than to a modern nuclear family. See further MacDonald, *Colossians and Ephesians*, 152–69, 324–42; Talbert, *Ephesians and Colossians*, 149–57.

81 In both letters, Paul employs the traditional "two ways" form of moral exhortation. On the background, form, and function of this type of ethical paraenesis, see my *Christ the Ideal King*, 221–26.

82 The discussion below of putting off vice and putting on virtue runs parallel to the argument in Barclay, *Paul and the Gift*, 493–519. In Rom 5–8 and 12–15, Paul is concerned with the replacement of a "deeply inculcated *habitus* of sin" by a new embodied Christian *habitus*. Virtues, like the "perceptions, goals,

dispositions, and values" that comprise a *habitus* (516), must be practiced and are embodied.

83   The discussion below will focus on the more concise treatment found in Colossians 3:5–17.

84   Brian J. Walsh and Sylvia C. Keesmaat, *Colossians Remixed: Subverting the Empire* (Downers Grove, Ill.: IVP Academic, 2004), 160–62. On the importance of sexual love to community life, and the community's sacred duty to protect it against the predation of the industrial economy, see Wendell Berry, *Sex, Economy, Freedom and Community: Eight Essays* (New York: Pantheon Books, 1993), 117–73, esp. 133–34.

85   Walsh and Keesmaat, *Colossians Remixed*, 164–68.

86   Walsh and Keesmaat, *Colossians Remixed*, 172–83.

87   See Johannes Behm, "καρδία," in Kittel and Friedrich, *TDNT*, 605–14, especially D.2.c.

88   It is often claimed that the spatialized eschatology in these two letters is at odds with the Jewish temporal eschatology one sees in Paul's undisputed letters. The temporal element, however, is not absent, e.g., the age to come, Eph 1:21; the coming of God's wrath, Col 3:6. See Lincoln, *Ephesians*, 65, 261, 422–24, 446; Sumney, *Colossians*, 192. The spatialized eschatology of these two letters is not a fully *realized* eschatology. Nor do these letters present what James K. A. Smith describes critically as "*spatialized* readings that imagine Jesus is carving up distinct jurisdictions of authority" (*Awaiting the King*, 75–80; emphasis original).

89   Walsh and Keesmaat argue that Paul is "denaturalizing these reified societal structures and unveiling them as the cultural lies they are" (*Colossians Remixed*, 173).

90   Newbigin, *Gospel*, 222–33.

91   "Remembering" here may imply more than literal memory, especially if the tradition of infant baptism was practiced in the NT church, as implied by the baptism of entire households (Acts 10:44–48; 16:13–15; 18:8; 1 Cor 1:16). On this question see Oscar Cullmann, *Baptism in the New Testament*, trans. J. K. S. Reid, SBT (London: SCM, 1950), who regards infant baptism to be biblical in practice even if the practice in the NT church is only indirectly observable. On the baptismal anamnesis in Colossians and Ephesians, see Walter T. Wilson, *The Hope of Glory: Education and Exhortation in the Epistle to the Colossians*, NovTSup 88 (Leiden: Brill, 1997), 113–31. See also Wayne A. Meeks, "In One Body: The Unity of Humankind in Colossians and Ephesians," in *God's Christ and His People: Studies in Honour of Nils Alstrup Dahl*, ed. Nils Alstrup Dahl, Jacob Jervell, and Wayne A. Meeks (Oslo: Universitetsforlaget, 1977), 210.

92   MacDonald, *Colossians and Ephesians*, 150.

93   In this regard, note Paul's conclusion to his lengthy ethical exhortation in Eph 4:17–5:21: "Do not get drunk with wine, for that is debauchery; but be filled with the Spirit, as you sing psalms and hymns and spiritual songs among yourselves, singing and making melody to the Lord in your hearts, giving thanks to God the Father at all times and for everything in the name of our Lord Jesus Christ" (Eph 5:18–20). Although editors of modern English translations typically insert a paragraph break after this sentence, there are good grammatical reasons for seeing them as connected to what Paul writes next: "Be subject to one another out of reverence for Christ" (Eph 5:21). The verb "be subject" is actually a participle (*hupotassomenoi*) dependent upon the finite verb in the previous sentence. Taking these sentences together suggests that mutual submission grows out of, or is nurtured by, giving thanks to God. Paul's exhortation to exercise mutual submission also serves to introduce the

following "household code" (5:21–6:9). Paul expects that the mutual submission borne out of worship will spread throughout domestic life.

94   The discussion in Talbert, *Ephesians and Colossians*, 149–57, provides a helpful orientation to the main issues.

95   These explanations are not mutually exclusive, and all three may in fact help to understand Paul's intentions.

96   James K. A. Smith, *Imagining the Kingdom*, 157–58.

97   Rhodes, "Formative Feasting," 301; emphasis added.

98   Talbert, *Ephesians and Colossians*, 39.

99   In Eph 1:11 Paul writes, "In Christ we also have obtained an inheritance," which I interpret, in light of Eph 2:11–22, as a reference to Gentiles having been incorporated into the "commonwealth of Israel" through the death of Christ (cf. Eph 2:12).

100 In Greek, as in English, to indicate a *might*—a possible state of affairs—one typically uses the subjunctive mode. Paul expresses his thought here using an articular infinitive (*to einai*), which is used to indicate the result (or sometimes the purpose) of the action of the finite verb.

101 Here I am in substantial agreement with Barclay, *Paul and the Gift*, 518, commenting on Romans: "Because the life of the believer is thus *derived* from Christ, Paul does not have to play the agency of the believer off against the agency of Christ/the Spirit; he does not need to insist that the *real* agent is the Spirit"; emphasis added.

5 Creation

1   In fall 2018, Purdue University's College of Agriculture (ranked #12 in the world) boasted its largest undergraduate enrollment since 1980: 2,803 students (https://www.purdue.edu/newsroom/releases/2018/Q4/college-of-agriculture-hits-milestone-undergrad-enrollment), accessed October 2, 2019.

2   Wendell Berry, *The Art of Loading Brush: New Agrarian Writings* (Berkeley, Calif.: Counterpoint, 2017), 25.

3   Berry, *Art of Loading Brush*, 43, cites the following example, in a letter from John Logan Brent, Judge Executive of Henry County, Kentucky, dated October 3, 2016: "'The good news is that for a young man wishing to earn a middle, to slightly below middle class annual salary of $45,000 farming cattle full-time, he only has to have $3,281,000 in capital to get started. If he can find 780 acres to rent, he only has to have $551,000 for used cows and equipment. I say this is the good news, because the reality is that this was based on a weaned calf price of $850 from June of this year. According to today's sales reports, that same calf is now $650 at best.'"

4   Marilynne Robinson, "Fear," *New York Review of Books* 62/14 (September 24, 2015): 28–30.

5   Wendell Berry, *The Unsettling of America: Culture and Agriculture* (San Francisco: Sierra Club Books, 1977), 21.

6   Wendell Berry wrote *The Unsettling of America* in 1977 to document and explain this ecological catastrophe. In a recent collection of essays, he observes that the conditions described in this landmark book "have persisted and become worse over the last twenty-five years" (*Citizenship Papers* [Washington, D.C.: Shoemaker & Hoard, 2003], 143).

7   Berry, *Unsettling of America*, 22.

8   Agrarian writers such as Wendell Berry would prefer to speak of "membership" within a community rather than "citizenship."

9   Davis, *Scripture, Culture, and Agriculture*, 1.

10   Davis, *Scripture, Culture, and Agriculture*, 29.

11   The following discussion borrows from my monograph, *Christ the Ideal King*, 48–55.

12   Wallace-Hadrill, "Golden Age," 20.

13   H. C. Baldry, "Who Invented the Golden Age?" *CQ* 2 (1952): 83–92; Bodo Gatz, *Weltalter, goldene Zeit und sinnverwandte Vorstellungen*, Spudasmata 16 (Hildesheim: Olms, 1967), 28–51, 114–53.

14   The child's identity is not made clear. R. G. M. Nisbet, "Virgil's Fourth Eclogue: Easterners and Westerners," *Bulletin of the Institute for Classical Studies* 25 (1978): 70–71, believes that the poem's enigmatic ending may be a deliberate effort to show that the child is out of the ordinary, and perhaps will have a superhuman destiny.

15   The influence of Jewish sources (Isa 11:6–9; *Sib. Or.* 3.743–759) may lie behind the descriptions of this golden age. See Nisbet, "Virgil's Fourth Eclogue," 65–67; Wallace-Hadrill, "Golden Age," 21; Gatz, *Weltalter*, 79–83.

16   This last descriptor refers to Augustus having ended civil strife, prompting the resolution by the Senate to shut the gates of the temple of Janus (cf. *Res gest.* 13).

17   In the vision of a people for whom law is no longer necessary to produce righteousness, one may detect a faint echo of the concept of the king as a living law (*nomos empsuchos*). At the same time, it must be acknowledged that the peoples' righteousness is not dependent upon the ruler's possession of the animate law. Furthermore, note that elsewhere Saturn is described as giving humanity laws: "First from heavenly Olympus came Saturn . . . He gathered together the unruly race, scattered over mountain heights, and gave them laws" (*Aen.* 8.321). The reign of Saturn is further characterized by peace (*Aen.* 8.325–327), and the absence of personal property or greed (*Georg.* 1.125–128).

18   R. J. Getty, "Romulus, Roma, and Augustus in the Sixth Book of the *Aeneid*," *CP* 45 (1950): 1–12; J. Rufus Fears, Princeps a Diis Electus: *The Divine Election of the Emperor as a Political Concept at Rome*, Papers and Monographs of the American Academy in Rome 26 (Rome: American Academy in Rome, 1977), 123–25. Dvornik, *Political Philosophy*, 2:491–94, claims that Cicero's "Dream of Scipio" (*Rep.* 6.13, 24), in which rulers are envisioned as coming from and returning to heaven, represents an earlier stage in the development of the belief that rulers are the divinely elected vicegerents of the gods.

19   Wallace-Hadrill, "Golden Age," 24. The close of Virgil's first *Georgic* implies that the people's *scelus* is responsible for the current age of civil war (*Georg.* 1.463–68). As to the solution, Virgil prays to the "gods of our fathers" not to prevent Caesar from saving the world from ruin (*Georg.* 1.498–500).

20   Wallace-Hadrill, "Golden Age," 29.

21   Francis Cairns, *Virgil's Augustan Epic* (Cambridge: Cambridge University Press, 1989), 60–62.

22   See further the examples taken from Augustus' life gathered in Dvornik, *Political Philosophy*, 2:483–86. An encomion, according to the *progymnasmata* (preliminary composition exercises) of Aelius Theon, is "language revealing the greatness of virtuous actions and other good qualities belonging to a particular person" (*Prog.* 109 in Kennedy, *Progymnasmata*, 50). The extant *progymnasmata* indicate that elementary rhetorical training commonly involved learning to craft both the encomion and its opposite, the invective.

23   M. P. Charlesworth, "The Virtues of a Roman Emperor: Propaganda and the Creation of the Belief," *Proceedings of the British Academy* 23 (1937): 105–33. See further Lothar Wickert, "Princeps (Civitatis)," in *Paulys Realencyclopädie der classischen Altertumswissenschaft*, vol. 22, no. 2, ed. Georg Wissowa et al. (Stuttgart: Druckenmüller, 1954), 2222–31. Wallace-Hadrill, "Virtues," 298–323, argues that in fact there was no fixed "canon" of imperial virtues. Instead, a multiplicity of virtues and personifications were used in imperial coinage not so much as intentional propaganda, but rather as response to the pressure from the elites that the emperor conform to a set of virtues that would ensure stability.

24   The Roman Cult of Virtues also allowed for innovation, since new virtues could be emphasized as the hallmark of the new emperor's reign (e.g., Tiberius—*Clementia, Moderatio*; Claudius—*Constantia*); see Fishwick, *Imperial Cult*, 456–59.

25   Wallace-Hadrill, "Virtues," 316.

26   Steven J. Friesen, *Imperial Cults and the Apocalypse of John: Reading Revelation in the Ruins* (Oxford: Oxford University Press, 2001), 122–31, demonstrates the ways in which the imperial cult functioned as religion: worship of the imperial family fit within the symbolic world of Greco-Roman polytheism, fulfilling functions of cosmogony, cosmology, human maturation, and eschatology.

27   Friesen, *Imperial Cults*, 4.

28   Augustus famously boasted of his grain distributions to Rome (*Res gest.* 18).

29   Willem M. Jongman, "The Early Roman Empire: Consumption," in *The Cambridge Economic History of the Greco-Roman World*, ed. Walter Scheidel, Ian Morris, and Richard Saller (Cambridge: Cambridge University Press, 2007), 606–7.

30   Elio Lo Cascio, "The Early Roman Empire: The State and the Economy," in *The Cambridge Economic History of the Greco-Roman World*, ed. Walter Scheidel, Ian Morris, and Richard Saller (Cambridge: Cambridge University Press, 2007), 639–41.

31   Robert Sallares, "Ecology," in *The Cambridge Economic History of the Greco-Roman World*, ed. Walter Scheidel, Ian Morris, and Richard Saller (Cambridge: Cambridge University Press, 2007), 28–34. Peter Garnsey and Richard Saller argue that the Roman economy during the principate was underdeveloped; the extent of economic activity such as trade, manufacturing, transportation, construction and the like paled in comparison to subsistence farming, the occupation of the majority of the population (*The Roman Empire: Economy, Society and Culture* [Berkeley: University of California Press, 1987], 43–63).

32   K. D. White, *Roman Farming*, Aspects of Greek and Roman Life (Ithaca, N.Y.: Cornell University Press, 1970), 11–12; Dennis P. Kehoe, "The Early Roman Empire: Production," in *The Cambridge Economic History of the Greco-Roman World*, ed. Walter Scheidel, Ian Morris, and Richard Saller (Cambridge: Cambridge University Press, 2007), 568–69; Garnsey and Saller, *Roman Empire*, 43–46; Aldo Schiavone, *The End of the Past: Ancient Rome and the Modern West*; trans. Margery J. Schneider, Revealing Antiquity 13 (Cambridge, Mass.: Harvard University Press, 2000), 103. See the comments of Cicero, *De officiis* 1.42.151.

33   For an overview of ancient sources, see K. D. White, *Roman Farming*, 14–46. The primary extant technical treatises are: Cato, *De Agri Cultura* (mid-second c. BCE); Varro, *De Re Rustica* (37 BCE); and Columella (ca. 4 BCE–65 CE), *De Re Rustica*. Pliny the Elder's *Natural History* (77–79 CE) frequently sheds insight on improved farming techniques outside Italy but uses sources uncritically. Non-technical agrarian writers include Horace (65–27 BCE), Cicero (106–43 BCE), Virgil (70–19 BCE) and Pliny the Younger (61–113 CE).

34   Sallares, "Ecology," 15–37; K. D. White, *Roman Farming*, 47–49; Kehoe, "Production," 551–53; Geoffrey Rickman, *The Corn Supply of Ancient Rome* (Oxford: Clarendon, 1980), 3–7; Richard Duncan-Jones, *The Economy of the Roman Empire: Quantitative Studies* (Cambridge: Cambridge University Press, 1974), 37.

35   John Percival, *The Roman Villa: An Historical Introduction*, Batsford Studies in Archaeology (London: Batsford, 1976), 111. See, for example, Virgil's old man of Tarentum (*Georgics* 4.125–126). See further Magen Broshi, "Agriculture and Economy in Roman Palestine: Seven Notes on the Babatha Archive," *IEJ* 42, nos. 3–4 (1992): 234, who notes that it required one hundred and fifty labor days per hectare to cultivate date palms in Roman Palestine.

36   K. D. White, *Roman Farming*, 346; Percival, *Roman Villa*, 119. After fifteen days, Cincinnatus resigned his office and returned to his farm. This story was frequently told as an illustration of Roman virtue. Cicero reports that he was again summoned from his farm in 439 BCE (*De sen.* 56). See also Pliny's reference to the event in *Natural History* 18.20–21. Percival, however, doubts the historical accuracy of the account, given the disparity between large and small landowners inherent within a social and political system based upon land ownership. One *iugerus* is approximately five-eighths of an acre. A farm of seven *iugera* would be less than four and a half acres. Columella indicates that a seven-*iugera* vineyard could be cultivated by one person; see K. D. White, *Roman Farming*, 327–33.

37   There is now considerable debate over the former consensus that Italy suffered a decline in the free rural peasantry during this period. For an overview of this debate concerning demography, see Alessandro Launaro, *Peasants and Slaves: The Rural Population of Roman Italy (200 BC to AD 100)* (Cambridge: Cambridge University Press, 2011), 1–3. Launaro argues, on the basis of extensive landscape archaeological surveys, that free peasant farms and slave-run villas (on which see below) increased, remained stable, or declined at approximately the same rates (166–68).

38   Percival, *Roman Villa*, 119. He cautions that this account may be exaggerated. State-owned land (*ager publicus*) was allotted to citizens and veterans in colonies in an effort to restore small-scale proprietors. Nevertheless, land ownership and use were fundamentally changed in Italy as a result of these wars.

39   Walter Scheidel, "Slavery," in *The Cambridge Companion to the Roman Economy*, ed. Walter Scheidel (Cambridge: Cambridge University Press, 2012), 93. The number of slaves in Italy in the first three centuries of the principate cannot be known with confidence; estimates range between 250,000–750,000 agricultural slaves and between 500,000–1,000,000 urban slaves. This would constitute between 15–25 percent of the total Italian population. Walter Scheidel, "Demography," in *The Cambridge Economic History of the Greco-Roman World*, ed. Walter Scheidel, Ian Morris, and Richard Saller (Cambridge: Cambridge University Press, 2007), 64, estimates cautiously that in the last two centuries of the Republic, "several million slaves must have been transferred to Italy."

40   Kehoe, "Production," 546–50; Garnsey and Saller, *Roman Empire*, 56–57. These surpluses resulting from slave labor were also required to supply Rome's massive army at a cost of some 450–500 million *sesterces* per year, which was probably over half the imperial budget. See Neville Morley, "The Early Roman Empire: Distribution," in *The Cambridge Economic History of the Greco-Roman World*, ed. Walter Scheidel, Ian Morris, and Richard Saller (Cambridge: Cambridge University Press, 2007), 575–76; Garnsey and Saller, *Roman Empire*, 88–97; Keith Hopkins, "Taxes and Trade in the Roman Empire (200 B.C.–A.D. 400)," *JRS* 70 (1980): 124–25.

41   K. D. White, *Roman Farming*, 26–27. Kehoe, "Production," 554, points to Villa Settefinestre at Cosa, an estate of several hundred hectares, as an example of a typical slave-run estate. Supervised by a slave-bailiff (*vilicus*), such a property would have required the labor of fifty to one hundred slaves.

42   Percival, *Roman Villa*, 13. See further Annalisa Marzano, *Roman Villas in Central Italy: A Social and Economic History*, Columbia Studies in the Classical Tradition 30 (Leiden: Brill, 2007), who distinguishes between the *villa maritima* and the *villa rustica*.

43   Michael I. Rostovtzeff, *The Social and Economic History of the Roman Empire*, 2nd ed., 2 vols (Oxford: Clarendon, 1957), 2:564 n. 23. See further K. D. White, "Latifundia," *Bulletin of the Institute of Classical Studies of the University of London* 14 (1967): 76. See, however, Marzano, *Roman Villas in Central Italy*, 125–53, who contends that the *villa rustica* may have been farmed by a combination of both slaves and tenants. The argument turns upon whether the supposed *ergastulum* (slave quarters) identified at Villa Settefinestre was in fact used for other purposes. Marzano concedes that, even so, slaves may well have been housed in wooden outbuildings that have left no archaeological trace.

44   Percival, *Roman Villa*, 146. See also Hopkins, "Taxes and Trade," 104–5.

45   Scheidel, "Slavery," 102–4. Scheidel, "Demography," 64, notes that in the absence of sufficient population pressure, the effort-intensive cultivation in the villa system required coerced labor.

46   Lin Foxhall, "The Dependent Tenant: Land Leasing and Labour in Italy and Greece," *JRS* 80 (1990): 97–114. Foxhall observes that tenants remained in exploitative leases often because they were the "least worst" option available to them (111–13). Paul Erdkamp, *The Grain Market in the Roman Empire* (Cambridge: Cambridge University Press, 2005), 23–33, points out, however, that the social and economic conditions of tenants ran the gamut from prosperous to poor. Even Launaro, *Peasants and Slaves*, 170–77, who argues overall for a more limited role of slavery in the economic rise of Roman Italy, concedes that the vast majority of tenants were of humble status.

47   Kehoe, "Production," 555–56. See further the evidence from the alimentary inscription at Veleia in Garnsey and Saller, *Roman Empire*, 66–71.

48   See K. D. White, "Latifundia," 64–72, for the ancient literary evidence. The extant evidence of the actual size of actual estates is slender. Based on the calculation of one thousand *sesterces* per *iugerum* as a middling price, White estimates that Pliny the Younger's Tuscan estate was approximately five thousand *iugera*, or three thousand acres. Garnsey and Saller, *Roman Empire*, 64–66, describe Pliny's wealth of 20 million *sesterces* as "modest."

49   K. D. White, "Latifundia," 72–75. Strabo, writing ca. 17 CE, observes that the previously flourishing market town of Murgantia in Sicily had disappeared, and that the northern and western sides of the island were deserted. White infers that this is the result of large-scale conversion of arable land to pasture. The damaging effects of this change in land usage over time are reflected in the changing meaning of the term *saltus*, which refers to land used for stock-grazing. Livy (59 BCE–17 CE) uses the term to refer to virgin woodland rather than land cleared for cultivation (*History of Rome* 27.12). But Isidore, writing over five centuries later (560–636 CE), equates *saltus* with *vasta et silvestria loca* ("waste and wooded areas"), suggesting that land used exclusively for pasturage inevitably suffered neglect over time. White concludes that in between these two writers "lies a tale of centuries of neglect and positive misuse of the land" ("Latifundia," 74).

50   Pliny is referring to Virgil, *Georg.* 2.412.

51   Percival, *Roman Villa*, 119. K. D. White, "Latifundia," 78, finds Pliny's comments "so vague as to be virtually without value."

52   K. D. White, *Roman Farming*, 26–27. White's comment pertains to Columella, writing in the middle of the first century, who similarly had a dim view of current agricultural practices. Although K. D. White, "Latifundia," 78, finds Pliny's comment vague, he nevertheless concludes that "what Pliny meant was that the *latifundia*, which dominated many parts of the south, were so large that they could not be cultivated by their owners, and had been allowed to develop into vast tracts of *agri deserti* [deserted fields]."

53   Hopkins, "Taxes and Trade," 104; Duncan-Jones, *Economy of the Roman Empire*, 37. Jack Morato, "*Praecipitia in Ruinam*: The Decline of the Small Roman Farmer and the Fall of the Roman Republic," *International Social Science Review* 92, no. 1 (2016): 1–28, argues convincingly that the decline of subsistence farming originated in the late third century BCE of the Republic.

54   K. D. White, *Roman Farming*, 336–76; Garnsey and Saller, *Roman Empire*, 43–46, 97–103.

55   Bruce W. Longenecker, *Remember the Poor: Paul, Poverty, and the Greco-Roman World* (Grand Rapids: Eerdmans, 2010), 44–53, estimates that those living at (and often below) the subsistence level comprised 30 percent of the population, while those living below subsistence, 25 percent. Steven J. Friesen, "Poverty in Pauline Studies: Beyond the So-Called New Consensus," *JSNT* 26 (2004): 323–61, had earlier estimated those groups at 40 percent and 28 percent respectively.

56   Jongman, "Consumption," 617. See further Garnsey and Saller, *Roman Empire*, 64–66; Duncan-Jones, *Economy of the Roman Empire*, 343–44; Peter Temin, "The Economy of the Early Roman Empire," *Journal of Economic Perspectives* 20 (2006): 136.

57   Duncan-Jones, *Economy of the Roman Empire*, 288–319.

58   For an overview of the debate, see Sallares, "Ecology," 22–27. J. Donald Hughes, "Ancient Deforestation Revisited," *Journal of the History of Biology* 44 (2011): 43–57, argues that Roman agricultural practice had a major effect on deforestation; his argument is based on evidence from anthracology, palynology, and computer modeling.

59   Rickman, *Corn Supply*, 1–3.

60   Rickman, *Corn Supply*, 8–13, 94–119, 173–74; Lo Cascio, "State and Economy," 639–41.

61   William V. Harris, "The Late Republic," in *The Cambridge Economic History of the Greco-Roman World*, ed. Walter Scheidel, Ian Morris, and Richard Saller (Cambridge: Cambridge University Press, 2007), 530–32, points to the negative effects of the grain tithe on Sicily for example. In an average year, Sicily's wheat tax equaled 3 million *modii* (20,640 tons), or the equivalent of the entire produce from 51,150 ha (out of 500,000 ha under grain cultivation). The tax thus represented over 10 percent of the grain produced on the island. Garnsey and Saller, *Roman Empire*, 20–40, 51–56, 97–103, observe that while the overall tax burden in the Roman empire was modest, it disproportionately affected subsistence farmers, whose entire surplus would have been siphoned off by taxes and rents.

62   Broshi, "Agriculture and Economy," 236. Daniel Sperber, "Aspects of Agrarian Life in Roman Palestine I: Agricultural Decline in Palestine During the Later Principate," *ANRW* 2.8 (1977): 400, argues that by the Rabbinic period, the increasing

load of taxation was causing the progressive abandonment of land. See further
Hopkins, "Taxes and Trade," 101–3, 122.

63   Wendell Berry, *What Matters? Economics for a Renewed Commonwealth* (Berkeley,
Calif.: Counterpoint, 2010), 64; emphasis added.

64   Berry, *Sex, Economy, Freedom and Community*, 21.

65   Wendell Berry, *The Hidden Wound* (Berkeley, Calif.: Counterpoint, 1989), 65.

66   Berry, *The Hidden Wound*, 112, argues that racism was not the cause of slavery
in America, but rather became its justification: "The root of our racial problem
in America is not racism. The root is in our inordinate desire to be superior—not
to some inferior or subject people, though this desire leads to the subjection of
people—but to our condition. We wish to rise above the sweat and bother of taking
care of anything—of ourselves, of each other, or of our country. We did not enslave
African blacks because they were black, but because their labor promised to free us
of the obligations of stewardship, and because they were unable to prevent us from
enslaving them."

67   Berry, *The Hidden Wound*, 78.

68   An historian might wish to quibble with Berry's observation here. This might be
said of parts of the antebellum South, though with large qualifications; however, it
certainly was never true in the northern United States, where preserving the dignity of "free soil" and "free labor" was part of the Republican Party's appeal from its
beginnings in 1854. Much northern farming outside New England was both highly
remunerative and well regarded through the late nineteenth century. I am indebted
to my colleague Mel Piehl for this insight.

69   Berry, *The Hidden Wound*, 81; emphasis added.

70   Berry, *The Hidden Wound*, 105.

71   This point is supported by Schiavone, *End of the Past*, 40, who contends that Aristotle's characterization of a slave as such "by nature" (*Pol.* 1252a) reflected a "social division of labor that linked slavery indissolubly with production." Schiavone
contends that in the ancient mindset, "all agricultural and manufacturing labor of
a subservient nature—whether slave labor or not—contained such a heavy burden
of discrimination and oppression, and was conjoined so forcibly with compulsion
without consensus, that it was very difficult to include it in the moral universe and
the mental sphere of vision of the higher classes. . . . ethics and intellect were allotted no part in this lowly and degraded world."

72   On Paul's self-identification as a Pharisee and its significance for his thinking, see
Wright, *The New Testament and the People of God*, 181–203; Wright, *Paul and the
Faithfulness of God*, 75–196. On the importance of narrative tradition for ethics, see
Alasdair MacIntyre, *After Virtue: A Study in Moral Theory*, 2nd ed. (Notre Dame,
Ind.: University of Notre Dame Press, 1984), 204–25. MacIntyre's moral theory, in
particular his conceptualization of practices, will prove important below as we seek
to use Paul's argument in Romans as a hermeneutical resource for thinking about
agrarian virtues in our own context.

73   Treatment of the biblical tradition in this section is heavily indebted to Davis,
Scripture, Culture, and Agriculture.

74   Davis, *Scripture, Culture, and Agriculture*, 19. On the ancient Greek view of *physis*
(translated "nature") as the power inherent in a thing, see Wirzba, *From Nature to
Creation*, 33–39. Such an understanding has certain ethical implications: one can
seek both to contemplate nature as well as to harness or exploit its powers.

75   Davis, *Scripture, Culture, and Agriculture*, 26; emphasis added. Davis goes on to
describe the Bible's "land ethic," which is comprised of four elements: 1) "the land

comes first," and thus humankind must learn to serve the land, learning from and respecting its limits; 2) a "forthright embrace of ignorance," implying the willingness to accept the limits of the human condition as well as the reliance on God's wisdom, especially with respect to agriculture; 3) "exacting concern with the *materiality* of human existence," implying a concern to meet human needs without inflicting human and ecological damage; and 4) the land is invaluable, not a commodity to be bought and sold as private property (21–41).

76   For the argument that Scripture presents us with a coherent narrative, see Bauckham, "Reading Scripture," 38–53. See further Bauckham, *The Bible and Ecology*, 141–78, in which the author describes Scripture as a "christological eco-narrative" in which salvation is envisioned not as the replacement, but rather the renewal of creation.

77   So, famously, Lynn White Jr., "The Historical Roots of Our Ecological Crisis," *Science* 155 (1967): 1203–7. Among the many perceptive critiques of White's argument, see in particular Richard Bauckham, *Living with Other Creatures: Green Exegesis and Theology* (Waco, Tex: Baylor University Press, 2011), 14–62.

78   Davis, *Scripture, Culture, and Agriculture*, 53–63. To confirm the suspicion that the use of the verb *kbš* in Gen 1 is ironic, Davis compares this poem of creation with another, Psalm 104, in which the reader is "stung" by moral judgment only at the very end (63).

79   Bartholomew, *Where Mortals Dwell*, 24–25, sees a narrative movement of "progressive implacement" in Gen 1–2. For further elements of continuity between Gen 1–2, see Davis, *Scripture, Culture, and Agriculture*, 43; Middleton, *Liberating Image*, 290–91; McConville, *Being Human in God's World*, 31; Bauckham, *The Bible and Ecology*, 20.

80   Davis, *Scripture, Culture, and Agriculture*, 30.

81   On the *imago Dei* as royal prerogative, see Middleton, *Liberating Image*, 88–89. On the intrinsic aspects of the *imago Dei*, see McConville, *Being Human in God's World*, 21–23.

82   McConville, *Being Human in God's World*, 26.

83   Davis, *Scripture, Culture, and Agriculture*, 64.

84   Davis, *Scripture, Culture, and Agriculture*, 101–19.

85   Davis, *Scripture, Culture, and Agriculture*, 106–7. The term can refer to land acquired through conquest, but Davis thinks its primary notion is "possession 'from below,' based on care."

86   The expression "kindly use" is a favorite of Wendell Berry. The "economics of permanence" is from E. F. Schumacher, *Small Is Beautiful: Economics as if People Mattered* (New York: HarperCollins, 1989), 33–34.

87   This is a marked contrast with the Roman institution of slavery.

88   Davis, *Scripture, Culture, and Agriculture*, 125.

89   Davis, *Scripture, Culture, and Agriculture*, 120–38.

90   The Chronicler casts the specialized agriculture of Uzziah in a positive light, giving as a reason for this development that the king "loved the soil" (2 Chron 26:9–10). The analysis of eighth-century crown agriculture by Davis, *Scripture, Culture, and Agriculture*, 120–38, as seen through the poetry of the prophets, is decidedly more critical.

91   Davis, *Scripture, Culture, and Agriculture*, 129.

92   Davis, *Scripture, Culture, and Agriculture*, 128.

93   Davis, *Scripture, Culture, and Agriculture*, 131.

94   Davis, *Scripture, Culture, and Agriculture*, 136.

95   Davis, *Scripture, Culture, and Agriculture*, 138; emphasis added.

96   To characterize Paul's eschatological perspective in this way—"already and not yet"—is commonplace in Pauline studies.

97   *Elpis* and cognates appear in Rom 4:18; 5:2, 4, 5; 8:20, 24, 25; 12:12; 15:4, 12, 13, 24. *Hypomonē* and cognates appear in Rom 2:7; 5:3, 4; 8:25; 12:12; 15:4–5.

98   In speaking of the "faithfulness *of* the Messiah Jesus," I am reflecting a particular translation of the phrase *pistis Christou*, which is found throughout Paul's letters (Rom 3:22; Gal 2:16; 3:22; Phil 3:9). Traditionally, this phrase has been rendered as "faith *in* Christ," taking Christ to be the *object* of faith (in grammatical terms, the "objective genitive"). Richard B. Hays, *The Faith of Jesus Christ: An Investigation of the Narrative Substructure of Galatians 3:1–4:11*, 2nd ed. (1983; repr., The Biblical Resource Series, Grand Rapids: Eerdmans, 2002), 141–61, argues that Christ should rather be understood as the *subject* of the verbal idea of *pistis*, or "faithfulness" (in grammatical terms, the "subjective genitive"). Paul would thus be talking about the "faithfulness *of* Christ," referring to his faithful obedience to God the Father, even to the point of death on the cross. Many scholars have been persuaded by Hays' argument, although cogent arguments have been adduced for taking *pistis Christou* as an objective genitive (faith *in* Christ): see Dunn, *Theology of Paul the Apostle*, 379–85, with helpful discussion of the scholarly debate. In an attempt to mediate this debate, Wolter, *Paul: An Outline of His Theology*, 75–77, takes *pistis Christou* to mean "Christian faith" or better, "Christ-faith." It is important to add that Hays is not simply arguing *against* the necessity of placing one's faith *in* Christ. This is also vitally important for Paul, as is clear, for example, in Gal 2:16 (the very same verse in which he speaks of justification through *pistis Christou*); there Paul speaks of believing *in* Christ Jesus (*eis Christon Iēsoun episteusamen*).

99   The term *dikaiosunē* and its cognates present a particular difficulty for translation: *righteousness* and *justice* are both possibilities. N. T. Wright often renders the term as *covenant justice* in order to capture the sense of faithfulness to the covenant relationship between Israel and YHWH that is implicit.

100 Recall the earlier discussion of Phil 2:5–11 in ch. 2.

101 As David Bentley Hart points out in his recent translation of the NT, the adjective *aiōnios* properly means "of the ages" and only in a derivative sense means "eternal" (David Bentley Hart, trans., *The New Testament: A Translation* [New Haven: Yale University Press, 2017], 537–42).

102 Paul casts his argument in 7:7–25 in the form of a fictive "I", representing the Jew under Torah who is unable to do what Torah commands. For this reading, see N. T. Wright, "Romans," in *The New Interpreter's Bible*, ed. Leander E. Keck, vol. 10, *Acts–First Corinthians* (Nashville: Abingdon, 2002), 569–72. This section also echoes the lament of Greco-Roman moralists who found themselves failing morally despite their best efforts. The echo may subtly suggest that, even as the Messiah is the fulfillment of Torah, he also surpasses the best efforts of pagan culture to achieve moral behavior.

103 Wright, "Romans," 555.

104 Laurie J. Braaten contends that in Rom 8, as normally in the Hebrew Bible, "the *labor pangs connote pain and judgment*, without reference to an immediate positive outcome" ("All Creation Groans: Romans 8:22 in Light of the Biblical Sources," *HBT* 28 [2006]: 141; emphasis original). However, see J. P. Davies, "What to Expect When You're Expecting: Maternity, Salvation History, and the 'Apocalyptic Paul,'" *JSNT* 38 (2016): 301–15, who finds that in Jewish and Christian apocalyptic

literature, childbirth imagery connotes not simply pain and judgment, but rather the decisive action of God in history.

105   Such a claim is entirely consistent with the pattern of the Messiah's suffering and subsequent glorification that Paul sets forth paradigmatically in Phil 2:5–11. See ch. 2 of this book and Gorman, *Becoming the Gospel*, 106–41, who contends that this represents Paul's "master story."

106   This claim requires qualification, as it is not true for all conceivable objects of hope. One might *hope* for a free trip to Disneyland, but would not really "suffer" its absence. This conception of hope, however, is rather what one might call "wish," an unfounded desire.

107   These comments can also be applied to the metaphor of the Exodus, which according to N. T. Wright, also provides the metaphorical background for Paul's argument in this section ("Romans," 510).

108   Thus the sense of "already and not yet" pervades the argument of Rom 5–8. Already God's children, yet we eagerly await adoption; already saved, yet we wait for our salvation patiently in hope (8:23–25). This present-and-future orientation furthermore helps make sense of the emphasis upon changed behavior in Rom 6: the new status of freedom from sin conferred by baptism; the reckoning of behavior appropriate to this new life; and the practice of bodily disciplines that lead towards sanctification.

109   The unbounded accumulation of wealth, Aristotle contended, was incompatible with the character of citizenship. See the discussion in Pellegrin, "Aristotle's *Politics*," 566.

110   Herman E. Daly, foreword to Berry, *What Matters?* x.

111   Wright, *Paul and the Faithfulness of God*, 1070.

112   Wright, *Paul and the Faithfulness of God*, 1014.

113   Davis, *Scripture, Culture, and Agriculture*, 72.

114   Davis, *Scripture, Culture, and Agriculture*, 78.

115   Berry, *The Hidden Wound*, 135.

6 Paul and the Good Life

1   Often the immediate cause for persecution was Christians' refusal to participate in the imperial cult. Christians came to see this participation in civil religion as tantamount to endorsing Caesar as Lord, which they could not with integrity do while at the same time proclaiming Jesus as Lord. Note, for example, the mid-to-late second-century *Martyrdom of Polycarp*, in which the magistrate implores the elderly bishop of Smyrna, "Swear by the oath [to Caesar], and I will release you; revile Christ." Polycarp replies, "For eighty-six years I have been his servant, and he has done me no wrong. How can I blaspheme my King who saved me?" (9.3). For a historically grounded, lively, fictionalized account of the persecution early Christians faced as a result of allegiance to Jesus, see Bruce W. Longenecker, *The Lost Letters of Pergamum: A Story from the New Testament World*, 2nd ed. (Grand Rapids: Baker Academic, 2016).

2   English translation from *Tertullian*, ed. Alexander Roberts and James Donaldson, vol. 3 of *The Ante-Nicene Fathers*, rev. A. Cleveland Coxe (Buffalo, N.Y.: Christian Literature Co., 1885–1896), 54–55.

3   Philip Schaff and Henry Wace, eds., *The Nicene and Post-Nicene Fathers* (Grand Rapids: Eerdmans, 1978–80), 2.1:581–610. For further discussion, see Fears, "Theology of Victory," 749–52, 818.

4   The "sign" to which Eusebius refers is the sign of the cross, which Constantine had spread throughout the empire by building and restoring Christian churches (*Laud. Const.* 9.13–19).

5   Newbigin, *Foolishness*, 101. See further Wright, *Paul and the Faithfulness of God*; Newbigin, *Gospel*, 104.

6   I agree with Newbigin's frequent assertions that the church cannot go back to the "Constantinian dream"; see Newbigin, *Foolishness*, ch. 5; Newbigin, *Gospel*, 232–33; Newbigin, *Open Secret*, 109. Nevertheless, one must resist the easy assertions that Constantine's Christian commitment was inauthentic or that his conversion marked the fall of the church. See the careful historical argument in Peter J. Leithart, *Defending Constantine: The Twilight of an Empire and the Dawn of Christendom* (Downers Grove, Ill.: InterVarsity, 2010).

7   See Bockmuehl, *Philippians*, 64: the Philippian believers are Paul's partners in the "public advocacy and corroboration of the gospel's truth and credibility."

8   See the discussion of the "missional locatedness of readers" and the "missional engagement with cultures" in Hunsberger, "Proposals," 313–16.

9   Although I refer to "North America" throughout, my discussion of contemporary politics that follows is intended to describe specifically the United States.

10   Michael Kelley, "THE 1992 CAMPAIGN: The Democrats—Clinton and Bush Compete to Be Champion of Change; Democrat Fights Perceptions of Bush Gain," *New York Times*, October 30, 1992.

11   Perhaps the biggest loser of all, as we now clearly see but seem powerless to respond to adequately, is the earth itself.

12   My point is not that capitalism is *necessarily* or universally a zero-sum game. Competition within a capitalist economy often results in a "rising tide" of shared wealth, even if it neither requires nor guarantees this result. It is, however, problematic to think of competition, as we often do, as a "law" governing economic activity. As Wendell Berry opines in his essay "The Total Economy": "The 'law of competition' does *not* imply that many competitors will compete indefinitely. The law of competition is a simple paradox: Competition destroys competition. The law of competition implies that many competitors, competing on the 'free market' without restraint, will ultimately and inevitably reduce the number of competitors to one. The law of competition, in short, is the law of war" (*What Matters?* 184; emphasis original).

13   Newbigin, *Foolishness*, ch 5. Elsewhere, he contends that Adam Smith's "invisible hand" represents a contemporary iteration of the Roman divinizing of luck (Fortuna) "which mysteriously converts private selfishness into public good. . . . Thus in our economic life we are no longer responsible to Christ; we are not responsible at all, for economic life has been handed over to the goddess Fortuna" (Newbigin, *Gospel*, 206–7). This is, I fully admit, a tendentious view of modern economics. While I cannot hope to convince readers who disagree, I can at least point to those who have articulated the argument forcefully and persuasively. In addition to the works cited in the notes above, see: Paul Heyne, *"Are Economists Basically Immoral?": And Other Essays on Economics, Ethics, and Religion* (Indianapolis: Liberty Fund, 2008); Wendell Berry, "Faustian Economics," in *What Matters?* 41–53; David Bentley Hart, "What Lies Beyond Capitalism?" *Plough Quarterly* 21 (Summer 2019): 30–38.

14   Newbigin, *Truth to Tell*, 81.

15   John Stuart Mill's *On Liberty* (1860) provides a classic articulation of this vision. Mill himself never articulates the *telos* towards which enlightened society

progresses, a symptom of modernity's inability to arrive at a commonly agreed upon *telos* or accept a divinely given one.

16   Of course, a strong economy is protected by the threat (and frequent use) of military force.

17   This fall in the Revised Common Lectionary (2017; year A), the majority of Philippians is read during the four Sundays of Proper 20–24.

18   Oakes, *Philippians: From People to Letter*, 77–84; Friesen, "Poverty."

19   Recent decades have seen the reversal of this trend, as certain urban areas are "revitalized" and become attractive living environments for wealthy urban professionals. The resulting gentrification, however, does not often benefit the poorer residents who, unable to now afford the higher cost of housing, must move away.

20   Such relocations of houses of worship recall perhaps Jeroboam's decision to construct shrines at Dan and Bethel, born out of the anxiety that the northern tribes, having seceded from Solomon's kingdom, might be enticed back by continuing to worship in Jerusalem (1 Kgs 12:25–33).

21   Ken Massey, pastor of Calvary Baptist at the time, credits this decision to the influence of women who had only recently been ordained to the church's diaconal ministry. He recalls, "Had it been just men, the church might have decided to relocate. . . . But the women were the driving force in saying, 'Well no, God put us here for a reason, and we should have some kind of ministry in this location'"; quoted in Marly Ramsour, "Jezebel or Servant of God?: How Julie Pennington-Russell Became the First Female Pastor in Texas" (unpublished master's thesis, Waco, Tex.: Baylor University, 2008), 38.

22   During the six years that I pursued a Ph.D. at Baylor, our family lived in the Sanger Heights neighborhood and worshiped at Calvary; the experience has made an indelible imprint on our lives. Space does not permit me to share stories of our sojourn with Calvary, but one may read of other churches who have similarly decided to remain in urban neighborhoods. See C. Christopher Smith and John Pattison, *Slow Church: Cultivating Community in the Patient Way of Jesus* (Downers Grove, Ill.: InterVarsity, 2014); David E. Fitch, *Faithful Presence: Seven Disciplines That Shape the Church for Mission* (Downers Grove, Ill.: InterVarsity, 2016).

23   As we saw above, James K. A. Smith, *Desiring the Kingdom*, argues compellingly that "cultural liturgies" profoundly shape our desires.

24   By embracing suffering, we can, for example, pursue trade deals that are equally as good for poorer countries as they are for us, meaning that in relative terms, we will suffer as a consequence. Domestically, we can pursue policies that benefit those of lower socioeconomic status, even while those of higher status suffer in relative terms. We can suffer higher energy costs in order to conserve limited resources and constrain pollution. We can suffer higher food prices to promote sustainable agriculture.

25   See MacIntyre, *After Virtue*.

26   N. T. Wright offers compelling examples illustrating the claim that "*virtue* is what happens when wise and courageous choices have become 'second nature'" through a lifetime of appropriate habituation (*After You Believe*, 18–26; emphasis original).

27   Paul is clearly urging an ethic of disinvestment in the normal routines of human life in 1 Cor 7:29–31, not because of the "imminence of the end," but rather because a more important allegiance to Jesus is called for; so John M. G. Barclay, "Apocalyptic Allegiance and Disinvestment in the World: A Reading of 1 Corinthians 7:25–35," in *Paul and the Apocalyptic Imagination*, ed. Ben C. Blackwell, John K. Goodrich, and Jason Maston (Minneapolis: Fortress, 2016), 257–74.

28   Commenting upon Gal 1:11–12, in which Paul elucidates the source of his gospel, J. Louis Martyn explains that for the Apostle, the gospel "cannot be measured
by any tradition, for at every juncture without exception *apocalypse takes primacy
over tradition*" (*Galatians: A New Translation with Introduction and Commentary*,
AB 33A [New York: Doubleday, 1997], 151; emphasis added). The readings of Paul
as an apocalyptic theologian have tended to diminish the importance of salvation
history (the idea of God's ongoing efforts at redemption, e.g., through the covenant
with Israel) in his letters. My own argument (recall the prominence of the covenant with Israel in my discussion of 2 Cor 3 and Rom 5–8) has endeavored to read
Paul as *both* a covenantal and apocalyptic theologian. See further David A. Shaw,
"Apocalyptic and Covenant: Perspectives on Paul or Antinomies at War?" *JSNT* 36
(2013): 155–71; Davies, "What to Expect When You're Expecting," 301–15.

29   Martinus C. de Boer, "Paul's Mythologizing Program in Romans 5–8," in *Apocalyptic Paul: Cosmos and Anthropos in Romans 5–8*, ed. Beverly Roberts Gaventa
(Waco, Tex.: Baylor University Press, 2013), 13. See further his excursus on apocalyptic eschatology in Galatians, a letter in which, as he notes, scholars typically
find scant evidence of Paul's apocalyptic thought (*Galatians: A Commentary*, NTL
[Louisville: Westminster John Knox, 2011], 31–36). De Boer is here following in
the footsteps of J. Louis Martyn, whose highly influential Galatians commentary
pioneered an apocalyptic reading of Paul; see Martyn, *Galatians*, 97–105. For a
critical assessment of the apocalyptic reading of Paul advanced by Martyn and
de Boer, see Wright, *Paul and His Recent Interpreters*, 155–86.

30   Paul can speak of Sin (capital s) as an enslaving power (Rom 3:9; 5:21) and sin
(small s) as a human act. J. Louis Martyn insists that Sin as slavemaster is primary
in Paul's thought, while sin as human act is secondary. He accounts for this tension
by explaining that for Paul, under the enslavement of Sin, we become "*actively
complicit* with the jailer" ("Afterword: The Human Moral Dilemma," in *Apocalyptic
Paul: Cosmos and Anthropos in Romans 5–8*, ed. Beverly Roberts Gaventa [Waco,
Tex.: Baylor University Press, 2013], 163).

31   In disagreement with Philip G. Ziegler, *Militant Grace: The Apocalyptic Turn and
the Future of Christian Theology* (Grand Rapids: Baker Academic, 2018), 133–34.

32   Consider the balanced judgment of Barclay: "Paul does not seem anxious to pref-
ace every reference to believer-agency with mention of its prior grounding in grace.
There is no doubt that 'life in Christ' is sourced and constituted in the Christ-event,
but the believer is thereby created, not diminished, as an actor. Paul's language
requires us to banish 'zero-sum' calculations of agency (the more God, the less
human); it seems better to speak of a pattern of 'energism' in Pauline agency. His
paraenesis points simultaneously to divine- and believer-agency, as the expression
and realization of the good news" (*Paul and the Gift*, 442).

33   My response to the challenges posed by apocalyptic readings of Paul has been
helped tremendously by Rhodes, "Formative Feasting," 208–21. Rhodes argues
persuasively that the "apocalyptic understanding of renewed agency creates the
proper frame for an account of ongoing moral formation through practice. Christ-
followers are transformed agents engaged in ongoing moral formation through
practice as they live with Christ as their 'very context' within a world still influenced by the defeated but active anti-God powers of Sin and Death" (213).

34   On the generic compatibility between apocalyptic and wisdom literature, see J. P.
Davies, *Paul among the Apocalypses: An Evaluation of the 'Apocalyptic Paul' in the
Context of Jewish and Christian Apocalyptic Literature*, LNTS (London: T&T Clark,
2018), 51, 55. Ellen Davis finds within the tradition of Israelite wisdom literature

a rich source for biblically inspired character formation ("Preserving Virtues: Renewing the Tradition of the Sages," in *Character and Scripture: Moral Formation, Community, and Biblical Interpretation,* ed. William P. Brown [Grand Rapids: Eerdmans, 2002], 183–201).

35   English translation from Niccolò Machiavelli, *The Prince,* trans. Harvey C. Mansfield (Chicago: University of Chicago Press, 1998), 62. Machiavelli further explains his point in the following chapter, "Of Liberality and Parsimony," in which he argues that the prince must prudently determine when it is expedient to exercise liberality, that is, the generous benefaction expected of a ruler. While prudence is indeed an essential intellectual virtue within Aristotle's moral framework, Machiavelli employs it in a fashion Aristotle could hardly have approved. Prudence, according to Machiavelli, enables the prince to determine when it is expedient to abandon liberality and choose instead the vice of parsimony, or meanness: "A prince should esteem it little to incur a name for meanness, because this is one of those vices which enable him to rule" (*The Prince,* 64).

36   Cesare Borgia was aided in this endeavor—and indeed in all of his political pursuits—by his father Rodrigo Borgia, who in 1492 had become pope, taking the name Alexander VI.

37   Machiavelli, *The Prince,* 30. The brilliance of Borgia's action, in Machiavelli's eyes at least, is that he "satisfies" the peoples' desire to have the cruel man punished, while at the same time sending the clear message that those who oppose him will meet the same fate. Thus are the people "stupefied." The same strategy—usually minus the bloodshed—is still in currency today.

38   Jonathan Powell, *The New Machiavelli: How to Wield Power in the Modern World* (London: The Bodley Head, 2010), 135. Powell served as the Chief of Staff to British Prime Minister Tony Blair for thirteen years and his book, a memoir of sorts, addresses the need for a "modern handbook to power and how to wield it" (3). The maxim is from Machiavelli, *The Prince,* 66.

39   This is precisely what Newbigin insists the church must not do if it is to function as the hermeneutic of the gospel (*Foolishness,* 124).

40   This is reflected in the emphasis Aristotle places upon friendship in books 8–9 of *Nicomachean Ethics.* For Aristotle, virtuous friendship would seem to lead one ineluctably towards virtue.

41   My earlier argument (see previous section) implied that the privilege of citizenship within a nation-state is often little more than a partnership in nationalism and capitalist covetousness. It *might* seem to follow that citizenship within the heavenly *politeuma* should require Christians to renounce citizenship in any recognized polity. I am not, however, arguing for an ethic of complete withdrawal. Rather, I am trying to hold together two convictions in tension with each other. Hauerwas and Willimon express it well: "Christianity is mostly a matter of politics—politics as defined by the gospel. The call to be part of the gospel is a joyful call to be adopted by an alien people, to join a countercultural phenomenon, a new *polis* called church." And yet they do not advocate an ethic of withdrawal: "The church is not out of the world. There is no other place for the church to be than here. . . . The church's only concern is *how* to be in the world, in what form, for what purpose" (Hauerwas and Willimon, *Resident Aliens,* 30, 43). See also James K. A. Smith, *Awaiting the King,* 53–89. Smith is keen to correct what he regards as a persistent misreading of Hauerwas' "resident alien" trope as an endorsement of withdrawal: "To see the church as an 'alternative' *polis* does not entail the superlative claim that Christian

citizens in the *saeculum* ensconce themselves in *only* the church. Resident aliens are *resident* where they are alien" (*Awaiting the King*, 54).

42 Dallas Willard acknowledges that "the magnitude of evil in human deeds is also a result of the institutional structures or common practices that emerge at the social level in politics, art, business, journalism, education, the intellectual life, government service, sexual and family relations, and sports and entertainment." On the one hand, it is correct to say that structural evil must be addressed structurally. Nevertheless, Willard insists, the evil present within such social structures "totally depend for their existence and power upon the *readinesses* that are in us individually" (*Spirit of the Disciplines*, 229; emphasis original). Systemic change must therefore be coupled with individual transformation.

43 This of course raises the question: To *what* should politicians be held accountable? It is unreasonable to hold them accountable to religiously based ethical norms, which they may not share. On the other hand, to hold politicians accountable to their *own* standards might be problematic for Christians. The complexity of this question cannot be satisfactorily addressed here. Two points must suffice. First, as Slavica Jakelić has demonstrated through her analysis of the Polish Solidarity movement, religious and secular humanists have collaborated in the past to address pressing historical issues ("Engaging Religious and Secular Humanisms," in *At the Limits of the Secular: Reflections on Faith and Public Life*, ed. William A. Barbieri Jr. [Grand Rapids: Eerdmans, 2014], 305–30). Second, therefore, to the extent that religious and secular humanists can find common ground in a shared conception of the common good, they should work to hold politicians accountable to working for this good rather than bowing to special interests. Wendell Berry expresses it well: "The time is past when it was enough merely to elect our officials. We will have to elect them and then go and *watch* them and keep our hands on them, the way the coal companies do" ("Think Little," in *The Art of the Common-Place: The Agrarian Essays of Wendell Berry*, ed. Norman Wirzba [Washington, D.C.: Counterpoint, 2002], 83; emphasis original).

44 Newbigin, *Foolishness*, 116.

45 Wendell Berry, "Solving for Pattern," in *The Art of the Common-Place: The Agrarian Essays of Wendell Berry*, ed. Norman Wirzba (Washington, D.C.: Counterpoint, 2002), 267. He continues: "But I could just as easily be talking about sanitation systems that pollute, school systems that graduate illiterate students, medical cures that cause disease, or nuclear armaments that explode in the midst of the people they are meant to protect."

46 Berry, "Solving for Pattern," 269.

47 Berry, "Solving for Pattern," 269; emphasis added.

48 Berry, "Solving for Pattern," 275; emphasis added.

49 Willard, *Spirit of the Disciplines*, 232–33; emphasis added. Willard freely acknowledges the appropriateness of legislative and social reform but only within the context of the radical transformation of human character and relationships (234).

50 One may well ask whether my argument is at all relevant to the multitudes of people who have no interest in being transformed into the likeness of Jesus. To such a reader I would stress that my argument for a christocentric spiritual formation shares much in common with arguments for moral formation broadly speaking. In response to such fundamental questions as—"What makes our lives go as they do? What could make them go as they ought?"—Dallas Willard contends that "thoughtful people through the ages have tried to answer these questions, and they have with one accord found . . . that what matters most for how life goes and

ought to go is what we are on the 'inside.' . . . This 'within' is the arena of spiritual formation and, later, transformation" (*Renovation of the Heart*, 16). Although Willard goes on to make an argument, as I do, for a christocentric version of spiritual formation, he also insists that spiritual formation *per se* is not inherently religious: "*Spiritual formation, without regard to any specifically religious context or tradition, is the* process *by which the human spirit or will is given a definite 'form' or character*" (19; emphasis original). Aaron Preston makes explicit what is implicit here and throughout Willard's writing on spiritual formation, namely that for Willard, "spiritual formation is the same as Platonic moral formation" ("Redeeming Moral Formation: The Unity of Spiritual and Moral Formation in Willardian Thought," *Journal of Spiritual Formation & Soul Care* 3, no. 2 [2010]: 214). Preston observes, for example, that while philosophical construals of *dikaiosunē* (justice, or righteousness) differ from Jesus' notion of *dikaiosunē*, they are not fundamentally opposed (216). Like Willard and Preston, I believe there are significant areas of overlap between Christian and non-Christian traditions of spiritual formation. Even though Paul would insist that we are only truly liberated from the deforming power of sin through the reign of Jesus, I believe that he nevertheless would affirm human efforts, however faltering, to pursue the good. He knows, after all, of those outside Israel's covenant family "who do not possess the law," and yet "do instinctively what the law requires" (Rom 2:14).

51   Martin Luther King Jr., *Strength to Love* (Philadelphia: Fortress, 1981), 102. King attributes the observation to Prof. Liston Pope.

52   See the analysis of this failure in Willard, *Divine Conspiracy*, 35–59.

53   This pattern of spiritual transformation is laid out in Willard, *Renovation of the Heart*, 85–92.

54   James K. A. Smith, *Imagining the Kingdom*, 188–89. Smith contends that this problem is best remedied by "liturgical catechesis," intentionally reflecting on what we are doing in worship, and why.

55   The phrase comes from the *Book of Common Prayer* and is part of the opening of the eucharistic liturgy of the Anglican Church.

56   This insight is true of the larger tradition of virtue ethics. Aristotle recognized both that individual virtues cannot be pursued to proper effect in isolation, and that a virtuous person cannot be fully human outside of a flourishing *polis*. Thus Aristotle conceives of justice, the harmonious functioning of all the virtues together, as "complete virtue" (*Nic. Eth.* 1129b25). Wendell Berry takes this claim one step further, insisting that individual and communal health is integrally connected to the health of the land and our relationship to it ("Health Is Membership," in *The Art of the Common-Place: The Agrarian Essays of Wendell Berry*, ed. Norman Wirzba [Washington, D.C.: Counterpoint, 2002], 144–58).

57   To better understand *how* worship "stories" us, see the exegesis of a Christian worship service in James K. A. Smith, *Desiring the Kingdom*, 155–214.

58   Francis Watson uses the *fall/redemption model* to explain what he regards as a "seriously deficient construal of Christian faith and the biblical witness," although he acknowledges that this model is an ideal type that probably has never existed historically in the pure, unqualified form in which he presents it. Nevertheless, I agree with Watson that the model does serve to illuminate the anthropomonistic tendency in certain strains—both ancient and modern—of Christian thought ("In the Beginning," 129–30).

59   For an account of the biblical narrative along these lines, see Middleton, *New Heaven*, 21–73. See further Bauckham, "Reading Scripture," who responds to the

critiques of biblical scholars and postmodern readers to this way of reading the Bible. Finally, see Francis Watson, "In the Beginning," 130–38, whose analysis of Irenaeus' response to the Gnostics provides evidence of reading Scripture as a narrative unity already in the second century.

60   For the argument that human culture is implied within the divine mandate to "fill the earth and subdue it" (Gen 1:28), see Middleton, *New Heaven*, 41–55.

61   James K. A. Smith, *Awaiting the King*, 15–16.

62   James K. A. Smith, *Awaiting the King*, 62–63; emphasis added.

63   James K. A. Smith, *Awaiting the King*, 67.

64   The question of where to draw the line with respect to technological innovation is difficult but it must be asked. Berry offers a set of nine standards by which he evaluates technological innovation in his own work as a writer. They can, I believe, be meaningfully applied more broadly as well. They are as insightful as they are challenging, in particular the last: Any technological innovation "should not replace or disrupt anything good that already exists, and this includes family and community relationships" ("Why I Am Not Going to Buy a Computer," in *What Are People For? Essays* [San Francisco: North Point, 1990], 172).

65   Aldo Leopold, *A Sand County Almanac, and Sketches Here and There* (1949; repr., New York: Oxford University Press, 1968), 224–25.

66   Berry, *Sex, Economy, Freedom and Community*, 131.

67   Berry, *Hidden Wound*, 135.

68   MacIntyre, *After Virtue*, 181–203.

69   Stanley Hauerwas, *In Good Company: The Church as* Polis (Notre Dame, Ind.: University of Notre Dame Press, 1995), 153–68; Hauerwas and Willimon, *Resident Aliens*, 60–66, 80–83; see also James K. A. Smith, *Imagining the Kingdom*, 151–91.

70   In our own context this means freedom from the pernicious source of industrial agriculture. For a primer on the human, social, and ecological costs of the global food system, much of which is borne by the most vulnerable lands and communities, see Jennifer R. Ayres, *Good Food: Grounded Practical Theology* (Waco, Tex.: Baylor University Press, 2013), 13–52.

71   Berry, "Think Little," 88–89. Additionally, such a person "is also enlarging, for himself, the meaning of food and the pleasure of eating" (88). This is a small, but important, step in the journey to what Jennifer Ayres describes as "local food sovereignty" (Ayres, *Good Food*, 99–116).

72   See the discussion of church-supported farming in Ayres, *Good Food*, 79–97.

73   Urban agriculture is making a surprising comeback, as Ellen Davis observes, in Detroit, which is emerging as a "postindustrial green city" (*Scripture, Culture, and Agriculture*, 175–78).

74   See Presian R. Burroughs, "Christlike Feasting: Attentiveness, Solidarity, and Self-Restraint in Romans," in *Practicing with Paul: Reflections on Paul and the Practices of Ministry in Honor of Susan G. Eastman*, ed. Presian R. Burroughs (Eugene, Ore.: Cascade Books, 2018), 157–79. Burroughs presents Christian feasting as a practice requiring attentiveness to the agricultural practices whereby food is produced.

75   Laura Dunn, *Look and See*. See the discussion of Berry in ch. 1.

Conclusion

1   The cross was designed by the architect Charles E. Stade, the sculpture by David Elder. The sculpture was dedicated in January 1965.

2   "Homeless Jesus" was first unveiled in 2013 in Toronto and was later blessed by
     Pope Francis at the Vatican. The installation on the campus of Valparaiso Univer-
     sity in 2015 was made possible by a gift from Ron '58 and Janet Reimer.

BIBLIOGRAPHY

Allan, John A. "The 'In Christ' Formula in Ephesians." *NTS* 5 (1958): 54–61.

Alston, Richard. *Rome's Revolution: Death of the Republic and Birth of the Empire*. Ancient Warfare and Civilization. Oxford: Oxford University Press, 2015.

Amador, J. D. H. "Revisiting 2 Corinthians: Rhetoric and the Case for Unity." *NTS* 46 (2000): 92–111.

Andreassen, Cecilie Schou, Joël Billieux, Mark D. Griffiths, Daria J. Kuss, Zsolt Demetrovics, Elvis Mazzoni, and Ståle Pallesen. "The Relationship Between Addictive Use of Social Media and Video Games and Symptoms of Psychiatric Disorders: A Large-Scale Cross-Sectional Study." *Psychology of Addictive Behaviors* 30, no. 2 (2016): 252–62.

Aristotle. *Nicomachean Ethics*. 2nd ed. Translated by Terence Irwin. Indianapolis: Hackett. 1999.

———. *Politics*. Translated by H. Rackham. LCL. Cambridge, Mass.: Harvard University Press, 1944.

Ayres, Jennifer R. *Good Food: Grounded Practical Theology*. Waco, Tex.: Baylor University Press, 2013.

Baldry, H. C. "Who Invented the Golden Age?" *CQ* 2 (1952): 83–92.

Barclay, John M. G. "Apocalyptic Allegiance and Disinvestment in the World: A Reading of 1 Corinthians 7:25–35." In *Paul and the Apocalyptic Imagination*, edited by Ben C. Blackwell, John K. Goodrich, and Jason Maston, 257–74. Minneapolis: Fortress, 2016.

———. *Paul and the Gift*. Grand Rapids: Eerdmans, 2015.

———. *Pauline Churches and Diaspora Jews*. Grand Rapids: Eerdmans, 2016.

Barker, Ernest, trans. *The Politics of Aristotle*. New York: Oxford University Press, 1962.

Barnett, Paul. *The Second Epistle to the Corinthians*. The New International Commentary on the New Testament. Grand Rapids: Eerdmans, 1997.

Barram, Michael. *Missional Economics: Biblical Justice and Character Formation*. The Gospel and Our Culture Series. Grand Rapids: Eerdmans, 2018.

Bartholomew, Craig G. *Where Mortals Dwell: A Christian View of Place for Today*. Grand Rapids: Baker Academic, 2011.

Bartholomew, Craig G., and Michael W. Goheen. *The Drama of Scripture: Finding Our Place in the Biblical Story*. Grand Rapids: Baker Academic, 2004.

Bates, Matthew W. *Salvation by Allegiance Alone: Rethinking Faith, Works, and the Gospel of Jesus the King*. Grand Rapids: Baker Academic, 2017.

Bauckham, Richard. *The Bible and Ecology: Rediscovering the Community of Creation*. Sarum Theological Lectures. Waco, Tex.: Baylor University Press, 2010.

———. *Living with Other Creatures: Green Exegesis and Theology*. Waco, Tex.: Baylor University Press, 2011.

———. "Reading Scripture as a Coherent Story." In *The Art of Reading Scripture*, edited by Ellen F. Davis and Richard B. Hays, 38–54. Grand Rapids: Eerdmans, 2003.

Bauer, W., F. W. Danker, W. F. Arndt, and F. W. Gingrich. *A Greek-English Lexicon of the New Testament and Other Early Christian Literature*. 3rd ed. Revised by F. W. Danker. Chicago: University of Chicago Press, 2000.

Beard, Mary. *The Roman Triumph*. Cambridge, Mass.: Belknap, 2007.

———. *SPQR: A History of Ancient Rome*. New York: W. W. Norton, 2015.

Behm, Johannes. "καρδία." In *Theological Dictionary of the New Testament*, edited by Gerhard Kittel and Gerhard Friedrich, 3:605–14. Translated by Geoffrey William Bromiley. Grand Rapids: Eerdmans, 1964.

Beker, Johan Christiaan. *Paul the Apostle: The Triumph of God in Life and Thought*. Philadelphia: Fortress, 1980.

Ben Zeev, Miriam Pucci. "Jews among Greeks and Romans." In *The Eerdmans Dictionary of Early Judaism*, edited by John J. Collins and Daniel C. Harlow, 237–55. Grand Rapids: Eerdmans, 2010.

Berger, Peter L., and Thomas Luckmann. *The Social Construction of Reality: A Treatise in the Sociology of Knowledge*. Garden City, N.Y.: Doubleday, 1966.

Berry, Wendell. *The Art of Loading Brush: New Agrarian Writings*. Berkeley, Calif.: Counterpoint, 2017.

———. "The Burden of the Gospels." *Christian Century* 122, no. 19 (September 2005): 22–27.

———. "Christianity and the Survival of Creation." In *Sex, Economy, Freedom and Community: Eight Essays*, 93–116. New York: Pantheon Books, 1993.

———. *Citizenship Papers*. Washington, D.C.: Shoemaker & Hoard, 2003.

———. *The Country of Marriage*. New York: Harcourt Brace Jovanovich, 1973.

———. "Faustian Economics." In *What Matters? Economics for a Renewed Commonwealth*, 41–53. Berkeley, Calif.: Counterpoint, 2010.

———. "Health Is Membership." In *The Art of the Common-Place: The Agrarian Essays of Wendell Berry*, edited by Norman Wirzba, 144–58. Washington, D.C.: Counterpoint, 2002.

———. *The Hidden Wound*. Berkeley, Calif.: Counterpoint, 1989.

———. "Manifesto: The Mad Farmer Liberation Front." In *The Country of Marriage*, 14–15. New York: Harcourt Brace Jovanovich, 1973.

———. *Sex, Economy, Freedom and Community: Eight Essays*. New York: Pantheon Books, 1993.

——. "Solving for Pattern." In *The Art of the Common-Place: The Agrarian Essays of Wendell Berry*, edited by Norman Wirzba, 267–75. Washington, D.C.: Counterpoint, 2002.

——. "Think Little." In *The Art of the Common-Place: The Agrarian Essays of Wendell Berry*, edited by Norman Wirzba, 81–90. Washington, D.C.: Counterpoint, 2002.

——. *The Unsettling of America: Culture and Agriculture*. San Francisco: Sierra Club Books, 1977.

——. *What Matters? Economics for a Renewed Commonwealth*. With a foreword by Herman E. Daly. Berkeley, Calif: Counterpoint, 2010.

——. "Why I Am Not Going to Buy a Computer." In *What Are People For? Essays*, 170–77. San Francisco: North Point, 1990.

Bilbro, Jeffrey. "When Did Wendell Berry Start Talking Like a Christian." *Christianity & Literature* 68 (2019): 272–96.

Black, Matthew. "The Pauline Doctrine of the Second Adam." *SJT* 7 (1954): 170–79.

Blackwell, Ben C., John K. Goodrich, and Jason Maston, eds. *Paul and the Apocalyptic Imagination*. Minneapolis: Fortress, 2016.

Blass, Friedrich, Albert Debrunner, and Robert Walter Funk. *A Greek Grammar of the New Testament and Other Early Christian Literature*. Edited by Robert Walter Funk. Chicago: University of Chicago Press, 1961.

Bloom, Irene, trans. *Mencius*. Edited by Philip J. Ivanhoe. Translations from the Asian Classics. New York: Columbia University Press, 2009.

Bockmuehl, Markus. *The Epistle to the Philippians*. Black's New Testament Commentary. London: A & C Black, 1997.

Borgen, Peder. "Moses, Jesus, and the Roman Emperor: Observations in Philo's Writings and the Revelation of John." *NovT* 38 (1996): 145–59.

Boulton, Matthew Myer. *Life in God: John Calvin, Practical Formation, and the Future of Protestant Theology*. Grand Rapids: Eerdmans, 2011.

Bourdieu, Pierre. *The Logic of Practice*. Translated by Richard Nice. 1980. Reprint, Stanford: Stanford University Press, 1990.

Braaten, Laurie J. "All Creation Groans: Romans 8:22 in Light of the Biblical Sources." *HBT* 28 (2006): 131–59.

Brewer, R. R. "The Meaning of Politeuesthe in Philippians 1:27." *JBL* 73 (1954): 76–83.

Breytenbach, Cilliers. "Paul's Proclamation and God's 'Thriambos': (Notes on 2 Corinthians 2:14–16b)." *Neot* 24 (1990): 257–71.

Bréhier, Émile. *Chrysippe*. Les grands philosophes. Paris: Félix Alcan, 1910.

Bringmann, Klaus. "The King as Benefactor: Some Remarks on Ideal Kingship in the Age of Hellenism." In *Images and Ideologies: Self-Definition in the Hellenistic World*, edited by A. W. Bulloch, E. Gruen, A. Long, and A. Stewart, 7–24. Hellenistic Culture and Society. Berkeley: University of California Press, 1993.

Broshi, Magen. "Agriculture and Economy in Roman Palestine: Seven Notes on the Babatha Archive." *Israel Exploration Journal* 42, nos. 3–4 (1992): 230–40.

Brunt, P. A., and J. M. Moore, eds. *Res Gestae Divi Augusti: The Achievements of the Divine Augustus*. Oxford: Oxford University Press, 1967.

Bultmann, Rudolf. "πιστεύω κτλ." In *Theological Dictionary of the New Testament*, edited by Gerhard Kittel and Gerhard Friedrich, translated by Geoffrey William Bromiley, 7:145. Grand Rapids: Eerdmans, 1964.

Burns, J. Patout, trans. and ed. *Theological Anthropology*. Sources of Early Christian Thought. Philadelphia: Fortress, 1981.

Burroughs, Presian R. "Christlike Feasting: Attentiveness, Solidarity, and Self-Restraint in Romans." In *Practicing with Paul: Reflections on Paul and the Practices of Ministry in Honor of Susan G. Eastman*, edited by Presian R. Burroughs, 157–79. Eugene, Ore.: Cascade Books, 2018.

Burrows, William R. "Newbigin's Theology of Mission and Culture After Twenty-Five Years: Attending to the 'Subject' of Mission." In *The Gospel and Pluralism Today: Reassessing Lesslie Newbigin in the 21st Century*, edited by Scott W. Sunquist and Amos Yong, 49–69. Missiological Engagements. Downers Grove, Ill.: InterVarsity, 2015.

Bush, Harold K. "Hunting for Reasons to Hope: A Conversation with Wendell Berry." *Christianity & Literature* 56 (2007): 214–34.

Busse, Ulrich. "Metaphorik und Rhetorik im Johannesevangelium: Das Bildfeld vom König." In *Imagery in the Gospel of John: Terms, Forms, Themes, and Theology of Johannine Figurative Language*, edited by Jörg Frey, Ruben Zimmermann, J. G. Van der Watt, and Gabriele Kern, 279–318. WUNT 200. Tübingen: Mohr Siebeck, 2006.

Caird, G. B. *New Testament Theology*. Edited by L. D. Hurst. Oxford: Clarendon, 1994.

Cairns, Francis. *Virgil's Augustan Epic*. Cambridge: Cambridge University Press, 1989.

Carrez, Maurice. "Odeur de mort, odeur de vie (à propos de 2 Cor 2:16)." *RHPR* 64 (1984): 135–42.

Cartledge, Paul. "Greek Political Thought: The Historical Context." In *The Cambridge History of Greek and Roman Political Thought*, edited by Christopher Rowe and Malcolm Schofield, 11–22. Cambridge: Cambridge University Press, 2005.

Castelli, Elizabeth A. *Imitating Paul: A Discourse of Power*. Literary Currents in Biblical Interpretation. Louisville: Westminster John Knox, 1991.

Charlesworth, James H., ed. *The Old Testament Pseudepigrapha*. 2 vols. Anchor Bible Reference Library. Garden City, N.Y.: Doubleday, 1983–85.

Charlesworth, M. P. *Documents Illustrating the Reigns of Claudius Collected by M. P. Charlesworth*. Cambridge: Cambridge University Press, 1939.

———. "The Virtues of a Roman Emperor: Propaganda and the Creation of the Belief." *Proceedings of the British Academy* 23 (1937): 105–33.

Chesnut, Glenn F. "The Ruler and the Logos in Neopythagorean, Middle Platonic, and Late Stoic Political Philosophy." *ANRW* 2.16.2 (1978): 1310–32.

Cochrane, Charles Norris. *Christianity and Classical Culture: A Study of Thought and Action from Augustus to Augustine.* New York: Oxford University Press, 1944.

Collins, John J. *The Sibylline Oracles of Egyptian Judaism.* SBLDS 13. Missoula, Mont.: Scholars' Press, 1974.

Collins, Raymond F. *I and II Timothy and Titus: A Commentary.* NTL. Louisville: Westminster John Knox, 2002.

Columella. *De Re Rustica.* Translated by Harrison Boyd Ash. 3 vols. LCL. Cambridge, Mass.: Harvard University Press, 1941–55.

Cousar, Charles B. *Philippians and Philemon: A Commentary.* NTL. Louisville: Westminster John Knox, 2009.

Coutts, John. "Ephesians 1:3–14 and 1 Peter 1:3–12." *NTS* 3 (1957): 115–27.

Cover, Michael. *Lifting the Veil: 2 Corinthians 3:7–18 in Light of Jewish Homiletic and Commentary Traditions.* BZNW 210. Berlin: De Gruyter, 2015.

Cullmann, Oscar. *Baptism in the New Testament.* Translated by J. K. S. Reid. SBT. London: SCM, 1950.

Dahl, Nils Alstrup. "Adresse und Proömium des Epheserbriefes." *Theologische Zeitschrift* 7 (1951): 241–64.

Davies, J. P. *Paul among the Apocalypses: An Evaluation of the 'Apocalyptic Paul' in the Context of Jewish and Christian Apocalyptic Literature.* LNTS. London: T&T Clark, 2018.

———. "What to Expect When You're Expecting: Maternity, Salvation History, and the 'Apocalyptic Paul.'" *Journal for the Study of the New Testament* 38 (2016): 301–15.

Davies, W. D. *Paul and Rabbinic Judaism: Some Rabbinic Elements in Pauline Theology.* 2nd ed. London: SPCK, 1955.

Davis, Ellen F. "Preserving Virtues: Renewing the Tradition of the Sages." In *Character and Scripture: Moral Formation, Community, and Biblical Interpretation,* edited by William P. Brown, 183–201. Grand Rapids: Eerdmans, 2002.

———. *Scripture, Culture, and Agriculture: An Agrarian Reading of the Bible.* New York: Cambridge University Press, 2009.

de Boer, Martinus C. *Galatians: A Commentary.* NTL. Louisville: Westminster John Knox, 2011.

———. "Paul's Mythologizing Program in Romans 5–8." In *Apocalyptic Paul: Cosmos and Anthropos in Romans 5–8,* edited by Beverly Roberts Gaventa, 1–20. Waco, Tex.: Baylor University Press, 2013.

Deissmann, Adolf. *Light from the Ancient East: The New Testament Illustrated by Recently Discovered Texts of the Graeco-Roman World.* Translated by Lionel Richard Mortimer Strachan. London: Hodder & Stoughton, 1910.

DeMaris, Richard E. *The New Testament in Its Ritual World.* London: Routledge, 2008.

deSilva, David A. "Exchanging Favor for Wrath: Apostasy in Hebrews and Patron-Client Relationships." *JBL* 115 (Spring 1996): 91–116.

———. *Introducing the Apocrypha: Message, Context, and Significance.* Grand Rapids: Baker Academic, 2002.

Dick, Philip K. *Philip K. Dick's Electric Dreams*. New York: Houghton Mifflin Harcourt, 2017.

Dillenberger, John, ed. *Martin Luther: Selections from His Writings*. Garden City, N.Y.: Doubleday, 1962.

Dio Chrysostom. *Dio Chrysostom*. Translated by J. W. Cohoon and H. L. Crosby. 5 vols. LCL. Cambridge, Mass.: Harvard University Press, 1932–1951.

Diogenes Laertius. *Lives of Eminent Philosophers*. Translated by R. D. Hicks. 2 vols. LCL. Cambridge, Mass.: Harvard University Press, 1925.

Duff, Paul Brooks. "Metaphor, Motif, and Meaning: The Rhetorical Strategy Behind the Image 'Led in Triumph' in 2 Corinthians 2:14." *CBQ* 53 (1991): 79–92.

———. *Moses in Corinth: The Apologetic Context of 2 Corinthians 3*. NovTSup 159. Leiden: Brill, 2015.

———. "Transformed 'from Glory to Glory': Paul's Appeal to the Experience of His Readers in 2 Corinthians 3:18." *JBL* 127 (2008): 759–80.

Duncan-Jones, Richard. *The Economy of the Roman Empire: Quantitative Studies*. Cambridge: Cambridge University Press, 1974.

Dunn, James D. G. *The Theology of Paul the Apostle*. Grand Rapids: Eerdmans, 1998.

Dupont, Jacques. "Le Chrétien, miroir de la gloire divine d'après II Cor., III, 18." *Revue biblique* 56 (1949): 392–411.

Dvornik, Francis. *Early Christian and Byzantine Political Philosophy: Origins and Background*. 2 vols. DOS 9. Washington, D.C.: Dumbarton Oaks Center for Byzantine Studies, 1966.

Eastman, Susan Grove. *Paul and the Person: Reframing Paul's Anthropology*. Grand Rapids: Eerdmans, 2017.

Engberg-Pedersen, Troels. *Paul and the Stoics*. Louisville: Westminster John Knox, 2000.

Erdkamp, Paul. *The Grain Market in the Roman Empire*. Cambridge: Cambridge University Press, 2005.

Fears, J. Rufus. "The Cult of Virtues and Roman Imperial Ideology." *ANRW* 2.17.2 (1981): 827–948.

———. *Princeps a Diis Electus: The Divine Election of the Emperor as a Political Concept at Rome*. Papers and Monographs of the American Academy in Rome 26. Rome: American Academy in Rome, 1977.

———. "The Solar Monarchy of Nero and the Imperial Panegyric of Q. Curtius Rufus." *Historia* 25 (1976): 494–96.

———. "The Theology of Victory at Rome: Approaches and Problems." *ANRW* 2.17.2 (1981): 736–825.

Feldman, Louis H. "Josephus' Portrait of Solomon." *HUCA* 66 (1995): 103–67.

———. *Philo's Portrayal of Moses in the Context of Ancient Judaism*. CJAS 15. Notre Dame, Ind.: University of Notre Dame Press, 2007.

Finney, Mark T. "Honor, Rhetoric and Factionalism in the Ancient World: 1 Corinthians 1–4 and Its Social Context." *BTB* 40 (2010): 27–36.

Fishwick, Duncan. *The Imperial Cult in the Latin West: Studies in the Ruler Cult of the Western Provinces of the Roman Empire*. 7 vols. Leiden: Brill, 1991–2004.

Fitch, David E. *Faithful Presence: Seven Disciplines That Shape the Church for Mission*. Downers Grove, Ill.: InterVarsity, 2016.

Fitzmyer, Joseph A. "Glory Reflected on the Face of Christ (2 Cor 3:7–4:6) and a Palestinian Jewish Motif." *TS* 42 (1981): 630–44.

Foster, Richard J. *Celebration of Discipline: The Path to Spiritual Growth*. San Francisco: Harper & Row, 1978.

Fowl, Stephen. "Christology and Ethics in Philippians 2:5–11." In *Where Christology Began: Essays on Philippians 2*, edited by Ralph P. Martin and Brian J. Dodd, 140–53. Louisville: Westminster John Knox, 1998.

———. "Know Your Context: Giving and Receiving Money in Philippians." *Int* 56 (2002): 45–58.

Foxhall, Lin. "The Dependent Tenant: Land Leasing and Labour in Italy and Greece." *JRS* 80 (1990): 97–114.

Frede, Dorothea. "The Political Character of Aristotle's *Ethics*." In *The Cambridge Companion to Aristotle's* Politics, edited by Marguerite Deslauriers and Pierre Destrée, 14–37. Cambridge: Cambridge University Press, 2013.

Friesen, Steven J. *Imperial Cults and the Apocalypse of John: Reading Revelation in the Ruins*. Oxford: Oxford University Press, 2001.

———. "Poverty in Pauline Studies: Beyond the So-Called New Consensus." *JSNT* 26 (2004): 323–61.

Furnish, Victor Paul. *II Corinthians*. AB 32A. Garden City, N.Y.: Doubleday, 1984.

Garnsey, Peter. *Social Status and Legal Privilege in the Roman Empire*. Oxford: Clarendon, 1970.

Garnsey, Peter, and Richard Saller. *The Roman Empire: Economy, Society and Culture*. Berkeley: University of California Press, 1987.

Garthwaite, John. "The Panegyrics of Domitian in Martial Book 9." *Ramus* 22 (1993): 78–102.

Gatz, Bodo. *Weltalter, goldene Zeit und sinnverwandte Vorstellungen*. Spudasmata 16. Hildesheim: Olms, 1967.

Gauger, Jörg-Dieter. "Antiochos III. und Artaxerxes: Der Fremdherrscher als Wohltäter." *JSJ* 38 (2007): 196–225.

Georgi, Dieter. *The Opponents of Paul in Second Corinthians*. Philadelphia: Fortress, 1986.

Getty, R. J. "Romulus, Roma, and Augustus in the Sixth Book of the *Aeneid*." *Classical Philology* 45 (1950): 1–12.

Glancy, Jennifer A. "Boasting of Beatings (2 Corinthians 11:23–25)." *JBL* 123 (2004): 99–135.

Goheen, Michael W., ed. *Reading the Bible Missionally*. The Gospel and Our Culture Series. Grand Rapids: Eerdmans, 2016.

Goldschmidt, Victor. *Les dialogues de Platon: Structure et méthode dialectique*. 1947. 4th ed. Reprint, Paris: Presses Universitaires de France, 1988.

Goodenough, Erwin R. "Kingship in Early Israel." *JBL* 48 (1929): 169–205.

———. "Philo's Exposition of the Law and His De Vita Mosis." *HTR* 26 (1933): 109–25.

———. "The Political Philosophy of Hellenistic Kingship." *Yale Classical Studies* 1 (1928): 55–102.

Gorman, Michael J. *Apostle of the Crucified Lord: A Theological Introduction to Paul and His Letters*. 2nd ed. Grand Rapids: Eerdmans, 2017.

———. *Becoming the Gospel: Paul, Participation, and Mission*. The Gospel and Our Culture Series. Grand Rapids: Eerdmans, 2015.

———. "Pauline Theology: *Perspectives, Perennial Topics, and Prospects*." In *The State of New Testament Studies: A Survey of Recent Research*, edited by Scot McKnight and Nijay K. Gupta, 197–223. Grand Rapids: Baker Academic, 2019.

Gray, Benjamin. "Scepticism About Community: Polybius on Peloponnesian Exiles, Good Faith ('Pistis') and the Achaian League." *Historia: Zeitschrift für Alte Geschicthe* 62 (2013): 323–60.

Gray, Patrick. *Opening Paul's Letters: A Reader's Guide to Genre and Interpretation*. Grand Rapids: Baker Academic, 2012.

———. *Paul as a Problem in History and Culture: The Apostle and His Critics through the Centuries*. Grand Rapids: Baker Academic, 2016.

Gruen, Erich S. *Heritage and Hellenism: The Reinvention of Jewish Tradition*. Hellenistic Culture and Society 30. Berkeley: University of California Press, 1998.

Guthrie, George H. "Paul's Triumphal Procession Imagery (2 Cor 2.14–16a): Neglected Points of Background." *NTS* 61 (2015): 79–91.

Guthrie, Kenneth Sylvan, trans. *The Pythagorean Sourcebook and Library: An Anthology of Ancient Writings Which Relate to Pythagoras and Pythagorean Philosophy*. Edited by David R. Fideler. Grand Rapids: Phanes, 1987.

Hadot, Pierre. *Philosophy as a Way of Life: Spiritual Exercises from Socrates to Foucault*. Edited by Arnold I. Davidson. Translated by Michael Chase. Malden, Mass.: Blackwell, 1995.

———. *What Is Ancient Philosophy?* Translated by Michael Chase. Cambridge, Mass.: Belknap, 2002.

Hafemann, Scott J. *Paul, Moses, and History of Israel: The Letter/Spirit Contrast and the Argument from Scripture in 2 Corinthians 3*. Paternoster Biblical Monographs. Milton Keynes: Paternoster, 2005.

———. *Suffering and Ministry in the Spirit: Paul's Defense of His Ministry in II Corinthians 2:14–3:3*. Grand Rapids: Eerdmans, 1990.

Harmon, A.M., trans. *Lucian*. 8 vols. LCL. Cambridge, Mass.: Harvard University Press, 1913.

Harrill, J. Albert. *Paul the Apostle: His Life and Legacy in Their Roman Context*. Cambridge: Cambridge University Press, 2012.

Harrington, Daniel J., and James F. Keenan. *Paul and Virtue Ethics: Building Bridges Between New Testament Studies and Moral Theology*. Lanham, Md.: Rowman & Littlefield, 2010.

Harris, William V. "The Late Republic." In *The Cambridge Economic History of the Greco-Roman World*, edited by Walter Scheidel, Ian Morris, and Richard Saller, 511–39. Cambridge: Cambridge University Press, 2007.

Hart, David Bentley, trans. *The New Testament: A Translation*. New Haven: Yale University Press, 2017.

———. "What Lies Beyond Capitalism?" *Plough Quarterly* 21 (Summer 2019): 30–38.

Hauerwas, Stanley. "The Difference of Virtue and the Difference It Makes: Courage Exemplified." *Modern Theology* 9 (1993): 249–64.

———. *In Good Company: The Church as* Polis. Notre Dame, Ind.: University of Notre Dame Press, 1995.

Hauerwas, Stanley, and William H. Willimon. *Resident Aliens: Life in the Christian Colony*. Expanded 25th anniversary ed. Nashville: Abingdon, 2014.

Hays, Richard B. *The Conversion of the Imagination: Paul as Interpreter of Israel's Scripture*. Grand Rapids: Eerdmans, 2005.

———. *Echoes of Scripture in the Letters of Paul*. New Haven: Yale University Press, 1989.

———. *The Faith of Jesus Christ: An Investigation of the Narrative Substructure of Galatians 3:1–4:11*. 2nd ed. 1983. Reprint, The Biblical Resource Series. Grand Rapids: Eerdmans, 2002.

———. *First Corinthians*. Interpretation. Louisville: John Knox, 1997.

Heath, Jane M. F. *Paul's Visual Piety: The Metamorphosis of the Beholder*. Oxford: Oxford University Press, 2013.

Heilig, Christoph. *Paul's Triumph: Reassessing 2 Corinthians 2:14 in Its Literary and Historical Context*. BTS. Leuven: Peeters, 2017.

Heyne, Paul. *"Are Economists Basically Immoral?": And Other Essays on Economics, Ethics, and Religion*. Indianapolis: Liberty Fund, 2008.

Hill, Wesley. *Paul and the Trinity: Persons, Relations, and the Pauline Letters*. Grand Rapids: Eerdmans, 2015.

Hoehner, Harold W. *Ephesians: An Exegetical Commentary*. Grand Rapids: Baker Academic, 2002.

Holmes, Michael William, ed. and trans. *The Apostolic Fathers: Greek Texts and English Translations*. Grand Rapids: Baker, 1999.

Hopkins, Keith. "Taxes and Trade in the Roman Empire (200 B.C.–A.D. 400)." *JRS* 70 (1980): 101–25.

Hughes, J. Donald. "Ancient Deforestation Revisited." *Journal of the History of Biology* 44 (2011): 43–57.

Hull, Robert F., Jr. "Constructing Euodia and Syntyche: Philippians 4:2–3 and the Informed Imagination." *Priscilla Papers* 30, no. 2 (2016): 3–7.

Hunsberger, George R. "Proposals for a Missional Hermeneutic: Mapping a Conversation." *Missiology: An International Review* 39 (2011): 309–21.

Isocrates. *Isocrates*. Translated by George Norlin and Larue van Hook. 3 vols. LCL. Cambridge, Mass.: Harvard University Press, 1954.

Irwin, T. H. "Conceptions of Happiness in the *Nicomachean Ethics*." In *The Oxford Handbook of Aristotle*, edited by Christopher Shields, 495–528. New York: Oxford University Press, 2012.

Jakelić, Slavica. "Engaging Religious and Secular Humanisms." In *At the Limits of the Secular: Reflections on Faith and Public Life*, edited by William A. Barbieri Jr., 305–30. Grand Rapids: Eerdmans, 2014.

Jewett, Robert. *Paul's Anthropological Terms: A Study of Their Use in Conflict Settings*. AGJU 10. Leiden: Brill, 1971.

Jipp, Joshua W. *Christ Is King: Paul's Royal Ideology*. Minneapolis: Fortress, 2015.

———. "Sharing in the Heavenly Rule of Christ the King: Paul's Royal Participatory Language in Ephesians." In *"In Christ" in Paul: Explorations in Paul's Theology of Union and Participation*, edited by Michael J. Thate, Kevin J. Vanhoozer, and Constantine R. Campbell, 251–79. WUNT 2/384. Tübingen: Mohr Siebeck, 2014.

Jongman, Willem M. "The Early Roman Empire: Consumption." In *The Cambridge Economic History of the Greco-Roman World*, edited by Walter Scheidel, Ian Morris, and Richard Saller, 592–618. Cambridge: Cambridge University Press, 2007.

Kehoe, Dennis P. "The Early Roman Empire: Production." In *The Cambridge Economic History of the Greco-Roman World*, edited by Walter Scheidel, Ian Morris, and Richard Saller, 543–69. Cambridge: Cambridge University Press, 2007.

Kennedy, George Alexander, ed. and trans. *Progymnasmata: Greek Textbooks of Prose Composition and Rhetoric*. WGRW 10. Atlanta: Society of Biblical Literature, 2003.

King, Martin Luther, Jr. *Strength to Love*. Philadelphia: Fortress, 1981.

Kirby, J. C. *Ephesians: Baptism and Pentecost: An Inquiry into the Structure and Purpose of the Epistle to the Ephesians*. London: SPCK, 1968.

Kittel, Gerhard, and Gerhard Friedrich, eds. *Theological Dictionary of the New Testament*. Translated by Geoffrey William Bromiley. 10 vols. Grand Rapids: Eerdmans, 1964.

Klauck, Hans-Josef. *Ancient Letters and the New Testament: A Guide to Context and Exegesis*. Waco, Tex.: Baylor University Press, 2006.

Kloppenborg, John S. "Isis and Sophia in the Book of Wisdom." *HTR* 75 (1982): 57–84.

Koester, Helmut. "The Purpose of the Polemic of a Pauline Fragment." *NTS* 8 (1962): 317–32.

Kooten, George H. van. "Why Did Paul Include an Exegesis of Moses' Shining Face (Exod 34) in 2 Cor 3?: Moses' Strength, Well-Being and (Transitory) Glory, According to Philo, Josephus, Paul, and the Corinthian Sophists." In *Significance of Sinai*, 149–81. Leiden: Brill, 2008.

Koperski, Veronica. "Feminist Concerns and the Authorial Readers in Philippians." *Louvain Studies* 17 (1992): 269–92.

Koukouli-Chrysantaki, Chaido. "Colonia Iulia Augusta Philippensis." In *Philippi at the Time of Paul and After His Death*, edited by Charalambos Bakirtzis and Helmut Koester, 5–35. 1998. Reprint, Eugene, Ore.: Wipf and Stock, 2009.

Kraut, Richard. "Aristotle on Becoming Good: Habituation, Reflection, and Perception." In *The Oxford Handbook of Aristotle*, edited by Christopher Shields, 529–57. New York: Oxford University Press, 2012.

Kügler, Joachim. "Spuren ägyptisch-hellenistischer Königstheologie bei Philo von Alexandria." In *Ägypten und der östliche Mittelmeerraum im 1. Jahrtausend v. Chr*, edited by Manfred Görg and Günther Hölbl, 231–49. ÄAT 44. Wiesbaden: Harrassowitz, 2000.

Lambrecht, Jan. "The Defeated Paul, Aroma of Christ: An Exegetical Study of 2 Corinthians 2:14–16b." *Louvain Studies* 20 (1995): 170–86.

Launaro, Alessandro. *Peasants and Slaves: The Rural Population of Roman Italy (200 BC to AD 100)*. Cambridge: Cambridge University Press, 2011.

Leithart, Peter J. *Defending Constantine: The Twilight of an Empire and the Dawn of Christendom*. Downers Grove, Ill.: InterVarsity, 2010.

Leopold, Aldo. *A Sand County Almanac, and Sketches Here and There*. 1949. Reprint, New York: Oxford University Press, 1968.

Lewis, C. S. *Mere Christianity*. New York: HarperOne, 2001.

Lincoln, Andrew T. *Ephesians*. WBC 42. Dallas: Word, 1990.

———. *Paradise Now and Not Yet: Studies in the Role of the Heavenly Dimension in Paul's Thought with Special Reference to His Eschatology*. Society for New Testament Studies Monograph Series 43. Cambridge: Cambridge University Press, 1981.

Litwa, M. David. "Transformation Through a Mirror: Moses in 2 Cor. 3.18." *JSNT* 34 (2012): 286–97.

Lo Cascio, Elio. "The Early Roman Empire: The State and the Economy." In *The Cambridge Economic History of the Greco-Roman World*, edited by Walter Scheidel, Ian Morris, and Richard Saller, 619–47. Cambridge: Cambridge University Press, 2007.

Long, Fredrick J. *Ancient Rhetoric and Paul's Apology: The Compositional Unity of 2 Corinthians*. Society for New Testament Studies Monograph Series 131. Cambridge: Cambridge University Press, 2004.

Longenecker, Bruce W. *The Lost Letters of Pergamum: A Story from the New Testament World*. 2nd ed. Grand Rapids: Baker Academic, 2016.

———. *Remember the Poor: Paul, Poverty, and the Greco-Roman World*. Grand Rapids: Eerdmans, 2010.

Lord, Carnes, trans. *Aristotle's Politics*. 1984. Reprint, Chicago: University of Chicago Press, 2013.

Lutz, Cora E. "M. Rufus, 'The Roman Socrates.'" *YCS* 10 (1947): 3–147.

Lüderitz, Gert. "What is the Politeuma?" In *Studies in Early Jewish Epigraphy*, edited by Jan Willem van Henten and Pieter Willem van der Horst, 183–225. AGJU 21. Leiden: Brill, 1994.

Ma, John. "Kings." In *A Companion to the Hellenistic World*, edited by Andrew Erskine, 177–95. Blackwell Companions to the Ancient World. Oxford: Blackwell, 2003.

MacDonald, Margaret Y. *Colossians and Ephesians*. SP 17. Collegeville, Minn.: Liturgical, 2000.

Machiavelli, Niccolò. *The Prince*. Translated by Harvey C. Mansfield. Chicago: University of Chicago Press, 1998.

MacIntyre, Alasdair. *After Virtue: A Study in Moral Theory*. 2nd ed. Notre Dame, Ind.: University of Notre Dame Press, 1984.

Mack, Burton L. "Imitatio Mosis: Patterns of Cosmology and Soteriology in the Hellenistic Synagogue." *SPhilo* 1 (1972): 27–55.

Malherbe, Abraham J. *Paul and the Popular Philosophers*. Minneapolis: Fortress, 1989.

Malina, Bruce J. *The New Testament World: Insights from Cultural Anthropology*. Rev. ed. Louisville: Westminster John Knox, 1993.

Malinowski, Francis X. "The Brave Women of Philippi." *BTB* 15 (1985): 60–64.

Marcus, Joel. "Mark—Interpreter of Paul." *NTS* 46 (2000): 473–87.

Marshall, Peter. "A Metaphor of Social Shame: ΘPIAMBEYEIN IN 2 Cor 2:14." *NovT* 25 (1983): 302–17.

Martin, Ralph P. *2 Corinthians*. WBC. Nashville: Thomas Nelson, 1986.

Martyn, J. Louis. "Afterword: The Human Moral Dilemma." In *Apocalyptic Paul: Cosmos and Anthropos in Romans 5–8*, edited by Beverly Roberts Gaventa, 157–66. Waco, Tex.: Baylor University Press, 2013.

———. *Galatians: A New Translation with Introduction and Commentary*. AB 33A. New York: Doubleday, 1997.

Marzano, Annalisa. *Roman Villas in Central Italy: A Social and Economic History*. Columbia Studies in the Classical Tradition 30. Leiden: Brill, 2007.

Matera, Frank J. *II Corinthians: A Commentary*. NTL. Louisville: Westminster John Knox, 2003.

McConville, J. Gordon. *Being Human in God's World: An Old Testament Theology of Humanity*. Grand Rapids: Baker Academic, 2016.

Meeks, Wayne A. *The First Urban Christians: The Social World of the Apostle Paul*. New Haven: Yale University Press, 1983.

———. "In One Body: The Unity of Humankind in Colossians and Ephesians." In *God's Christ and His People: Studies in Honour of Nils Alstrup Dahl*, edited by Nils Alstrup Dahl, Jacob Jervell, and Wayne A. Meeks, 209–21. Oslo: Universitetsforlaget, 1977.

———. *The Moral World of the First Christians*. Philadelphia: Westminster Press, 1986.

———. "Moses as God and King." In *Religions in Antiquity: Essays in Memory of Erwin Ramsdell Goodenough*, edited by Jacob Neusner, 354–71. Leiden: Brill, 1968.

———. *The Prophet-King: Moses Traditions and the Johannine Christology*. NovTSup 14. Leiden: Brill, 1967.

Merleau-Ponty, Maurice. *Phenomenology of Perception*. Translated by Donald A. Landes. 1945. Reprint, London: Routledge, 2012.

Metzger, Bruce M. *The Canon of the New Testament: Its Origin, Development, and Significance*. Oxford: Clarendon, 1987.

Middleton, J. Richard. *The Liberating Image: The Imago Dei in Genesis 1*. Grand Rapids: Brazos, 2005.

———. *A New Heaven and a New Earth: Reclaiming Biblical Eschatology*. Grand Rapids: Baker Academic, 2014.

Miller, Ernest C. "Πολιτεύεσθε In Philippians 1.27: Some Philological and Thematic Observations." *JSNT* 15 (1982): 86–96.

Minear, Paul S. "Singing and Suffering in Philippi." In *The Conversation Continues: Studies in Paul and John in Honor of J. Louis Martyn*, edited by Robert Tomson Fortna and Beverly Roberts Gaventa, 202–19. Nashville: Abingdon, 1990.

Mitchell, Margaret M. *Paul, the Corinthians and the Birth of Christian Hermeneutics*. Cambridge: Cambridge University Press, 2010.

Morato, Jack. "*Praecipitia in Ruinam*: The Decline of the Small Roman Farmer and the Fall of the Roman Republic." *International Social Science Review* 92, no. 1 (2016): 1–28.

Morgan, Teresa. *Roman Faith and Christian Faith: Pistis and Fides in the Early Roman Empire and Early Churches*. Oxford: Oxford University Press, 2015.

Morley, Neville. "The Early Roman Empire: Distribution." In *The Cambridge Economic History of the Greco-Roman World*, edited by Walter Scheidel, Ian Morris, and Richard Saller, 570–91. Cambridge: Cambridge University Press, 2007.

Mulgan, R. C. *Aristotle's Political Theory*. Oxford: Clarendon, 1977.

Neusner, Jacob, and Bruce D. Chilton, eds. *In Quest of the Historical Pharisees*. Waco, Tex.: Baylor University Press, 2007.

Newbigin, Lesslie. *Foolishness to the Greeks: The Gospel and Western Culture*. Grand Rapids: Eerdmans, 1986.

———. *The Gospel in a Pluralist Society*. Grand Rapids: Eerdmans, 1989.

———. *The Open Secret: An Introduction to the Theology of Mission*. Rev. ed. Grand Rapids: Eerdmans, 1995.

———. *Truth and Authority in Modernity*. Christian Mission and Modern Culture. Valley Forge, Pa.: Trinity Press International, 1996.

———. *Truth to Tell: The Gospel as Public Truth*. London: SPCK, 1991.

Nisbet, R. G. M. "Virgil's Fourth Eclogue: Easterners and Westerners." *Bulletin of the Institute for Classical Studies* 25 (1978): 59–78.

Novenson, Matthew V. *Christ among the Messiahs: Christ Language in Paul and Messiah Language in Ancient Judaism*. New York: Oxford University Press, 2012.

Nussbaum, Martha C. *The Therapy of Desire: Theory and Practice in Hellenistic Ethics*. Martin Classical Lectures. Princeton: Princeton University Press, 1994.

Oakes, Peter. *Philippians: From People to Letter*. Society for New Testament Studies Monograph Series. Cambridge: Cambridge University Press, 2001.

O'Connor, Flannery. *Mystery and Manners*. Edited by Sally Fitzgerald and Robert Fitzgerald. New York: Farrar, Straus & Giroux, 1957.

Oostendorp, Derk William. *Another Jesus: A Gospel of Jewish-Christian Superiority in II Corinthians*. Kampen: Kok, 1967.

Parsons, Mikeal C. *Acts*. Paideia. Grand Rapids: Baker Academic, 2008.

Patzia, Arthur G. *The Making of the New Testament: Origin, Collection, Text and Canon*. Downers Grove, Ill.: InterVarsity, 1995.

Pellegrin, Pierre. "Aristotle's *Politics*." In *The Oxford Handbook of Aristotle*, edited by Christopher Shields, 558–85. New York: Oxford University Press, 2012.

Pennington, Jonathan T. *The Sermon on the Mount and Human Flourishing: A Theological Commentary*. Grand Rapids: Baker Academic, 2018.

Percival, John. *The Roman Villa: An Historical Introduction*. Batsford Studies in Archaeology. London: Batsford, 1976.

Pfitzner, Victor C. *Paul and the Agon Motif: Traditional Athletic Imagery in the Pauline Literature*. NovTSup 16. Leiden: Brill, 1967.

Philo. *Philo*. Translated by F. H. Colson. LCL. 12 vols. Cambridge, Mass.: Harvard University Press, 1929.

Pietersma, Albert, and Benjamin G. Wright, eds. *A New English Translation of the Septuagint*. Oxford: Oxford University Press, 2007.

Plato. *The Republic*. Translated by Paul Shorey. LCL. 2 vols. Cambridge, Mass.: Harvard University Press, 1937.

———. *Timaeus, Critias, Cleitophon, Menexenus, Epistles*. Translated by R. G. Bury. LCL. Cambridge, Mass.: Harvard University Press, 1929.

Pliny. 1938–63. *Natural History*. Translated by H. Rackham, W. H. Jones, and D. E. Eichholz. LCL. 10 vols. Cambridge, Mass.: Harvard University Press.

Plutarch. *Lives*. Translated by Bernadotte Perrin. LCL. 11 vols. Cambridge, Mass.: Harvard University Press, 1914–26.

———. *Moralia*. Translated by Frank Cole Babbitt et al. LCL. 15 vols. Cambridge, Mass.: Harvard University Press, 1927–69.

Powell, Jonathan. *The New Machiavelli: How to Wield Power in the Modern World*. London: The Bodley Head, 2010.

Preston, Aaron. "Redeeming Moral Formation: The Unity of Spiritual and Moral Formation in Willardian Thought." *Journal of Spiritual Formation & Soul Care* 3, no. 2 (2010): 206–29.

Ps-Cicero. *Rhetorica Ad Herennium*. Translated by Harry Caplan. LCL. Cambridge, Mass.: Harvard University Press, 1954.

Purcell, Nicholas. "Romans in the Roman World." In *The Cambridge Companion to the Age of Augustus*, edited by Karl Galinsky, 85–105. Cambridge: Cambridge University Press, 2005.

Rabinowitz, Peter J. "Truth in Fiction: A Reexamination of Audiences." *Critical Inquiry* 4 (1977): 121–41.

Ramsour, Marly. "Jezebel or Servant of God?: How Julie Pennington-Russell Became the First Female Pastor in Texas." Unpublished master's thesis. Waco, Tex.: Baylor University, 2008.

Reese, James M. *Hellenistic Influence on the Book of Wisdom and Its Consequences*. Analecta Biblica 41. Rome: Biblical Institute Press, 1970.

Reumann, John. *Philippians: A New Translation with Introduction and Commentary*. AB 33B. New Haven: Yale University Press, 2008.

Rhodes, Michael J. "Formative Feasting: Practices and Economic Ethics in Deuteronomy's Tithe Meal and the Corinthian Lord's Supper." PhD diss., University of Aberdeen, 2019.

Rickman, Geoffrey. *The Corn Supply of Ancient Rome*. Oxford: Clarendon, 1980.

Rillera, Andrew Remington. "*Tertium Genus* or Dyadic Unity? Investigating Socio-Political Salvation in Ephesians." *BR* 65 (2020).

Roberts, Jean. *Aristotle and the* Politics. Routledge Philosophy Guidebooks. London: Routledge, 2009.

Robinson, Marilynne. "Fear." *New York Review of Books* 62/14 (2015): 28–30.

Roetzel, Calvin J. "The Language of War (2 Cor. 10:1–6) and the Language of Weakness (2 Cor. 11:21b–13:10)." In *Violence, Scripture, and Textual Practice in Early Judaism and Christianity*, edited by Ra'anan S. Boustan, Alex P. Jassen and Calvin J. Roetzel, 77–98. Leiden: Brill, 2009.

———. *Paul: The Man and the Myth*. 1997. Reprint, Minneapolis: Fortress, 1999.

Rostovtzeff, Michael I. *The Social and Economic History of the Roman Empire*. 2nd ed. 2 vols. Oxford: Clarendon, 1957.

Rowe, C. Kavin. *Early Narrative Christology: The Lord in the Gospel of Luke.* BZNW 139. Berlin: De Gruyter, 2006.

———. *World Upside Down: Reading Acts in the Graeco-Roman Age*. Oxford: Oxford University Press, 2010.

Rowe, Christopher. "The *Politicus* and Other Dialogues." In *The Cambridge History of Greek and Roman Political Thought*, edited by Christopher Rowe and Malcolm Schofield, 233–57. Cambridge: Cambridge University Press, 2005.

Ruden, Sarah. *Paul among the People: The Apostle Reinterpreted and Reimagined in His Own Time*. New York: Pantheon, 2010.

Ruppel, W. "Politeuma: Bedeutungsgeschichte eines staatsrechtlichen Terminus." *Phil* 82 (1927): 268–312, 433–54.

Salkever, Stephen. "Reading Aristotle's *Nicomachean Ethics* and *Politics* as a Single Course of Lectures: Rhetoric, Politics, and Philosophy." In *The Cambridge Companion to Ancient Greek Political Thought*, edited by Stephen Salkever, 209–42. New York: Cambridge University Press, 2009.

Sallares, Robert. "Ecology." In *The Cambridge Economic History of the Greco-Roman World*, edited by Walter Scheidel, Ian Morris, and Richard Saller, 15–37. Cambridge: Cambridge University Press, 2007.

Saller, Richard. "Status and Patronage." In *The High Empire, A.D. 70–192*, edited by Alan K. Bowman, Peter Garnsey, and Dominique Rathbone, 817–54. Vol. 11 of *The Cambridge Ancient History*. Cambridge: Cambridge University Press, 2000.

Schaff, Philip, and Henry Wace, eds. *The Nicene and Post-Nicene Fathers*. Grand Rapids: Eerdmans, 1978–1980.

Scheidel, Walter. "Demography." In *The Cambridge Economic History of the Greco-Roman World*, edited by Walter Scheidel, Ian Morris, and Richard Saller, 38–86. Cambridge: Cambridge University Press, 2007.

———. "Slavery." In *The Cambridge Companion to the Roman Economy*, edited by Walter Scheidel, 89–113. Cambridge: Cambridge University Press, 2012.

Schiavone, Aldo. *The End of the Past: Ancient Rome and the Modern West*. Translated by Margery J. Schneider. Revealing Antiquity 13. Cambridge, Mass.: Harvard University Press, 2000.

Schmeller, Thomas. "No Bridge Over Troubled Water? The Gap Between 2 Corinthians 1–9 and 10–13 Revisited." *JSNT* 36 (2013): 73–84.

Schnelle, Udo. *Apostle Paul: His Life and Theology*. Translated by M. Eugene Boring. Grand Rapids: Baker Academic, 2005.

Schofield, Malcolm. "Aristotle: An Introduction." In *The Cambridge History of Greek and Roman Political Thought*, edited by Christopher Rowe and Malcolm Schofield, 310–20. Cambridge: Cambridge University Press, 2005.

Scholtissek, Klaus. "'Ihr seid ein Brief Christi' (2 Kor 3,3)." *BZ* 44 (2000): 183–205.

Schumacher, E. F. *Small Is Beautiful: Economics as if People Mattered*. New York: HarperCollins, 1989.

Scott, Kenneth. "Statius' Adulation of Domitian." *AJP* 54 (1933): 247–59.

Scroggs, Robin. *The Last Adam: A Study in Pauline Anthropology*. Philadelphia: Fortress, 1966.

Sellin, Gerhard. *Der Brief an die Epheser*. 9th ed. KEK 8. Göttingen: Vandenhoeck & Ruprecht, 2008.

Seneca. *Apocolocyntosis Divi Claudii*. Translated and edited by Apostolos N. Athanassakis. Lawrence, Kans.: Coronado, 1973.

———. *Epistles*. Translated by Richard M. Gunmere. LCL. 3 vols. Cambridge, Mass.: Harvard University Press, 1917–25.

Shaw, David A. "Apocalyptic and Covenant: Perspectives on Paul or Antinomies at War?" *JSNT* 36 (2013): 155–71.

Sherlock, Mary, and Danielle L. Wagstaff. "Exploring the Relationship Between Frequency of Instagram Use, Exposure to Idealized Images, and Psychological Well-Being in Women." *Psychology of Popular Media Culture* 8, no. 4 (2019): 482–90.

Sherwin-White, A. N. *The Roman Citizenship*. Oxford: Clarendon, 1939.

Slingerland, Edward, trans. *Confucius: The Essential Analects*. Indianapolis: Hackett, 2003.

Smith, C. Christopher, and John Pattison. *Slow Church: Cultivating Community in the Patient Way of Jesus*. Downers Grove, Ill.: InterVarsity, 2014.

Smith, James K. A. "Alternative Liturgy: Social Media as Ritual." *Christian Century*, March 6, 2013, 30–33.

———. *Awaiting the King: Reforming Public Theology*. Cultural Liturgies 3. Grand Rapids: Baker Academic, 2017.

———. *Desiring the Kingdom: Worship, Worldview, and Cultural Formation*. Cultural Liturgies 1. Grand Rapids: Baker Academic, 2009.

———. *Imagining the Kingdom: How Worship Works*. Cultural Liturgies 2. Grand Rapids: Baker Academic, 2013.

Smith, Julien C. H. *Christ the Ideal King: Cultural Context, Rhetorical Strategy, and the Power of Divine Monarchy in Ephesians*. WUNT 2/313. Tübingen: Mohr Siebeck, 2011.

Snodgrass, Klyne R. *Who God Says You Are: A Christian Understanding of Identity*. Grand Rapids: Eerdmans, 2018.

Sperber, Daniel. "Aspects of Agrarian Life in Roman Palestine I: Agricultural Decline in Palestine During the Later Principate." *ANRW* 2.8 (1977): 397–443.

Sprague, Rosamond Kent. *Plato's Philosopher-King: A Study of the Theoretical Background*. Columbia: University of South Carolina Press, 1976.

Stalnaker, Aaron. *Overcoming Our Evil: Human Nature and Spiritual Exercises in Xunzi and Augustine*. Washington, D.C.: Georgetown University Press, 2006.

Steers, Mai-Ly N., Michelle C. Quist, Jennifer L. Bryan, Dawn W. Foster, Chelsie M. Young, and Clayton Neighbors. "I Want You to Like Me: Extraversion, Need for Approval, and Time on Facebook as Predictors of Anxiety." *Translational Issues in Psychological Science* 2, no. 3 (2016): 283–93.

Stendahl, Krister. "The Apostle Paul and the Introspective Conscience of the West." *HTR* 56, no. 3 (1963): 199–215.

Sternberg, Meir. *The Poetics of Biblical Narrative: Ideological Literature and the Drama of Reading*. ILBS. Bloomington: Indiana University Press, 1985.

Suadi, Soham-al. "The Meal in 1 Corinthians 11." In *T&T Clark Handbook to Early Christian Meals in the Greco-Roman World*, edited by Soham Al-Suadi and Peter-Ben Smit, 227–39. London: T&T Clark, 2019.

Suetonius. *Lives of the Caesars*. Translated by J. C. Rolfe. LCL. Cambridge, Mass.: Harvard University Press, 1914.

Sumney, Jerry L. *Colossians: A Commentary*. NTL. Louisville: Westminster John Knox, 2008.

———. *Identifying Paul's Opponents: The Question of Method in 2 Corinthians*. JSNTSup 40. Sheffield: Sheffield Academic, 1990.

Sunquist, Scott W., and Amos Yong, eds. *The Gospel and Pluralism Today: Reassessing Lesslie Newbigin in the 21st Century*. Missiological Engagements. Downers Grove, Ill.: InterVarsity, 2015.

Svensson, Ludvig. "Paul in the Roman Triumph: Possibilities in the Interpretation of θριαμβεύω (2 Cor 2:14)." *Svensk Exegetisk Årsbok* 83 (2018): 86–100.

Talbert, Charles H. *Ephesians and Colossians*. Paideia. Grand Rapids: Baker Academic, 2007.

———. *Reading the Sermon on the Mount: Character Formation and Decision Making in Matthew 5–7*. Columbia: University of South Carolina Press, 2004.

Taylor, Charles. *Modern Social Imaginaries*. Public Planet Books. Durham: Duke University Press, 2004.

———. *A Secular Age*. Cambridge, Mass.: Belknap, 2007.

Temin, Peter. "The Economy of the Early Roman Empire." *Journal of Economic Perspectives* 20 (2006): 133–51.

Tertullian. Edited by Alexander Roberts and James Donaldson. Revised by A. Cleveland Coxe. Vol. 3 of *The Ante-Nicene Fathers*. Buffalo, N.Y.: Christian Literature Co, 1885–1886.

Thesleff, Holger. *The Pythagorean Texts of the Hellenistic Period*. Acta Academiae Aboensis 30.1. Åbo: Åbo Akademi, 1965.

Thiselton, Anthony C. *The First Epistle to the Corinthians: A Commentary on the Greek Text*. New International Greek Testament Commentary. Grand Rapids: Eerdmans, 2000.

Thrall, Margaret E. *A Critical and Exegetical Commentary on the Second Epistle of the Corinthians*. ICC. 2 vols. London: T&T Clark International, 2004.

Thurston, Bonnie B., and Judith Ryan. *Philippians and Philemon*. SP 10. Collegeville, Minn.: Liturgical, 2005.

Uro, Risto, Juliette E. Day, Richard E. DeMaris, and Rikard Roitto, eds. *The Oxford Handbook of Early Christian Ritual*. Oxford: Oxford University Press, 2019.

Versnel, H. S. "What Did Ancient Man See When He Saw a God? Some Reflections on Greco-Roman Epiphany." In *Effigies Dei: Essays on the History of Religions*, edited by Dirk van der Plas, 42–55. Leiden: Brill, 1987.

Virgil. *Works*. Translated by H. Rushton Fairclough. LCL. Rev. ed. 2 vols. Cambridge, Mass.: Harvard University Press, 1934.

Volkmann, Hans. "Ἔνδοξος δουλεία als ehrenvoller Knechtsdienst gegenüber dem Gesetz." *Phil* 16 (1956): 52–61.

Völker, Walther. *Fortschritt und Vollendung bei Philo von Alexandrien: Eine Studie zur Geschichte der Frömmigkeit*. Texte und Untersuchungen zur Geschichte der altchristlichen Literatur 49, no. 1. Leipzig: Hinrichs, 1938.

Walbank, F. W. "Monarchies and Monarchic Ideas." In *Cambridge Ancient History*, edited by F. W. Walbank, A. E. Astin, M. W. Frederiksen, and R. M. Ogilvie, 62–100. Vol. 7.2. Cambridge: Cambridge University Press, 1984.

Walker, William. "2 Corinthians 3:7–18 as a Non-Pauline Interpolation." *JSPL* 3 (2013): 195–217.

Wallace, Daniel B. *Greek Grammar Beyond the Basics: An Exegetical Syntax of the New Testament*. Grand Rapids: Zondervan, 1996.

Wallace-Hadrill, Andrew. *Augustan Rome*. 2nd ed. Classical World Series 10. London: Bloomsbury Academic, 2018.

———. "The Emperor and His Virtues." *Historia* 30 (1981): 298–323.

———. "The Golden Age and Sin in Augustan Ideology." *Past and Present* 95 (1982): 19–36.

Walsh, Brian J., and Sylvia C. Keesmaat. *Colossians Remixed: Subverting the Empire*. Downers Grove, Ill.: IVP Academic, 2004.

Watson, Burton, trans. *Xunzi: Basic Writings*. Translations from the Asian Classics. New York: Columbia University Press, 2003.

Watson, Francis. "In the Beginning: Irenaeus, Creation and the Environment." In *Ecological Hermeneutics: Biblical, Historical and Theological Perspectives*, edited by David G. Horrell, Cherryl Hunt, Christopher Southgate, and Franscesca Stavrakopoulou, 127–39. London: T&T Clark, 2010.

Welborn, Laurence L. "The Identification of 2 Corinthians 10–13 with the 'Letter of Tears.'" *NovT* 37 (1995): 138–53.

———. "Like Broken Pieces of a Ring: 2 Cor 1.1–2.3; 7.5–16 and Ancient Theories of Literary Unity." *NTS* 42 (1996): 559–83.

Wengst, Klaus. *Pax Romana and the Peace of Jesus Christ*. Translated by John Bowden. Philadelphia: Fortress, 1987.

White, Adam G. *Where Is the Wise Man? Graeco-Roman Education as a Background to the Divisions in 1 Corinthians 1–4*. London: Bloomsbury T&T Clark, 2015.

White, K. D. "Latifundia." *Bulletin of the Institute of Classical Studies of the University of London* 14 (1967): 62–79.

———. *Roman Farming*. Aspects of Greek and Roman Life. Ithaca, N.Y.: Cornell University Press, 1970.

White, Lynn, Jr. "The Historical Roots of Our Ecological Crisis." *Science* 155 (1967): 1203–7.

Wickert, Lothar. "Princeps (Civitatis)." In *Paulys Realencyclopädie der classischen Altertumswissenschaft*, edited by Georg Wissowa, Wilhelm Kroll, Karl Mittelhaus, and Konrat Ziegler, 1998–2296. Vol. 22, no 2. Stuttgart: Druckenmüller, 1954.

Wiedemann, Thomas. "Reflections of Roman Political Thought in Latin Historical Writing." In *The Cambridge History of Greek and Roman Political Thought*, edited by Christopher Rowe and Malcolm Schofield, 517–31. Cambridge: Cambridge University Press, 2005.

Willard, Dallas. *The Divine Conspiracy: Rediscovering Our Hidden Life in God*. San Francisco: HarperSanFrancisco, 1998.

———. *Renovation of the Heart: Putting on the Character of Christ*. Colorado Springs: NavPress, 2002.

———. *The Spirit of the Disciplines: Understanding How God Changes Lives*. San Francisco: Harper, 1988.

Williamson, Lamar, Jr. "Led in Triumph: Paul's Use of Thriambeuō." *Int* 22 (1968): 317–32.

Wilson, Walter T. *The Hope of Glory: Education and Exhortation in the Epistle to the Colossians*. NovTSup 88. Leiden: Brill, 1997.

Windisch, Hans. *Der Zweite Korintherbrief*. Edited by Georg Strecker. 9th ed. KEK. Göttingen: Vandenhoeck & Ruprecht, 1924.

Winston, David. *The Wisdom of Solomon: A New Translation with Introduction and Commentary*. AB 43. Garden City, N.Y.: Doubleday, 1979.

Winter, Bruce W. *After Paul Left Corinth: The Influence of Secular Ethics and Social Change*. Grand Rapids: Eerdmans, 2001.

Wirzba, Norman. *From Nature to Creation: A Christian Vision for Understanding and Loving Our World*. The Church and Postmodern Culture. Grand Rapids: Baker Academic, 2015.

Witherup, Ronald D. "Functional Redundancy in the Acts of the Apostles: A Case Study." *JSNT* 48 (1992): 67–86.

Wolter, Michael. *Paul: An Outline of His Theology*. Translated by Robert L. Brawley. Waco, Tex.: Baylor University Press, 2015.

Woolf, Greg. "Provincial Perspectives." In *The Cambridge Companion to the Age of Augustus*, edited by Karl Galinsky, 106–29. Cambridge: Cambridge University Press, 2005.

Wright, N. T. *After You Believe: Why Christian Character Matters*. New York: HarperOne, 2010.

———. *The Climax of the Covenant: Christ and the Law in Pauline Theology*. Minneapolis: Fortress, 1992.

———. *The New Testament and the People of God*. Christian Origins and the Question of God 1. Minneapolis: Fortress, 1992.

———. *Paul: A Biography*. San Francisco: HarperOne, 2018.

———. *The Paul Debate: Critical Questions for Understanding the Apostle*. Waco, Tex.: Baylor University Press, 2015.

————. *Paul and the Faithfulness of God*. Christian Origins and the Question of God 4. Minneapolis: Fortress, 2013.

————. *Paul in Fresh Perspective*. Minneapolis: Fortress, 2005.

————. *Paul and His Recent Interpreters: Some Contemporary Debates*. Minneapolis: Fortress, 2015.

————. "Romans." In *Acts–First Corinthians*, 393–770. Vol. 10 of *The New Interpreter's Bible*, edited by Leander E. Keck. Nashville: Abingdon, 2002.

————. *Scripture and the Authority of God: How to Read the Bible Today*. San Francisco: HarperOne, 2005.

————. *Surprised by Hope: Rethinking Heaven, the Resurrection, and the Mission of the Church*. New York: HarperOne, 2008.

Wu, Tim. *The Attention Merchants: The Epic Scramble to Get Inside Our Heads*. New York: Vintage, 2017.

Ziegler, Philip G. *Militant Grace: The Apocalyptic Turn and the Future of Christian Theology*. Grand Rapids: Baker Academic, 2018.

INDEX OF MODERN AUTHORS

INDEX OF SCRIPTURE AND ANCIENT SOURCES

Other Authors